SOME CONCEPTUAL APPROACHES TO THE STUDY OF MODERNIZATION

SOME CONCEPTUAL APPROACHES TO THE STUDY OF MODERNIZATION

DAVID E. APTER
University of California, Berkeley

PRENTICE-HALL, INC., Englewood Cliffs, New Jersey

Library of Congress Catalog Card No.: 68-31840

Current printing (last digit):
10 9 8 7 6 5 4 3 2 1

PRENTICE-HALL INTERNATIONAL, INC., *London*
PRENTICE-HALL OF AUSTRALIA, PTY. LTD., *Sydney*
PRENTICE-HALL OF CANADA, LTD., *Toronto*
PRENTICE-HALL OF INDIA PRIVATE LTD., *New Delhi*
PRENTICE-HALL OF JAPAN, INC., *Tokyo*

Printed in the United States of America

For WACAPS

Acknowledgments

"Theory and the Study of Politics," from the *American Political Science Review*, LI, No. 3 (1957). Reprinted by permission.

"A Comparative Method for the Study of Politics," from *The American Journal of Sociology*, LXIV, No. 3 (November 1958), 221–37. Reprinted by permission of The University of Chicago Press.

"Nationalism, Government, and Economic Growth," from *Economic Development and Cultural Change* (January 1959), pp. 117–36. Reprinted by permission of The University of Chicago Press.

"Some Reflections on the Role of a Political Opposition in New Nations," from *Comparative Studies in Society and History* (The Hague, January 1962). Reprinted by permission of the Society for Comparative Society and History.

"Bureaucracy, Party, and Constitutional Democracy: An examination of political role systems in Ghana" (with Robert A. Lystad), from *Transition in Africa: Studies in Political Adaptation*, eds. Gwendolen M. Carter and William O. Brown (Boston: Boston University Press, 1958). Copyright 1958 by the Trustees of Boston University. Reprinted by permission of the Boston University Press.

"The Role of Traditionalism in the Political Modernization of Ghana and Uganda," from *World Politics*, XIII, No. 1 (October 1960). Reprinted by permission.

"The Politics of Solidarity in Ghana," from *Political Parties and National Integration in Tropical Africa*, eds. James S. Coleman and Carl G. Rosberg (Berkeley: University of California Press, 1964). Reprinted by permission.

"Political Religion in the New Nations," reprinted by permission of The Macmillan Company from *Old Societies and New Nations*, ed. Clifford Geertz. © 1963 by The Free Press.

"Ideology and Discontent," reprinted by permission of The Macmillan Company from *Ideology and Discontent*, ed. David E. Apter. © 1963 by The Free Press, a division of The Macmillan Company.

"System, Process, and the Politics of Economic Development," from *Industrialization and Society*, eds. Bert F. Hoselitz and Wilbert E. Moore (The Hague: UNESCO-Mouton, 1963), pp. 135–59. Reprinted by permission.

"Notes for a Theory of Non-Democratic Representation," from *NOMOS X* (1968). Reprinted by permission.

Contents

Introduction
1

Theory and
the Study of Politics
10

A Comparative Method
for the Study of Politics
23

Nationalism, Government,
and Economic Growth
48

Some Reflections on
the Role of a Political Opposition
in New Nations
72

Bureaucracy, Party, and
Constitutional Democracy:
An examination of political role systems
in Ghana
88

The Role of Traditionalism
in the Political Modernization
of Ghana and Uganda
113

The Politics of Solidarity
in Ghana
136

Political Religion
in the New Nations
193

Ideology and Discontent
233

System, Process, and
the Politics of Economic Development
272

Notes for a Theory of
Non-Democratic Representation
295

Political Systems and Developmental Change

329

A Paradigm for Political Analysis

351

SOME CONCEPTUAL APPROACHES TO THE STUDY OF MODERNIZATION

Introduction

This book represents some of the steps I have taken over the past ten years in an attempt to merge functional theory with a developmental design. My problem has been to avoid what might be called "raw" empiricism on the one hand and the "static" implications of equilibrium theory implicit in functional studies on the other.[1] My emphasis has been on a series of analytical questions: What is the relationship between macro and micro units of analysis? What effect has the revolution in technique—and particularly computers—had upon both our ability to do effective empirical work and our ability to bring the accumulation of data into a tighter analytical network?

One indication of how important these matters have become is the growing concern with "meta-theory" in the social sciences; I have tried not to ignore such questions, even though my own interest—less philosophical than applied—has focused on what happens in the "real world" of development and change. Nor can we wait for the philosophers to dispose of the metaphysical problems posed by contemporary analytical and empirical work, even though much of our experimental theory remains, perhaps because of this, at a primitive level. Certainly, many of our ideas seem mechanical and contrived, as in the past when the early innovators in the physical sciences were engineers and good craftsmen rather than mathematicians and physicists. Indeed, despite our desire for scientific status in the social sciences, our critical faculties remain a good deal more advanced than our scientific capabilities.

[1] "Theory in Anthropology: Developmental or Causal?" in *Sociological Theory: Inquiries and Paradigms*, ed. L. Gross (New York: Harper & Row, Publishers, 1967), p. 154.

Discussion of these and more empirical matters with members of the Politics of Modernization Project at Berkeley has, nevertheless, shown the intimate and practical need of dealing with such large questions in the context of immediate research. Indeed, the idea of publishing these essays was proposed to me by several Latin American scholars in our Project. A few of these articles had been circulated in Spanish and Portuguese in mimeographed form; only a small number of students in Latin America were likely to have encountered them. My colleagues suggested, therefore, that I make available the essays represented here in a single volume in Spanish as well as English, despite the obvious fact that many of the attempted formulations have proven inadequate (some due to excessive complexity or descriptive diffuseness; others, although analytically clear, were impossible to operationalize). I remain concerned that this group of essays may add to the considerable confusion already existing in political studies, which as a discipline has already been subjected to more "cracker barrel theorizing" than most. Nevertheless, there seems to be some merit in showing the various steps by which I have come to hold my present views.

Perhaps an additional word of justification is in order. Political analysis is, in my view, moving from a more descriptive to a more analytical basis. At the same time, it is becoming more and more quantitative. At first glance, it would seem that these two tendencies in the field go hand in hand—in many ways they do; but, in many ways they do not. The more descriptive categories of politics are most likely to be quantified first. Hence there is a danger that "premature" quantification, in this special sense, prolongs the descriptive life of the field, while preventing its analytical development. For this reason I prefer working at the "conceptual" level, trying to establish a better analytical basis for quantification, but with the latter as a definite, or long-run goal.

Whether qualitatively or quantitatively oriented, however, many contemporary theorists have tried to establish a new theoretical grounding of the field. The thinking of scholars like Deutsch, Dahl, Easton, and Almond, to name a few, has had important results in this direction. Some have taken analogies from the physical and natural sciences as bases for their analytical thinking. I prefer to take mine from philosophy (although I do not claim any real or putative relationship to that discipline), concentrating meanwhile on modernization as a process which affects choice. The modernization focus helps to make sense of the choices likely to be at our disposal.

The period in which these essays were written was an extremely dynamic one, and included some remarkable events: the growth of nationalism, the massive retreat of European colonialism, and a concern with direct methods of planning for development. Equally unusual was the emotional climate of postwar reconstruction and innovation, which produced a variety of unanticipated "experiments" in political form and method. (They caused a sometimes heady mixture of buoyancy and hope, moral interest and goodwill, which could not fail to impress the outside observer.) In other words, the events studied possessed unusual intrinsic interest. Many of the politicians best symbolizing these processes took on special significance, with their names personalizing big events: Nkrumah, Sukarno, U Nu, Azikiwe, Olympio, to name a few. They are mostly gone from the scene. A few survivors from this "heroic" period remain—Nasser, Kenyatta, Nyerere, Touré—but their roles are different now, the consequences of their actions less dramatic, and their expectations perhaps more realistic.

The mood is also different for the observer. What we tended to see as quick and sudden change, startling in its intensity, has turned out not to be so. Perhaps we used the wrong indicators to evaluate all that was taking place in the great transformation from traditional to modern life. Indeed, today we are more impressed with what appears to be the infinite malleability of culture, its persistence and toughness and capacity to perform many functions and serve many masters. Despite this malleability, however, one point remains clear: even if certain traditional cultural characteristics appear to die out at a normative level and few structural opportunities appear to sustain them, they may continue to have behavioral relevance for a long time. This does not make change any less real—from subsistence agriculture to manufacturing, from country-rural to town-urban, from ethnic or linguistic "primordial" loyalties to national and federal citizenship, and from local organizational affiliation to mass parties. All this is occurring. Nevertheless, older forms of life persist which, latent under the surface, can erupt in turbulence, instability, and political strife. We need to be able to comprehend such matters analytically, if only to see how important they are in enriching our understanding of our own problems. It is true that as time goes on, our world becomes more difficult to understand, but simplistic formulae only leave us the more confused and dismayed. Yet, how far we have come. Only a short time ago political analysts dealing with decolonization customarily concentrated on constitutionalism. They viewed the formation of new nations primarily as a series of measured steps by which (with each devolution of authority, each enlargement of local responsibility) a new stage would be reached leading to the eventual achievement of simultaneous goals, independence and democracy. How archaic that all seems now![2]

Equally quaint, from the vantage point of today, were efforts by local

[2]One is bemused today by the amount of effort which went into devising formulae for the "right" mixtures of *ex officio* and popularly elected governments, functional and popular representation in legislatures, the formulation of modified list systems to ensure stable majorities, or, for that matter, popular single-member constituencies.

leaders to create stable regimes at home while establishing Pan-Asian or Pan-African movements, fraternal party and trade union links which, at independence, were intended to bring strong government at home and the "Bandung spirit" abroad. Independence, it was widely held, would be the opening wedge leading to the establishment of a "tiers-monde," designed to prevent new nations from becoming a residual collection of poor countries and pawns of the great powers. Indeed, the nations were to become new moral centers of the modern world.

Such objects have manifestly failed. Independence with strong government, independence plus an organized third world—all are illusions, or at least appear to be less than what was anticipated. Certainly the aims were contradictory. (Perhaps what is surprising is how well some of them have succeeded.) Yet I believe all this will occur again. We will see a new round of constitution-making, and perhaps fresh efforts to establish transnational links and associations and better collective agreements for economic and technical assistance. The present generation of "new realists" tends to exaggerate the ideological claims made by former leaders while at the same time it understates their significance, pays little attention to the difficulties of achieving such goals, but also treats the goals themselves as illusions. Illusions they may well be, but such illusions are the promises men live on. Indeed, we cannot afford the growing tendency to shrug off national problems and political institutions in developing countries—regardless of the formal style of government or the professed intentions of leaders (what is called socialism in one country or capitalism in another seems in actuality much the same thing)—as basically so similar that there is not much point in comparing them. We need to compare, to treat each system as an experiment, and, in addition, to go back to the way people think and feel and act in order to improve our direct acquaintance with the immediate circumstances of their lives.

This point of view should not be taken for a new parochialism. There is always the danger that we will not see the forest for the trees. The local is no more real than the national. Nor should we confuse a strategy of research (in which units are selected for analysis) with the ideas by which analysis can take place. However, we need to test the universalism of ideas in more and more particular contexts, using micro as well as macro units and quantitative data. The search for a method, then, is dictated very much by a recognition of these methods. Little "is as it seems." The self-conscious concern with universal or functional categories must be designed to make the study of many cases through a comparative method yield useful correlations.

My interest in structural analysis stems from its use in comparison. In its modern "systems" form, it has been extended beyond descriptive typologies. The purpose is to test propositions and to stimulate new ideas, i.e., to identify new variables and to relate old ones in a more sensitive manner. From such types of analysis a corpus should emerge representing that "theoretical increment" which lies behind the events of the day, of which the abstracted wisdom represents an important part of the substance of social science or political knowledge. This is the point of view put forward in the first essay in this book and to which I continue to subscribe.

Having said all this, it remains true that systems-analysis of the structural variety presents many problems. It is, on the whole, a tiresome method of working. It remains excessively pompous. There is a sort of neo-Hegelianism about it, stemming as much from the jargon with which it is associated as any analytical analogy. Moreover, the formidable problems of operationalization seriously curtail its immediate usefulness. The final essay in this book is an attempt to sketch out some of the main dimensions of systems-analysis; the rest deal, in one way or another, with limiting its focus for political studies, articulating sub-units and their relationships, and offering some hypotheses about the way governments and societies work in terms that lend themselves to quantitative operationalization.

If there is a lesson to be learned from these essays, it is this: the empirical world is too complex to admit any single definition of it. Analytical systems are ways of delimiting reality for various purposes and for ultimately acting upon it. Each analytical system should be, in the long run, a basis for policy on a concrete system. One need not apologize for making that effort. These were the objectives of the classical political theorists and Marx. They remain valid today, with due allowance for our more modest piecemeal objectives and ambitions. The problem, then, is not *whether* to "support" a systemic approach or to reject it, but to discover *which* system is meaningful and useful for *what* purpose. These essays represent attempts to find some meaningful and useful systems for the political analysis of development. They have been clustered according to principal concerns, not always chronologically, and it should be possible to see how the various approaches have been modified, both in logical form and in the face of empirical necessities, errors of interpretation and mistakes in judgment.[3]

[3]I suspect that, whatever the difficulties, structural analysis in one form or another will be with us for a long time. Nevertheless, whatever the merit of the various arguments and points of view suggested, I must also confess to a certain idiosyncrasy in these matters. The truth is that I have always been fascinated by both the real world and "systems," of both the more abstract and complex philosophical sorts as well as the operational (and even abstract models in economics). Bounded relationships linked together by logically meaningful statements seem exciting in their own right, despite their often absurd and elephantine qualities, their architectonic pretensions, or, as in the case of economics models, their elegance. Systems are far from reality, to be sure, but their intellectual challenge, as I see it, is to perceive some piece of reality in a fresh way which illuminates and excites the imagination. Structural analysis particularly intrigues me because it is possible to set up dimensions

The required refinements are many. They include greater logical coherence (the problem of adequate formalization) and the ruthless elimination of ambiguity in order to take advantage of the possible application of computer techniques. It should be possible to test both the formal and operational aspects of these and other systems by using descriptive variables as data. For this reason formulation of adequate "systems" and description of the models employed in them represents the state of the professional arts in the study of politics.

Such matters have more than purely technical significance. As soon as one tries to combine better explanations with prediction, one meets moral dilemmas similar to those confronting all social observers from Plato onwards. The ultimate measure of morality is man, and on this point there is no argument. But precisely what morality? If we can contribute to the moral debate and suggest new dimensions for it, then to that extent we widen our concerns for the predicaments men encounter and avoid the narrow prescriptive formulations of modern technocrats, whose preoccupation with technique and limited prediction obscures the larger view. We need then, as one test of meaning, a better balance between the moral and technical aspects of our endeavors. (In my view this has been an overriding concern in political science for a long time, and it is one reason why I prefer political science as a discipline to those analytically adjacent to it.)

Of course, by taking any set of *ad hoc* categories and putting them in the hands of a reasonably skilled and sensitive research observer, good results will follow. But it is not enough to take words like culture or role, function or structure, development or change, put the word "political" in front of them, and assume that this will produce a theoretical advance. As contrasted with a purely descriptive emphasis, an inner coherence and logical relationship between the variables employed is required. On the other hand, if we carry this too far we run into the same problem posed for Marxists. Marxism today represents such a highly generalized system that it "pre-cuts" all relevant experience for the observer. The result is a kind of theoretical "over-kill." One danger of all excessively generalized theoretical systems is that if one knows "everything" of relevance by means of a small number of variables, empirical work becomes

---

within which variables can be rotated in such a manner that the various ways of sorting them out constitute an explanation or a predication. Surely this is not for the fastidious, because the machinery is too crude and the concepts too vague. I mention it partly to "put the record straight" and partly in order to explain why I use the "property-space" device as an operational model. See Allen H. Barton, "The Concept of Property-Space in Social Research," in *The Language of Social Research*, eds. Paul Felix Lazarsfeld and Morris Rosenberg (Glencoe, Ill.: The Free Press, 1955).

mere window dressing. Still another danger is common with the type of crete system: the total societal, the political, and critical sub-groups, such general systems-theory which requires one to know "everything" before it is possible to know "anything." If Marx sinned on the first count, Parsons does on the second.

These are partly matters of taste and discretion, of course. But there are also involved rules and intellectual styles which vary according to the appropriateness of analytical and empirical methods. In addition, such issues are related to the actualities of politics. It is a serious practical matter in socialist countries that Marxism as an explicit orthodoxy is declining, though its language remains. It is equally significant that as a form of established political ethics, it has emerged among younger intellectuals in France and the United States, to shape their research designs and formulations. Similar trends occur not only between societies but also between disciplines; i.e., Parsonian analysis has begun to lose its impact in sociology (where it originated) and is becoming prominent in political science under the generic term "functionalism." Such changes are not improper. We cite them, not as criticism but rather, to indicate how theories "move about" in response to the differing needs they can satisfy and the meanings and utilities they can support. Nevertheless, such "movement" is never random (and should not be self-cancelling). If forms move, content must change.

For this and other reasons, a better fit between the problems examined and the systems employed for their analysis is needed. The improved research technology at our disposal today allows us to form such theories on an intermediate level, with large numbers of variables (too large for elegance) from which we can derive new hypotheses while testing old ones. Computer technology also allows us to use multiple sets or systems in combination with both indicator data and correlations. Given this point of view, it is not surprising that these essays in one manner or another deal with finding an appropriate set of categories for a system. Nor should it be strange that I choose to try these out ("test" would be misleading under the circumstances) in developing areas, new and old, Africa and Latin America. I feel a responsibility to help create an intellectual space—small, not large—pitched somewhere between the great and powerful systems of a Marx or a Parsons, to discover something looser, more proximate, more empirical, and eventually quantitative, which defines the task for the present analytical generation. In my own case choice is the problem, politics the "venue" of analysis, development the empirical focus, and comparison the method.

Hence these essays are offered as "working papers," which I have employed over the past ten years—nothing more. They are not marching orders for field work, nor do they represent plans for the capture of commanding heights. They sort themselves out into three levels of concrete system; the total societal, the political, and sub-groups, such as parties, armies, bureaucracies, and the like. Three analytical levels emerge with increasing clarity: normative, structural, and behavioral. These concrete and analytical sets represent both the theoretical and concrete boundaries of choice.

Hence the single thread that unites these essays is the concern with choice in the context of modernization. Politically this is a problem of how to deal with the changing fit and relationships arising normatively, structurally, and behaviorally between society, government, and various sub-groups. Specifying the conditions of these and the types of theoretical systems which we can use to articulate the relationships between them has been the overriding methodological concern. There is overlap in the formulations (sometimes causing as much confusion as clarification). Promising leads have been discarded. Many early definitions of political system and stratification have turned out to be less fruitful than anticipated.

Whatever the fate of these efforts, they share in a tradition established in the works of Levy, Shils, Smelser, Fallers, Geertz, and Lipset (to name a few) in sociology and anthropology, and Dahl, Easton, Deutsch, Almond, Pye, Binder, and Riggs in political science. However, if I may be permitted to make some predictions about the future of development studies in these fields, I would suggest (using the terms I like to employ) that the scholars just named have worked largely at the intersection between normative and structural theory. They are "neo-institutionalists." The "new wave" will work at the intersection between structural and behavioral theory. One can only hope that in the more empirical structural methods and behavioral quantitative techniques, the normative dimension will not be lost.

Most of the earlier essays presented here were written in the context of the changing political scene in Africa, while the more recent ones were undertaken in a Latin American context. This change in area emphasis required a review and reappraisal of the earlier categories as well as an evaluation of new categories to see if they represented any improvement. My first efforts were undertaken in the context of the West African Comparative Analysis Project, whose members include Professors James Coleman, Robert Lystad, and L. Gray Cowan. The more recent ones were undertaken in the Politics of Modernization Project, particularly in collaboration with José Nun, Torcuato Di Tella, Magali Sarfatti, and Carlos Strasser. The approaches taken in these essays were thus stimulated by constant methodological discussions, and while the participants in these groups are in no way responsible for the essays themselves, except in the collaborative essay with Lystad, whatever merit these essays retain is in large measure due to their critical imagination.

David E. Apter

Theory and the Study of Politics

I

In the omnibus philosophy of an earlier day the pursuit of knowledge was the pursuit of science. Political science became a specialized discipline only very recently, and while it gained by its specialization it also suffered because of it. One of the nice tasks of modern political science is to avoid the effects of descriptive detail as a substitute for theory and once again relate political phenomena to broader patterns of human activity, without losing the advantages, particularly in research, of the specialized knowledge and lore so laboriously acquired.

We cannot return to "omnibus philosophy." What is perhaps required is the reintroduction of problem oriented empirical philosophy, which has gained considerable currency in other social science disciplines. The results have been most striking at those points in knowledge where in the past reliable information was weakest and the need for knowledge greatest. A few such areas are perhaps worth a brief mention here: *concept-formation* with its dual aspects of basic perception and logic, *motivation* with its associated factors of objectives, expectations, and norms, and *organization*, including the basic supply of means and structures of choice thrown up in group activity and association. An enormous amount of research in the area of linguistics, logic, and indeed both the philosophy of science and the philosophy of knowledge has gone into the first. Widely differing approaches to the general area tolerate very little parochialism and social psychologists, logical positivists, mathematical logicians and others have pounded happily away at associated problems. The same thing can be said for the other two basic problem areas mentioned. A battery of approaches, rather than an array of disciplines, is brought to bear with cumulative and productive results. Consequently social science literature is increasingly problem-clustered, a healthy sign, and the selective reading of social scientists requires cutting through a variety of disciplines. If one is interested in bureaucracy, or certain aspects of organizational behavior his choice of literature will necessarily be very diverse. It may vary from articles on feed-backs and servo-mechanisms and communications nets, to the Weberian approaches to formal disinterested behavior in bureaucratic agencies.

All this puts very different burdens upon students. What should they learn and emphasize? Weighed down by curricula which have emerged out of the era of specialization in political science, political scientists are unsure how much to stress detailed information which should be part of the intellectual apparatus of every student who plans to continue in the field, and the amount of "non-political science" materials with which he should be familiar. If he is inadequately trained, a student may attempt a slow milk run through a diverse literature which turns sour before it can be consumed. Given the limited time available to him there are difficult priorities: information versus theory, disciplinary theory versus general analytical theory; these are only a few of the problems which we face both in the teaching of our subject and in our own approach to research.

One approach to minimizing this difficulty for those who expect to be professional political scientists has been a revamping of the traditional curricula of postgraduate work to deal less with descriptive data and information (assuming the student has some background knowledge on which to build), and to present a broader training, first in the canons and criteria of scientific work generally, and secondly in the general principles of social behavior and organization.

There is of course nothing new in this approach to studies. Classical approaches to scholarship emphasized basic information early in education, with abstraction proceeding at the level of higher scholarship. Indeed, if higher education, particularly postgraduate work is to mean anything at all, it must deal with the manipulation of abstractions and generalizations in relation to problems posed. The art or science of analysis is the application of principles to fact.

The problem is aggravated for political science because the field lacks clean boundaries. An emphasis on science does not end specialization; it merely shifts the specialist function first to an appreciation of scientific technique, second to concept formation and organization, and third to technical information of a highly specific sort. Unfortunately in political science today specialization often means compartmentalization, with the result that we turn out better mechanics than we do creative scholars.

Students recognize this difficulty with political science more quickly than professors. They are "voting with their feet." The best students in the social sciences today tend not to go into political science, but into those disciplines where a genuine body of research theory is emerging. It is already highly doubtful that undergraduate work in political science, particularly in some institutions where a heavy program in political science is possible, is in fact the best preparation for postgraduate work in the field. The same query can be raised in regard to the majority of postgraduate students preparing themselves to be professional political scientists. Presently constituted curricula tend to be theoretically parochial and laden with descriptive data without an adequate appreciation of the conceptual pegs to hang such data.

Curricula tend to reflect secular tendencies in a discipline, and rightly so if there is to be a stable body of knowledge out of which the field is constituted. The price paid for this is that curricula tend to remain too conservative and turn out people ill-equipped for present day needs. However, as soon as one raises queries pertaining to curriculum changes, vested interests, convictions, and indeed the cultural traditions of political science are set in motion. Questions about "education for what" vie with queries about the basic stuff of education itself. Styles and schools in professional education, each with their virtues and angry in defense, sometimes end by obfuscating real issues. Too often it is fashion which wins the day rather than a sober assessment of our needs and problems. Perhaps it might be worth while to try to point out certain tendencies and trends in political science which have bearing on both the teaching and the needs of political scientists today.

Two "trends" have crystallized since the war. One, the neo-institutionalist," is a result of dissatisfaction with the legal-historical approach to analysis in politics, as well as an accompanying recognition that "sociological" factors are significant in any kind of political analysis. Much of the work in this direction reveals itself in a search for the meaning of a set of organized groupings in society: the church, the state, the family, the economic system, etc. It avoids some of the pitfalls of simple pressure group analysis and tends to emphasize the ideological conventions which surround each of the institutions in contact with one another. Explanation, in part, consists of unravelling the ideological commitments of each of these institutions as they are joined together, in an effort to reveal the basic pattern or ground plan of social life and organization.

Another trend has grown out of dissatisfaction with both the traditional legal-historical approach in political analysis, and the neo-institutionalist approach. We can generally call this behavioral because it deals with selected aspects of patterned behavior and includes three major features: (1) a formal institutional feature (or organizational feature), (2) a qualitative feature, and (3) an attributive feature. The formal institutional feature refers to the organization of membership structures of a given unit of analysis. The qualitative feature refers to the norms and values operative in action within a given unit, including standards of judgment and moral expressions. The attributive feature refers to the inferred motivational qualities of patterns of action.

These two trends as can readily be seen, have much in common, but their major differences appear in their approach to questions of science and method. This is not to say that the neo-institutionalists would reject science. Not at all. To date they have probably contributed more along scientific lines than the behaviorists have. But, to the behaviorists, their standards vary somewhat, and the neo-institutionalist's use of science tends to be *ad hoc* and imprecise.

Perhaps another trend has arisen as a result of the fact that people in other disciplines are becoming concerned with problems of politics, attacking them often from substantially different but no less important research needs. For instance, more and more attention to specialized instruments of social control is being paid by anthropologists and social psychologists. Suffering from a lack of knowledge of traditional political science, but often unencumbered by it, some of them are attacking political problems with a fresh eye. Many of their remarks are certainly not new. Yet they are closely tied in with immediate problems of the social world which give their statements a ready relevance sometimes lacking in political analysis. Often it is "the political system" which is regarded as the most crucial set of institutional structures for the integration and maintenance of a given society. It is looked upon as the most generalized structure for the performance of control functions and as an expression of generalized wants to be translated into legal and normative role prescriptions in all aspects of a given society. Approached systematically such a viewpoint demands broad knowledge and theoretical expertise if treatment is to be effective and meaningful.[1]

If we admit the need for scientific canons, we immediately raise a set of epistemological questions which are appropriate to science in general. Problems of experiment and control, of research design, and of operating assumptions become part and parcel of the training of political scientists. An emphasis on method is an emphasis on the rules of the game, and a description of how the rules can be put to work. Without such an effort neither the logic of science, nor science itself is of much use to us. The working assumptions we use should themselves be either defined as given,

[1]Examples of particular interest are L. A. Fallers, *Bantu Bureaucracy* (Cambridge: W. Heffer & Sons, Ltd., 1956), which deals with the development of a civil service system of chieftaincy in an important district in Uganda, and J. A. Barnes, *Politics in a Changing Society* (London: Oxford University Press, Inc., 1954), which gives an interesting thesis of the "snowball state," and which deals with another African group, the Fort Jameson Ngoni, as the subject for intensive empirical work.

or else substantiated through the theoretical works of others. At least part of what can become operating assumptions for us would result from experiment in other fields.

If we are to examine the behavioral aspects of man as a political being, using the notion of behavior described above, we are at once forced to make certain assumptions about his nature and functioning. Either this is to be done arbitrarily, or else our conceptions of him must be abstracted from his range of activities in organized settings. In order to reveal the latter, across-the-board empirical research is the foundation for useful generalization.

Hence in viewing the work of other social scientists and their theoretical assumptions there is no injunction intended here about our own levels of specialized work, other than to note that we have to bring in other ranges of explanatory concepts and premises than those we are accustomed to in our work, depending upon our problems for analysis, and the units of research. This is not a plea for integration of concepts into a single "social science."[2]

What contributions can political scientists make in careful and controlled observation of human action as patterned behavior, and in the kinds of generalizations drawn? Can they illuminate different aspects of questions with which other social scientists have concerned themselves? Indeed the aspect of their work of most interest to us is that they may articulate much that has been implicit in political science, or rather crudely drawn in recent years, e.g., such matters as unit change and response, the absorption limits of unit variations, the way in which group activity is sustained, etc., in such fashion that new bits of knowledge can be used to negate, advance, or rephrase questions. Political scientists constantly deal with these items. Efforts to discuss democracy, industrialization, cabinets and parliaments, voting and political parties, the spread of communism, how revolutions occur, threats to freedom and liberty, all deal with human motivations, activities in organized groupings, and a range of cultural and symbolic behavioral expressions about which those in other disciplines have important things to say.

Unless these questions are made theoretically pertinent to a larger

[2]See M. Mandelbaum, "Societal Facts," in *The British Journal of Sociology*, VI, No. 4 (December 1955), for a good discussion of this problem. Speaking of the problem of reductionism Mandelbaum says, "There can scarcely be any doubt that there is at present a considerable measure of disagreement among social scientists concerning the relations which obtain among their various disciplines. For example there is little agreement as to how the province of 'social psychology' is related to general psychology on the one hand or to sociology on the other. There is perhaps even less agreement as to how sociology and history are related, or whether, in fact history is itself a social science. Even the province of cultural anthropology which, in its earlier stages, seemed to be capable of clear definition, is now in a position extremely fluid. This type of fluidity in boundaries of the various social sciences, and the ease with which concepts employed in one discipline spread to other disciplines, has been

body of theory, a research enterprise remains at the level of either satisfying idle curiosity, or simple acceptance of disciplinary tradition. Usually, of course, some implicit notions of significance are built into the question raised. Whether the question is cabinet stability in France, or voting behavior in a rural American county, "significance" lies in much more than a more certain knowledge of the data pertinent to such questions. It lies in the abstraction of generalizable patterns about human propensities within certain types of institutional settings. "It is always the search for, and the exposition of, typical and recurring elements *within the unique course of the world* that is the subject of science."[3]

Is the question for a political scientist one of retaining or eliminating the field, if he pays singular attention to behavior? Certainly not. There is a wealth of accumulated wisdom and information which the discipline itself represents. Nevertheless, much of this wealth still needs to be sorted, tested, evaluated, and brought into better theoretical frames of analysis so that its content, its meaning, its true value, can be assayed. The difficulty which remains is one of grasping general propositions of social science without getting lost in ambiguities and conflicts within each of the social science disciplines themselves, and without losing sight of the problems which we are ourselves most concerned with. There is the problem of individual efficiency in ranging over the literature, and the problem of boundaries. They are problems that each man must answer for himself according to his needs, his interests and his rigor. Equally they are problems which seem more formidable at first glance than they really are.

The only way in which questions can be phrased in terms of their

---

quite generally regarded as a promising augury for the future of the social sciences. One notes the frequency with which 'integration' is held up as an important programmatic goal for social scientists. But such pleas for integration are ambiguous. On the one hand, they may merely signify a recognition of the fact that attempts to understand some concrete problems call for co-operation between persons trained to use the concepts and methods of different social sciences, or that workers in one discipline should be aware of the methods and results of those who work in other fields. On the other hand, what some who plead for 'integration' seem to demand is that the various disciplines should merge into one larger whole. On such a view the goal of integration would be the achievement of a state in which all persons who work in the field of social science would operate with the same set of concepts and would utilize the same methods of inquiry." The latter position is of course absurd if only because of the wide variety of research needs in the differing social sciences and because specialized theory is not easily transferred from one discipline to another.

[3]See Richard Von Mises, *Positivism, A Study in Human Understanding* (Cambridge: Harvard University Press, 1951), p. 8. The extremely stimulating introduction of this work covers nicely some of the problems current in political science today when the issues of science, method, and technique are raised as a legitimate course for the political scientist to pursue. In the same work there is a very clearly written discussion of the language used not only in interdisciplinary work, but as a barrier to logical analysis, and the need for specialized categories and concepts for technical purposes.

maximum significance is to articulate the body of research theory to which the problem is relevant. If a problem is phrased concerning, say, the rise of the Falangist movement in Spain, for example, what ranges of theory do we typically provide? One political scientist might answer, "theories of revolution." Another might say that it involves "theories" of fascism, referring to doctrinal differences between different expressions of fascism. Another may "generalize" the material to "theories" of authoritarianism, while still another political scientist might argue that in truth the Falangist movement in Spain was the product of a peculiar and unique set of circumstances in history and that the relative value of generalization is small, subject to all the ills of analogical thinking. This is scarcely an overstatement of the case. Not only do we have different things in mind when we deal with "theory," but we are concerned with phenomena as having "obvious" descriptive boundaries which are often reified by many observers as they begin to analyze their materials.

Much of what seems to be a maze of jargon in social science is a direct result of the effort to cut through so called common sense terms which, upon intensive probing, prove themselves to be of limited usefulness. Concepts of "class" and "ideology" or other terms characteristic of post-Marxian-type analyses, for example, while very productive in general sociological work, have had to be sharpened by categories having more immediate operational value, e.g., status, role, factors of perception, normative structures in typologies of systems, etc. Indeed, much of what remains the most sophisticated theory in political science today uses nineteenth century constructs of action developed by the Marxians, their commentators and glossators up until the end of the Second World War,[4] while others in other disciplines have gone far beyond this. Many of the most useful constructs in present day social science came from pushing on from the specific assumptions and models implicit in Marxian and post-Marxian hypotheses[5]—a task in which political science has been notably weak, Bentleyan pressure group analysis notwithstanding.

We are rapidly pushing beyond the sheer manipulation of common sense, except insofar as common sense is constantly being modified by the absorption and useful vulgarization of more rarefied knowledge. Common sense knowledge today is substantially different from the common sense knowledge of yesterday in many crucial ways. This is particularly noticeable in the physical science world and to a lesser extent in the world of "social engineering" where a kind of trickle-down theory of scientific capital applies in regard to such items as slum clearance,

[4]See David Easton's general thesis that properly speaking there is no political theory today in *The Political System* (New York: Alfred A. Knopf, Inc., 1953), *passim.*

[5]See Merton's paradigm of functional analysis and Marxian analysis in *Social Theory and Social Structure* (Glencoe, Ill.: The Free Press, 1949), Chap. i.

race relations, industrial efficiency of the working force, etc. This has been least true, however, in the world of politics where the "hero-villain" approach to analysis has not yet died out, and we are sometimes so concerned with establishing the superiority of one kind of system over another, that some of us have dubbed our "science" "the authoritative allocation of values."

Interestingly enough, the development of modern political theory has been affected by those trained in Germany in the more classical omnibus pattern of philosophy and historical jurisprudence, the American parallels for which are found not in political science, but in sociology. In the British and American traditions of political science, the Barkers and Laskis are far more brilliant commentators and publicists than theory builders.[6]

How do we phrase questions in a manner maximizing their scientific utility, and their cumulative value? To answer such a question one must first point up some of the things we see or have in mind when we ask a question. Second, we need to articulate "significance." Third, we must relate the question to other questions. Finally, we need to develop useful research schemes in order to gather valid data.

II

It may well be asked whether or not the effect of "rephrasing" political science questions for their maximum behavioral implications is not simply a kind of reductionism, to return to a point raised earlier, i.e., that political science is reducible to action or behavior generally, and action is reducible to physiological processes. With such reductionism little is left but the psychologist. Certainly political science as we know it would disappear. Of course, this partly depends upon how we consider political science itself, the kind of boundaries we put upon it. Then, too, in its most extreme form, the reductionist argument is partly misleading because the reductionism is phrased in terms of disciplines rather than theory. The matter is certainly not a question of political scientists becoming psychologists.

"Reductionism," properly considered, represents the exhaustion of relevant factors of explanation at each analytical level of the phenomenon under consideration. Obviously processes of politics cannot be explained

[6]For a good view of Barker's efforts at positive theory construction one need only look at his *Principles of Social and Political Theory* (London: Oxford University Press, Inc., 1953) where "out of his later years" he begins to deal in systematic analytical fashion with the materials he had previously worked in brilliant intuitive fashion. The volume is not only a failure as theory construction, but points up how far he has strayed from the tradition of Maitland, or for that matter, Gierke.

solely in terms of psychological theory. But equally, problems of politics insofar as they have crucial interaction processes as their foundation can rely on the data and findings of those studying other aspects of social interaction or behavior. This is not to say that theory regarding social interaction is sufficient to analyze political phenomena. It is to say that if political analysis is to reach a high state of theoretical sophistication it must have a specialized set of behavioral assumptions and theories which build on the more general.

It is essential to draw up fundamental behavioral propositions which can tell us about the interaction and learning processes which may appear in many specific or concrete groupings, like a Congress, an administrative agency, or a labor union. The groupings are identified by the problems one may wish to examine. The problem will help determine the range and degree of general theory to be used in examination, the choices to be made in this regard, and the specialized and further considerations which emerge from research findings about this problem.

In this connection much discussion can be simplified by examining models used in research and theory in a variety of disciplines. Behavioral models are of two general sorts. The first can be called a *nuclear* model containing predicating assumptions. As such it is a way of expressing theory in highly abstracted form since it sets up crucial patterns of interrelationships between variables. The second form of behavior model can be called the *experimental* model. Here the nuclear model or several nuclear models are brought together into a research design for purposes of identifying and relating new materials and for holding some factors constant and measuring changes in others. These can be of various kinds. For example, one type of experimental model, an equilibrium model, is being used in connection with several different kinds of disciplines, economics, psychology, etc., in which input-output analysis is being done. It must be pointed out that the two types of models discussed here are not concretely separable but rather deal with aspects of the same thing. The classic S-R model in psychology is both a nuclear model from a theoretical point of view and an experimental model from an operational point of view.

Stating our intuitive themes sharply and explicitly in both types of models is necessary to provide coherence and intelligibility in what have in political science been somewhat murky realms of intuitive speculation. This will serve us to organize more clearly the kinds of behavioral assumptions and implicit experimentation or hypothesizing that we are making all the time. No one studying politics today can ignore, for example, the communications aspects of pressure groups, legislative bodies, administrative units, etc., both as a guide to understanding how they achieve their work product, and their relation to authority or power, the making of law, etc. Yet if we have certain propositions tested under varying conditions which can be applied to the study of the communications aspect of such groupings, we will have a more fruitful base for analysis. If we know that a communication is more likely to occur between two persons if their orientations to the object of communication differ in some respect than if they do not, and if we also know that following communication between *A* and *B* in regard to *X*, *A*'s knowledge and *B*'s knowledge will have greater similarity, we can ask some pertinent questions about consensus, about political beliefs, and about the political activities of individuals in "political" groupings. If these propositions are true, for example, does it follow that the greater the difference in orientation toward an object of communication the greater the likelihood of communication? Does it also follow that with continuing communication, if there is greater similarity in the knowledge held by the communicators, communication in fact will fall off, other things being equal? Could we say that the probabilities of communication of a given object vary jointly with the discrepancy in orientation among the potential communicators and with the strength of positive attraction among them? Indeed if our experimental model consisted of multiple *ABX* systems phrased in equilibrium terms, we might find that our research problem could deal with data derived from "summit" conferences, assuming for the moment that such data were available. The experimental model might take the form of multiple *AP* systems set up in equilibrium terms. The nuclear model might be a form of the S–*R* model.

Experimental models are immediately useful in the development of methodologies of social science; they can provide a way in which order and control can be brought into the analysis of empirical political problems. If we assume, for example, that our S–*R* model as a nuclear model has relevance to basic factors in general behavior theory, particularly in learning, it is conceivable that it could form part of an operational model for the analysis of basic factors in political behavior. Certainly operational models for the analysis of groups which are involved in political processes could be developed. Insofar as government activity is small group or organizational activity, models which deal with variables crucial to any governmental activity, e.g., problem solving variables, emotional and leadership variables, allow us to ask several kinds of questions. First, we can ask questions about political groupings, as groupings, that is, the specific behavioral aspects of governmental organization in terms of general small-group variables. Secondly, we can ask what are the special factors that arise in the nature of political tasks which governmental groups are created to handle. Out of the latter approach it is possible to build up a range of empirically verified propositions to add to the fund of knowledge about specialized political activities.

The utility of the various theoretical approaches in the building of systematic theory in political science is not that they substitute a more rarefied set of theories for those that we already have, but rather that they help to bring back to political science both respectability and purpose in the general attempts of social scientists to solve problems in the human sphere. Problems of government as such demand both general statements utilizing propositions pertaining to those characteristics of politics which arise from the fact that governmental structures are social organizations in which human personalities interact, have peculiar systems of roles which are institutionalized by members of a given society, and have special problems which give rise to statements unique to the "political" aspects of these structures. Where political scientists have most to offer and as yet have been relatively hesitant about coming forward, is in the analysis of authority (coordination and communication), the specialized attributes of a political system (the patterned power relationships in a social system), and related problems.

In putting forward this view, however, we do not disparage the discipline of political science as compared with other disciplines. The plea here is simply for more training of the political scientist in research theory. The specialists' knowledge he will get when dealing with a range of data and problems, i.e., those pertinent to politics. Political scientists on the whole are not adequately equipped for behavioral studies partly because inherited course titles have become a substitute for analytical categories. A "typical" political science curriculum which has a variety of subject and areal *foci* tends to give a wealth of facts, but only the most primitive means for discussing those facts. It does not provide training in research theory and experimental design.

No one discipline or branch of science will provide complete answers to any of the problems to which political scientists have customarily addressed themselves. But, more and more, politics as a part of general behavior is becoming recognized, just as economists have more and more recognized the importance of non-economic factors in economics. The difference is that economists have a more manageable universe in which to work than do political scientists, and as well, have a series of currently useful systematic theories of their own on which to build, as on the whole we do not. This makes it all the more crucial that we organize our theoretical assets before we discard what we have, while not overlooking our theoretical liabilities. Indeed in many cases we have denied the place of what might be deemed the "scientific spirit" in favor of the pulpit and the sacrament. Surely we do not have to deny the one in order to accept the other.

If we attempt to absorb the scientific lore of other disciplines, will we simply become amateurs in other areas on which professional knowledge will be based? This issue has two sides. On the one hand we can ask whether we do not do this anyway, except that we are clumsy amateurs and not knowledgeable in the rules of the game. On the other hand we can be more than amateurs. This latter depends on knowing what general theory consists of, how to specialize conceptually both for the purpose of analysis and for organizing concepts. It does demand a difficult reading schedule. Too often perhaps it means that political scientists have to re-orient their thinking. This is difficult, but we are not making a plea here for pushing the field in an uncertain direction, rather merely for certain kinds of specialists to come forward in the field of politics who are willing to absorb a different kind of knowledge, and to put that knowledge to the tests which political scientists well know how to administer.

Aside from the value in theoretical development, research work, and cumulative results which are implicit in the use of behavioral theory in political science as we have used the term, one can perhaps put forward an assumption which helps reaffirm the significance of political science both as a moral and an experimental discipline. There has never yet been heard a definition of political science, or politics, or the place of political science or politics in the scheme of social affairs, which seemed to meet wth general satisfaction. We feel vaguely dissatisfied with attempts to define away subtle areas of our discourse and knowledge. We often feel that the scope of our work is greater than any definition would allow, or that a definition gets us nowhere since we pay no attention to it anyway. Confusion in definitions helps to evade rather crucial issues in political science. While we may define politics by what it "does," the fact is that it intervenes in all major aspects of social life, and organization. The assumption offered here is that what sets off politics, and makes some people regard politics as both coterminous with society and coterminous with moral and ethical imperatives, is the assumption that government as a particular group of organizations and agencies at its most general level is responsible for seeing that at least the minimal conditions for the perpetuation of a society are in fact achieved. In analytical terms these conditions must be abstracted from a wide range of "sociological" and "psychological" phenomena which go on in any functioning society. If this latter assumption is correct, then one is constantly, in political science, dealing with a discipline which has for theoretical boundaries any functioning system of which it is a part, and all theories relevant to how that system functions have possible relevance to an understanding of politics, depending upon the enquiry.

Our job as political scientists is perhaps the most complex of all the social sciences, dealing as we do with a special aspect of the totality of social activity and interpersonal behavior. All the more striking, therefore, is our need for effective control of our material, and the development of theory through the application of scientific canons characteristic of all the disciplines. Insofar as our work deals with a specialized branch of human activity, we need to know some of the fundamentals of human behavior.

We need greater understanding of the epistemological foundations of science. Too few political scientists get specific training in theory construction, while at the same time keeping contact with empirical problems manipulable by scientific means. We need, too, a greater appreciation of the difference between analytical theory and synthetic categories which simply add jargon rather than effective tools for greater understanding. We need a picture of other theories in social science relevant to our own basic assumptions as analysts of a segment of social behavior, which is impossible to obtain without an understanding of what theory is and how it works in relation to problems, and how it can be generalized to other areas.

A Comparative Method for the Study of Politics

INTRODUCTION

This essay presents a method which is, at present, inelegant, not parsimonious, and which combines both analytic and descriptive categories. Its purpose is to create a framework for the treatment of governments in diverse social settings in order to make possible some generalization about how the presence, absence, or clustering of certain combinations of variables affect politics.

Implicit in this scheme is a model of politics. Every society has a social stratification system. The dominant motive of social behavior is assumed (whether rightly or wrongly) to be the increased mobility toward the higher ends of the stratification hierarchy. Members of the public join in political groups in order to expand mobility opportunities and, in this respect, make representations to government or to influence or control government in some manner. Government policy must then in part be responsive to the interests of political groups. Depending upon who the group represents, we see that government policy is geared as well to the ultimate alteration of social stratification or aspects thereof. This is, of course, both a traditional and a respectable view of politics. Government is viewed as a maximizer, sending out streams of satisfactions. One is to political group leaders who represent both an information and organizational dynamic. A second is to followers who, depending upon their group composition, represent in some measure the prevailing social stratification system. Assuming that no one is ever truly satisfied with the system of social stratification except conservatives, we find that the basic motive of politics is a striving motive to expand mobility opportunities, either for some special group or for large segments of the society.[1]

The scheme laid out here attempts to delineate sets of useful variables in each of three main dimensions—social stratification, political groups, and government—in order to produce manipulative theory out of comparative research. It stems from a tradition associated with Pollock and Maitland, Austin, Maine, and Vinogradoff, and the functionalist tradition in modern anthropology and sociology. It is designed to cover societies whether they are industrial or not, whenever they are tribal, traditional, or technologically advanced.[2] The core of such a scheme is a set of general analytical categories called the "structural requisites" of any government. These represent a minimal set of concerns for any government, whether it be formalized or not. The demands put upon government, initiated in some measure through parties and originating in mobility strivings, must be met through activities in one or a combination of the structural requisites.

Nor does the format of government have to be democratic. The possible range of representativeness will limit the manner in which actions within each of the structural requisites can be performed. Such structural requisites are more than simply a heuristic device, as we shall hope to indicate.

The problem for which this scheme was undertaken deals with the development of parliamentary government in Africa. Thus cultural and technological data range from aspects of the most secular and complex of European governments to tribal life, all within the compass of single societies. Stated generally, we are studying rapidly changing underdeveloped areas in order to indicate some of the general conditions pro-

[1]The model can be stated as follows:

$$\text{Time 1: } \underset{1}{[ss]} \rightarrow \underset{2}{[pf + pl]} \rightarrow [govt] \rightarrow \underset{3}{(sr + format)}$$

$$\underset{4}{[pf + pl]} \rightarrow \underset{5}{[ss]} \text{ Time 2}$$

ss = social stratification system
pf = party following (composition)
pl = party leadership
$govt$ = government in terms of:
(*a*) sr = structural requisites
(*b*) format = type determined by degree of representativeness

[2]Vinogradoff has argued that "we must begin by ascertaining whether certain fundamental ideas recurring in various combinations may be traced as elements of the institution. If such elements exist, the work of each one ought to be analyzed as far as possible by itself before the ways in which it combines with other materials can be studied. The materials for such an analysis may be drawn from a broad and comprehensive collection of ethnological data, because it is only in this manner that we can make sure that nothing essential has escaped our observation." Paul Vinogradoff, *Outline of Historical Jurisprudence* (New York: Oxford University Press, 1920), I, 93 and 167).

duced by change as reflected in the conditions which are necessary for the development of parliamentary government.[3] The range of events and the materials to be dealt with require treatment in systematic fashion—a treatment that is not methodologically harsh, inappropriate, or stultifying, yet which is sufficient to provide a meaningful focus in comparative work.[4]

We shall in this discussion sketch very briefly the major components of each of the three dimensions—social stratification, government, and political groups—with emphasis upon the last. It is a major assumption here that extensive comparative study will eventually result in typical clusterings of those variables. Departures from typical clusterings should also prove challenging and interesting as we attempt to develop theory to explain the phenomena observed.

UTILITY OF SOCIAL STRATIFICATION

Social stratification and government are closely connected. Ultimately, the actions of government affect stratification in some significant manner. Of particular interest are the changes occurring in stratification in hitherto tribal societies under the impact of commercial, colonial, nationalist, and technological forces. Changes in culture include alteration in ideologies, with their expressed valuations on patterns of stratification. Most of all, however, the values and ideas of a changing social system can be expressed in the activities which take place to modify or protect the given pattern of stratification in a particular area.

[3]This methodological scheme represents work done by the author in conjunction with his colleagues on the West African Comparative Analysis Project. The members of this project are James S. Coleman (University of California at Los Angeles), Gray Cowan (Columbia University), Robert A. Lystad (Tulane University). The work of this group has been made possible through a grant from the Carnegie Corporation, to which gratitude is hereby expressed.

[4]More specifically, the concern here is to produce a system of comparative analysis which is integrated with real research. We are not concerned with the basic properties of system qua system. We are concerned here with the treatment of empirical systems in general through the comparative observation of empirical systems in particular. In other words, we are concerned with characteristics which mediate between the most highly general (any system) and the most specific (system x), so that we can discuss regularities and irregularities in the variables of systems $x_{1,\ 2,\ 3,\ \ldots\ n}$.

There are, of course, special difficulties involved in doing comparative work at the gross data level. Analytical categories in use are hard to operationalize for purposes of rigorous manipulation. Scaling techniques seem the most favorable for much of the data-gathering. Another difficulty is that the higher the degree of control over the variables, i.e., the more selectivity employed, and the more precise the operations performed upon them, the lower is the degree of control over the parameters. Testing by other means is difficult because (1) a small data unit may simply affirm general system properties, (2) a small data unit may not exhibit equivalent variables, and (3) criteria of validation are difficult to specify.

Stratification is, as well, a useful way of indicating the degree of internal flexibility in a system. Relatively undifferentiated systems tend to be fragile and unable to adapt with ease to changes in the social or political environment. An important query then is similar to the one that Durkheim posed: In systems in which there is limited division of labor there is little flexibility (a lack of pluralism) or, to put it another way, there is fragility. Hence in such systems the most powerful expression of social solidarity is through an extensive system of repressive law which regards a wide range of socially unsanctioned acts as crimes against basic morality. With an increase in the division of labor there is not only specialization of function but also an increase in local solidary affiliations which become mutually dependent, and a decline in repressive law. These affiliations give rise to defined hierarchies of power and prestige, some based upon ascriptive evaluations and others based upon achievement. These, as well as other factors directly derivative from the pattern of alteration in stratification, set limiting conditions both for the activities of government and for the actions of political parties.[5]

Nor is the utility of stratification limited to societies undergoing industrialization. Its application is more general, applying as well to "mature" industrial systems, where it retains its intimate association with government and party actions.

Where active modification of the stratification system is going on, members characteristically (1) are status-conscious (i.e., they are aware of their position in the social system vis-à-vis others and, in addition, are aware of the advantages and disadvantages of a given status position which they might occupy); (2) are engaged in role-testing (i.e., they explore the legitimate limits of their roles and experiment to the point where they can expect sanctions of one kind or other to be initiated); and (3) are future-oriented (i.e., they look to changes in their life-chances and attempt to produce conditions leading to secure expectations proximate to what they desire).[6] Where these three conditions prevail, the implications for political development are great.

Three questions about the stratification system need to be answered before it is possible to make meaningful statements about the conse-

[5]See Émile Durkheim, *The Division of Labor* (New York: The Free Press, 1947), *passim*; and Reinhard Bendix, "Social Stratification and Political Power," *American Political Science Review*, XLVI (June, 1952).

[6]Parsons notes: "It has come to be rather widely recognized in the sociological field that social stratification is a generalized aspect of the structure of all social systems, and that the system of stratification is intimately linked to the level and type of integration of the system as a system" (Talcott Parsons, "A Revised Analytical Approach to the Theory of Social Stratification," in *Reader in Social Stratification*, eds. Reinhold Bendix and Seymour Lipset (New York: The Free Press, 1957). See also S. F. Nadel, *The Theory of Social Structure* (New York: The Free Press, 1957), Chap. iv.

quences of changing stratification. The first asks what the system is from the point of view of the members. How are *roles* defined in a given system and how are they ranked in a status hierarchy? Second, what are the institutionalized criteria of stratification? Are they economic, political, religious, generational, educational, etc.? Third, what are the recruitment patterns to the major groups which comprise the system? Are the institutional criteria such that recruitment is relatively open or closed, achievement-based or ascription-based?

For example, common in systems which are undergoing rapid industrialization and commercialization is a decline in power accorded to generational factors and religious factors, although prestige may persist a bit longer. High valuations for both power and prestige result from economic and sometimes political factors. Interesting situations are produced when groups which formerly had economic power and prestige lose the first and seek to maintain the second. The set of variables to be specified under the dimension of social stratification, once the rank order of status positions has been described, is shown in the following diagram.

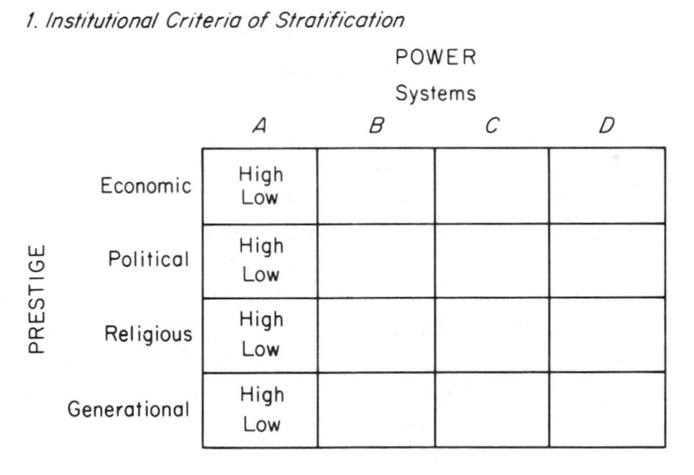

Figure 1.

These categories should, first, indicate what group values and "vested interests" exist in a system. Second, they should illuminate the institutionalized barriers to social mobility, and, third, they should demonstrate the nature of political groupings to the degree such groups reproduce or fail to reproduce the stratification range in their recruitment and membership. Finally, they should provide some guides to the degree of commitment members have to the system, leading to hypotheses about the direction of change. As it is used here, change means the degree of alteration in the basic characteristics of the stratification system itself, reflecting alteration in the concrete groupings of the unit under observation.

Our ultimate concern here is therefore the relationships between government and social stratification. However, the crucial connecting link between them is political party, association, or movement, as the case may be. To give equal treatment to each of the three dimensions discussed here is impossible because of lack of space. We shall therefore concentrate our discussion on the *political group* dimension after first specifying its relationship to government and to stratification. Before going on to discuss political groups, therefore, a discussion of government is essential.

GOVERNMENT

Very narrow definitions of government exclude a great deal that we intuitively know is relevant to government. Broad definitions tend to have limits which are loose. Legal definitions obscure the relationship between government and the social system of which it is a part.

As used here, "government" refers to a concrete group. It is defined as follows: In a system "government" is the most generalized membership unit possessing (1) defined responsibilities for the maintenance of the system of which it is a part and (2) a practical monopoly of coercive powers.[7] Using this definition we can speak of the government of a society, or a church, or a trade union. The same characteristics analytically defined would hold whatever empirical form the activities of government might take. We can call these general characteristics "structural requisites." In addition, the manner of participation in government of members of a unit can vary. Types of variation we shall call "format." The variation of format will depend upon the degree of representativeness of government. Finally, we are saying that government, although a concrete unit, is distinct from others in the following respect: *it is a concrete structural requisite for any social system.* We are saying, for example, that, while

[7]This definition is by no means unusual. A similar one has most recently been put forward by Bertrand dé Jouvenel. See *Sovereignty* (Chicago: University of Chicago Press, 1957), p. 20.

any substructure of a society (or other social system) has relationship to the maintenance of society, government is the most strategic of these. We do not say that, if you set up a government, you automatically create a society. Rather, the minimal requirements for the maintenance of government must be related to society in such a way that both can exist.

The crucial concerns of government are those which threaten the existence of the unit of which it is part. With its practical monopoly of coercive powers, government has an indivisible responsibility for protecting the system. It handles its responsibilities in terms of certain minimal structures. If any of these structures should fail to operate, government itself must undergo drastic modification, and/or the system itself will undergo drastic modification. Therefore, important threats to the system are, first, threats to the ability of government to work in terms of its structural requisites, and second, threats deriving from inadequate performance of government within the structural requisites from the point of view of the system as a whole, i.e., bad policy, inadequate action, etc. We shall discuss these structural requisites very briefly.[8]

The Structural Requisites of Government

Of the broad range of activities which governments undertake, some are "vitally" necessary if the unit is to keep going. Some of the means to insure the performance of such activities are, in a loose way, what we mean by structural requisites. A tentative set of goals can be listed for any government, as follows: (1) the structure of authoritative decision-making; (2) the structure of accountability and consent; (3) the structure of coercion and punishment; (4) the structure of resource determination and allocation; and (5) the structure of political recruitment and role assignment.

Decision-making by government involves the posing of alternatives and the selection of one or more for effectuation. Decision-making is presumed to be prompted by demands made outside the government or demands placed upon government by its own plans or the logic of previous actions. Here the important questions are: (1) Who makes the decisions? (2) What is the nature of the issues posed? (3) What is the range of supervision by decision-makers? Significant characteristics to be specified are as follows: the method of arriving at decisions, the scope of those decisions, and the degree of centralization in decision-making (in-

[8]Applications and discussion of the structural requisites of government are given much fuller treatment in another paper, "Nationalism, Government, and Economic Growth," in *Economic Development and Cultural Change*, January, 1959. [Reprinted in this volume.]

cluding federal and unitary forms). Decisional legislation can take two forms: *framework legislation,* or broad enabling legislation with scope for initiative and innovation in application left to effectuating agencies, and *supervisory legislation,* involving detailed and continuous scrutiny by decision-makers.[9]

Patterns of accountability and consent involve reference groups for decision-makers significant to the extent that decisions will be made with such groups in mind. Such groups will either modify decisions at the request of government or require formal approval before a final decision is made. In democratic societies there are legally defined and ordered accountability groups (e.g., standing committees of a legislature) and consent groups (e.g., parliaments). In such instances there is symmetry between decision-making and accountability. Where decision-makers can more arbitrarily shift their accountability (e.g., to interest groups or special groups in a party), they have considerable autonomy. "Asymmetry" in such instances can involve a genuine difference between formal and substantive accountability, as in the case of "rubber-stamp" parliaments.[10]

Indeed, where decision-making does not have effective accountability, there is a genuine lack of information on the part of decision-makers, who very often cannot control the consequences of their own decisions or make useful predictions in this regard. Each decision involves an evaluation of consequence. Systems which posit goals of a distant nature and force the pace to their accomplishment normally cannot remain accountable to representatives of the public for very long periods of time. Instead, they would be more likely to be responsible to the technicians and others who are concerned with carrying out the goals. They use specialist information rather than information about public desires.

Where accountability is asymmetrical and shifting (i.e., where deci-

[9]We do not have space for a genuine discussion of this structural requisite. It is strategic from a research point of view as well. If a content analysis is done, for example, on sample legislation in a given area and work can be done on the initiation and direction of bills (or other forms of decisions like orders or commands, etc.), then considerable information about the responsiveness of government can be elicited, along with patterns of leadership and autonomy in government. For a useful discussion of decision-making see R. C. Snyder, H. W. Bruck, and B. Sapin, *Decision-making as an Approach to the Study of International Politics* ("Foreign Policy Analysis Project," Series No. 3; Princeton: Princeton University Press, 1954).

[10]It is held here that even dictators are accountable in some measure to groups in the system. They will normally "spread" that accountability in such fashion that no crucial accountability group can challenge authority. Indeed, many of the crises of dictatorial regimes arise because it is difficult to keep the distribution of accountability such that it does not limit the autonomy of the dictator. The ultimate accountability group in democratic systems is the toal responsible and adult membership of the system, i.e., where there is universal suffrage. This represents a residual accountability. Interesting combinations occur where the two extremes merge, i.e., where effective dictatorship occurs with maximum support as expressed in universal suffrage or some equivalent. Popular radical dictatorships are of this nature.

sion-makers have considerable autonomy), coercion and punishment are normally extensive. Coercion may take the form of positing new norms, concepts of ideal citizenship (the "New Soviet Man," for example), and social pressures of a variety of kinds. Types of coercion may range from social pressure to the modern arsenal of technological refinements. Both coercion and punishment are consequences of actions taken without knowledge of consequences. Insofar as the costs of coercion and punishment are financially high and morally corrosive (they break down all solidarity except the solidarity of complicity), they reduce the ability of government to devote as much of its resources to modifications in stratification as are perhaps necessary (except by using party, police, or army as patronage).

The general ability of decision-makers to act and the costs of their decisions to the public are determined by the ability of government to define, exploit, and allocate resources. Included here are the important problems of taxation and revenue assessment, which might result in reapportionment of wealth. In the modern social welfare state (and this would include most colonial and recent former colonial states as well) welfare measures are among the most important ways of gradually modifying social stratification. Equally important, they are a means of ensuring the commitment of members to the system itself.

Finally, links between social stratification, party, and government itself are in part determined by the method of recruitment to and the definition of the roles of government. As Duverger has shown very adequately, types of electoral systems, for example, play an important part in determining the pattern of government accountability, the important units of decision-making, and the ability of government to recruit effective participants.[11] In some systems elections are the only permissible warrant for making decisions. In others there is co-optation and election. In some systems there are appointments germane to the perpetuation of an oligarchy. In large part the structure of political recruitment and role assignment determine the format of government. Format is extremely important because it is an indication of the formal responsiveness of a regime.

Format of Government

As we have indicated, we mean by "format" the degree of representativeness of the regime. All regimes can be regarded as oligarchical in some respects, but the important question is whether or not the oligarchy

[11]For a general discussion of the relationship between party, government, and stratification see M. Duverger, *Political Parties* (London: Methuen & Co., 1954), *passim*. A detailed, if at times unorthodox, discussion of the consequences of differing electoral systems applicable to systems of indirect representation can be found in J. F. S. Ross, *Elections and Electors* (London: Eyre & Spottiswoode, 1955).

serves the wider purposes of the system or is free to serve its own. On the other hand, even totalitarian regimes have some representative feature. Format, then, represents types of systems with respect to their representativeness, as follows: (1) dictatorial; (2) oligarchical; (3) indirectly representational; and (4) directly representational. These types are important insofar as variations in them involve differences in the performances of structural requisites and indicate degrees of sensitivity to the social stratification system. Depending upon format, political parties have differing roles to play, have different potentialities, and have limits put upon their own actions.

It is important that we recognize, first, the crucial and strategic role of government in a going social system; second, that the format of government in part determines its actions, and third, that these actions occur within the framework of five structural requisites, failure to perform in any one of which entails the breakdown of government itself. Insofar as government is regarded as a concrete structural requisite of any social system, the social system itself will be altered.

From the point of view of theory, the empirical variations in possible actions in each of these structural requisites should be the core of comparative treatment. Ideally, a battery of data would have to be built up based on analysis of widely differing social systems and societies before the theoretical value of many empirical activities could be ascertained. At a minimum, then, these structures should have heuristic value. At a maximum they should produce useful theories.

POLITICAL GROUPS

Modifications in the stratification system can be brought about by two major groups of entrepreneurs: (1) those who use the factors of production and are primarily *economic*, and (2) those whose entrepreneurial activities are essentially devoted to the recruitment of followers who attempt to modify the system either by participation in government or by directing their action against it. These latter will be regarded as *political*. Of groups called "political," those which seek to find positions for their members in government will be regarded as political *associations* if they are composed of intimates and associates (like clubs) and political *parties* if there are regularly subscribed rules for membership and if the members are governed by the rules rather than personal association. If the rules of a political group are vague, not based upon norms for the behavior of intimates, it will be called a *movement*. To be effective, movements require mass membership; they are extraordinarily dependent upon personal leaders. They tend to transform themselves into parties if a stable framework of legitimate government is sufficiently flexible.

Historically, in most western countries political associations appeared before political parties, but only recently have political movements transformed themselves into parties. Political movements emerge particularly in a system where there are fundamental disequilibria in social stratification and where economic entrepreneurship does not appear as a feasible means of increasing public commitment to that system. In some instances political movements transform themselves into parties if they can capture government and combine economic entrepreneurship with political entrepreneurship through state enterprise. Political movements are normally monopolistic—opposition groups are despised or their members are regarded as traitors.

The actions of political groups depend ultimately upon the social stratification system insofar as there is a search for basic issues and grievances and insofar as recruitment to political groups is deeply affected by social strata. Depending upon who is recruited, considerable limitations are normally imposed upon political parties, upon political associations in particular, and, to a lesser extent, upon political movements. However, political groups have both contingent properties and their own "system" properties. They have certain organizational characteristics which produce changes in their activities and ideologies. Some refer to leadership and to the abilities of a political group to take advantage of a given situation. Others refer specifically to recruitment and scope. A constant rejuxtaposition of such characteristics provides differences in political group activity. We shall discuss political groups therefore under two general rubrics: the structure of leadership and the structure of membership.

The Structure of Leadership

Four characteristic types of leadership shall be encompassed here. They are: (1) bureaucratic and durable; (2) personal and fragile; (3) bureaucratic and fragile; and (4) personal and durable.

Normally, bureaucratic and durable parties, such as the Social Democratic party of Germany or the Conservative and Labour parties in England, require a stable and highly participant structure of government with a format of indirect democracy. The leadership in such a party may itself be oligarchical but only within the larger compass of a democratic state. Hence the oligarchical aspect of bureaucratic and durable parties tends to reinforce the democratic system by using its machinery to bring about a correspondence between public demands and government decisions. Democracy within a party does not necessarily lead to effective democracy in government.

Bureaucratic and durable parties have stable oligarchical (and usually middle-aged) leaders. The supporters are normally middle-class and are "majoritarian" in their outlook, requiring mass membership less than a stable mass support. Such parties have a large corps of functional experts whose position in the party may involve a full-time appointment and is based upon "expertise" (functionally specific roles). There is, at the very top, a leadership composed of a few persons whose roles are widely varied and who can play, simultaneously, public spokesman, symbol of ideas, parliamentary leader or prime minister, and chief "organizer" of talent. Such leaders are characteristically "political entrepreneurs."[12]

Bureaucratic and durable parties require a stable government format and help to produce one. They draw their following from widely differing groups in the social stratification system, but they differ substantially from political movements, which also draw their support from widely differing groups in the social stratification system insofar as they are not temporary amalgams of unhomogeneous elements. Such political parties are normally progressive or conservative and gain their flexibility by appealing to voters within the generally middle-class ranges of the social stratification system. These parties are possible, however, only where the stratification system is relatively wide in range and open in mobility. Bureaucratic and durable parties which do not find such a social stratification system are normally impossible to organize unless they transform the political format of government into a single-party state, in which case the party oligarchy becomes the government oligarchy. The case of Turkey has, until recent years, been very instructive here.

The complete obverse of bureaucratic and durable political party leadership is that which is personal and fragile. Normally, in such patterns of leadership, a single figure exercises an extremely powerful moral and legitimizing influence. Members partake of his grace and are a chosen people or the carriers of a special mission. In its extreme form this is the type of leadership that Weber called "charismatic." In its more usual form it involves a highly personal type of control over followers which should not be confused with charisma[13] but which is dependent upon offices and rewards to be supplied by the leader for his followers and,

[12]For a discussion of functionality and bureaucracy see D. E. Apter and R. Lystad, "Bureaucracy, Party and Constitutional Democracy," in *Transition in Africa: Studies in Political Adaptation*, eds. G. Carter and W. O. Brown (Boston: Boston University Press, 1958). [Reprinted in this volume.]

[13]The term "charismatic" has become misused. Charisma is a most unusual phenomenon and does simply refer to personal magnetism on the part of a leader. Properly speaking, charisma involves special qualities of grace and legitimization which are deeply spiritual and profound. See Max Weber, *The Theory of Social and Economic Organization*, trans., Alexander Morell Henderson and Talcott Parsons (Edinburgh: William Hodge & Co., 1947).

most of all, upon the access to high positions in the social stratification system which the party makes possible.

Personal and fragile parties need crises in order to maintain their followings. Very often they require a revolutionary ideology, although in practice they may not be at all opposed to the social stratification system, but are merely interested in opening avenues for party members to the high power and prestige roles. This is certainly the case for Fascist parties, which characteristically have a "revolutionary" ideology before they assume office—hence recruiting the most mobility-conscious of those in the population whose index of commitment to the stratification system is high but whose opportunities for advancement within it are low—and a conservative ideology as soon as they achieve control of the government. And, because they are fragile, they must produce a state bureaucracy in the absence of a party bureaucracy (i.e., the leader may have followers who perform bureaucratic tasks), but the essence of bureaucracy is that it has regularized and institutionalized roles which cannot be arbitrarily dealt with. Personal and fragile political parties show a constant change in officers. The government, then, serves to produce the bureaucracy which is under the control of the party leader. Such a combination can work quite well until the problem of leader succession arises —a problem which few personal and fragile parties have been able to solve satisfactorily.[14]

This problem of succession is adequately solved by personal and durable leaders. These are, characteristically, leadership roles in which the leader is not important as an individual but in which his position is intensely symbolic and mystical. Divine kingship is the classic example of such a position in government; others are provided by certain monarchical parties where a king or a pretender is in fact the party leader or figurehead in whose name a party leader operates. Personal and fragile parties must, over time, change into either bureaucratic and durable parties or personal and durable parties. An example of a partially unsuccessful attempt to make the transformation was demonstrated in the U.S.S.R. after the death of Lenin. Under Lenin's auspices it appeared as if the party would move more directly toward a bureaucratic and durable leadership. Under Stalin such a process became a menace to his own leadership autonomy, and, through purges and other means, bureaucratization of the party was halted—though there was a great increase in government bureaucracy, as was discussed above—and, indeed, personal control constantly increased. It is particularly difficult for personal and

[14]The Spanish example is instructive here, since Generalissimo Franco has apparently chosen to restore the monarchy (i.e., personal and durable leadership) to succeed himself.

fragile parties to maintain that type of leadership in systems of indirect representation (i.e., in democratic systems of government) and especially difficult where a single-member constituency parliamentary government is in operation. It is extremely useful to observe personal and fragile parties which develop out of nationalist movements in underdeveloped territories where colonial oligarchical governments have been displaced by European parliamentary forms of indirect representative government.

It is very difficult for personal and durable parties to operate for long periods in governments with indirect representation without changing the format of government to at least a nominal oligarchical format, as in Portugal. Also, personal and durable parties can be transformed into bureaucratic and durable parties by a conflict between a monarchical system and leaders of personal and durable parties. Such a situation expresses itself simultaneously in a widening of recruitment to the political party and in demands for more representative government. It helps to explain the phenomenon of Tory radicalism in nineteenth-century England and the expansion of constitutional monarchy.

Personal and fragile political parties usually develop out of political movements which cater to wide segments of the social stratification system. Personal and durable political parties usually develop out of select political associations which have a narrow recruiting base in the social stratification system. Such parties are often associated with religious legitimacy, in which the role of the leader has personal characteristics of a sacral nature, while the occupant of the role may change.[15] In personal and fragile parties, it is the person occupying the leadership position who carries with him these characteristics; hence the difficulty of succession.

Bureaucratic and fragile parties are particularly significant where the stratification system is widely disjointed or where membership is not on the basis of a movement but upon familiar linkages of social groups normally in contact with one another, such as with political associations based upon members of certain clubs, universities, occupational groups, and religious groups. Normally, these parties are held together by their overlapping membership in significant reference groups rather than by individual leaders, and they show a marked tendency to fission and reamalgamation with simply a reallocation of defined roles between members. Middle-class nationalist parties in colonial territories show that these propensities and parties break up and re-form with the same old faces and with only the party name being changed. Parliamentary party associations in nineteenth-century England showed some of these characteristics until they sought a more durable base among wider segments of the population dispersed throughout a social stratification system in

[15]An excellent example in the United States is afforded by the Mormons.

which middle ranges were increasing. The same has been true in British colonial territories. A mass following helps to produce a more stable bureaucracy in party leadership.

Very often, as a symptom as well as a cause of declining membership, a bureaucratic and durable party will transform itself into a bureaucratic and fragile party. This is particularly the case where substantial changes going on in the stratification system are not manifested in changes in the content of decisions in government, if such a party is in government, or if the government does not hold itself accountable to the party. If the index of commitment to the stratification system declines, then fission and fractionalization occur in the bureaucratic and durable party, changing it into a bureaucratic and fragile one. Normally, this situation is accompanied by the growth of personal and fragile parties, especially those having a revolutionary ideology.

The type of party leadership, then, depends a great deal upon what is going on in the region of social stratification (i.e., the sources of party recruitment) and its means and manner of representing those groups in relation to government. Personal and fragile parties have an affinity for oligarchical or dictatorial forms of government. Bureaucratic and durable parties have affinities for indirect representation systems of government. If the stratification system is such that the top positions are relatively narrow and closed, yet achievement criteria prevail, with widely developed groups in the population having obtained such achievements, a personal and fragile movement is possible. Such a movement would promise, in itself, to become a social stratification system, since by virtue of membership it accords both power and prestige. However, such situations are normally revolutionary, and, when the movement succeeds and takes over the government, it directs its effort toward drastic economic and social reforms. If it is to be successful, such reforms must accord the fruits of revolution to a significant number of followers at the expense of former high-ranking status-holders. Most bloody revolutions are of this character. On the other hand, if the movement becomes a party and the index of commitment to the system is high enough, it may be possible to satisfy enough of the followers by giving them political appointments without changing the social stratification system.

Both instances are normally found in association with some form of state socialism. In the first instance, the new stratification system comes into being by the party capturing the government, changing its format if necessary, and substantially altering property relations via massive nationalization. In the second instance, property relations are not basically altered, but positions are created in conjunction with the already existing high status positions to be found. The first instance is characteristic of the Communist pattern and the second of the Fascist pattern.

Bureaucratic and durable parties are normally pushed along the same lines by the same impulses in the social stratification system. However, if they are working within the framework of parliamentary government, they are characterized by progressive reform rather than revolutionary change. Much then depends upon how the structures of government are operated. Government may use its power of taxation and revenue allocation to minimize conflict in the social stratification sphere; indeed, it may do so drastically. But if the social stratification system is such that important groups in the population are highly resistant to such reform (as in the case of modern France), it is quite possible that government will not be able to carry out its functions. Such impotence will provide opportunities for a drastic change in the society itself.

Personal and fragile parties and movements thrive when changes in social stratification produce uncertainty in social and economic life and at their most extreme establish a system of legitimacy at variance with that of government. They can produce chaos by making it impossible for the government to carry out any or all of the structural requisites of government. If bureaucratic and durable parties are to be able to cope with such conditions in the social stratification system (which may be produced by depression, or plague, or a host of circumstances), they require a format of government in which the structure of accountability and consent and the structure of authoritative decision-making reflect both the needs and the demands of the population. Normally, a bureaucratic and durable party has a better awareness of incipient discontent in the members of the society and can reflect that awareness within the decision-making apparatus of a representative system of government. Totalitarian or oligarchical governments reach their maximum efficiency just after there has been a dramatic system change and the leaders are in close identification with the public. After that point they grow increasingly remote from the needs and the requirements of the public; hence they grow increasingly restrictive, and, normally, their decision-making is expressed in terms of a postponed goal which has a sentimental and historical attachment to the issues which gave rise to the movement or party in the first place, while they seek to demonstrate their achievements in the future rather than in the present.

If these totalitarian or oligarchical governments can provide sufficient satisfactions throughout a changing social stratification system to keep the public reasonably happy, it is possible for them to make their governmental format more representative, increase the accountability of the government, and change the party into a more bureaucratic and durable type. Some observers see signs of this process occurring in the social stratification system in the U.S.S.R. In some underdeveloped territories where a personal and fragile political movement has been transformed into a party operating a parliamentary government, there must either be enough commitment to the social stratification system for governmental activities not to be the exclusive concerns of members of society or the government system must be made oligarchic or dictatorial.[16] When economic entrepreneurship is a possible major means of reform, this is normally the case. Otherwise the political entrepreneurs transform themselves into economic entrepreneurs through the mechanism of state enterprise.

The impulses thus deriving from types of political group leadership strongly affect the way in which both government format and social stratification will be manifested in society. The activities of government and the social stratification system give rise to types of political group leadership. Such leadership reflects ideological positions which range in their degree of commitment to the social stratification system. The range itself, as a reflection of political group identification with the stratification system, can be specified as follows: *revolutionary* (i.e., a complete system change) and *progressiste* (i.e., extensive alteration in social stratification in any of the categories which describe it, such as changes from achievement rather than ascriptive eligibility to status, or extending or narrowing the range of participation). A *conservative* ideology involves maintenance of substantially the same structure of social stratification with only minor changes. A *revivalist* ideology seeks to restore an already altered social stratification system.

Political ideas can serve under more than one of these categories. For example, Communist political ideas are conservative in the contemporary U.S.S.R., according to this usage of ideology, but are revolutionary in the French Cameroons. Political groups of various types can subscribe to various of these ideological positions and can change over time. The National Socialist party of Germany, for example, showed elements of revivalism in its mythology, "revolutionaryism" before the SA purge, and conservatism for most of its governmental tenure. The Rassemblement Démocratique Africaine in French West Africa shows considerable

[16]When personal and fragile leaders working within a parliamentary system need to change the format of government in order to preserve their leadership, the modern pattern of populist or radical totalitarianism (which in modern times begins with Napoleon) produces leaders who prefer totalitarianism to oligarchy on the grounds that the former is more "democratic" or at least more compatible with fervent ideals. An oligarchy tends to create a specially privileged group in the social stratification system, while in radical dictatorships oligarchies can be removed. Indeed, this is implicit in the communism of both Leninists and Titoists, and only when it is discovered that a new oligarchy can emerge not based on actual ownership of property is there awareness of how "mischievous" is the doctrine. A good, yet pathetic, example of this "awareness" is to be found in Milovan Djilas, *The New Class* (New York: Frederick A. Praeger, Publisher, Inc., 1957). See also Ernst Cassirer, *The Myth of the State* (New Haven: Yale University Press, 1946).

Marxist influence yet remains *progressiste* in its ideology, and has a pragmatic approach aimed at gauging public demands for changes in the social stratification system without allowing Communist dogma to direct party programs and actions.

Types of leadership can strongly affect the type of ideological position taken, particularly in the case of personal and fragile political groups which feed on crises of increasing intensification, and make manifest latent disaffiliation of the public from the system of social stratification. If they push the government to decisions which contradict their position, or make active the structure of coercion and punishment they are forced into an increasingly revolutionary position. This is particularly true where they seek by means of strikes or parliamentary operations to make the structure of coercion and punishment inoperative, hence making government inoperative. Such political groups would require a revolutionary ideology both to justify their position with their following and to seek to create a new kind of society.

In underdeveloped areas nationalist movements are normally not of this type. They seek to throw out oligarchical colonial regimes, making them representative, take control by the use of electoral machinery, and then seek reform. Thus they are mostly *progressiste*, although their actual slogans and ideas may sound revolutionary. An excellent example is Ghana, where the Convention People's party is today in control of an independent country within a British-type parliamentary system of government, pushing toward moderate reform in the social stratification system. However, if under such circumstances the personal leadership of the party should fail, and the party, becoming more bureaucratic, show signs of fragility, it is possible that the government bureaucracy and the apparatus of the state power could be transformed into the personal weapon of the party leader, and the format of government could change to dictatorship or oligarchy, carrying a revolutionary ideology. The social stratification system would be altered or constrained as the case might be.

However, the range of possibilities open to political leaders is not only dependent upon the social stratification system and the format of government. Much depends on the characteristics of political group membership.

A diagram of leadership and ideological characteristics is shown in Figure 2.

The Structure of Membership

Variations in leadership patterns and ideology reflect the type of membership which obtains in a political group, whether a movement, a party, or an association. The first basic distinction is whether or not the political group is an *elite* or a *mass* organization. Normally, elite political groups are composed of narrow segments of the social stratification system or

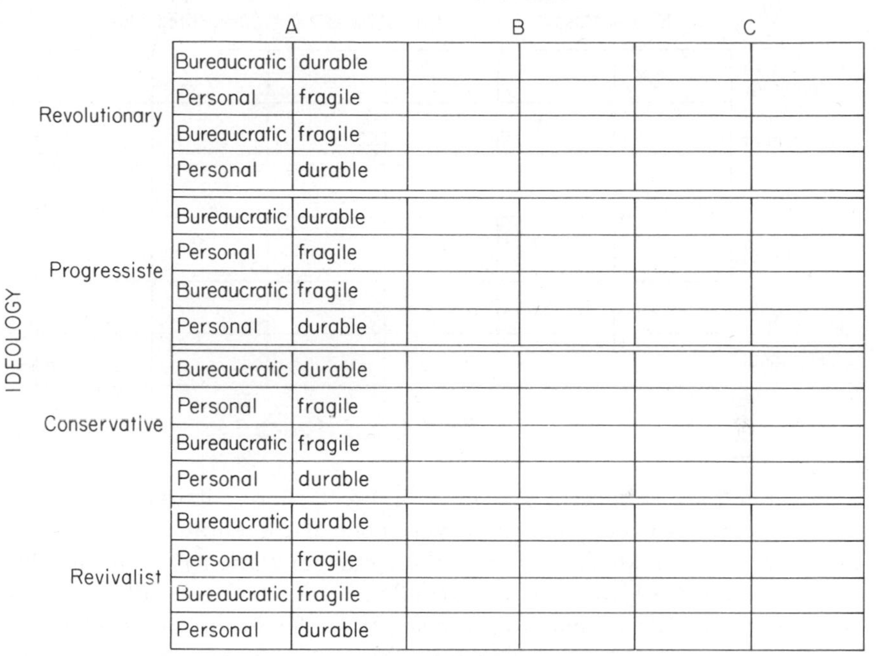

***Figure* 2.**

of people who have by some means "removed" themselves from it, as in the case of the bourgeois origins of many Communist party members. Where they seek a mass following, they form a party within a movement. An elite political group may or may not have strict rules of membership. Communist or Fascist parties normally do so; so may some nationalist parties which have their roots in situations where they were originally proscribed by governments and therefore show earmarks of operating illegally. Some elite parties openly do not want mass followings, for example, a political party in Uganda which identified itself as a party of "leaders" (i.e., the best people). Such an elite is a "weightier party" type of organization which seeks to influence others by the distinction of the membership.

Many of the characteristics of party leadership will also depend upon whether the organization, elite or mass as the case might be, is *urban-* or *rural-dominant*, *territorial* or *supraterritorial* in those it seeks to affiliate, and *ethnic* or *regional* in its scope.

Ethnic and/or regional groups, particularly if they are rural-dominant, mass political movements, or political parties, tend to push for local autonomy within a given territory and demand a federal system of gov-

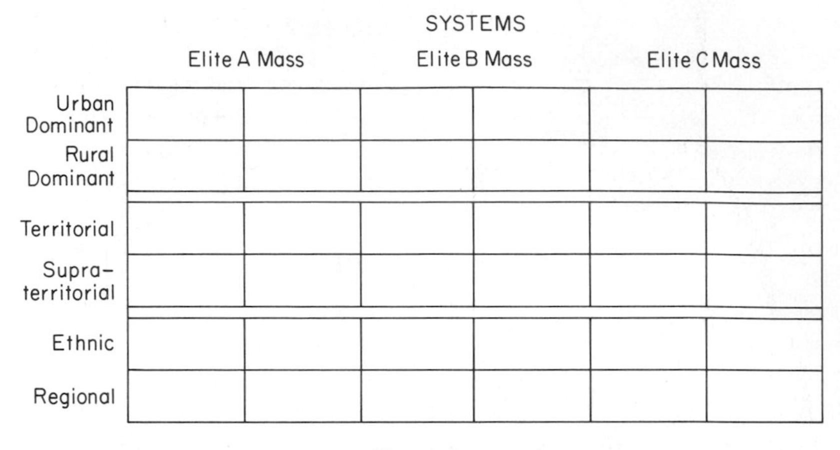

Figure 3.

ernment if they support a system of indirect representation and if the ethnic group is smaller than the government of the entire country. They may vary in their ideology, but, if the rural population is poor and disgruntled, and the leadership is urban-dominant, they normally push toward a *progressiste* system of reformism. If the leadership is personal and fragile, and especially if the membership is predominantly rural, this may quickly take the form of a revivalist ideology.

Urban-dominant elite parties, normally territorial in scope, may, depending upon how they recruit from the social stratification system, produce a bureaucratic and fragile leadership, as in the classic case of small, middle-class political parties which show fission and fusion and a conservative or *progressiste* ideology. If they recruit from a disinherited and disenfranchised group in the social stratification system, and if they are barred by an oligarchical government from effective participation, they are likely to produce a personal and fragile leadership moving toward a revolutionary ideology; on the other hand, an equivalent group which is rural- and ethnic-dominant is normally personal and durable in its leadership and revivalist in its ideology. This is particularly the case in some tribal societies existing in the context of a colonial oligarchical regime, such as the Bataka party in Uganda, and, among right-wing monarchical rural parties in some European countries with indirect representation, such as prewar France and Weimar Germany.

Occasionally, a situation exists in which an elite party forms an elect within a political movement with a personal and durable leadership and an elite membership urban-dominant and supraterritorial in its scope. Communist parties show some of these characteristics, the binding force being a revolutionary ideology reinforced by government actions which use against them the structures of decision-making, coercion and punishment, and sometimes revenue assessment and allocation. Their relative strength depends in large part upon the index of commitment to stratification. If it is high, Communist parties are relatively powerless, and, if it is low, they can be relatively powerful. Insofar as systems of government having indirect representation with bureaucratic and durable parties are normally most capable of determining the index of commitment, they are usually the most effective in resisting party activities. The least effective are oligarchical or totalitarian systems, unless they are constantly transforming the social stratification system.[17]

There are special problems when dealing with political parties which are themselves elites, such as a Communist party which bases its ultimate strength upon a number of factors which might be crucial for the Communist party, but for no other party which would normally abide by the more general rules of the game. Hence tactics and strategy for a Communist party, and often a Fascist party, in a parliamentary setting endangers that setting in a way which does not normally obtain. However, elite parties which are revolutionary in their ideology require a mass following, that is to say people who may belong to a movement but who are not, strictly speaking, allowed into the party itself. Now one characteristic of a movement is that, while it may have a well-defined goal, the goal must be ideologically diffuse. It cannot be narrowly programmatic, since movements usually recruit from a wide range of groups having relatively different positions in the social stratification system. The only exception is where a system has a dominant single class, like a working class, more or less permanently disbarred from high positions, as in classic Marxian doctrine. In practice this has not been very rare; even in Asia movements have been rural in recruitment and urban in leadership, with propensities for splitting apart with an increase in programming and scheduling political targets.

Communist parties, particularly in Europe, have the special problem of defining goals more narrowly for their members than for their followers (those in the movement which support the party). Such a circumstance increases the need for secrecy among party members and builds characteristics of control and discipline into the party which complement other reasons for control and discipline, such as subversion or capturing control of voluntary associations.

In addition, movements, as we have said, are normally "mass type." In classic Leninist doctrine, Communist party membership must remain small and fulfill vanguard functions. Party discipline does not extend to the movement. Hence there must be a considerable degree of symbolic

[17]They may transform the system by dramatic economic change (difficult without weakening the entire system), purges, changes in role occupants but not roles, etc.

representation of both persons and issues and a high degree of personalization of leadership, which is done less for the sake of the party members than for the followers of the movement. A Communist party, therefore, becomes an elect inside a movement with a double standard of behavior, one for members of the party acting as party members and another for members of the party working to rally the movement. Indeed, this situation prevailed in the U.S.S.R. to a large extent. Stalin's crime was to personalize himself to party members as well as to followers of the movement—hence the special sense of outrage in decrying the cult of personality.

Movements are characteristic of certain types of nationalist political groups. In underdeveloped areas they encompass members having regional and ethnic affiliations as well. In Nigeria this has produced political parties which range in their ideology from (1) conservative (the Northern People's party), (2) *progressiste* but dominated by a bureaucratic and durable chiefs' and middle-class leadership (Action Group), and (3) *progressiste* with a more radical program and a clearly urban leadership (the National Council of Nigeria and the Cameroons).

There can be considerable confusion between the broadly based, mass political party, such as those in this country, and a movement. Normally, mass political parties do not require much participation by members except at election time. A movement, on the other hand, tends to be aroused by an issue or series of issues which challenge the status quo in some fundamental manner, while mass parties in substance require the maintenance of the system as it stands. Hence mass parties do not challenge the legitimacy of government, although they might question its activities; that is, they will seek to manipulate and change the content of decisions but not the structure of decision-making. Movements, furthermore, require periodic manifestations of the loyalty of followers in a variety of activities and institutions (protest, strikes, petitions, special organizations like special schools, etc.). They surround their leaders with a mystique. They need considerable solidarity, which mass political parties do not. Their leadership is ordinarily personal and fragile or personal and durable.

Movements are charactertistic of those societies in which commitment to the social stratification system is low, and they normally change into parties of a mass type, or disintegrate. When an elect exists inside the movement, it tends to become dangerous, because it is difficult to control except by dramatic changes in the social stratification system which are normally brought about by the elect capturing the government and promulgating drastic reconstruction in society or by becoming extraterritorial in scope. Egypt under President Nasser is a case in point; here the extraterritorial basis of the movement is along ethnic lines (pan-Arabism), internal reform is extremely difficult, and the symbolic mystique of the leader is personal and fragile. Leadership could become personal and durable, as is true of some other Arab groups, by increasing the religious nature of its leadership, and a pseudo-papal Islamic religious role could be made out of the leadership position.

These additional aspects of political group structure, then, set limiting conditions upon the development of leadership and ideology in political groups. Each of the possible combinations produce different possible consequences and, taken together with the other elements of this comparative scheme, should (1) increase the ability of a research worker to make predictions about the outcome of a given state of affairs in politics and (2) generate theories on the basis of comparative treatment.

It should be possible to outline major consequences of structural relations between types of party organizations and types of government format, for example, modified by the performances of each, the seriousness of which can be measured in the degree to which they support or hinder government in carrying out its structural requisites—in turn, crucial for the maintenance of a given system. For example, when there are bureaucratic and fragile parties participating in a system of government which is indirectly representative (of the parliamentary type), party tendencies to fission produce multiple parliamentary party situations. Multiple parliamentary party situations emphasize differences between parties. Emphasis on differences produces (1) coalitions for government-forming purposes and (2) appeals to voters at the two opposite ends of the political spectrum (i.e., appeals to extremes). Appeals to extremes are modified by immediate coalition prospects and by electoral support, plus potential support of uncommitted voters to an opposition coalition. This is in large part determined by the degree of commitment which exists in the social stratification system.

Bureaucratic and durable parties tend to form middle-spectrum coalitions when there is a multiple-party system in parliament. Where there is a two-party system in parliament, the programs of the government party and the opposition party tend constantly to identify up to the point where marginal voters cease to prefer one party or the other.

Personal and durable parties tend toward a high degree of "traditionalistic" authoritarianism in which tendencies toward fission within the party are regarded as tantamount to treason. In a parliamentary setting they normally form a solid bloc and rarely have wide support, except in theocratic types of societies, and they prefer oligarchical government to indirect representative government.

Personal and fragile parties are dependent upon their degree of deviation from the social stratification system as it stands and cannot long endure under conditions of parliamentary government. They therefore seek to undermine the system or else to transform themselves into bureaucratic and durable parties with the same leadership maintained intact. This has been particularly true of political parties which have developed out of a special "struggle," whether in Europe, where the struggle was against a given form of oligarchy with changes sought in both the system of stratification and the format of government, or in underdeveloped areas attacking colonialism and, as a result, achieving self-government. Ghana, Indonesia, and Malaya are all interesting countries to compare in this latter regard.

CONCLUSION

The foregoing represents a "prolegomene" to a comparative method. It seeks to produce theories by developing a scheme in which by comparative treatment of many instances, it is possible to see combinations of these variables in action. If comparative analysis is to be effective, some such treatment is essential. The essence of this approach involves an examination of sample issues which are thrown up for government to deal with, particularly those which imply threats to the structural requisites of any government. Any research done in these terms would therefore, first of all, require a delimitation of core issues which, related to social stratification, on the one hand, and manifested in political group activity, on the other, specify how differing governments, in differing formats, deal with them. The structural requisites of any government then give a guide to the limits of variation to which governments may be subject without being destroyed, and their actual operations in terms of these structures gives us a guide to how well they are able to perform.

The possible empirical combinations of these variables are very great. Only a few possible combinations have been discussed. In this respect, as we have indicated, the scheme is very inelegant. It does not have precision. Much of it would be difficult, though hopefully not impossible, to operationalize for fine treatment. A wide variety of research techniques would be appropriate to its use. Refinements in comparative criteria would be essential.

Most of all, a careful comparison of differing societies and their governments can indicate some of the conditions necessary for the working of democracy, an especially acute question in those parts of the world where democratic institutions are new, their social bases weak, and governments are in the position of seeking social change while remaining able to control it. Oligarchical governments and totalitarianism are common, and we know some of the pressures which produce them. Can some of these same pressures be utilized for the working of modern democratic governments as well? In this respect we know far less about the potentialities of democracy than oligarchy. It is through the comparative analysis of democracies under widely differing conditions and through time that we can learn something about their potentialities and ultimate compatability with drastic social change. Equally, a study of some of the new governments round the world should help to produce a genuine theory of democratic government—a theory having practical as well as ethical implications for our times.

Nationalism, Government, and Economic Growth

INTRODUCTION

In this discussion we shall be concerned with newly independent countries which have emerged from colonial status in large part through the determined efforts of nationalist political leaders. Such leaders are faced with an overwhelming dilemma. They are faced with a need for wide and popular participation in political life necessary to retain support. They also need highly integrated and effective leadership—an oligarchy, if they are to produce satisfactions such as more education, greater social welfare, and increases in real income. How to produce both wide participation and effective oligarchy is thus the problem facing nationalist political leaders. We are familiar with the radical totalitarian solution to this problem. Our question is, how can we find an optimal solution which falls short of totalitarianism? We shall seek to demonstrate that, given the nature of pressures and demands put upon nationalist political leaders, an optimal solution can be found which allows for good sources of information, and provides for effective participation, and at the same time effective organization.

Most colonial governments are social welfare governments, in that they provide a great deal in the way of social benefits. Whatever the level of social welfare achieved, however, nationalists are professionally interested in making the public dissatisfied with it. They promise other kinds

Although they are not to be held responsible for the discussion presented here, I wish to acknowledge the valuable assistance offered by colleagues who read and commented on this paper: Harry Eckstein, Ronald Coase, and Clifford Geertz.

of satisfactions, of which one is greater status through improved social mobility, i.e., access to higher power and prestige positions in the society, not the least of which are political positions occupied by expatriate officials. Once in office, the pressure of such expectations upon political leaders is intense, and they cast about for radical solutions. One solution is to seek rapid industrialization. This, in turn, presumes tight organizational control, which in fact limits access to political positions.

SOURCES OF EXPECTATION—SOCIAL WELFARE COLONIALISM

The justification of colonialism has been increasingly expressed in terms of the social and economic benefits it has produced. Especially after the war, local areas were overrun with district medical officers, forestry officers, community development officers, cooperative and labor officers, veterinary officers, and so forth. Central government, composed of departmental establishments, provided health, housing, town and country planning, and the usual concerns of the contemporary welfare state in the west. These services were run at reasonably efficient levels by expatriate officers, and people came to expect their continual expansion as the justification of government itself.

Furthermore, there was financial assistance from the metropolitan power. Loans and assistance grants from F.I.D.E.S. in the French territories, the Colonial Development and Welfare funds in British territories, as well as shared costs for military forces, were among the tangible financial benefits received by colonial territories. With indepedence, a territory must find both the technical personnel to fill the positions of expatriate officers and the finances not only to provide welfare and public services but to expand them. In addition, it must allocate some funds to its own military establishments.

The structural framework which political leaders inherit includes legislative establishments, cabinet government composed of departmental heads, and an effective civil service which is increasingly local in its recruitment. "Progress" is measured by the ability of local personnel to meet the internal tasks imposed on government and by the smoothness and flow of government business on the metropolitan model. Achieving this kind of progress has been a concern for both nationalist leaders and colonial officials, and devolution of authority results in reconciliation of objectives between political leaders pushing for authority in the shortest possible time and colonial authorities seeking to prepare those leaders for effective government.

The legislative bodies provide for an expansion of shared political responsibility which facilitates the organization of political parties. The civil service opens its ranks to local recruitment. Indeed, a well-trained local civil service becomes a crucial organizational element in maintaining effective government when a transfer of power to nationalists takes place. Perhaps more than anything, however, colonial governments have been preoccupied with producing viable economies, less dependent upon a single cash crop, and possessing internal sources of savings, local investment, and markets. In the postwar development-conscious era, industrialization has been at least a tentative goal of colonial governments, unwilling as they were to make the drastic and forcible gestures which industrialization would require, because such gestures would place heavy reliance on coercion.

The situation is different for nationalists who see in industrialization the solution to a number of problems raised during the colonial period. To them, industrialization promises to increase wealth, social mobility, and opportunity. Education can expand and national status improve. The establishment of industrialization as a goal means that obstacles to it, whether in the form of institutional limitations or opposition to government, can be overridden because of the priority of service to the party and the state. Precisely because nationalists rush in where colonialists fear to tread, however, the entire framework of representative government with its integrated patterns of decision-making and execution is endangered. Support to nationalists becomes a matter not simply of volition, but of necessity, and the danger of government becoming omnivorous, of devouring all sources of pluralism and opposition, becomes very great if political leaders bent on industrialization do not become vulnerable. To remain exempt from vulnerability while marshalling the human and technical resources of a community takes highly effective leadership, a leadership more diversely skilled than that of the expatriates who are replaced, whose technical proficiency was its own justification, and whose oligarchy was only challenged by the nationalists themselves.

SOCIAL MOBILITY, RECRUITMENT, AND LEADERSHIP

The discussion so far can be simply summarized. When nationalists achieve self-government and succeed their colonial predecessors, the public expects continuation and expansion of former benefits. They also expect increases in participation, access to power and prestige positions in government and other forms of social life, and a speeding up of the tempo of social mobility. Nationalists are capable of absorbing some people into government as they replace departed expatriate officials. They can expand the number of positions in party and government. They can focus on development schemes of a local nature to provide both change and positions for local groups. Beyond a certain point, however, unless the economy is dynamically expanding, they can merely circulate elites.

Even the circulation of elites is limited because stabilization of leadership is required if effective government is to be carried out, and the number of skilled and experienced political leaders who have some knowledge of government is necessarily small. As the leadership becomes stabilized, thereby cutting off one channel to power and prestige, other alternative power and prestige positions must be created. The first concern of a new nationalist government, then, is recruitment. The question is, who will be recruited, and on what basis, to ensure both effective government and devotion to leaders, as the latter attempt to expand both social welfare and opportunity at the higher end of the stratification hierarchy. Participation in government seems to be characteristically determined in terms of the following: first, the importance of people whose support of the regime is required. These will determine the effectiveness with which evaluations of the political situation can be made, and decision-making will be realistic. The criteria of recruitment indicate to what extent the regime will place a high value on basic standards of rationality, expertise, and universalism. We can list these criteria, bearing in mind that they have important consequences for government.

1. *On the basis of political power.* People who have some following are politically significant, and failure to recruit them may well pose future problems for the government.
2. *On the basis of party loyalty.* Those who have served the party well expect that the party will care for them (and sometimes for their families). Furthermore, the party relies on them for carrying out party and government tasks which are necessary. Party loyalty needs to be rewarded if party discipline is to develop and maintain itself. Expulsion from the party would involve severe deprivation.
3. *On the basis of skill and talent.* Those with the necessary training to perform management and organizational tasks, or tasks necessary for the operation of technical services, must be recruited. In almost all newly developing countries, the job of increasing such cadres is the first target of government.

One indication of the status of a new government is the degree to which it mixes its proportions of these three types of recruitment. In many instances, the ministerial system of government is very useful here, since it allows political decisions to be made by political leaders who have been rewarded for party loyalty with cabinet posts. They in turn rely for their own sustained tenure on the effectiveness of their civil service staff or other experts who remain subordinate to them. Equally, a host of advisory boards, committees, etc., can be set up on which people with political power (having an important following) can be put. If there are important issues of land tenure, for example, a land tenure commission might become advisory to a minister of land tenure or a minister of local government. If the trade unions are important, some trade union leaders might be on a labor advisory commission to the minister of local government. If the trade unions are important, some trade union leaders might be on a labor advisory commission to the minister of trade and labor, or be given special tasks, such as the preparation of memoranda on labor conditions, housing, and the like. The government which is effectively able to blend these three forms of recruitment can promote the mutual interdependence of voluntary associations and semi-government commissions in actual participation in government.

The ability to do these things presumes a fairly extensive governmental framework. Because a government needs a great deal of trial and error in order to chart its course, its strength and structure must be relatively secure. Such strength is a function of political party support, which in turn depends upon recruitment. There is a tendency for parties to become the private patrimony of the leader. The party leader tries to alter the social stratification system by making its curve less sharp and reducing the upper strata. He needs to create a new managerial and bureaucratic elite. As Eisenstadt points out, there is then a marked tendency for the political elite and the bureaucracy "to direct all the social developments of the country, especially the raising of the standard of living and the development of new occupations and of mobility within them. In this way they hope to maintain their hold on most potential centers of power and to control their development. But these attempts may defeat their own ends, as the close control exercised by the bureaucracy may undermine the efforts of economic development, create more aspirants to new posts, etc., than are available and thus put the bureaucracy itself in an insecure position."[1] This is a particularly acute problem where nationalism is the main vehicle for national solidarity, and former nationalist political leaders find themselves in positions of political responsibility.

In most of the new countries, previous power and prestige holders either came from outside the system entirely, as in the case of former colonial territories, or their entry was based upon highly ascriptive grounds. The modern nationalist movements of today attack traditional oligarchies and replace them with their own. The main difference be-

[1]See S. N. Eisenstadt, "Changes in Patterns of Stratification Attendant on Attainment of Political Independence," in *Transactions of the Third World Congress of Sociology*, 1956, II, 32–41.

tween these old and new oligarchies is that in the new ones recruitment is on the basis of political power, party loyalty, or expertise. Each of these categories of entry is relatively democratic. People are not barred on such grounds as birth, color, or caste, unless they are regarded as foreigners or aliens, as are the Lebanese, Syrians, and Europeans in West Africa, or the Indians in East Africa. Sustained tenure of office depends upon achievement, which may be demonstrated in the skill by which a leader rallies others to support the government, or the skill in doing a particular administrative or entrepreneurial task. However, in each case, old restrictions have been swept away. Only if the category of party loyalty pre-empts all others is the new oligarchy in virtually the same position as the old one.

Indeed, it is in terms of social mobility and universalistic recruitment that democracy in such areas ought to be understood. More important than political rights of subjects and checks over the executive is the very faith that equality of opportunity has been granted. Equal opportunity demands that the government concentrate its energies on such forms of development as education, which is, in fact, normally the first interest of any new government. Through education come the skills and talents which will foster other types of development.

The character of a political party is shaped in part by the quality of its leadership and its membership. To take the latter first, if the party is a mass party, recruiting from widely differing parts of the social stratification system, it can stand for few specific objectives but requires general targets. Normally, mass nationalist movements are of this nature. They appeal to widely differing groups which are nevertheless in the party. On the other hand, class parties which recruit more narrowly from a certain class can tolerate a greater specificity within the program.

Elite parties tend to be totalitarian insofar as they must capture government and put forward measures without mass support behind them, or, where there is a multi-party system, be strategically placed in coalition governments.

Mass national movements provide a wide range of appeals to voters. Such movements are relatively stable coalitions of interests in many western countries and form loosely organized political parties, as in the United States. They tend to be less stable in developing countries, because each task with which the movement must deal helps to produce friction by favoring one or another group within the movement itself. Hence, a mass political movement which wishes to produce economic development requires some special social cement. It needs a monopoly over patronage. It needs to have some of the characteristics of a nonexclusive elite. It needs extensive decentralization, so that it becomes a village and local primary group, which, in the basic unit of organization, provides constant face-to-face association. It cannot have too much horizontal communication, or control over the party would become so decentralized that it would jeopardize the top leadership.

For maximum autonomy, such a movement or party needs to identify an enemy and produce myths of a new civilization. To the degree that it is organized around a single *personal and fragile* leader, it will be dependent upon the sense of personal identification members have with the leader himself. If the leadership is *bureaucratic and durable*, it will need a moderate yet coherent ideology, which supplies some of the same functions. Socialist parties are often of this type.

Elite parties are common. These may be based on an officer group or military caste, or on landowning or special interest groups. They may be based upon a professional, educated intelligentsia. In many instances this last type of elite party (professional elite) is the predecessor to mass parties, i.e., prepares the ground for a more rude, populist, socially mobile group to take over.

The combination of an elite core with a mass following is the most effective for development purposes. It provides the bureaucratic cadres to run the party and government and to act as the coordinating arm of the state, while the mass party organization provides the informational core. The differences and antagonisms between local party factions both provide competition in ideas and allow the membership to serve as a source of communications. This combination works best where there is a personal and fragile leader at the top, and when the elite has not become so bureaucraticized that it stifles initiative within the party itself. Personal and fragile leaders, furthermore, manipulate the elite cadres against the followers, in order to prevent premature loss of power.

In mass parties with elite cadres, there is an inevitable struggle for power between old and new elites. The form the struggle takes depends upon (1) whether the party is urban dominant or rural dominant, and (2) whether the party is regional/ethnic or territorial in focus. If the party is urban dominant, the "quality" of the elite must be based upon commercial skill or other related skills, which in fact are useful for development. If the party is rural dominant, such an elite may be attacked by the rural peasantry or by the "quality" elite of the traditional-minded rural groups. Hence, rural-urban disputes are common. Each has its own development commitments. Where such situations occur, an urban dominant party with an urban elite must either directly attack the traditional elite or modernize it by making some provisions for rural reform in its program.

If the party itself is territorial in focus, local elites may demand more recognition. If it is regional or ethnic, the elites are more often than not based on ascriptive criteria and promote tribalism or some form of regional parochialism which can threaten both party leadership and following. Ideally, *the party with an urban elite, organized around a territorial focus on a mass basis, produces the most effective and viable government.* Such a party then will have a wide range of information sources. As a mass party, it should be decentralized in its organization but hierarchical in its pattern of communication. It should be centralized in its decision-making and assist government in coordination. With a mass basis it provides government with a measure of stability. It furthermore serves as a basis for social mobility in society at large. It incorporates power groups and absorbs them. It provides patronage to its own members and maintains their support. If too strictly organized, such a party can become a punitive arm of the state. If it does, then the costs of coercion go up, and a very nasty situation can arise. Barring that situation, what we have just described is the typical nationalist, aggressive, congress-type political party which can be found in India, Indonesia, French West Africa, Ghana, Nigeria, Malaya, and elsewhere.

GOVERNMENT

By government, we mean *the most generalized membership unit possessing both defined responsibilities for the maintenance of the system of which it is part, and a practical monopoly of coercive powers.* Government refers to a concrete group of people whose job is to keep the social order intact, who must prevent it from being destroyed either by internal or by external forces. To accomplish these ends, this group requires authority or power, recognized by the public as legitimate, which gives it ultimate powers of deciding right and wrong. It is to these ends that a practical monopoly of coercive powers is necessary.

All governments need devices which can effectively produce choices. To make choices effectively, governments require knowledge and information about society generally, about the limits of public tolerance, and about the costs of development in terms of alternative courses of action. Government is in the business, so to speak, of estimating costs against consequences. Political costs and political consequences will therefore be the underlying theme of this discussion.

In systems where there is representative government, greater information is probably available to government than in other systems. However, in underdeveloped areas, representative institutions foster local particularism, opposition, and even separatism. Politicians, in order to gain supporters, search for issues which divide as well as amalgamate a public. Furthermore, where there is popular sovereignty, government actions tend necessarily to be defined within the institutional limits of social life. This must be so, or the government will lose its power. The pace of government can only be so fast as the electoral groups which provide the recurring majorities will permit.

On the other hand, where political arrangements give government a great deal of autonomy and where government has the freedom to choose its supporters, the problem of recurrent majorities enters only incidentally. In this case government actions are determined by fewer limitations. Normally such governments obliterate national differences, enforce integration, and are relatively insensitive to changes in public attitudes except where those attitudes entail threats to government itself. On the other hand, knowledge and information are not so freely available to governments that are more or less authoritarian. Most of all, where government acts as a leader, considerable estrangement will persist between some sectors of the community and government itself, a situation which will be of cost to the regime.

Thus the dilemma in most underdeveloped countries is clear. Few people in underdeveloped areas are willing or able to wait the "requisite" number of years for a "natural" development process to take place.[2] Indeed, if they did, most would still find themselves disproportionately behind the western industrial nations. Few countries have the resources to utilize the latest technological innovations today that imperial Germany was able to do with regard to nineteenth century Britain. Western nations, with their increasingly high living standards, seem a perpetual rebuke to those in new countries only beginning massive development. Questions of national pride and racial sensitivity make the tenure of representative governments uncertain if they do not act strongly in regard to development and endanger them if they do. Authoritarian governments mix the proportions of nationalism and ideology so that sacrifice and self-denial are regarded as social virtues. It is here that nationalist political parties become so important, especially where representative government is only partially effective; nationalism becomes the new religion, with its own galaxy of devils, angels, ascetics, militants, and priesthood. Such nationalist parties are modern in their organization and spirit. Duverger is right when he notes two essential characteristics of our time: "the revival of groups, the rebirth of religions . . . Today the

[2]By natural, we refer to the classic western pattern of private investment and entrepreneurship. This is one reason why forced savings, heavy discipline, and government investment have been more clearly successful in producing self-sustained economic growth than primarily private enterprise. Indeed, by "straddling" the issues of planning and industrialization on partly private and partly public terms, India has found herself in profound economic difficulties. By contrast, China has been more effective in efforts towards industrialization.

term party includes veritable churches with their clergy, their faithful, their belief, their orthodoxy, their intolerance."[3]

The big problem facing government, therefore, is how to remain accountable to the public without letting the public dictate the pace of change. Indeed, this is the meaning of the expression, "realistic" goals. In order to achieve such goals, governments must have some means of determining how political parties *and* the public would accept the duties and obligations which they entail. Where government and public possess adequate information about one another, the outcome of a particular goal can be judged more adequately by both. Governments engaged in development are, therefore, governments in search of certainty. They want information, and they seek to control that which might endanger their goals.

ELEMENTS OF GOVERNMENT VIABILITY[4]

The nature of party membership and leadership decides whether the government will be able to set goals autonomously, i.e., without much reference to public demands, or will have to keep its goals set within public tolerance. The degree of governmental autonomy is thus our first consideration.

Accountability and Consent

Autonomy in government is a function of accountability. To the degree that government is not accountable to parties, pressure groups, special interests, etc., it is free to make what decisions it likes. In effectively working representative government, accountability is regular and defined in legislative organs and a popular electoral system. Government needs the consent of some group in the legislature, whether a party majority or a coalition, before it can take action.

In many underdeveloped areas where there are large populations or

[3]See M. Duverger, *Political Parties* (London: Methuen & Co., Ltd., 1954), pp. 61–62.

[4]This discussion is focussed around five structural requisites of government: (a) accountability and consent; (b) authoritative decision-making; (c) political recruitment and role assignment; (d) resource determination and revenue allocation; and (e) coercion and punishment. For a methodological statement which expresses the variables under discussion here, see my article, "A Comparative Method for the Study of Politics", *American Journal of Sociology*, LXIV, No. 3 (November 1958). [Reprinted in this volume.] These structural requisites and the definition of government used here were worked out by the author and his colleagues on the West African Comparative Analysis Project. This Project was made possible through the generosity of the Carnegie Corporation, to whom acknowledgment is gratefully given.

a large territory, or where there are significant cleavages along ethnic or religious or regional lines, each group in the system wants a check upon government autonomy. Hence, federalism is a popular system because it builds limitations on the autonomy of government into the basic organization of government itself.

Where there is a mass party, territorial in scope, with personal and fragile leadership occupying governmental positions, the normal procedure is to produce a federal system in form, with little real accountability to regions or regional representatives. In a multi-party situation, accountability organs help the opposition parties and provide them with independent sources of power. In the latter instances, extensive accountability on the part of government weakens its preoccupation with development, as it must pay more attention to local needs. It may then have to spend a large proportion of its budget upon social welfare and local development, much of which may be considered part of general development in one sense but may retard the pace of net savings for investment.

To the extent that development takes place through government, the civil service is of basic importance as an accountability group. The bureaucracy will, under those circumstances, assume a critical significance and often engage in a deep struggle with a party or parties which operate government. The civil service is mostly oriented towards "task-performance." Its criteria are efficiency and skill. The more effective the civil service, the more the government relies on it for carrying out development objectives. The more it is relied upon, the more conscious are civil servants of their powers. The civil service then is a special elite which is in a sense subordinate to government, but which can hold government at its mercy. If a struggle over accountability should break out between party and bureaucracy and become sufficiently intense, it can easily produce chaos on the one hand, or totalitarianism on the other, either a totalitarianism of a bureaucratic oligarchy, or a party dictatorship. The special instance where elements of both combine to produce a "mixed type" of party-bureaucracy is exemplified in those areas where army officers form the nucleus of a political party, take over the government, and blend elements of both.

A third major source of accountability of government is private industry. That it is right and proper to act in such a way as not to antagonize business interests has acquired for some in the West the character of a doctrine. Leaders in newly developing countries take a dim view of it; it is what they sometimes mean by imperialism. Nevertheless, some accountability of government to industry in newly developing areas is necessary if private industry is to be attracted. It means that certain restrictions on the autonomy of government are at least implicit in the situation. Decisions not to nationalize industry, or to give tax rebates, or to discipline the labor force, or to promote training and welfare schemes may all be involved. More important, development decisions become dependent upon the actions of private investors. If resources are scarce, as they invariably are, government may reduce its own entrepreneurial activities in light of private development schemes.

It is precisely the effort to reduce these aspects of accountability that have led many governments to introduce the mixed government-private corporation. A general authority is set up, relatively independent of ordinary government control. Such corporations are under statute with government putting up a proportion of the capital in a particular enterprise out of the corporation's funds, while private entrepreneurs put up the rest. Run on a purely commercial basis, government has a policy stake, yet is less accountable to private investors. The fear of private investors is mostly a hangover from Marxian conceptions of exploitation, for almost any political party in developing territories uses some Marxian criteria in evaluating private enterprise, even where party and government leaders want private capital badly.

The most important feature of accountability, then, is that it indicates the groups to which government feels itself responsible. Government may become impatient with accountability, which limits the freedom and autonomy of decision-makers and tempers their decisions and their plans by potential opposition. In the process of development and planning, it may try to bypass such groups and create new ones more amenable to government control and manipulation. Hence, it is possible to reduce the position of an entrenched and hostile chamber of commerce, for instance, by creating new and more amenable business and cooperative associations having closer links to the centers of power than the chamber of commerce. The latter gradually becomes stifled and loses influence. Both the form and the content of accountability are therefore important, because they profoundly affect the pattern of decision-making on the part of government itself.

Authoritative Decision-Making

Decision-making by government involves the posing of alternatives and the selection of one for effectuation. Decision-making is prompted by demands made upon government from outside or demands placed upon decision-makers by their own plans. Decision-making may be limited to highly general issues. Its scope might be very broad, or it might be very detailed. Where its scope is broad, it is left to the bureaucracy or party to make a whole range of secondary decisions pertaining to the primary decisions themselves. Possibly detailed supervision may be left to the party. Hence, the method of decision-making and the scope of decision-making both help to determine the significance of both party and bureaucracy in the system.

Decision-making may be centralized or decentralized. Normally, it is more centralized where there is unitary government, and less so where there is a federal system. Decentralized decision-making may take some of the burden off central government, or it may complicate matters for government. The first instance occurs where local solutions are found for local problems; the second results where local solutions are not forthcoming, and government spends large sums in grant-in-aid, gifts, or pork-barrel operations, because it becomes politically impossible to do otherwise. In this case, development decisions may be held up because of local options and interests.

The range and scope of decision-making can be determined by taking a sample of developmental decisions. Some decisions will be in the form of *framework legislation*, broad enabling legislation with flexibility introduced through decentralized decision-making procedures. Such decentralization may occur through independent agencies. It may serve simply to stimulate economic growth in the private sphere; it may serve to channel self-help and community projects at the local level. Framework legislation may involve considerable integration and planning, yet provide scope for decision-making initiative beyond the precincts of the central government itself.

Supervisory legislation involves careful and continuous control by government. Here a heavy decision-making burden is imposed on government.

Other decisions will be in the form of *regional legislation*. Here, the question is the extent to which the center concerns itself with regional matters or allows the regions (or local areas) decision-making autonomy. Regional legislation can be of the framework or supervisory type.

Entrepreneurial legislation can be of the framework or supervisory type. Here, the government itself engages in economic activity. It may range from the operation of airlines, steamship companies, social services, to manufacturing operations, mining, and the like. If entrepreneurial legislation is combined with supervisory legislation, the government requires an exceptionally well-trained bureaucracy, with corps of technical specialists and planners. If entrepreneurial legislation is undertaken within the context of framework legislation, integration of efforts may be possible through financial controls such as grants-in-aid.[5]

The more government can decentralize its decisions and restrict itself to the most important planning and political issues, the more it is likely to be efficient in tackling developmental objectives. Once again it is important to point out the significance of party. If the recruitment of

[5]Supervisory and entrepreneurial legislation taken together reinforce the tendency towards government omnivorousness.

decision-makers is on an elite basis only, purely developmental considerations may lead to a great deal of trouble, because they might not accord with public sentiment. In the case of a mass party from which decision-makers are recruited, the temptation to use development as a huge pork-barrel is very great, precisely because public sentiment is well known and must be manipulated.

Political Recruitment and Role Assignment

Political recruitment and role assignment can here be described in terms of method. Is political recruitment on the basis of universal suffrage, voting constituencies, and competitive parties? Is there a western pattern of elections? Are roles assigned on the basis of plurality voting? To what extent are roles assigned through the vote, and to what extent by other means (co-option, appointment, bureaucratic promotion and transfer, etc.)? If there is a regular voting system, is the pattern one of single member constituencies or plural member constituencies? Is there a single ballot system or a list system? All these elements have a part to play in the analysis of government and how it operates.[6] Recognizing the importance of such issues, however, we shall be more concerned here with *political recruitment* as it provides satisfactions to the members of a party. We shall consider *role assignment* on the basis of qualities necessary to undertake political jobs.

We indicated earlier that the characteristic pattern of newly developing governments is an immediate expansion of "jobs for the boys" and a circulation of elites consequent upon coming to power. This situation rapidly stabilizes itself, and the members of government represent a party oligarchy. Whether there is a single- or multiple-party system, the same problem arises. The party oligarchy which controls government must still provide a flow of satisfactions (utilities) to party members, party supporters, and eventually the general public. Where there is universal suffrage and a legal opposition, the oligarchy finds it expedient to expand the range and number of positions open to party followers.

If there are periodic and genuine elections, these provide specific time intervals of a political nature. These time intervals tend to minimize the attractiveness of long-term planning. Projects may be requested by the people of an important constituency. In general, there is a bias against projects with a long postponed economic pay-off, unless there is considerable outside capital. Where elections are relatively meaningless and government does not have to contend with a regular machinery for its replacement, it can take a much longer view. Through forced savings

[6]Duverger, *op. cit.*, pp. 99–101; and A. Downs, *An Economic Theory of Democracy* (New York: Harper & Row, Publishers, 1957).

and disciplinary measures, it may concentrate on the development of primary facilities and heavy industry on the Soviet model.

The truly multi-party system of recruitment tends to sponsor governments which set goals in accordance with public perspective. Hence, there will be an emphasis on agricultural and land reform, commerce and distribution (retail trade), light industry. Government policy is devoted to the expansion of opportunity on a variety of fronts, depending upon pressure groups and what is thought to have the most influence over voters.

If capital is readily available to the private sector, then government in the role of advisor, mediator, and possibly stimulant, may increase and promote rapid economic growth, while remaining concerned with housing, town planning, health and education measures, which loom large because rewards so distributed gain voters' support. Here, the role of new governments is far more complex than it was in eighteenth and nineteenth century England, for example. Then, the franchise was very limited; government was accountable to few. Matters such as education were left mostly to private religious bodies. Health was at best left to what local authorities there were. Public works were mostly private, unless they concerned military operations in some manner. Justice was in the main locally administered.

Few newly developing countries with universal suffrage can ignore a direct concern with these matters, as could seventeenth and eighteenth century governments. Few have, moreover, the resources and talents to embark on major development programs in the private sector. Government tends to maximize available skills by recruiting them into the civil service, where the same set of skills can be utilized now for project A, and again for project B. How government will try to integrate its resources and talents with programs of development which rely on outside capital will depend partly upon how the party system operates.

Multi-party systems, tied as they are to recurrent majorities, tend to favor the employment of as much outside capital as possible. Where a single party prevails, the normal pattern of electoral recruitment is less significant. Here the allocation of offices must be made in accord with factions in the party. However, this practice results in pressures to add government posts or to expand the area of government control. Expansion of such posts requires new enterprises or a shuffling of roles, so that old elites are abolished.

Where there is, in effect, single-party democracy, the combination of mixed public and private entrepreneurship is highly regarded. Such a combination implies that party discipline is not overly tight, and that factionalism and internal party independence is possible. Here, too, a balance between long-run planning and immediate social welfare is more likely to be struck. The party can cajole, exhort, and otherwise ensure acceptance of long-term investment on the part of the government. It can do the ideological and propaganda work in order to win support. As it does so, it helps to produce a perspective and knowledge about economic development itself.

Single-party democratic systems are based upon support from recurrent majorities among factions in the party. Normally, they are pragmatic and socialist. Not afraid of private capital, they seek it actively and employ it side by side with government investment. Where there is a single-party totalitarian system, i.e., where the electoral system is a sham, it is possible for government to undertake long-range planning. Here, the widespread use of private capital is not favored, unless it can be directly controlled. Such controls normally frighten away would-be investors.

Hence, basic party structure and its significance in recruitment directly affect the direction of development and the forms which it can take.

We have not discussed the role of outside political and technical personnel. It can be stated as a principle that they are, of course, useful and valuable. They may, however, be received with scant courtesy by political leaders of lesser rank, because outsiders occupy jobs which might otherwise go to them and represent a source of authority which they often resent. Hence, there has often been a certain awkwardness about the role of outside experts. If the government conforms to the British model, such experts are often easy to employ as civil servants on contract, especially in the technical services of administrative departments like agriculture, forestry, rural development, and the like. However, if a new country comes into being after some bloodshed with the colonial regime, as in the case of Indonesia, the employment of outside experts becomes a delicate matter for the government.

Resource Determination and Revenue Allocation

Resource determination and revenue allocation include the kinds of economic activity pursued by government. We are concerned with how government defines and locates important resources, whether basic resources such as mineral, or human resources such as manpower, skills, etc. Revenue allocation refers to the distribution of income in the system, including taxation policy, government enterprise, etc. Involved are the following kinds of government policy making: regulation of consumption and savings, fiscal planning, currency stabilization, and credit facilitation and taxation policy which serve developmental ends. Political difficulties arise where the economy is dependent upon the production of a single cash crop, as in the case of Ghana, especially where that cash crop is grown only in a particular part of the country. The government cannot allow such a source of wealth to go untapped for development purposes.

Another important range of government activity concerns tariff policies, regulation of profits, customs and excise, and the range of related entrepreneurial activities which government can undertake in its own operations, such as government-owned railways, marketing boards, and participation in independent corporations. In addition, there are basic resource surveys, which involve the search for new products, new methods of manufacture, geological surveys leading to discovery of mineral resources, and development of hydroelectric resources. Finally, there is the range of regulatory legislation which deals with local markets, regulation of trade, inspection of cash crops, supervision of cattle or other livestock, etc.

The viability of government is dependent in great measure on basic financial policy. What are the reserve and lending policies of the banks? Is there credit available for rural development and for small entrepreneurs? Many governments have a strong tendency to expand control over the system through fiscal policy. They can then decide on major economic priorities with less reference to the politics of the situation. If the decision is to concentrate on heavy industrialization, for example, taxation and fiscal policy can then be devoted to that end.

Here the most difficult problem facing government arises if it is decided that forced savings should be the basis of economic growth. Politically, the government runs into the problem of maintaining support, while it penalizes the population now for promises in the future. A partially ameliorating device which kills several birds with one stone is to use taxation policy to redistribute income. This may simply involve lowering the standards of the few. Inhibitions to this process are great, however, when many of the wealthiest members of a community are the most skilled in business enterprise. The Chinese have, to some extent, been able to capitalize on this situation by keeping former owners of plants on as managers. Such former owners now become "ordinary" citizens, much to the gratification of the public, while the former owners, knowing the alternative fate in store for them if they object, are grateful for the opportunity to cooperate.

Often, developing countries do not have large enough internal markets to support major industry. It is possible then for several governments to form a common market. A common market tends to stimulate trade, raising the level of effective demand, which in turn produces greater investment opportunities. In time, if a government has been engaged in primary and secondary development activities, the basis for industrialization might develop. The nations which have the best opportunities for forming a common market are those which have been under a common colonial administration or have been dominated by the same colonial power. Hence, such arrangements are more effectively set up, for example, between Commonwealth countries.

The effectiveness of economic policy in government is, of course, the basis for development itself. If the question of "viability" of a government is at all pertinent, this is the place to raise it. Are money and banking, regulatory policies, taxation, etc., conducive to development, or not? What shall be the proportion of savings to be invested in social welfare, in heavy industry, etc.? What are the primary sources of new wealth? In general, it can be said that the higher the rate of forced savings a government can get away with, the more rapid the rate of development, if decision-makers have enough talented and skilled advisors and enough discipline so that resources are not simply wasted on jobs for the boys, abortive schemes, and grandiose politically popular projects. One way to ensure proper use of resources is the mixed public corporation, where a high proportion of investment comes from private sources.

Politically, a great deal depends upon the methods by which a government determines its budget. Important questions are: who prepares it—civil servants, politicians, financial experts outside of the government? Is it a major planning budget—does it provide a schedule of future project expenditures? How can it be modified—do modifications have to go through a parliament, or a planning commission, or a special committee?

Particularly if heavy government expenditures are contemplated and there is little in the way of external financial assistance, the tendency of government is to choose bootstrap economic measures. In this respect, labor does become a source of value. Such an approach is legitimized through the use of Marxian economic doctrine. The use of raw labor power to build roads, dams, irrigation projects, etc., is an initial source of wealth. Some nations have tried to use voluntary labor. Normally, this is only possible where very skilled manipulators of youth movements and voluntary associations can build up a sense of zeal and selflessness. In some areas, there are traditional forms of customary labor. In many tribal groups, a certain number of days are reserved for communal labor. If labor as a creator of goods becomes a major economic preoccupation of the regime, and it becomes simply a resource to allocate along with others, this normally involves extensive control by government itself.

Coercion and Punishment

Coercion and punishment is the last aspect of government that we shall discuss. Throughout this paper, a main theme has evolved around the advantages and disadvantages of the mass party in control of government. Leaders search for certainty; social life becomes organized; those who go along with the regime receive benefits and rewards; purpose and direction is provided; development of the state becomes the new religion in which the dominant political party is the home of the faithful, and the messiah is the party leader who controls the government. Within this general framework there can be considerable freedom, often even political freedom, although this depends partly on how determined the leadership is to promote goals involving postponed returns and forced savings.

The point at which public resistance to government becomes serious is the point at which coercion and punishment enter the picture. All governments have means of disciplining deviants in the society; some, however, use coercion as the key to certainty, instead of relying upon genuine support by the public. It is here that the multi-party representative governments have a great advantage over the single-party systems. If development in multi-party representative government is slowed to the pace of recurrent majorities, contemporary rewards cannot be displaced by future expectations. The stimulation of economic development must in large part come from the public itself. Heavy decision-making burdens are not the sole responsibility of government. Government knows pretty clearly what different sectors of the public want, and can manipulate accordingly. This may slow the pace of certain types of development, especially in heavy industry, but it can help produce voluntary support for the regime.

It is only under exceptional circumstances, however, that rapid development can occur under those terms. The nation which can afford democracy while attempting to produce rapid economic change is rather rare. Most governments try to maintain their own powers and discipline the public in order to achieve more rapid development. The assumption here is that development measures require a strong ideological commitment. Such a commitment is normally carried through a mass party with a determined elite. The elite recognizes that at least in the short run, ramrod measures may be necessary to organize the public for development purposes. An ideology is selected which supplies morality and legitimacy for coercive actions. Justification takes the position that strict measures are necessary in order to produce a satisfactory social life in the future. Coercion would thus help to produce greater public solidarity and the reduction of parochialism. To the extent that coercion is applied to achieve conformity, expenditures for weapons, security police, and army rise. Available resources for development are thereby reduced. If an opposition arises which increases the cost of coercion, it is the opposition which is expendable. Investment in propaganda and education must therefore be high enough and measures effective enough to reduce opposition, and by so doing, reduce the cost of punitive measures. This result rarely occurs, however.

One index of the degree of coercion being used by a government is the degree of *repressive*, as distinct from *restitutive*, law in the system. What is the extent of crimes against the state, or against the social order, which require symbolic punishment, and what is the extent of civil crimes for which restitution can be made? The greater the degree of repressive law, the greater the coercion in the system. In the Soviet Union during wartime, the extreme example was afforded by those shot for consistent lateness at work. Even lack of enthusiasm can be taken for sabotage. The upper ceiling on coercive action is reached when the costs of coercion begin to run higher than net developmental gains. The system which relies heavily on coercion is less efficient, has the greatest costs, and stifles imagination and initiative.

THE TENDENCY TOWARDS OMNIVOROUSNESS

We have said that government requires both knowledge of what people want and desire, and a means of checking upon the results of an action. It needs a constant flow of information between itself and the public it serves. Where there is popular sovereignty and representative government, information is more freely available to government, but there is restriction upon the freedom of government itself. Where popular sovereignty is vitiated by authoritarianism of one form or another, information is reduced, but freedom of action is increased.

The most important sources of information are the political parties. These are the most regularized means of determining public demands. Parties in two- or multi-party representative systems are more *transmitters* of information than *coordinators* of public action. The party in the single-party system is more a coordinator of public activity. In both systems, however, parties have some information and coordination roles. The more government requires a party to perform a coordinating role, the less effective will the party be in its information role. Such a role would be left to an opposition party. In systems where opposition parties do not exist, the problem of information is a severe one, and devices such as self-criticism and group discussion may serve.

None of the new governments are without opposition parties to face, though few opposition parties are effective in the sense that they can threaten a government with downfall. The typical situation seems to favor a two-party system, where the opposition is allowed participation in a legislature. Checks on government are provided by lax control over the backbench of the government party, so that it could conceivably combine with the opposition and therefore overthrow the government. Usually, the government has enough support to put through measures (some of which are bound to be unpopular) without having to take coercive measures. The opposition provides the information, while the party provides coordination (along with the bureaucracy) and serves to disseminate information about government down into the constituencies. Checks on government are limited to a potential coalition of the back-bench of the parliamentary party and a nominal opposition.

In this case, government has the advantages of a form of one-party government which focuses on national integration, allows wide representation, and retains oligarchy without incurring the costs of dictatorship. The government has considerable autonomy here. Turkey, after the revolution, was a good example of such a government which, after considerable development occurred, created a genuine multi-party system.

Party and government then recruit the talents which will serve the ends of economic and social development. They form the modern organizational nucleus. Depending upon the quality of the leadership, they demonstrate initiative, skill, and ability. With increasing control, there is an increase in certainty. This certainty refers both to public expectations and to government, for government is increasingly able to control the results of its actions. If such results are manifested in a resurgence of traditionalism, it directs its attack against the past and uses local government, financial, and voluntary associations to defeat a recrudescence of "reactionary" groups. If, on the other hand, there is no increase in control, local initiative may foster local particularism, and the position of the central government may eventually be in jeopardy.

One difficulty in such situations is that the more government controls, the more its costs rise. This is true in monetary terms and in real expenditures; it is also true in terms of consumption of talents and skills. In most newly developing systems, both financial resources and skills and talents are narrowly limited, so that by absorbing both money and skill, government restricts the degree of autonomous enterprise left outside the government sphere. Only the lesser talents remain outside the structure of government, and sources of wealth become reserves to be tapped by government, rather than employed on a private basis according to the skill and judgment of an entrepreneur.

Not only do costs rise with increased government control, but the proportion of value received declines. Governments engaged in simultaneous planning on a number of fronts rarely make the most efficient use of their financial and human resources. There is error from bad management, error in bad planning. Rare is the government which can increase its efficiency by decreasing its control, thereby releasing reserves of wealth and talent to private hands; mostly, the reverse is true. Since increasing costs must be borne by the public, there is normally a rise of dissatisfaction in all the organized sectors of social life. Social life, therefore, may even be kept constantly in flux, so that stable organizations which might be focal points of resentment cannot develop. The greater the measure of control, the more burdensome the planning requirements. More planning requires more information and certainty. The quest for certainty leads to greater control. This, then, is the tendency towards omnivorousness.

SUMMARY AND CONCLUSIONS

We have first discussed the role of government *vis-à-vis* developing society. Society has been viewed in terms of social stratification. The motivation for action has been defined as the striving of people generally to speed up social mobility. Ultimately, the strength of a government is based upon its ability to promote that end.

The satisfactions or dissatisfactions of people are expressed through organizations. Such organizations are political parties in the first instance, and relevant accountability groups in the second. Parties represent a regularized channel of communication to government, a source of recruitment to government, and a coordination arm of government.

Depending upon social stratification, composition of party membership, and leadership in party and government, accountability will be formal or informal, unitary or federal, centralized or decentralized. Where accountability is informal and at the discretion of the government, government has considerable autonomy. If accountability is limited, decision-making is restricted to the top levels of government. If it is extensive, it may be shifted in some form to various levels of government. If communications are both horizontal and vertical, much of the decision-making burden will be dispersed. If there are only vertical communications, central government is likely to control decisions of both wide and narrow range and large and small scope. In addition to "ecological" or geographic centralization or decentralization of decision-making, it may be functional as well, i.e., divided between bureaucracy and party organs, private entrepreneurs, etc.

Much depends upon the pattern of recruitment to office. Single-party electoral systems using the parliamentary form have some of the communications benefits of an opposition party, without being accountable to it. Multi-party systems using the parliamentary form require concurrent majorities, so that decision-making must be close to the demands of the public. Single-party systems have a tendency toward increasing omnivorousness, especially where there is universal suffrage.

Systems of any type which are attempting rapid development require bureaucrats and party personnel with managerial skills. Such skills are both organizational and technical. The pattern of role assignment in part will determine norms for recruitment in the system at large and affect the spread of ascription or achievement criteria. Such recruitment becomes particularly important in systems using fiscal controls and state entrepreneurial activities. Both managerial and technical skills become all-important where planning budgets are utilized.

Where fiscal controls are being utilized, government will seek to reduce accountability to the degree that decision-makers use forced savings and labor. Distributions of satisfaction may be in large measure initially accomplished through taxation policy to reapportion wealth. Important entrepreneurial activities are needed to provide economic growth, and power and prestige positions in the system. Where this is done through private means, government becomes less precarious, and the public's stake in the system is enhanced. Where it is done purely by government means, government must control all aspects of social life where a potential opposition can arise. Normally, mixed types of independent corporations and joint private and public investment are characteristic.

In addition, development needs to provide tangible benefits. Hence, considerable proportions of the budget are allocated for social welfare measures.

Depending upon the degree of control applied by government, coercion will represent a real cost and a political weapon to produce conformity. Coercion takes on a particularly significant aspect where there is universal suffrage. The degree of coercion in a system is measured by the proportion of activities coming under the category of repressive law, as compared with restitutive law. The upper limit to coercion is fixed by the proportion of its cost to net development gains.

On balance, the open, fraternal, mass, congress-type party which derives legitimacy from its large support and provides social mobility through party membership seems to be the most viable development-conscious party one can hope for. Such a party is characteristically socialist in its ideology and pragmatic in its actions. Emphasis upon democracy is provided by stressing economic development as a means to promote both equality of opportunity and, as well, greater shares for all. Contact with the public derives from the radical and populist nature of leaders and followers. Solidarity through party membership brings about social consensus, while burdensome reliance on costly coercive mechanisms characteristic of totalitarian regimes is not necessary.

Much depends upon the institutional framework of government within which the party works. If this framework provides a nominal opposition and recruitment is on the basis of universal suffrage, the basis for the development of genuine multi-party democracy is present. A potential opposition serves as a deterrent to extreme coercive mechanisms, thus providing a relatively advantageous portion of government revenues for development. Such a nominal opposition works best where factionalism in the mass party is considerable, especially in the parliamentary party. Here, the parliamentary form is of great value. Cabinet government can give the main party an effective working majority, and yet produce limitations on government itself, even where a multi-party situation does not yet exist. Furthermore, such a form provides a relatively autonomous bureaucracy with built-in standards of disinterested service.

Where the conditions of *mass party, nominal opposition, development focus, parliamentary form, universal suffrage, and effective civil service prevail*, the organizational, coordinational, and communications requirements of the system can be met. Hopefully, successful economic development would push such a political system towards eventual democracy.

Some Reflections on the Role of a Political Opposition in New Nations

THE ROLE OF A POLITICAL OPPOSITION

The role of a political opposition has proved ambiguous in most newly independent nations. New governments rarely see the necessity for a regular opposition party nor do they always accept the idea of opposition as a normal feature of government. There are many reasons why this is so. Most new nations have come into being after a prolonged period of struggle with colonial authorities which has caused nationalist leaders to monopolize loyalties. Also, opposition groups having themselves been associated with nationalism at some stage of their existence, often have an anti-government reflex common to those whose political actions have been aimed at changing the fundamental character of a country rather than accepting well established rules of political life and working within them. Indeed, many opposition leaders in new nations regard the new government much as they did their colonial predecessors, i.e., as basically illegitimate.

Considering such factors as these, we shall seek to show that an opposition in new nations needs a more limited and specialized role in order to safeguard its position and gain widespread acceptance. A great deal of discretion and responsibility is required on the part of those in the community whose views differ substantially from the government's. The key features of this role will be the subject of this paper.

In order to understand why an opposition needs to find a limited but indispensable role, we must recognize the special difficulties facing po-

A version of this paper was read at a Seminar held by the Congress of Cultural Freedom, Ibadan, Nigeria, March 1958.

litical leaders after independence. New nations are plagued with almost the entire range of political problems known to man. They are beset by an accumulation of immediate and often mundane tasks such as building up adequate medical, health, educational, transport, and other services, as well as improvement of housing, food supplies, and other basic necessities beyond the subsistence level. To state the case more sharply, in most of these countries per capita caloric intake remains far below that considered necessary for ordinary labor. Vivid in the minds of many political leaders are memories of the days when, not so long ago, they slept on the verandah and suffered from want of food and shelter. Some political leaders rose from poverty and obscurity to power in a short time. Politics is their only profession. For them to go out of office is, in effect, to become unemployed. Concern with the role of a political opposition thus appears to many such political leaders as an academic exercise, divorced from the realities of life, or at best suitable for wealthy countries where political life is less stern and the future more secure.

We shall seek to show that this evaluation of political opposition is shortsighted, even though understandable. In the day-to-day bread and butter politics of a nation, an opposition can help to determine the success or failure of a government wrestling with its problems. A political opposition is neither a luxury nor a danger. If it performs its functions well, an opposition can be of crucial service both to the government of the day, and to the people of a new nation.

In the West the idea of opposition is not often questioned. It is assumed to facilitate representation and channel diverse demands into constructive paths. This view is by no means common elsewhere. The western view of democracy as the open competition of political parties catering to diverse public needs and thereby transforming demands into policy, is not wholly accepted in most new nations. Since theirs is rather a perspective of struggle, political leaders do not regard struggle as at an end when independence is achieved. Instead they ask the public to work together for the "higher" phase, which might be liberation of a continent from colonialism, as is the aim of Ghana, or integration of a single nation out of several autonomous states, as is desired in the Middle East and in parts of former French West Africa.[1] In addition most new nations are anxious to industrialize. Whatever the obstacles, industrialization is attractive to political leaders. The urge is great to catch up with the West and modernize economic and social institutions. Whether cast in the role of crusader, or anxious to produce economic growth, political leaders easily accept the view that a political opposition is troublesome and dispensable, restricting the pace of development, at least in the early years following self-government.

[1] Such as the Sahel-Benin Entente.

Hence, when we look at many nations which attained independence since the war, the outlook for the opposition appears bleak. In Burma charges of party corruption and selfishness led to the army taking over government. It was the army rather than politicians who swept the squatters from the cities, and distributed food to the hungry. In its zeal and efficiency, the army made the politicians look foolish, more proficient at scrutinizing monastic texts than at dealing with the problems of the day. Facing similar problems, Indonesia is riddled with factionalism. Political party conflict can be found in every organized sector of life; in the army, the trade unions, the civil service and even in clan and village organizations. The country is so divided by party conflict that even "guided democracy" is impossible to achieve. If anything, opposition there is all-pervasive. Even the government is a coalition of oppositions.[2]

In the Sudan, the independence of the nation was challenged by political groups retaining strong ties with Egypt. The army took over in part to safeguard newly won autonomy. Even in Ghana, where the opposition has certainly not yet been extinguished, the entire executive committee of the Accra branch of the opposition United Party was put under preventive detention.

Fear that opposition will produce factionalism, corruption, and separatism is pervasive in new nations. The opposition is often blamed for producing a situation which in fact is inherent in the post-independence period of a nation. When the cement of nationalism is weakened a new basis for social solidarity must be found. Independence is an act of parliament or a stroke of the pen. Then the real difficulties begin. There is far more to self-government than a simple administrative transfer of power. Power is left to the nationalists like gold dumped in the streets, and many are bruised in the hectic scramble to gather it up again to place it in the strongbox of the nation where it can be used for public good.

New governments have a tendency to set impossible goals for themselves. To accomplish many of the objectives which they attempt to achieve, "human obstacles" have to be overcome. Some of these obstacles derive from the traditional conservatism of people who are loath to change familiar ways. But nationalist political leaders, fresh from their victory against the colonial powers, want to show the world what they can produce with freedom. They desperately desire to breathe a new vitality into their corner of the world. Hence no new nation is without its dramatic and expensive development plan. Set for five years or ten, emphasizing industry, or agriculture, or mining, each new nation seeks to fulfill the grand plan which will produce net growth, steady economic savings, high levels of investment, and material benefits for all.

[2]See Herbert Feith, *The Wilopo Cabinet, 1952–1953: A Turning Point in Post-Revolutionary Indonesia* (Ithaca: Modern Indonesia Project, 1958), pp. 165–93.

Impatient of the men in the villages who push the soil with outmoded implements and cling to rural ways, the new emphasis is upon discipline, education, and innovation. Unity is the demand of the hour—and cooperation. Join the party and the nation can be free and prosperous. A house divided cannot stand.

About such matters there is no "wrong" or "right" view. At the moment of independence the need for unity is great. It is easy for responsible leaders in government to take the view that an opposition simply magnifies grievance and exploits differences. Those who won independence know that it was not granted because of the kindness of colonial officials. Fought for by those willing to risk and dare, power has been captured by the nationalists, and having won it they intend to hold it by almost any means. The result is known. Rare indeed is the responsible opposition which can prosper in such a political climate.

TYPICAL PATTERNS IN NEW NATIONS

New nations tend to have either a great many parties, or a single dominant party with the opposition purely nominal. The Sudan was an example of the first, with the two main parties divided over the issue of closer union with Egypt. Government was a shaky coalition between large and small parties. India and Ghana are examples of the second. They possess a large mass "congress-type" party which grew out of the nationalist movement, while competing parties remain small and relatively helpless.

In the first instance, competition between the parties characteristically weakened the unity of the state. Indeed few examples of a successful post-independence multi-party system can be found among the new nations, with the exception of Israel. Others show a growing public dislike of party government. There develops a characteristic desire for a strong man who will be powerful and pure, leading the nation to harmony and achievement.[3] Hence it becomes possible for a single well organized group to be popularly preferred to several political parties. This is particularly so when bitter rivalry between parties divides the public. The greater the rivalry, the more people with passionate political attachments wish for an end of party conflict; but they are less willing to accept the dominance of any party other than their own. Hence they may look to an outside force (army, civil service) to save them from themselves. Excessive fear of tyranny thus produces oligarchy.

Where there is a dominant party of the congress type and a nominal

[3]See E. Shils, "The Concentration and Dispersion of Charisma," *World Politics*, XI, No. 1 (October 1958).

opposition, factionalism and intraparty intrigue become the prevailing political style. Politics then is similar to that in a bureaucracy, where each party official builds up his own support inside the party and seeks to outmanoeuvre the others.

To avoid this situation, mass party leaders attempt to impose discipline under the guise of fraternalism. Effectively organized, the single mass party system can become the weapon of change and discipline in a society. For example, political leaders in Ghana were struck with the Liberian system where the True Whig Party has prevailed for many generations. Conflict occurs within the ranks, but the party presents a united front to outsiders. Hence conflict and difference do not appear to challenge the unity of the party. Loyalty to the party becomes loyalty to the state.[4]

Political leaders in single mass party nations often discover that political opposition has not disappeared but is latent and underground. If, in order to prevent this, government tries to control information, public opinion (or expression of it), and voluntary associations like trade unions, democracy itself becomes hopeless. Often using the phrases of democratic socialism to mask a power position, government becomes the "organizational weapon" and seeks to eliminate all groups which might challenge its power. Opposition then becomes identified as an act of treason, and in such circumstances it must, of course, go underground. When the government becomes alive to its presence, it declares that the opposition is engaged in treason, sabotage, and other acts against the state.

THE FUNCTIONS OF AN OPPOSITION

The problems which we have discussed are not only the concern of leaders of governments in new nations. They are also problems for the opposition. Both need to discover issues which are popular but which will not so divide the public as to generate mutual contempt between citizens. The opposition must oppose but not obstruct. Both must nourish and preserve society by helping to transform private demands into acceptable public policy. To enlarge on this theme it is necessary to discuss the functions of an opposition in more specific terms.

Interest Representation

The opposition has an important task in representing *interests* which have been overlooked by the majority party. Otherwise groups in the

[4]This view is shared by other observers. For example, Pye indicates that "the fact that the ruling party in most non-western countries identifies itself with an effort

population whose interests have not been effectively represented can become discontented. One feature of democratic government is that while it cannot appease all interests simultaneously, it will not for long continue to give advantage to one group over another. The long-run prospect of equal treatment for all thus kindles an interest in government on the part of the public and creates a faith that government will deal, sooner or later, with the problems that plague it. Increasingly the public takes an interest in its government.

Still another factor enters here. Let us make a distinction between values and interests. Values are the basic beliefs and attachments held by the public. Interests are the immediate desires which it wishes to satisfy. A belief in freedom or equality is a value. A demand for assistance to cocoa farmers, or for an irrigation system, or for a local council is an interest. Interests and values are, of course, related, and the ensemble of interests is one means of judging values. However, value conflict differs from interest conflict. The latter is competition between groups for getting their demands met. If, for example, a government is to engage in development planning, interest groups will try to indicate types of development of immediate concern and benefit to them. They may ask for a scheme to be sited at points most beneficial to them. Value conflict, on the other hand, involves fundamental beliefs about what is right and wrong. *Value conflict challenges the foundations of society as a moral order, because at the value level, such conflict cannot be reconciled except by victory in a power struggle.*[5]

The task of an opposition, then, is to express interests as the basis for the perpetuation of the values to which it adheres, rather than to oppose government on value grounds. It can do so by advocating the interests of those who feel themselves aggrieved, and by suggesting alternative policies to the government. If, for example, it is proposed to create a semi-industrial area by the use of forced savings, planned allocations of the labor force, and the commitment of resources which might otherwise be available for other schemes, opposition might arise from the population affected by the program. Ancestral land might be violated for example, or control over land hitherto vested in a particular group might be upset. Pursuing the original plan at the expense of the wishes of the local people might engender value conflict. Government, taking as its primary value the need to produce material benefit and equality for all people, might assume that the original plan is of critical importance

to bring about total change in the society makes it difficult to limit the sphere of political controversy." See Lucian W. Pye, "The Non-Western Political Process," *The Journal of Politics*, XX (1958), 473.

[5]See Bertrand de Jouvenel, *Sovereignty*, trans. J. F. Huntington (Chicago: The University of Chicago Press, 1957), pp. 265–66.

in achieving its aim. If in its zeal government rides impatiently over the interests of the local population, the opposition might well charge that individual rights are being trampled underfoot, and that liberty is impaired. Value conflict develops. Value conflict produces rupture in social behavior between people who become scandalized at one another's behavior, and impairs, often irreparably, the relations between them. Government can easily leap to repair the damage by eliminating the aggrieved group in the interests of harmony and progress.

Hence, the opposition has a fundamental role to play here. It needs to act as a mediator, formulating and representing diverse interests in such a way that tact and compromise become the style of political life, rather than strife and persecution. The reconciliation of interests is one important means to this end.

Provision of Information

Another important function of an opposition is to provide otherwise unavailable *information* to government about public reaction to a particular official policy. In this respect, the opposition keeps the government informed about the consequences of official policy.

This function is particularly important in those nations dominated by a single mass party. Our assumption here is this: Where the leadership in control of government is aggressive, impatient, and progress-minded, the government soon begins to lack information, because the party itself becomes identified with the state. People will not care to make known their opposition to government leaders or the local followers of the dominant party because the risks might be too great. For example, a farmer who wants a loan for developing his farm might well understand that an agricultural loans board is dominated by people from the majority party who would be less likely to give favorable judgment on his application if they knew he belonged to an opposition. The same is true for families with children seeking scholarships from the government, or jobs and sinecures. The majority party controls all the patronage and all the avenues of opportunity. Political cynicism begins to spread and the public becomes adept at producing "spontaneous support" for the leaders even if in their hearts they despise them. This is a kind of political corruption which is far more harmful than such characteristic forms of corruption as misappropriation of funds, because society is then based on delusion and deception.

Indeed, if dissatisfaction remains hidden, only to break forward in sporadic but bloody intervals, the government sits on a powder keg. Its own party gets information pleasing to the ears of government officials. The true state of affairs remains uncertain, and political leaders therefore seek to control the entire organized life of the community. To reduce the consequences of ignorance when they are denied information, government leaders use coercion. By this means they seek to avoid blame for mistakes, and so remain invulnerable at the polls.

An opposition which indicates important centers of controversy and dissatisfaction is thus performing a valuable task. If people can freely ventilate their grievances by allowing the opposition to voice them, government is thereby provided with a knowledge of sensitive changes in public opinion and can modify its policies accordingly. Thus the existence of an open opposition helps to make political goals more realistic, and helps to avoid that kind of political ignorance which produces coercion. Just as the fluctuations in the glass of a barometer indicate information about the weather, so the rise and fall of support to an opposition indicates to government the effectiveness of its policies.

Exercising Criticism and Provision of Alternatives

The opposition has the responsibility of providing *criticism* and posing useful alternatives to government policies. This function, properly performed, helps government to set goals best qualified to produce public satisfaction. On matters of budget, welfare, and other major concerns, criticism keeps the government responsive to the public and aware of weaknesses in its program. This is a classic function of an opposition and does not require extended discussion here.

The three functions, representation of interests, provision of information, and constructive criticism, are the main contributions of an opposition. We shall see how these three functions relate to representative government.

OPPOSITION AND DEMOCRACY

An opposition capable of performing the functions we have listed is instrumental in preserving the structure and spirit of representative government if these functions operate within three important spheres. The first involves the *values of democracy* itself, the second refers to *conciliar or parliamentary control over the executive*, and the third involves *effective representation.*

Our conception of democracy is of a political system committed to democratic values, conciliar control, and representation, especially through universal adult suffrage. All democratic systems possessing these characteristics are, in the actual practice of government, operated by a party system. Competing parties can make each of these spheres active and meaningful, or they can dull them and make them inoperative.

Hence, in this sense, democracy depends upon the performances of political parties.

Israel, with a responsible multi-party system has been operating effectively in all these spheres. Ghana, for a time threatened with conflict over values, especially those pertaining to individual rights, seems now to be most effective in the first and third spheres, with conciliar control rather ambiguous. There was a time in 1957 when twenty-seven members of the backbench of the Convention Peoples Party, the government party, threatened to bolt to the other side. Government took strong action to bolster temporarily fading fortunes and has emerged triumphant. At the moment conciliar control in Ghana would appear to be weak. Other nations as well, show a mixed picture. In few can it be said that democracy is flourishing—but there is no doubt that democratic values are the dominant mode of politics. Even in Pakistan or the Sudan, there remains a strong commitment to democratic values even if, for the moment, conciliar control is in abeyance. Indeed in both those countries there remains a strong possibility that the political parties, having been chastened by the unexpected intervention of the military, will be restored to life when the army considers the moment propitious.

THE PRESERVATION OF VALUES

Political values are a reflection of preferences and beliefs and therefore underlie the formal or constitutional appearances of government. Political values must be shared and accepted by the people who need to be willing to support them. Confusion over political values can destroy the consensual basis for a viable nation.

To breathe life into representative institutions requires genuine commitment to democratic values. These provide the rationale for this relatively complex political form. No system can survive on purely instrumental grounds; values become the basis for emotional feeling about the society itself, and are the symbolic expression of political right or wrong.

What are the values with which we are particularly concerned? Those most characteristic of democracy are the product of four hundred years of struggle in the West. First there was struggle against religious orthodoxy, which was identified as a form of repression and dogma. *Liberty* was viewed as freedom of thought. Next, the idea of liberty was extended to include *individualism* and the political rights of men, and took the form of struggle against autocratic monarchs. *Political equality* subsequently led to demands for economic equality with an emphasis on opportunity, fair shares for all, and public education. Through socialist criticism along these lines, and through nineteenth century notions of progress, democracy thus acquired an economic dimension distinct from private property. Today we have the notion "psychic inequality," a consequence of social inequality, and there are efforts to obliterate those characteristics of a social order which breed feelings of inferiority and shame.

Although it took the West centuries to identify and realize these values, new nations strive to achieve them simultaneously. Modern nationalism is a demand for their realization. The problem is, however, that effort to achieve one can controvert the others. A paradox emerges. Overwhelming emphasis upon any one set of the values which are characteristic of democracy leads to a denial of others. The historical experience of the West was largely a process of realizing, *in turn*, each of the values we have identified. To achieve them all simultaneously is immeasurably more difficult.

Ghana, for example, emphasizes expansion of opportunity. Political leaders wish to emancipate people from ignorance and to utilize their talents. By this means they seek to restore respect to Africans and give people of color in all nations, including South Africa and the United States, courage to fight discrimination. Ghana also wishes to demonstrate through her own achievements after independence that the colonial powers cannot presume to judge the welfare of others and decide when a country is ready for independence. Ghanaians know that the best way to achieve these objectives is by demonstrating progress in Ghana. They concentrate on economic growth while attacking tribalism, separatism, and rural backwardness. However, conflict has arisen between those who are anxious to achieve "progress" and those whose ways are more set in favor of custom and tradition and who, if they are not bewildered, become antagonistic to government policy. Values are challenged because liberty and freedom have become practical questions of liberty and freedom for whom; they are no longer regarded as inalienable rights. From government's point of view the question is whether or not a part of the population is free to jeopardize the development of the country as a whole. The opposition charges that the majority cannot be allowed to ignore the minority on such issues. Each side challenges the legitimacy of the other's acts. Value conflict, hitherto incipient, can easily become open and manifest.

However, if we consider the case of Ghana further, it turns out that in practice most of the conflicts over value are directly derivable from inadequate reconciliation of interests. Rarely has it been the case that what the people want and what the government seeks to accomplish are as far apart as they appear to be. In performing its function, i.e., indicating to government what the interests of disaffected groups might be, pointing out the most crucial demands, communicating to government the depth of feeling and emotion involved, and proposing some compromise suitable for both groups, the actions of the opposition can prevent value conflict.

This is not simply a matter of niceties. If there is value conflict, government endangers its own success. Nothing is more desperate for progress-minded political leaders than to find that the public becomes not an asset, a pool of talent, and a reservoir of strength, but a weight to be shifted from one shoulder to the next, finally crushing those who are attempting to march forward with the burden.

Local support, and the transformation of interest conflict into satisfactory cooperation is thus possible if the opposition represents, communicates, and criticizes government policy. The public begins to share the burden of government. Otherwise plans worked out in Accra or Lagos or Cairo or Delhi have a way of being just enough out of perspective to have unanticipated consequences which jeopardize their success and perplex leaders.[6]

It can be argued that all this requires considerable nobility from political party leaders. Opposition leaders in new countries commonly complain that the opposition can scarcely perform its functions if its very existence is being threatened. Indeed, many of the differences which arise between government and opposition bear little relationship to problems of national progress. Quite the contrary, it is often the case that the government and the opposition shared much the same objectives in the past, i.e. national liberation and independence, and continue to support much the same aims. Often what is involved is personal conflict between men who share an intimate social environment. They know all about one another. The vulnerability of each is exposed, and exploited. It is by no means rare that when one side becomes politically dominant, the leader who is personally an anathema to members of the opposition taunts and goads them with displays of power. In such instances the surge of resentment and bitterness which comes over the opposition leads it into acts which play directly into the hands of government. Engaged in that kind of struggle, each side pre-empts the "public interest" as their party interest.

The problem is especially acute where the opposition is a combination of brilliant and educated men joined with embittered renegades from the dominant party, with a sprinkling of confused traditionalists. Characteristically, oppositions in new countries are a blend of traditionalists, renegades, and sophisticates. They fail to discipline themselves, perform erratically and inconsistently (although at times brilliantly), and do not give the government assurance that they can be relied on for responsible action.

Where the mass party is overwhelmingly preponderant numerically,

[6]See the discussion on planning by W. Arthur Lewis, "On Assessing a Development Plan," *The Economic Bulletin: The Journal of the Economic Society of Ghana* (June-July, 1959).

the opposition is not only small in numbers, but often composed of an elite antagonistic to popular and diverse membership of a mass party. Quite often a form of "class" conflict is built into the relationship between government and opposition in which the latter is alienated by being deprived of a share in power. Meanwhile the former may have leaders who take pleasure in humiliating the self-titled aristocrats who represent all that the mass parties dislike. If an opposition party is to survive in such a situation, it requires unusual discipline and self-control. Normally, however, such oppositions are incapacitated by their membership. Rarely can they resist personalizing the issues and maligning the motives of government leaders.[7]

A delicate tread is thus required, the more so because mass political organizations are themselves riddled with factionalism and easily threatened. The more powerful the mass party, the more intense will become intraparty intrigue and fighting. It is here that the mechanism of conciliar government becomes so important because, among other things, a legislature and an election system help to transform conflict between parties by putting them in a forum in which the performance is open to the public. The public makes the ultimate decisions about which side is preferred. If government and opposition carry their conflicts outside of the parliament and into all the other institutions of the country, public and private, a struggle for pure power soon emerges. Power then inheres in the dominant party, rather than in the institutions of government, to be won and lost, in turn, through the normal vagaries of electoral fortune. And if the power of the state inheres in the dominant party, then value conflict is profound, and violence and coercion lurk on all political paths.

CONCILIAR CONTROL OVER THE EXECUTIVE

The most burdensome problem for an opposition is to respect the legitimacy of government, when that government is dominated by a party which the opposition finds abhorrent. When the distinction between government and party breaks down, then representative government is at end, because embedded in the idea of democratic government is the concept that the party is a conveyer of the people's will through the institutions of government, but is not the repository of state power.[8]

[7]The question has been raised whether or not an opposition could survive at all. The assumption here is that such opposition members have the choice of nominal opposition or oblivion. The benefits of opposition are preferable to oblivion. Hence recruits to the opposition can be found, especially where they do have an impact on government policy.

[8]See D. E. Apter, and R. A. Lystad, "Bureaucracy, Party, and Constitutional Democracy," in *Transition in Africa*, eds. G. Carter and W. O. Brown (Boston: Boston University Press, 1958), pp. 42–43. [Reprinted in this volume.]

Here lies one of the fundamental differences between democratic and autocratic political belief. In the former, there is a respect for the limitations of office, a belief that such office is temporary for any occupant.

The opposition has an important responsibility to preserve these ideas through its action in parliament. It needs also to perform its function in ways helpful to government, and by doing so to facilitate the system of political representation.

An opposition has to strike that difficult balance between being an enemy and a contender for the government. If it poses a threat to a majority party such that it serves as a potential center of gravity, pulling members away from the majority party to the extent of destroying it, the opposition may be viewed as an enemy. We indicated that factionalism characterizes the mass party in power. The opposition can sometimes attract enough factions to split the dominant party. This is undesirable because it encourages mass party leaders (especially those trained in doctrine which assumes the party is "everything") to void such threats through punitive action. Majority party leaders may be propelled toward coercion under the guise of populism and discipline. And, since the mechanism of coercion is an application of state power, i.e., police or courts, the institutions of government are brought into contempt. Neither the government nor opposition parties can long have faith in their own government under such circumstances.

On the other hand, the opposition has to pose enough of an electoral threat to the dominant party so that both develop party discipline. Although we do not have space to discuss it adequately, an underlying feature of representative government is the coherence and discipline by which parties are organized so that they can represent the public, decide policy, and put it into practice.

Party discipline is important not only for representative purposes, but it is also crucial in the sphere of conciliar control over the executive. The opposition which finds the difficult point of balance between threatening government party and ensuring party discipline will be respected, and will be able to carry out its functions in a parliamentary setting. The opposition can do this by:

(1) convincing the government backbench of the correctness of opposition views on particular policy so that backbenchers bring pressure on their own party leaders; and (2) in rare circumstances, threatening the life of the government by a potential anti-government coalition, with disgruntled government backbenchers joining with the opposition to force a general election.

Parliamentary party discipline, however, has other effects. It promotes an atmosphere of constraint and propriety in the legislature so that reasonable discussion can prevail, despite moments when tempers become inflamed. Such a climate is necessary if the functions of an opposition are to be achieved. In such a climate issues can be more easily decided on the basis of general merit. Alternative policies can be more clearly phrased and made more comprehensible to the people themselves. In this way parliament itself can become more meaningful to the public, which expects so much from a new government and its leaders.

It takes a delicate combination of forces to produce a climate of repect for the institutions of government and a situation where issues can be made more clear, so that a concept of the public interest gradually can become identified. If such a pattern begins to take root, a whole series of subtle constraints upon the arbitrary power of the executive can be exercised, even when there is a preponderant government majority in parliament. Instead of "cabinet dictatorship," responsible government can develop. And instead of multi-party factionalism (as is often the case where parties are evenly divided) the government has assurance of a strong enough majority to carry through its program.

Party discipline then gives rise to coherence. Coherence allows policy alternatives to be posed in clearer fashion. Alternatives can provide government with knowledge of the best policies to carry out, and indicate necessary modification; in the forum of parliament, ministers can be made more responsive to legislators. In this fashion, the opposition can preserve the second sphere of representative government, i.e., conciliar control. At the same time, it can reflect more adequately those interests of which the government may not be cognizant, and help to prevent unforeseen political difficulties.

REPRESENTATION

Representation, the third sphere of democratic government, is as important as the other two. Political party competition, i.e., the struggle between the party in power and the opposition, is the lifeblood of democracy. Indeed one observer argues that "the democratic method is that institutional arrangement for arriving at political decisions in which individuals acquire the power to decide by means of a competitive struggle for the people's vote."[9]

By electoral means leaders are selected, a mandate for a program provided, and the public participates in the process of government. It is in competing for elections that the three functions of an opposition are carried out at the public level. It must seek out interests which it thinks

[9]See J. A. Schumpeter, *Capitalism, Socialism and Democracy* (London: George Allen & Unwin Ltd., 1943), p. 269.

are popular and which reflect public feeling. It needs to communicate this to the public by arranging their program and ideas in a package which shows the public at a glance what the contents are. Finally, the opposition attempts to sharpen the responsibilities of the electorate by criticizing the program and policies of the government and pointing out weaknesses and failures.

Hence, the representative aspect of government, underwritten by electoral competition, requires an opposition which is allowed to perform freely. Under these conditions generalized factionalism in the country becomes crystallized into main groups. And one of the practical rules of politics which works out in normally functioning democracies is that *when there is open party competition and free elections, both parties, government and opposition, seek the support of the large middle spectrum of voters*, i.e., those who comprise the bulk of the voting population. Hence, gradually, both parties draw closer together in their ideology and their program to the point where relatively minor differences become the issues on which elections are fought. This is the experience of every successful parliamentary system.[10]

Nor is it difficult to see why this is the case. If we take the simplest possible case, a government with a "radical" program and an opposition with a "conservative" program, we find that in real terms, most people in the country conform to neither one extreme nor the other, but fall somewhere in the middle. That is, they are in favor of some "radical" policies and some "conservative" ones. On the other hand, the extremists on either end of the political spectrum have no hope of winning elections themselves. The important electoral factor is the middle group, and in making coherent appeals to them, neither the government nor the opposition can have an extreme program. Hence the importance of free party competition—*it does not divide where all political parties are responsible—but instead exerts a constant pull on the parties drawing them together.* It neutralizes the extremists.[11] Thus party competition is basically not divisive, as is commonly thought, but most often unifying instead.

The forms of disunity which characterize governments in new nations are thus often premature. Equally, an opposition which fears and mistrusts the government of the day helps to magnify the fears of a majority party leadership that the opposition, in its efforts to achieve power is out to destroy all. In those first years of self-government both sides need to recognize how absolutely necessary each is to the other.

[10]There are, of course, exceptions. Where the middle spectrum does not show an identity of interest or is very small, political parties exacerbate differences. The Third and Fourth French Republics are good examples of what can happen in this situation.

[11]Where government is composed of the extremists these generalizations are of course inoperable. Rarely is it the case in new nations that extremists do in fact run the government.

CONCLUSION

We have indicated the challenge to opposition which has appeared in almost every new nation. Opposition, we have tried to show, is essential if the problems of governing new nations are not to engulf those in public office and impel them to coercive solutions. In representing interests, providing information, criticism, and alternative policies to government, the opposition can aid government in the three critical spheres of a democratic system, namely, preservation of a belief and acceptance of democratic values, helping to control the acts of the executive by conciliar control and advice, and giving coherence and meaning to the representative system.

In addition, by serving as a rallying ground and focal point for grievance, a responsible opposition can transform potential disenchantment with government into positive channels, preventing apathy, and avoiding cynicism about democracy.

New nations need more than bargaining power to gain the respect of the world. They need to demonstrate positive achievement. A responsible opposition can help win the struggle for unity, freedom, social betterment, and racial equality.

DAVID E. APTER / ROBERT A. LYSTAD

Bureaucracy, Party, and Constitutional Democracy:

An examination of political role systems in Ghana

INTRODUCTION AND METHOD

Nationalism in the British territories in Africa has resulted in a series of constitutional reforms. These have come as consequences of general patterns of development in the colonial territories. At some point in the history of the colonies an identifiable degree of coherence has emerged from the original inchoate and inarticulate antagonism to colonial administration. The perspectives of the colonials have sharpened. Their grievances have clarified, acquired solidity, and generated well-defined issues. Chiefs have realized their increasing inability to rule their districts as before. Education, commercialization, religion, urbanization, occupational specialization, all have come to exert pressures which have been subversive of both the traditional and the colonial systems and have led toward a new synthesis of political systems.

The Patterns

As these patterns have developed, simple reforms on an *ad hoc* basis have tended to multiply difficulties; instead of providing permanent solutions to problems, they have come mainly to herald subsequent major constitutional advances. In response to an increasingly strong nationalist call for self-government, these advances have embodied a progressive

This analysis was read at the APSA meetings in September, 1956, in unrevised form. This study was done in conjunction with the West African Comparative Analysis Project under a grant from the Carnegie Foundation. The authors wish to acknowledge their debt to the Foundation and to the other members of the project.

change from emphasis upon local government and reliance upon local groups to emphasis upon a national government, national political parties, principles of representation by election, and upon decision-making by conciliar means, that is, by representative assemblies empowered to consult, advise, and legislate. These changes have been incorporated into successive interim constitutions prepared by the Colonial Office in the attempt to introduce at least a measure of stability and controlled advance in rapidly changing situations.

One of the major problems which must be faced by the writers of constitutions is to prepare a document which can be understood by the people governed under it. The understanding—or lack of understanding—of the constitution by the public affects the manner in which it can be made to operate. In Africa, constitutions tend to be understood by rather narrow segments of the population for whom they are drawn, and in order to prevent this problem from hampering future development, the device of the interim constitution has been used.

This device rests upon the assumption that interim constitutions gradually establish both the procedures of constitutional government and the public's understanding of them. By the time full self-government does occur, therefore, parliamentary and administrative procedures will have become institutionalized, that is, widely understood and accepted because they have been built into the total pattern of social life. When the permanent constitution is eventually written, the public will have come to share attitudes and beliefs about government and its functions to a degree which permits the resolution of conflicts by constitutional means.

In contrast to this "gradualist" assumption is that which maintains that even the short-term existence of colonial relationship is an affront to modern day political ethics. Such a position argues for immediate self-government in colonial territories, premised on the right of a people to make its own errors and to decide in its own fashion what sort of a political system it will enjoy. That there are problems involved in this "sink or swim" approach to political democracy seems clear even to those who regard colonialism as anathema.

The British have based their colonial policy on the first alternative assumption and have directed their efforts toward the establishment of national independence via the causeway of constitutionalism. This paper will examine some of the processes used by them in developing a parliamentary system of government in Ghana and will examine some of the present consequences of this policy.

The new state of Ghana, granted independence by the British on March 6, 1957, came into being after a series of interim constitutions, the last of which in 1954 had already brought full internal responsibility under a system of Cabinet Government. Public support for the Convention People's Party, the principal nationalist party, had been interpreted by the British as a clear public demand for independence. Subsequent conflict between the Convention People's Party and the opposition over the terms of self-government was not viewed by the Colonial Office or the British Parliament as a lack of "readiness" for independence.

It is not the purpose of this paper to discuss these internal conflicts. It is sufficient to say that Ghana remains divided on many fundamental issues but that all political parties appear committed to the basic framework of constitutional democracy within which their difficulties must be resolved.

The method adopted for this analysis is to rank interrelated roles and membership groups in terms of their functional specificity or their functional diffuseness. These are not the only qualities of role relationships.[1] These qualities, however, are of crucial importance for the understanding of roles which have varying degrees of authority or subordination to authority vested in them. Governmental roles clearly fall within this category, although any roles which have aspects of authority may be understood more clearly and compared more readily by means of this method.

As used in this study, the terms of this method have the following meanings:

Role: any identifiable position in a social relationship between two or more persons. Each role is considered as having a function to perform, goal(s) to be achieved, a desired state of affairs to be established. In achieving its goal(s), a role makes use of certain means defined by the society as appropriate to the role. Perhaps the most familiar synonym for "role" is "office" when dealing with certain processes of government, as in this study.

Membership groups: a system of interacting roles, in which there is a preponderance of shared goals and shared means to the achievement of the goals. Among the membership groups frequently referred to in this study will be the Cabinet, the Parliament, the national political party, the parliamentary party, the party bureaucracy, the civil service government bureaucracy, and the public. As the study will make clear, membership groups within membership groups must also be distinguished because of the degrees of difference which emerge with respect either to goals or the means to goals.

Functional specificity and functional diffuseness: the qualities of goals,

[1]See Marion Levy, *The Structure of Society* (Princeton, N.J.: Princeton University Press, 1952), for other "analytic aspects of relationship structures" and for a discussion of functional specificity and diffuseness which has served as a point of departure for the development of the method used in this paper.

and means to goals, which characterize different roles and membership groups. "Specific" and "diffuse" represent the two poles of characteristic role action between which varying degrees of specificity or diffuseness may be differentiated. Degrees between the poles are designated as predominantly specific, specific-diffuse, and predominantly diffuse.

Ranking: determination of the degree of specificity or diffuseness characteristic of the action of a role or of a membership group. The system of ranking uses three sets of criteria stated in terms of polar variables. Both the goals and the means of each role or membership group are ranked on the following bases:

1. Required goal(s), mean(s)—Alternative goal(s), mean(s).
2. Explicit goal(s), means(s)—Implicit goal(s), mean(s).
3. Narrow scope goal(s), mean(s)—Wide scope goal(s) means(s).

These polar terms are used as follows:

1. Required: without alternative goal(s), mean(s).
   Alternative: the role or membership group enjoys a choice of goal(s), mean(s), any one of which is considered equally desirable or valid.
2. Explicit: clearly defined criteria for goal(s), mean(s).
   Implicit: vaguely defined criteria for goal(s), mean(s).
3. Scope: range within which the goal(s), mean(s) have effect. The scope of a role or membership group is judged as being narrow or wide.

The technique used in ranking is as follows:

A score of "1" is given for each of the polar variables to the left; a score of "0" is given for each of the polar variables to the right.

A functionally specific role or membership group would have a score of "6" (goals: required "1," explicit "1," narrow "1"; means: required "1," explicit "1," narrow "1").

A functionally diffuse role or membership group would have a score of "0" (goals: alternative "0," implicit "0"; wide "0"; means: alterna- "0," implicit "0," wide "0").

The complete set of terms used in ranking functional specificity or diffuseness is as follows:

Specific (Score 6).
Predominantly specific (Score 5 or Score 4).
Specific-diffuse (Score 3).
Predominantly diffuse (Score 2 or Score 1).
Diffuse (Score 0).

Throughout this paper the adverb "functionally" will be omitted; however, it is to be implied in each case.

THE ORIGINS OF GHANA CONSTITUTIONALISM IN THE CIVIL SERVICE

Ghana was first ruled by a colonial administration in which administrators in the Colonial Service were responsible to the British Parliament through the Colonial Office. During the years prior to 1957 many of the administrative roles came to be filled by Africans. The administration today is conducted by the Ghana Civil Service responsible to the Ghana Parliament through the Prime Minister.

In its internal structure the colonial administration is specific (Score 6; goals: required, explicit, narrow; means: required, explicit, narrow), a structure characteristic of bureaucracies generally. They involve a complexly organized hierarchy of clearly defined roles, an elaborate set of rules, and they place a heavy emphasis on administrative efficiency toward achievement of well defined goals. In its relationship with the public, however, the colonial administration is predominantly diffuse (Score 1; goals: required, implicit, wide; means: alternative, implicit, wide). It enjoys wide latitude in its authoritative decision-making and in the scope of its effect on the public. The reason for this difference in scores is that the diffuse policy-making roles and the specific, bureaucratic, policy-implementing roles are parts of a single membership group, the colonial administration; frequently both types of roles are filled by a single person alternating between them. In stable democratic governments the bureaucracy has no direct relationship with the public and is solely specific in its relationship with policy-making groups.

Within the colonial administration itself, particular roles vary in their degrees of specificity or diffuseness. In their relationship to other roles in the administration, such roles as Governor, Colonial Secretary, and Financial Secretary are diffuse (Score 0), while the role of District Officer is predominantly specific (Score 4; goals: required, implicit, narrow; means: required, implicit, narrow). In their relationship to the public the roles of Governor, Colonial Secretary, and Financial Secretary are also diffuse (Score 0). In its relationship to the public, however, the role of the District Officer becomes predominantly diffuse (Score 2; goals: required, implicit, wide; means: required, implicit, wide) because of the high degree of discretionary power placed in his hands. Within the colonial administration the District Officer has relatively little authority, but in relation to the public his role has a relatively high degree of authority and is characterized, therefore, by a greater degree of diffuseness. The area he administers depends upon him for many of the important decisions by which the structure of traditional society is altered.

Due to the immediacy of this role relationship and the degree of discretion permitted the District Officer during the earlier years of colonial administration in the Gold Coast, the District Officer was often more important than most of his colleagues in the Secretariat. Upon this role depended the actual functioning of the colonial government, the maintenance of an orderly legal framework of political life, the improvement of health and sanitation, the collection of taxes, and the enforcement of other financial regulations depending upon the economic and financial status of the territory under its jurisdiction. The scope of the District Officer's authority widened as the colonial administration widened its interests to include education, agriculture, forestry, husbandry, mining, commerce, and other activities.

Africans entered into the colonial administrative system at the level of the most specific roles. In performing his role, the District Officer made use of chiefs and native authorities, both groups being specific in nature (Score 6) in contrast to his predominantly diffuse role (Score 2). Elsewhere in the system Africans gradually came to be employed as clerks and police (Score 6).

Except in certain individual cases, the concerted efforts of the early nationalistic movements to fill the more diffuse, more authoritative roles higher in the administration met with British opposition. To the British, colonial administration in the classic pattern was unthinkable with a corps of locally recruited people, and, of course, in the early period few Africans could meet the educational standards of recruitment. But even when a group of professionally qualified Africans gradually developed, they were generally barred from entrance into the more diffuse, more authoritative roles in the civil service.

Nationalism, in its early phases, directed itself as much to this problem of Africanization of the existing colonial administration as to the more fundamental problem of the right of a colonial administration to rule. Blocked by British opposition to rapid, indiscriminate Africanization, nationalists began to demand the establishment of membership groups which had at least local advisory status, a demand toward which the British were favorable. In theory, at least, these groups were specific (Score 6), being severely delimited and restricted in scope of authority; in practice, however, they came to perform in a somewhat more diffuse, authoritative manner as educated politicians assumed more and more of the roles once vested in traditional leaders. Nationalists came to dominate territorial councils and town councils. Eventually they became members of the Gold Coast Legislative Council, partly as a result of their own efforts, partly as the result of changes in colonial administrative practice. Until 1951 this Council was the most authoritative conciliar body in the Gold Coast, although it remained predominantly specific in nature (Score 4; goals: alternative, explicit, narrow; means: alternative, explicit, narrow) because of its largely advisory status.

Nationalism, in the radical phase opened by the Convention People's Party (CPP), was little concerned with the gradual widening of participation in politics by a conservative African elite. It demanded that absolute control of all political membership groups and roles, diffuse and specific, be given to Africans without any responsibility to such a higher, diffuse, authoritative group as the British Parliament. Although it upheld the creation of a completely independent, diffuse parliamentary authority within Ghana as its fundamental objective, the CPP also recognized that government requires a dependent, specific, civil service bureaucracy to carry out the tasks assigned to it by the parliament. The CPP, therefore, stressed the maintenance of the civil service with a clear understanding of its specific role in the governing of an independent state.

In summary, early nationalism appeared content to play roles and to support membership groups which were specific or, at the most, predominantly specific in character, because its primary relationship was with the diffuse, authoritative British Parliament through the Colonial Office. The radical nationalism of the CPP made clear it would be content only if it controlled all the governmental roles and membership groups, free from any responsibility to the British Parliament.

The transition from the Gold Coast as a colony to Ghana as an independent constitutional democracy required a change in the qualities of the roles and membership groups within the government. Under the British the colonial administration was specific in its internal organization, diffuse in its relationship with the public. In the absence of any representative, conciliar assemblies, there was no real differentiation between administrative and policy-making groups. In relationship to the public these actually compromised a single, diffuse group with both specific and diffuse aspects. Being manned only by Europeans and moreover being exclusive in its standards of recruitment and behavior, the colonial administration provided a focal point at which to direct public antagonism.

Once the CPP was granted increasing degrees of authority, however, it recognized how much its performance depended upon the colonial administration in its specific aspects. With nothing less than control of all roles, specific and diffuse, as its goal, the CPP came to differentiate sharply between the administrative and the policy-making membership groups within government. It regarded the conciliar groups as properly diffuse, the civil service administrative groups as properly specific; the conciliar groups were to ascertain public needs and demands and to put them into the form of orders and legislation which were then to be carried out by the civil service administrative groups.

The progressive changes under the interim constitutions allowed for this differentiation between policy-making and policy-implementing groups during the transitional period when the CPP was given effective internal authority within the Gold Coast. The consequence was to keep government operating at a high level of efficiency while the new ministers and legislators became familiar with the procedures and canons of government.[2]

The relationship between the specific, bureaucratic membership groups and the diffuse, conciliar or representative membership groups in government is the most crucial one in modern constitutionalism. Development of a harmonious relationship between them poses difficult problems in a colonial territory which is moving toward self-government, because the bureaucratic groups, in the form of the colonial administration, have long been functioning, whereas the conciliar groups are just coming into being.[3] The conciliar groups are composed, furthermore, of politicians, trained in the rough and tumble of independence-movement politics, far removed from the setting which prepared British administrators to move with ease between specific, bureaucratic roles and diffuse, parliamentary roles.

During the transition period of the interim constitutions, while Africans were achieving genuine political authority in such conciliar bodies as the Cabinet and the Legislature, heavy reliance was placed upon bureaucratic roles for guidance. The Permanent Secretaries, civil service roles filled exclusively by British personnel, provided information at Cabinet meetings, prepared politically feasible alternatives for the Ministers to propose in Parliament when problems arose, and sat in the spectators' gallery during sessions of the Legislative Assembly in order to give support to their African seniors. It was hoped, furthermore, that the Permanent Secretaries could introduce into both the Cabinet and the Legislature the awareness and the practice of such bureaucratic concepts as the integrity and responsibility of the group, efficiency, division and specialization of function, coordination, recognition of hierarchy and authority, and rational decision-making.

There is evidence of the success of these attempts in the way in which

[2]This statement does not imply a clear-cut distinction between "politics and administration." Nevertheless the subordinate position of administrative roles and groups is a characteristic of the system. The very term "civil servant" is an expression of this position. During the last stages of British rule, the civil service was able to maintain a dominant or "mentor" position while remaining constitutionally and functionally subordinate.

[3]This was not the case in the western world, where bureaucracy and conciliarism developed simultaneously in keeping with a pattern of cultural and structural changes pervasive throughout the societies. Here bureaucracy and conciliarism shared some of the same characteristics: a mutual subordination to principles of government shared with the public, a pattern of the division of labor and the division of power, a concept of the public interest, means of determining the public interest, etc. Bureaucracy was not dissociated from the general social organization, and it changed along with changes in public beliefs. Bureaucratic units do have their own sub-cultures, but these are not incompatible with other sub-cultures in the society, however different they may be.

the CPP has relegated to unimportant roles or even denied candidacy to certain politicians who have seemed unable to work under the framework of constitutionalism. It is not yet certain, however, that the diffuse membership groupings in Ghana's political system fully comprehend the nature of the relationship between each other and between them and the specific, bureaucratic groups in the government.

THE CONVENTION PEOPLE'S PARTY

The task of a nationalist movement in a colonial territory such as the Gold Coast is a complex and difficult one. Such a movement must determine the means for uniting numerous, separate, traditional societies, each with its own history, loyalties, and vested interests, into a single, cohesive group. To do so it must provide a wide range of satisfactions to widely differing groups of people possessed of many types of social organization. In addition a nationalist movement must continue to expand. It requires increasing power and resources. As a consequence of its difficult task, it postpones the attempt to reconcile the requirements of its own existence with the requirements of socially responsible action. But eventually this reconciliation must be attempted, and this is done at that point where members of the nationalist movement begin to analyze the roles they have been playing and the roles they must play if they are to provide responsible government.

In its initial phases, a nationalist movement is predominantly a diffuse group (Score 1; goals: required, implicit, wide; means: alternative, implicit, wide). But as it begins to take form, it tends to become more and more specific. When it becomes sufficiently specific to function as a "party," it has developed a corps of functionaries, regionally and nationally identified as "patriots." Some of these may have undergone "suffering," as in the case of Ghana's "Prison Graduates." Their loyalty is to the party, and they form the basis of a stable party organization.

Party funds become subject to accounting, and financial laxity, which in Ghana was a characteristic of the nationalist movement, declines. The roles of party officials become more clarified, regularized, and specialized. The leadership must become expert in propaganda and education, in organizational techniques, in mass persuasion; its "thinkers" must find popular issues and phrase them in popular terms. The growing division of labor extends downward to the activation of such roles as "vote organizers," and hierarchies of control on national, regional, district, and local levels, both rural and municipal, come into being.

Within this increasingly specific party framework, leaders emerge. They are frequently men who have displayed superior skill in specific roles but who also appear qualified to play more diffuse roles at the organizational top of the party. Just as there are differences in degrees of specificity and diffuseness between roles within the colonial administration, so are there differences between roles within the internal structure of a political party.

The most diffuse, the most authoritative of these may be called "all-purpose roles." Within the party, these roles and the persons filling them serve as sources rather than as executors of power and policy; they are superior in position to roles of a more specific nature and to those persons who fill them. Such all-purpose roles select the goals and the means for achieving them; they make explicit the nature of the goals and the means to them, and their range of influence is wide (Score 0). They stand in contrast to the lesser degree of discretionary power permitted to the persons in the more specific, bureaucratic roles within the party. Whereas the bureaucratic roles in the party minimize the effects of the personality of the person playing the role by clearly defining the boundaries of action, the all-purpose roles permit much greater expression of the personality of their occupants.

Similar, diffuse all-purpose roles are found both in the Parliament and in the Cabinet. Furthermore, because the civil service bureaucracy is controlled by the Cabinet, the all-purpose roles in the Cabinet may also be regarded as all-purpose roles in the civil service.

In Ghana the persons filling the all-purpose roles of the CPP also fill the all-purpose roles in the Parliament, in the Cabinet, and, therefore, in the civil service, and herein lies one of the difficult problems that must be solved before democratic government in Ghana can become meaningful. The problem may be stated in this way: In a situation in which the all-purpose roles in both the government and the political party are filled by the same persons, can the occupants effectively distinguish between their roles in the two membership groups in which they function simultaneously? The questions may be more specifically phrased in this fashion: Is the CPP to be regarded as identical with Ghana? Is constitutional government to be regarded simply as the expression of the government structure of the CPP? Is the diffuse, all-purpose role of the Life-Chairman of the CPP, Kwame Nkrumah, indistinguishable from the diffuse, all-purpose role of the Prime Minister, Kwame Nkrumah? Is Ghana in fact a one-party state?

For some members of the CPP the answers to these questions seem to be affirmative, though it is probable that most party members are unsure. It is partly in fear of an ultimate affirmative answer that the National Liberation Movement has developed in Ashanti. Depending upon its as yet unconvincing answers to these questions, the CPP either will usurp to itself alone the right to speak in the name of Ghana, or it will accept its obligation to claim authority only on the basis of victory in elections conducted under the terms of the constitution.

If the former alternative is chosen, Ghana government under the CPP will be indistinguishable in its functional qualities from the Gold Coast under colonial administration. In its internal structure it will be specific in nature (Score 6); in its relationship with the public it will be predominantly diffuse (Score 1). And it will have failed to solve the problem, present in all constitutional democracies, of the crucial relationship between specific bureaucratic groups and diffuse conciliar groups. It will have failed because in practice the role occupants failed adequately to distinguish between their roles.

THE CONCILIAR SYSTEM

During the period of interim constitutions, the Gold Coast Government established several types of conciliar systems, that is, systems of representative assemblies established to debate, advise, or legislate. Those concerned with local government are outside the scope of this discussion, but those concerned with the central government are crucial. They comprise the legislative system.

Insofar as African participation is concerned, the change in the functional qualities of the legislative system has been a change from specific to diffuse groups and roles, from solely advisory African groups and roles to completely responsible African groups and roles. At first the Legislative Council was primarily composed of official members, that is, individuals from the higher ranks of the Colonial Service. Gradually its membership was supplemented by unofficial members, both African and European, until in 1946 a majority of the Legislative Council members were African. In the constitutional revision of 1950 a Cabinet system was established. At that time a single political party, the CPP, became the parliamentary party which organized and controlled the predominantly African Legislative Assembly and filled all of the Cabinet roles except for three *ex-officio* British members. In the constitutional revision of 1954 the Cabinet became all-African, although the parliamentary system remained responsible to the British Parliament through the Colonial Office. On March 6, 1957, the parliamentary system assumed full responsibility for the affairs of Ghana.

The Legislature

The device of the interim constitution has accomplished a remarkably smooth transition, in certain respects at least, from African participation in specific advisory or clerical groups to diffuse authoritative groups. In the early period of the Legislative Council the official members, most of them senior in the Colonial Service, set the procedural patterns for parliamentary operations, and the Africans who were subsequently elected or appointed to the Council accepted the patterns. Many of the Africans, furthermore, had enjoyed previous training in the civil service or in specific conciliar groups like the municipal authorites in local government. Even after 1946, when the Legislative Council had an African majority, high procedural standards prevailed.

After 1951, when a much more popularly elected Legislative Assembly came into being, the standards of debate dropped somewhat, but the conduct of the Assembly continued to conform to the rules of "the dignity of the House." Even the misconceptions, misunderstandings, errors, and sheer prejudice revealed both in committees and in open debate could not obscure the obvious seriousness of purpose manifested by the legislators. If parliamentary propriety was occasionally abused, rarely were the offenders responsible members of the government. These standards of propriety have continued down to the present.

The legislature is the fount of political authority in constitutional government (Score 0). Whether or not it has achieved this status in Ghana is as yet uncertain. The opposition charges that Nkrumah and the CPP do not differentiate between themselves and the legislature, and the government replies that the opposition is without faith in the constitution. It is still possible to say, however, that despite the depth of feeling on constitutional matters and despite the degree to which the government and the opposition have been driven apart, they both appear to be committed to parliamentary supremacy in principle and to oppose overt identification of a political party with the legislature.

The CPP Parliamentary Party

Since the CPP as the dominant party organizes and controls the Parliament, an analysis of its structure as it functions in the Parliament is essential to the understanding of the Ghana conciliar system.

In the internal structure of the CPP a differentiation has developed between the role of "delegate" and the role of "representative." With respect to the qualitative aspects of these roles in their relationship with the parliamentary party, the delegate is specific (Score 6), the representative is specific-diffuse (Score 3; goals: required, implicit, narrow; means: alternative, implicit, narrow).

Persons playing the role of delegate are persons, usually without special talents, who are completely responsive to the demands of their public constituencies. Because of this strong public support, they can be used by the CPP to state the popular issues and to announce the CPP position on them. Ordinarily they are firm in their adherence to CPP discipline.

Persons playing the role of representative are less responsive to the demands of their constituents, more directed by their own discretion or "conscience," and capable of nonconformity to CPP discipline, even though actual nonconformity is rare. If either a delegate or a representative behaves too independently, an attempt is made to remove him from politics. If, however, the delegate is too powerfully supported by his public constituency, he may be incorporated into the Cabinet or into the policy-making group within the CPP. The nonconforming representative may either be removed from politics or appointed to a specific, nonauthoritative role in some government agency such as a marketing board.

Delegates of special interest groups, such as a trade union, a voluntary association, or a trading association, tend to enact the role of representative on matters not pertinent to their special interest. The importance of these delegates in matters of national significance, however, is relatively minor.[4]

In addition to the roles of delegate and representative, a third role, that of the "party core," has been differentiated. It is a predominantly specific role, similar to that of the delegate, though different in its content. The person filling this role is regarded as qualified for Parliament primarily because of his effective service to the CPP. He is a hero to his constituency, which accepts rather than determines his actions. His actions, in turn, are determined by the CPP, to which he is loyal both inside and outside of Parliament. As a group, the party core is in closest touch with the CPP bureaucracy, and individuals may actually be members of the party bureaucracy. If they show a tendency toward nonconformity to CPP discipline, they are dropped, but if in addition to complete reliability they are intelligent, are effective organizers, have strong independent backing, or are in any way crucial to success either in government or within the party, they may be appointed as Government Whips or given other responsible tasks in the government.

Within the parliamentary party these roles are combined to form the "back bench," a membership group which, in its relationship with the CPP, is predominantly specific in nature (Score 4; goals: required, explicit, wide; means: required, explicit, wide).

A fourth role which must be distinguished in the parliamentary party is that of the Ministerial Secretary, a particularly complex role because of the position it holds with respect both to the more diffuse role of the Minister, to which it is subordinate, and to the more specific roles and membership groups over which it can exert its dominance. Among the latter roles and membership groups are the CPP, the back bench of

[4]An exception to this generalization are the Trade Union Congress representatives who are assuming an increasingly important and aggressive role in their constituencies and in the union organizations themselves.

the parliamentary party, the Parliament itself, and the civil service bureaucracy.

In its relationship with the role of Minister, that of the Ministerial Secretary is, in theory, specific (Score 6). When, however, the person filling this role is better trained and possessed of a more deft sense of judgment than his superior, the Minister, his role may in actuality become as predominantly diffuse as that of the Minister. In such cases, his role may possess considerable power to make decisions, even though it is a delegated rather than an official power. When the Minister is himself a person of ability or power, the role of Ministerial Secretary may require simply the performance of routine, clerical tasks.

In its relationship with the back bench of the parliamentary party, this role is more diffuse. The Ministerial Secretary is frequently a person who has performed well in some other specific capacity in the CPP or in the government. In this case he may become useful as a communicator between his Minister or the Cabinet and the back bench as a determiner of back bench action. His relationship with the more specific roles within the CPP is similar to that with the back bench, as is his relationship with the civil service. But in all of these relationships (and this is characteristic of the more diffuse roles in any relationship), the personality of the role occupant affects the function of the role. He may range from a highly responsible figure, being groomed for future office, to a much more irresponsible, self-seeking figure, who may attempt to exploit his political following on the back bench and in the political party by dispensing political patronage.

This complex role is important, furthermore, in that it is the principal means by which the relationship between the civil service bureaucracy and the Parliament is regulated. The English rules governing access by Members of Parliament to civil service administrators have been retained in Ghana. These rules are reflected in a statement by Professor Robson: ". . . the dangers of a too close relationship between Members of Parliament and civil servants might be considerable. A civil servant might be deflected by political influence of an MP or a group of MP's. He might be made to feel that his own future depended to some extent on the favour or disfavour in which he stood with members of the legislature. A Minister's authority in his department might be undermined by legislative support for a particular division or branch."[5] Standing as it does between the Member of Parliament and the Minister, the role of the Ministerial Secretary provides its occupant with considerable discretionary power to determine who may and who may not approach the

[5]See William A. Robson, ed., *The Civil Service in England and France* (London: The Hogarth Press, 1956), Chap. 1, p. 10.

Minister or any of the civil servants in his department. According to the rules, there is no other legitimate access to the civil servant except through his Minister, and the Ministerial Secretary guards that approach. It may also be pointed out that the opportunity for corruption at this diffuse level of authority is considerable.

The final membership group, or system or roles to be distinguished in the parliamentary party is that of the "front bench." It is comprised of the Ministers and the Prime Minister, and it is a diffuse group in all its relationships (Score 0). Certain of the Ministries which dispense patronage, such as the Ministry of Works, may be more specific in nature than others. Certain of the Ministers in the front bench, furthermore, may also play such predominantly specific roles as "party core" or technically competent "administrators." But the group itself is diffuse in its relationships with all other roles and groups.

It is through the front bench that the civil service must exert its influence. It is the front bench which gives the entire Ghana Parliament its vitality by demanding proper parliamentary behavior from the members of the parliamentary party. It is the front bench which exerts great control over the CPP itself and which is associated with the Prime Minister in his role as political party leader.

Within the front bench, the most important, the most authoritative Ministers play "all-purpose" roles. They have a prestige and a position which allows them considerable personal latitude in the exercise of discretion. In their role they are capable of combining the characteristics of the party core and the technical expert. In addition, the persons occupying these all-purpose roles—of whom the Prime Minister, Kwame Nkrumah, the Minister of Finance, K. A. Gbedemah, and the Minister of Interior (1957), Krobo Edusei, are outstanding examples—possess personalities which give them a symbolic position in the conciliar system and in the entire nation.

In their special relationship with the public, these men in their all-purpose roles function as symbols for the nation—as do all political leaders of great stature—and they need no justification for their actions other than their own symbolic positions. It is as public symbols that these men, in their most diffuse, all-purpose roles in the political party, in the parliamentary party, and in the Parliament, can serve either to strengthen or weaken the patterns of constitutional government in Ghana.

The Cabinet

In its relationship with the parliamentary party, the Cabinet, comprised of the Ministerial roles, is a diffuse membership group. But the Cabinet is a complex group which also has relationships with the civil service bureaucracy, Parliament, and with the political party. Each of these relationships requires analysis.

In its relationship with the civil service bureaucracy, the Cabinet is a predominantly specific group (Score 4; goals: required, explicit, wide; means: required, explicit, wide). It is, however, more diffuse than is the civil service itself, for the Cabinet is the most authoritative part of the civil service. In this relationship the civil service is specific, since the scope of its goals and means is narrower than that of the Cabinet, whose Ministers are responsible heads of the departments of the civil service. In his capacity as head of a department, the Cabinet Minister is a specialist in local government, housing, education, and the like, of whom efficient performance is required. In order to achieve his goals, he must share in certain respects the perspectives and skills of the senior civil service personnel and must have an understanding of the operations and procedures of the bureaucratic department for which he is responsible.

During the period of the interim constitutions, the Ministers learned the requirements of their roles in their civil service relationships from the British Permanent Secretaries, who not only continued their former specialist roles but also served as "mentors" to the Ministers under whom they worked. So important was this latter function that often the qualities of the roles were reversed, the Ministerial role being more specific than that of the Permanent Secretary. Despite the occasional complaint that a Minister was hampered by his Permanent Secretary, the strikingly effective record of successive Gold Coast Cabinets during the interim period is one indication of the success of this "training period." Cabinet Ministers were enabled by this device to approach decisions with the necessary information and criteria for judgment.

The ministerial skills developed through this relationship with the civil service also served to establish the Cabinet as a diffuse group in its relationship with Parliament and to make possible a high standard of procedures in that body. The Minister, equipped with information and experience in decision-making which Members of Parliament did not possess, was frequently able to control and even to intimidate his less knowledgeable party colleagues and the opposition.

The relationship of the Cabinet with the political party demonstrates the complexity and difficulty of the Minister's role. With respect to many issues, of course, the Cabinet is diffuse and the political party specific, for the Ministers possess not only technical skill, but also the symbolic position of recognized leadership which other party members do not possess in equal degree. But on many issues and over a long time-span, the Cabinet as a group and each Minister individually must be responsive to the party, for without party support and the public support which it represents, the Cabinet fails. In this aspect of the Cabinet's relationship with the political party, therefore, the Cabinet is specific-diffuse (Score 3; goals: required, explicit, narrow; means: alternative, implicit, wide). The Cabinet retains sufficient diffuseness to determine the means to goals, but the political party defines the goals themselves. The Cabinet Minister must remain a party politician; he must cater to his party membership. Some of the latter, in fact, have been brought into the Parliament and the Cabinet, where they play, among their other roles, the role of party core.

Because of the nature of its relationships with all of these groups, the Cabinet serves as the principal integrator of governmental and political party groups. The person who fills the role of Minister, therefore, must be capable of finding the means to balance these groups; he must have parliamentary agility, political shrewdness, judgment and sagacity and, above all, he must have the ability to combine in himself all the alternative roles which he, as Minister, must play as leader of his civil service department, as party politician, as parliamentarian, as leader of the parliamentary party, and as public symbol. He must be able to integrate all other political roles and groups and he must be able to do so in a way which strengthens his role and his own position in it.

It has been pointed out above that during the period of the interim constitutions, the Cabinet was diffuse in its relationship with Parliament, primarily because of its superior knowledge and experience in decision-making gained through the training provided by the British members of the senior civil service. This is not the relationship characteristic of constitutional democracies. In this system of government, the Cabinet provides leadership for the parliamentary party, for the public, and for the civil service bureaucracy, but it is subordinate to Parliament, to which it is responsible. In the ideal relationship, therefore, it is Parliament which is the diffuse group and the Cabinet which is specific.

The Ghana Parliament has not yet assumed this essential control over the Cabinet, and it will be unable to do so as long as the opposition remains comparatively ineffective. The distinctions between the civil service bureacracy, the parliamentary party, the Cabinet, Parliament, and the political party have not yet been clearly defined. It is not that the roles have been poorly filled. Radical-populist as the CPP is, it has selected leaders for Cabinet positions who, for the most part, are men with higher educations, with old school ties, and with experience in other cultures. They have played their roles effectively. Some of them are fully as technically skilled as the African specialists who fill specific roles in the higher ranks of the civil service. As nationalist leaders they have achieved their nationalist goals. In the Cabinet they have succeeded in reconciling the different relationships of their role in such a way as to provide effective leadership acceptable to the public.

But the question of the Cabinet's relationship to Parliament remains unanswered. If the political party regards itself as the government of Ghana, then the Cabinet is only a device to cloak authority in constitutional garb. If the party differentiates clearly between itself and the government, then the Cabinet will become subordinate to Parliament, and this essential requirement of constitutional democracy will be met.

ROLE INTEGRATION AND AUTHORITY

The significant roles and membership groups and the complex network of relationships between them which have arisen under the policy of interim constitutions have now been analyzed. The assumption on which this policy has been based is that gradual, progressive devolution of authority to Africans provides the time and experience necessary for coming to understand and to institutionalize the patterns of constitutional democracy. Has this assumption as yet been justified?

In many respects, the transition from colonial administration to constitutional self-government has enjoyed marked success. A sufficient degree of integration between the roles and the membership groups has been achieved to enable the government to function without breakdown. The system has succeeded in filling the crucial political roles with men of technical skill who also possess the qualities of leadership. The policy, furthermore, has succeeded in gaining public acceptance of certain of the values of a constitutional democracy: the public has come to accept the new political roles which are part of the constitutional system, and they have come increasingly to rely upon the constitutional means of political action available to the public in the vote, in petitions and memorials, etc. In keeping with the goal of the policy of interim constitutions, therefore, two types of authoritative political membership groups, broadly defined, have in fact been developed: these two groups are comprised of the political elite, those with authority in the governmental system, and the public, that group whose support is necessary in order to maintain the elite in their positions.

In order effectively to capture and use the authority of the public group, political parties develop their own bureaucracies. When governmental political roles (previously unavailable to Africans or filled by the politically conservative African elite representative of the earliest stages of nationalism) become open, the nationalist party tends to fill them only from among the leaders of the party itself. The party also develops specialists in organization, propaganda, communications, tactics, and strategy. In so doing a twofold differentiation of function emerges: certain roles come to be regarded as specialist, others as all-purpose. The specialist roles are integrated into a true party bureaucracy, the all-purpose roles supply legitimacy and leadership for the bureaucracy, which then is regarded as subordinate to the all-purpose roles.

Ghana's political system has thus come to include two types of bureaucracy: a political party bureaucracy, and a government civil service bureaucracy. In both their internal structure and in their relationships to the groups to which they are responsible—the government bureaucracy being responsible to Parliament through the Cabinet, the party bureaucracy responsible to the party leadership—these two bureaucracies have identical qualities: they are both specific (Score 6). Both of them, furthermore, have relationships with the same two membership groups within the government, Parliament and the Cabinet, both of which are diffuse (Score 0) in these relationships. In their interaction with these membership groups, however, the goals of the two bureaucracies are quite different. The goal of the party bureacracy is to strengthen its own position, and it tends to view Parliament and the Cabinet as groups to be manipulated in order to gain its goal. The goal of the government bureaucracy, on the other hand, is to provide effective government, and it tends to view Parliament and the Cabinet as groups which may restrict its attempts to improve government and, therefore, as groups which threaten the status of the bureaucracy itself. The two bureaucracies do not interact directly with each other but do so indirectly through their mutual relationships with Parliament and the Cabinet.

An important tentative conclusion emerges at this point of the analysis. *The party bureaucracy and the government bureaucracy exert opposing pressures upon those persons filling all-purpose roles in Parliament and the Cabinet.*

The logic which underlies this conclusion is as follows: (1) With the formalization of constitutional practice, both bureaucracies become more developed in order to achieve their respective goals. (2) With the development of the bureaucracies, the specialist roles are differentiated more precisely; they become more specific in quality. (3) The more specific a role becomes, the more the role occupant comes to view his own narrow membership group as most crucial to the entire system. (4) The more the role occupant acts in terms of his own group, the more he seeks to avoid threats to his group, regardless of the consequences of his action for constitutional development or abtsract political values.

Both bureaucracies, therefore, exert opposing pressures upon Parliament and the Cabinet in order to assure achievement of their own goals. Some CPP bureaucrats regard the government ideally as a simple reflection of the party. Some government bureaucrats regard the government ideally as a simple reflection of the civil service—a viewpoint reinforced during the period of interim training under the British—and most of those who have been disappointed by political developments to the contrary have resigned, retired, or been transferred.

If the goals of the two bureaucracies differ, the means at their disposal also differ, because they stand in different relationships to the public, that basic authority group to which both are ultimately responsible in a constitutional democracy. In this relationship the government bureaucracy is specific (Score 6). It has specifically defined responsibilities; it is a dependent group, specifically responsible to Parliament through the Cabinet; it operates under a formal, constitutional mandate which removes it from any direct relationship with the public. The party bureaucracy, on the other hand, has only diffusely defined responsibilities: it is an autonomous group, responsible to the party; it operates only under an informal mandate, that of public approval and allegiance. Both bureaucracies have real sources of power. Each possesses advantages which the other does not. And each, with the different means at its disposal, seeks to affect the way in which government will develop by attempting to maximize its control over Parliament and the Cabinet.

The pressures exerted by both of these bureaucracies are directed primarily toward those members of Parliament and the Cabinet who play the most important all-purpose roles. Nkrumah recognizes that his continuance in office is in part dependent upon the specialist roles in the party bureaucracy which are necessary to capture and maintain public allegiance. But he recognizes as well that his continuance in office is in part dependent upon the specialist roles in the government bureaucracy which are necessary to carry out the policies of his government and thus enable him to wage an effective campaign before the public. This latter dependence is even greater in an underdeveloped area like Ghana, where governmental rather than nongovernmental groups are directly involved in a high proportion of the social and economic institutions of the country.

One of the major goals of the Prime Minister, the Cabinet, and the parliamentary party, therefore, is to maximize the utility of the two bureaucracies and to minimize the conflict between them.[6] This is, perhaps, one of the features of the parliamentary system in Ghana which distinguishes it from the more stabilized parliamentary systems in Europe. It gains its peculiar importance from the fact that both the Cabinet and Parliament are comprised of numerous persons who must play overlapping, diffuse roles; that is, they simultaneously hold analogous positions of authority in two theoretically and ideally separate political member-

[6]It must be emphasized that the conflict is an indirect one. It rarely becomes overt, although it may do so through the entrance into the conflict of another political party, such as the National Liberation Movement, which may deliberately point up the existence of opposing pressures.

ship groups. The Cabinet and the front bench of the parliamentary party consist of the same individuals who are the authoritative leaders of the political party and, hence, of the party bureaucracy. On the back bench of the parliamentary party are found the roles of "delegate" and "party core," both of which conform in their actions to the party bureaucracy; indeed, the party core is made up of some of the more important party bureaucrats. The overlapping between political party roles and parliamentary roles is thus considerable.

The overlap of roles in the Cabinet has a different but analogous pattern. Here the Cabinet members simultaneously play diffuse roles in the civil service government bureaucracy, in the parliamentary party (to which the government bureaucracy is responsible), and in the political party. Ideally, the Cabinet Minister judges the proposals of the government bureaucracy solely on the criteria of logicality and governmental efficiency, but often his overlapping roles of parliamentary party member or of political party leader prevail, and judgments are made on the criteria of what is considered politically feasible or utilitarian by the party bureaucracy.

Nkrumah's ability to maximize the utility of both bureaucracies and to minimize the conflict between them has depended until now upon his peculiar all-purpose role, a role possibly filled also by Gbedemah and Edusei. This type of role differs from overlapping roles in that the latter consist of several separate, well-defined roles which may successively or alternately be filled by the individual playing each. The all-purpose role is much more diffuse in its definition and permits the individual playing it great freedom of action, including domination of any of the overlapping roles in the bureaucracies and in Parliament. Authority for this role derives from the public, whose complete acceptance gives it a symbolic quality enjoyed by no other role. It is in this role that Nkrumah has thus far successfully maintained both his own position and an effective political system in Ghana.

The question of whether or not he can continue to do so gives rise to a second tentative conclusion: *The parliamentary system permits leaders to fill overlapping roles only; all-purpose roles, therefore, are gradually abolished.* The symbolic status of a leader declines, and he becomes the occupant of several, well-defined, specialist roles.

Nkrumah's symbolic position has already undergone such a decline, one measure of which is the revived symbolic position of chiefs whose role in the traditional society approached that of "all-purpose." There are many reasons for Nkrumah's apparent decline—though he remains the most significant and powerful individual in Ghana—but the most far-reaching reason is the nature of the parliamentary system itself. Once it becomes stabilized or institutionalized, this system does not permit the existence of all-purpose roles.

The logic which underlies this conclusion is as follows:

1. As the parliamentary system stabilizes, the actions of the Cabinet Minister are more and more dominated by his specialist, specific roles rather than by his diffuse party roles. This is the reverse of the relationship between his overlapping roles in the early stages of a parliamentary system. The Cabinet Minister comes to identify himself with the civil service government bureaucracy, with whose senior members he shares attitudes and outlook as a result of similar educations, social backgrounds, technical skills, and responsibilities for effective government. The effect of this identification is to raise the status of the government bureaucracy.

2. As the party bureaucracy becomes stabilized, continues to recruit new party leaders, and gains experience, the persons filling specialist roles begin to acquire and exert greater authority; they move into roles which are more diffusely defined.

3. As the Cabinet Ministers on the front bench come to identify themselves more completely with the government bureaucracy, the party core, drawn primarily from the party bureaucracy, assumes increased control over the back bench of the parliamentary party because it is the party bureaucracy which enforces party discipline and selects party candidates for office.

4. The diffuse, all-purpose role, previously dominant over both bureaucracies, is less and less able to exert its dominance. In the Cabinet it takes on the characteristics of a specialist role, though still more diffusely defined than any of the roles subordinate to it in either the Cabinet or the government bureaucracy. Similar consequences occur in the political party aspects of the all-purpose role. As party leaders emerge in the party bureaucracy, the undivided support of the public for the all-purpose role is weakened, and it loses its symbolic status for the public, that group in the political system which initially sanctioned it.

If this conclusion is substantiated, certain consequences appear inevitable. The conflict between the party bureaucracy and the government bureaucracy, always implicit, becomes more open and intense. This is followed by a decline in responsible government, since each bureaucracy "tends to view the entire nation in its own image." Ghana appears, therefore, to be entering a phase marked by an interesting political dilemma, not unlike that of the French political system. In the absence of an effective opposition political party in the country, there is a strong possibility that the CPP will resolve this dilemma by itself becoming the government.

In the terms of this analysis, then, Ghana faces the problem of reducing a personalized, diffuse all-purpose role—in itself a potential threat to constitutional democracy—to a system of predominantly specific overlapping roles without precipitating a struggle in government even more threatening to constitutional democracy. Thus far Nkrumah and the various membership groups in Parliament have kept the conflict indirect and subtle without impairing the operations of government.

If Ghana can develop a responsible opposition, an alternative government in a real sense, committed to the constitutional order, capable of recruiting candidates for political office who possess a sense of party discipline and party organization, and capable of filling overlapping roles with qualified persons, the dilemma can be resolved in a satisfactory manner. Eisenstadt has pointed out that "insofar as other groups tend to participate more actively in political life, the monopoly of power and prestige breaks down, and the bureaucracy may thus become only one among a number of status groups, deriving many of its symbols from other groups and strata in the society. As the pressure from these groups becomes stronger, the bureaucracy tends to lose some of its autonomy.[7] The government bureaucracy becomes a neutralized, specific membership group in government, seeking the goal of effective government compatible with the basic, general rules of the society. The party bureaucracy becomes a neutralized, specific membership group in the political system but outside of direct intervention in government, because it must contend and compromise with strong opposition party bureaucracies for public support.

In this respect, the National Liberation Movement in Ghana has thus far been unable to provide the necessary kind of opposition, for the results of its efforts have been simply to strengthen the relationships between the party bureaucracy of the CPP and the Prime Minister and his Cabinet. The NLM cannot at the present time be regarded as a source of political pluralism.

CONCLUSION

The series of interim constitutions has not been able to establish a functioning democratic system in Ghana. It is apparent that the system will be less stable than before, at least during the early stages of self-government, for reasons discussed in this analysis. There is one other factor contributing to the instability of government in the near future, however, to which attention must be given. This factor is the omission from the pattern of constitutional development of any feature equivalent to the British Crown, that is, some symbol as meaningful to Ghana as "The Crown" has been to the British.[8]

Ultimately the concept of the state as a moral trust is essential to

[7]See S. N. Eisenstadt, "Political Power in Bureaucratic Societies," *World Politics*, IX, No. 1 (October, 1956), 34.

[8]Constitutionally—unless Ghana should declare itself a republic—the Crown plays the same part in Ghana that it does in the United Kingdom.

the functioning of a constitutional democracy, and it is solely to this aspect of "The Crown" that reference is here made (and not to such aspects as historical derivation from feudalism, the inheritance of office, the nobility, the class system, and all the other formal aspects of the concept). Perhaps the most crucial feature of the British constitutional system is the incorporation of this concept of moral trust into every role of the governmental system to a degree found in no other system. The concept of "The Crown" expresses the subordination and responsibility of each person filling a political role to that symbolic role. In a real sense, each role becomes a specific role; only "The Crown" is diffuse, all-purpose. This single role is the "property" of Her Majesty's Government. The sovereign is relatively powerless, but the symbol is powerful, and responsibility to it becomes peculiarly and personally the requirement of the occupant of every political role, including the sovereign himself. In the British pattern, there is almost a direct correlation between the rise in symbolic status of "The Crown" and the decline of personalized diffuse roles in the British Parliament. This is perhaps nowhere better brought out than in the position of Sir Winston Churchill, whose powerful personality was combined with an awesome respect for the limits and traditions of his office.

The interim constitutions in Ghana have created a set of political roles which interact and are integrated with each other. Roles have become increasingly specific and the degree of indeterminacy and freedom of action based upon personality or upon irresponsibility has been reduced. Up to the present time, however, the most crucial role in the government has not been sufficiently depersonalized. The Prime Minister still carries a "mystique" of public morality, not only in the eyes of his followers but also in his own eyes as well. He personally is indeed the symbol of Ghana, of anti-imperialism, of self-government, of freedom, and in certain respects he regards the state of Ghana as his own creation and as an extension of his own personality and life.

"The Crown" cannot perform a function in Ghana similar to that which it performs in Great Britain or, to a lesser degree, in New Zealand, Australia, or Canada. It is to be hoped, however, that a functional equivalent will emerge which will supply that component essential to constitutional democracy, a sense of political propriety in the public and in those chosen for public office, a responsibility to the state itself as a moral trust. Perhaps this has been best stated by T. H. Green when he argues that the "real" function of government is "to maintain conditions of life in which morality shall be possible, and morality consisting in the disinterested performance of self-imposed duties."[9]

In the last analysis interim constitutions establish the bases from which

[9]T. H. Green, *Principles of Political Obligation* (London: Longmans, Green & Co., Ltd., 1950), p. 40.

further political development can take place. These bases have been well provided in Ghana. But interim constitutions are no guarantee of effective government. They can at best provide the mechanisms for resolving conflict. The public and those it chooses to represent it must decide if it wants those conflicts to be resolved.

The Role of Traditionalism in the Political Modernization of Ghana and Uganda

Social analysts have long been preoccupied with those features of traditional culture and belief which affect the direction of change and the receptivity of a society to innovation. In spite of the very considerable literature concerned with acculturation, there have been few efforts to examine different types of traditional systems with respect to the problems they pose for political modernization. We attempt this form of analysis here. The plan is to examine two countries, Ghana and Uganda, both of which are engaged in the effort to build a national society. Each is experimenting with constitutional forms, and each has had to deal with the problem of traditionalism. Indeed, the central problem of those concerned with building national, as distinct from local, political institutions has been to create overarching political parties, voluntary associations, and governmental forms that bridge older parochialisms. Moreover, just as tradition is a source of parochial strengths and social pride, so its characteristics vary widely. There are some who argue that any understanding of modernity in Africa must be based on an examination of the variants of the traditional systems.

In an earlier form, this article was presented at the Dobbs Ferry Conference of the SSRC Sub-Committee on Comparative Government in 1959.

Research by the author in West Africa was first made possible through the generosity of the Social Science Research Council in 1952. Subsequent work was done in West Africa under the auspices of the West African Comparative Analysis Project, a Carnegie-supported research project that is still under way. Work on Uganda was undertaken in 1955–1956 through a Ford Foundation Area Research Training Fellowship. None of these agencies is responsible for the opinions expressed in this article.

In this article, we shall compare recent political events in Ghana and Uganda to try to show how they have been shaped by the nature of traditionalism. By this means we can illustrate the implications of two different kinds of traditionalism and the problems they pose for modern nation-builders.

TRADITIONALISM

The importance of traditional factors in change was not the discovery of Max Weber, as some have thought. Such antecedent greats as Marx and Coulanges sought to link to the problem of modernization those stable symbols, artifacts, and values transmitted by the people of a society through generations. Marx was particularly concerned with its economic aspects; Coulanges with its religious aspects. Since that time, the study of tradition has been either directly or indirectly brought into the most contemporary concerns. Most recently, Lerner has observed the behavioral consequences and durability of tradition by exploring degrees of participation in mass media of communication. Fallers has dealt with it in terms of bureaucracy. My own concern has focused on the functional implications of traditional political forms for modern ones.[1]

Nor is interest in tradition a peculiarity of social scientists. Politicians, no less than academics, recognize that traditional factors which under some circumstances seem to create immobilities in social structure, and abort or minimize innovation, at other times can open the door to an entirely different range of behaviors. Administrators who in Mali Federation (formerly Senegal and French Sudan) for years sought with only small success to establish effective local units of government, possessing cultural and solidary features satisfying to the population, now find the very same measures enthusiastically taken up by African leaders and interpreted as peculiar to the genius of Africans. Under the ideology of *negritude*, the meaning attached to community development, cooperation, and communalism has been transformed into a living and continuous feature of the African past. By this means, innovation has been "traditionalized" and made comfortable. Change is not strange or foreign, requiring new roles or learning. Traditionalism puts novelty on trial rather than the people that novelty is supposed to serve. The lesson of Mali is that contemporary administrators and political leaders in Africa who can learn to enlist traditionalism in the service of innovation will indeed be contributing to successful political modernization.

[1]See D. Lerner *et al., The Passing of Traditional Society* (Glencoe, Ill.: The Free Press, 1958); L. A. Fallers, *Bantu Bureaucracy* (Cambridge: W. Heffer & Sons, Ltd., 1956); and D. E. Apter, *The Gold Coast in Transition* (Princeton: Princeton University Press, 1955).

Traditionalism, as distinct from tradition, we can define as validations of current behavior stemming from immemorial prescriptive norms. It is not that traditionalist systems do not change, but rather that innovation—i.e., extra-systemic action—has to be mediated within the social system and charged to antecedent values. Modernism, in contrast, presupposes a much remoter relationship between antecedent values and new goals. Modern systems, with their complex and highly differentiated social structures, value change itself.

These distinctions between modernism and traditionalism, valid as they are, leave unanswered the question why some traditional systems can innovate more easily than others. Answers have been sought in the structural features of traditional societies, while traditionalism has remained a more or less undifferentiated concept.

The discussion here accordingly distinguishes between two types of traditionalism. The first can be called *instrumental*, the second, *consummatory.*[2] Each kind exhibits certain structural tendencies. The combination of value type and structural tendency determines the problems that confront political leaders as they seek to build modern nations. We shall examine these combinations in Ghana and Uganda.

As we are using the term, instrumental systems are those which can innovate easily by spreading the blanket of tradition upon change itself. In such systems, those who are called upon to arbitrate in matters of custom and to interpret in some official capacity are easily persuaded to find traditional counterparts in contemporary events. Such systems can innovate without appearing to alter their social institutions fundamentally. Rather, innovation is made to serve immemoriality. The characteristic structural expression of instrumental traditionalism is a military

[2]As we are using the terms, "instrumental" systems are those characterized by a large sector of intermediate ends separate from and independent of ultimate ends; "consummatory" systems are those characterized by a close relationship between intermediate and ultimate ends. The terms are derived from Parsons' categories of "cognitive-instrumental meanings" and "expressive-integrative meanings." See T. Parsons *et al.*, *Working Papers in the Theory of Action* (Glencoe, Ill.: The Free Press, 1953), p. 105.

The difference between instrumental and consummatory values, in the sense we are using them here, can be illustrated by the following example. Consider two traditional systems, one consummatory and the other instrumental in value type. Both are short-hoe cultures and an effort is made to introduce new agricultural techniques in each, particularly the use of tractors. In the consummatory system, changing from the short hand-hoe system will so corrupt the ritual of hoe-making, the division of men's and women's work, the religious practices associated with both, and the relationship between agricultural rituals and the authority of chiefs that it would be impossible to consider introduction of the tractor only in terms of increasing agricultural productivity. In the instrumental system, by contrast, the tractor would simply be viewed in terms of its ability to expand agricultural output and would not affect the ultimate ends of the system. In the first instance, such an innovation represents a threat to the system. In the second instance, it is far likelier to strengthen the system by increasing farm income.

type of system, with hierarchical authority stemming from a single king or command figure.[3] Appointive ranks in the system tend to underwrite the king as the central source of authority. Here, a heavy reliance on performance is a characteristic of office, and the chief who fails to serve his king loyally and well is subject to removal or death. Religion is decidedly secondary in such a system, which has as a primary value service to the king or state. Examples of such systems are Morocco, Ethiopia, and Buganda.[4]

The traditionalism of consummatory systems is much more complex. They were first described by Fustel de Coulanges when, deploring the simplistic interpretations of Greece and Rome as prototypes for modern societies, he wrote that examining the institutions of those two systems without a knowledge of their religious notions left them "obscure, whimsical, and inexplicable." He went on to say: "A comparison of beliefs and laws shows that a primitive religion constituted the Greek and Roman family, established marriage and paternal authority, fixed the order of relationship, and consecrated the right of property, and the right of inheritance. This same religion, after having enlarged and extended the family, formed a still larger association, the city, and reigned in that as it had reigned in the family. From it came all the institutions, as well as all the private laws, of the ancients. It was from this that the city received all its principles, its rules, its usages and its magistracies."[5]

Thus society, the state, authority, and the like are all part of an elaborately sustained, high-solidarity system in which religion as a cognitive guide is pervasive. Such systems have been hostile to innovation. Change has produced fundamental social upheavals such as migration to towns. Broken are warmth and intimacy of custom. Not only were ancient Greece and Rome examples of such systems, but so was Ashanti.[6]

[3]For a discussion of hierarchical authority, see A. Southall, *Alur Society* (Cambridge: W. Heffer & Sons, Ltd., 1956) especially Chap. 6. See also D. E. Apter, *The Political Kingdom in Uganda: A Study of Bureaucratic Nationalism* (Princeton: Princeton University Press, 1961).

[4]The reader should note that the name Uganda refers to the entire country, the Uganda Protectorate, which includes many different tribes; Buganda is a tribe within Uganda; the Baganda are the people (plural) of Buganda; a Muganda is a single member of the Buganda tribe; and Kiganda is the adjective form.

[5]Fustel de Coulanges, *The Ancient City* (New York: Doubleday & Company, Inc., n.d.), p. 13.

[6]Such systems can innovate, however. Indeed, the philosophy prevailing in Senegal today is similar to that described by Coulanges, but the religious system is pervaded by humanistic socialism. Hence to build upon traditional solidarities, the emphasis on family, corporatism in institutions, personalism, and the like go hand in hand with joint participation in communal economic efforts. By this means, work is ennobled and given new meaning in traditional terms. See, for example, the expression of this point of view by M. Mamadou Dia in *L'Economie africaine*, Paris, 1957, and "Economie et culture devant les élites africaines," *Présence africaine*, Nos. 14–15 (June-September 1957), pp. 58–72.

Our general hypothesis is that the instrumental-hierarchical type of system can innovate with ease until the kingship principle is challenged, at which point the entire system joins together to resist change. In other words, such systems are highly resistant to political rather than other forms of modernization, and in particular cannot easily supplant the hierarchical principle of authority with a representative one.

Consummatory values are most significantly rooted where the structural expression of authority is pyramidal rather than hierarchical. Pyramidal structure means that patterns of subordinacy and superordinacy are limited to such activities as war or court appeals. For most purposes a chief or political leader is responsible to his social group rather than to a senior chief or official. The chiefs at each level of the pyramid thus have similar powers and are relatively autonomous in respect to one another. Such a structural form relies heavily on semi-segmental kinship relationships. The autonomy of the chief or political leader is thus a reflection of the autonomy of the kinship unit itself.

Consummatory-pyramidal systems are highly resistant to all forms of innovation, and the consequences of change are external political groupings that form as new solidary associations cutting across the older ones. In other words, new social structures with a political focus emerge, with the object of tearing down the older ones. Let us examine these processes in Ghana and Uganda.

TWO TRADITIONAL SYSTEMS

Buganda, one of the most important kingdom states in the lake area of Eastern Africa, was regarded very favorably by Europeans who first came upon the country in the latter half of the nineteenth century. First Arabs, and then British and French missionaries, were welcomed by the king, or *Kabaka*, of Buganda. Kabaka Mutesa I encouraged competitive performances by the three religious groups—Muslim, Catholic, and Protestant. Although he died a pagan, he was intensely interested in Christianity.

To the Baganda, adoption of Christianity came to denote a superior technological and educational status. The older religious system, associated with the institution of clanship which was itself giving way to a hierarchical chieftaincy system, disappeared without producing much internal strain. Christianity easily passed muster as an aid to the Baganda in maintaining their society. The only point of concern was the fact that missionaries, in gaining adherents, tended to usurp the functions of chiefs. Since the latter remained responsible to the Kabaka, while the missionaries were not, a disturbing element was introduced into the political system.

Competition among religions, however, resulted in religious wars. These were eventually resolved by allocating fixed numbers of chieftaincies to Catholics, Protestants, and Muslims. The religious factions became tantamount to political parties within Buganda.

The missionaries themselves commented on how quickly the Baganda took to education and became ardent religionists as well.[7] After British intervention and the establishment of the Protectorate over Uganda, regular Catholic and Protestant school systems were established. The chiefs were the best-educated group in the population. Catholic chiefs were products of Kisubi, the Catholic school, and Protestant chiefs were products of King's College, Budo. Both were modeled after British public schools.

Moreover, freehold land tenure was introduced and 8,000 square miles were distributed among 1,000 chiefs and notables, who thereby became a kind of squirearchy. The recipients of the land were mainly Catholics and Protestants.

Whatever the innovated structure, whether civil-service chieftaincy, a parliament and council of ministers, modern education, or freehold tenure, it strengthened the system. The instrumental quality of hierarchical kingship was never defeated. The innovations that were most easily accepted were those that strengthened the Buganda government and also facilitated the individual's efficiency within it.

As a result, the organization of political life, which had been the crucial social structure in Buganda, was regarded as continuing from the past, with each innovation simply perfecting and strengthening an established system. All novelty came to be regarded as a device for strengthening tradition. As we shall indicate below, the main form of nationalism which emerged was that of a modernizing autocracy in which the government of the Kabaka and the Kabaka himself represented effective nationalism.

In Ashanti, on the other hand, responses to innovation were relatively complicated. Chieftaincy, despite its tiers of relatively autonomous powers with respect to various units of government, was nevertheless hemmed in with restrictions. Chieftaincy faced inward to the people to whom, by lineage and totem, the chief or headman was related. Instead of the individual atomism of Buganda, which was held together by regard for the Kabaka and the external force of hierarchical authority, the Ashanti chief was linked with an elaborate system of religiously sanctioned self-restraints on behavior. When land alienation began to occur in undue measure, for example, chieftaincy was affected and the stable

[7] See R. P. Ashe, *Chronicles of Uganda* (New York: Randolph & Co., 1895); and A. R. Tucker, *Eighteen Years in Uganda and East Africa* (London: Edward Arnold, 1908), *passim.*

confines of the social system were undermined. When Christianity was introduced, it helped to weaken the traditions of chieftaincy and removed the control that the dead ancestors exercised over the living. The result was excesses by chiefs, who turned to British authorities for their support. When education was introduced, chiefs had to be ordered to send their children to school. While they could not disobey the orders of district officers, they often sent the children of their slave lineages rather than the children of royal blood. The succeeding generations of chiefs were thus by no means the best educated.

The support required for the authority of the chiefs violated customary restraints on behavior. The excesses of the chiefs soon came to be regarded as perversions of traditional society, from which younger and more educated elements began to disaffiliate. Christianity helped ease the process of disaffiliation and there developed, along with an increase in urbanization and the growth of villages, the phenomenon of the urban village Christian and the rural village pagan. Most important, a series of wars between the British and the Ashanti was a token of the inability of Ashanti to absorb those innovating effects of a system of colonial rule which was basically common to both Buganda and Ashanti. In the end the *Asantehene*, or king of Ashanti, had to be exiled. Indeed, from 1901 to 1935, the Ashanti Confederacy did not exist as such.[8]

Within the context of the term "traditional," both Ashanti and Buganda were traditional systems. Both required validations of current behavior by appeal to immemoriality. Both had myths of origin involving a powerful figure associated with the formation of the society, and with whom the king had claims to ancestry. In the case of the Ashanti, the powers of origin descended to the Golden Stool rather than to a person. In Buganda, descent was reckoned through the line of kings, or Kabakas. That the preservation of power and continuity should reside in an object in the case of Ashanti—as distinct from a person, as in Buganda—is not without significance. For, in Ashanti, those in power serve the present by serving the past. It is a symbol of ancestral concern which is the visible repository of authority. In Buganda the king was, as both Roscoe and Fallers have called him, despotic.[9] While there was—and still is—pomp and ceremony around the king, he was not regarded as a descendant of living ancestors. He was rather the punishing, aggressive, and virile representative of a dynamic people expanding their military hegemony in the Lake Victoria region. Hence the essentially religious and theocratic nature of the Ashanti state, and the more secular and military character of Buganda.

[8]J. N. Matson, *Warrington's Notes on Ashanti Custom*, 2nd ed. (Cape Coast: Prospect Printing Press, 1941).

[9]See, in particular, John Roscoe, *The Baganda* (London: 1911), p. 232.

There were other important differences between these societies. In Ashanti, the system of political organization had its prototype in the extended family, which included up to a hundred members, possessing strong solidary affiliations. Families lived together in villages and it was unusual for an Ashanti to live alone or with only his immediate family.

In addition, the Ashanti had an elaborate lineage system whereby recruitment to office and the allocation of rights and duties were organized. The core political unit was the village. The largest unit was the division, over which there was a paramount chief. Kumasi, which established a compact with the other Ashanti divisions in a historical episode veiled in mystery and magic, became the center of a Confederacy. An elaborate balance of checks and controls on authority extended from the village level to the division, including restrictions on the exercise of power by the Asantehene, or king of the Ashanti Confederacy.

The system in Buganda was much simpler in one respect, and much more complex in others. Unlike the chief in Ashanti, who was a religious figure, a lineage figure and, moreover, elected to office, the chief in Buganda was appointed by the king, or Kabaka, and was responsible to him. The chief was subject to summary dismissal at the pleasure of the Kabaka. Much closer to the Ashanti pattern was an earlier, pre-Kabaka, clan system which continued to play a part in subsequent periods. The king was both *Sabataka* (head of all the clans) and Kabaka.

Every Muganda is a member of a clan. Clans are hereditary. The elders of clans had responsibilities over the family, the social conduct of individuals, and inheritance. Chiefs, who were appointed, reflected the powers of the Kabaka. Clan elders, who were elected from eligible lineages, reflected religious and immemorial powers. These two principles of authority were in constant conflict. Increasingly, performance in serving the Kabaka and thereby the state became the basis of chieftaincy. Performance and service became readily identifiable since Buganda, as a military system, was in process of expanding at the expense of her neighbors.

The acceptance of hierarchical authority thus was associated with successful national aggrandizement and the pure authority of the Kabaka was not mitigated by any other countervailing principle. Tension within the system was produced by conflicts between clanship and chieftaincy. But the Kabaka represented the central authority in both systems—i.e., Sabataka or head of all the clans, and Kabaka or head of all the chiefs.

Two effects were immediately observable from the twin systems of organization in Buganda united by a system of autocratic and hierarchical kingship. Clans were scattered throughout the country. In any area an individual on the move could find a clansman and receive certain benefits from him. This not only facilitated mobility but also ensured considerable uniformity of custom and behavior throughout the system.

The chiefs, who were territorial governors for the king, were also military leaders. Their followers were loyal to the chief because the chief reflected the Kabaka's authority. This military-administrative system of organization included a massive network of military roads converging, radially, upon the center or capital. Yet the capital itself was often moved, so that there was no "center" and "hinterland."

The result was a "suburban" pattern of life in which clanship counterpoised chieftaincy in daily life, but each man's eyes centered upon the king. In time of war, which was often, the military administrative system required almost no modification. The necessary mobilizations took place under the chiefs. Food continued to be produced, and family life managed to go on quite well. In contrast, Ashanti had to shift to a quite different military formation in time of war, and then returned to their peacetime pyramidal organization when war was over.[10]

What were some of the controversial issues which the Kiganda system was unable to absorb? The most characteristic one was an inability to adjust to any permanent limitation on the power of the Kabaka. Whether a Muganda were chief or peasant, educated or not, he maintained the same unabashed veneration for the office of the Kabaka. Or, to put the matter another way, the principle of national aggrandizement was never lost, and the Kabaka was its symbol. Each of the major conflicts which aroused the Baganda and posed serious problems for the Protectorate government centered around possible dangers to the autonomy of Buganda or diminutions of the authority of the Kabaka.

In contrast to Ashanti, then, the Baganda have instrumental values. Ends are relatively well defined and essentially patriotic.

Both Baganda and Ashanti developed their own forms of tribal parochialism. The former were adept in retaining considerable political autonomy, and the Uganda Agreement of 1900, which stipulated the relations between Baganda and British, became a legal bulwark of ethnic nationalism and political parochialism. In Ashanti, where no such constitutional relationship existed, internal conflict was widely manifested throughout the entire area, creating instabilities which eventually led to mass nationalism. In more contemporary terms, in Buganda nationalist

[10]Ashanti had a complex hierarchy of chiefs. At the pinnacle of the hierarchy was the *omanhene*, or divisional chief. Independent in his sphere of authority, he was nevertheless hedged about with restrictions. His was a religious role symbolizing lineage relationships to ancestors, and only members of a founder's or royal lineage were eligible to be elected to chieftaincy. The same held true for village chiefs and headmen. During war a division chief and others would take a position in the army and a more hierarchical system of authority would come to prevail. See E. Meyerowitz, *The Sacred State of the Akan* (London: Faber & Faber, Ltd., 1951), especially Chap. 10.

politicians have so far been able to make little headway and are regarded by the Buganda government as malcontents and ne'er-do-wells. One finds there an absorbing situation, in which the British authorities are anxious to see nationalist political parties develop on an all-Uganda pattern as the solution to building a modern state.[11] In Ghana, the party nationalists have become tantamount to the state itself, regarding chiefs dimly, to say the least. Not only have they taken active steps to break the chief's power, but the Asantehene, the paramount chief of Ashanti, has been their particular target. In the last encounter between the Asantehene and the party government, it was the former who had to admit defeat. The quasi-religious character of traditional society has been replaced by the quasi-religious character of modern nationalism in Ghana. We can analyze these developments more closely.

CONTRASTING EFFORTS AT POLITICAL MODERNIZATION

Uganda and Ghana are in the process of modernization. Practically, this has meant establishing parliamentary institutions by means of which the whole country is governed. Ghana achieved the level of political development in 1950 which Uganda now hopes to achieve. In other respects as well, Ghana has developed more rapidly. National income per head in Ghana is double that of Uganda. More effective internal transport and trade facilities are found in Ghana and Africans participate actively in all aspects of technical and commercial life. In Uganda, Asians and Europeans still monopolize the more important sectors of the economy and are the predominant racial groups in the civil service. In contrast, Africanization of the civil service in Ghana is virtually complete, with only a few senior positions and technical services still performed by Europeans, and these mostly on contract.

Ghana is economically well off for an African country.[12] Since 1951, 80 percent of its internal savings has been based upon a single cash crop, cocoa. Other sources of income are gold, bauxite, manganese, industrial diamonds, and timber. It has advanced economically under a series of development plans, the first of which was primarily concerned with expanding basic transportation facilities. Railways were extended, a deep-water port built at Takoradi. The principle of a reserve fund for eco-

[11]See *Report of the Constitutional Committee, 1959* (Wild Report; Entebbe: Government Printer, 1959), pp. 33–35.

[12]A population of approximately 5 million in an area of over 90,000 square miles is divided into several main tribal groups. The northern peoples are chiefly grouped in Muslim kingdoms. The central group is the seat of the once-powerful Ashanti Confederacy. The southern groups—Fante, Ga, Ewe, and others—have had the longest contact with western commerce and education. There are old families inhabiting the former "factories" of early traders who intermarried with the local people and established their own family dynasties.

nomic contingencies was established early. The first ten-year development plan was launched at the end of World War I and, except during the period of the world depression, Ghana has been development-conscious. Both under the latter stages of colonialism and under her present nationalist government, she has been a social-welfare state.

What was the effect of innovation? Traditional chieftaincy and social organization increasingly became a focus for internal resentments. Bitter conflict over land developed. The pattern of self-restraints on behavior was upset. Land alienation in the form of concessions was common. Considerable friction developed between chiefs, who took their seats not only in traditional councils but on the legislative council and other conciliar bodies set up by the government, and the urban, educated elites which emerged with the spread of modern commerce. Each emerging group thought itself destined to inherit political power. The result was cultural withdrawal which prepared the ground for mass nationalism in Ghana after the Second World War. The chiefs, failing to consider the sources of mass nationalism, regarded it as simply an event in a long and stable cultural tradition which would only help to restore chieftaincy to its proper role.

The western-educated elites regarded the nationalists as usurpers of their roles. The British viewed them as dangerous malcontents, subversive of public peace and good order. Such rejection gave fervor to the nationalists of the Convention People's Party (CPP), who by adherence to the party gave a new coherence to Ghana as a national society. They brought about a closer integration of the different peoples making up the territory, and they made economic and political institutions African rather than foreign by using them in the interests of self-government. Politics had already become polarized between traditional and secular authorities during the colonial period. Now the fundamental issues of traditionalism and modernity became wrapped up in more complex conflicts over democracy itself.

The major achievement of the CPP in Ghana was the organization and maintenance of an effective mass political organization. This resulted in centers of communication in the towns and villages, requiring members who could co-ordinate the activities of others. By building the CPP into a social group, a fraternity of the disadvantaged was encouraged to mold society in its favor by means of national political institutions and political freedom. A widely diverse membership was provided with a feeling of confidence in the future. Self-government was the goal. New opportunities were to be achieved thereby. A vision of a new society which was as vague as it was powerful was the moral claim of the CPP.

Yet in creating a mass political organization devoted to achieving independence, the CPP incorporated elements which had no long-run natural inclinations toward one another. More particularly, traditional groupings formed centers of opposition to Dr. Nkrumah both inside and outside the party. The main source of opposition was Ashanti. The Asantehene and his council helped plan the organization of an opposition, the National Liberation Movement (NLM), which itself renewed an old alliance between intellectuals and traditional authorities.[13]

With demands for a federal system of government, the situation rapidly grew dangerous. One Cabinet minister, a leading CPP figure from Ashanti, was ambushed outside his house and his sister killed. Government leaders did not dare to go to Ashanti for almost two years. Moreover, the appearance of successful traditionalism in Ashanti encouraged other opposition groups to form. In Accra, in Nkrumah's own constituency, there was formed an Accra people's movement which was essentially parochial and anti-Nkrumah. Everywhere traditionalism and the natural organization of the ethnic and tribal group seemed the only possible alternative to party rule by the Convention People's Party.

The conflicts over traditionalism and the future of democracy were sharpest during the period just prior to independence. In the general election of 1956, the candidates of seven parties and 45 independents ran for office. In spite of the fact that the NLM was able to put only 39 candidates in the field, and the CPP was well enough organized to contest all 104 seats, the latter received only 398,141 votes and the combined opposition received 299,116. This opposition vote was extremely high, considering the fact that a vote for the CPP was considered a vote for independence. Approximately 50 percent of the electorate voted. In the post-independence period, the opposition was smashed. A series of acts rushed through Parliament were designed to break the power of traditional authorities. So successful were these efforts that, when elections to the Kumasi Municipal Council were held in February 1958, the CPP won 17 out of 24 seats—a remarkable achievement.

In attacking traditionalism, movements of the CPP type take on the characteristic of inviolability. They have a tendency to brand splinter groups and the opposition as playing into the hands of the "feudal" elements in society. The idea of party fealty is stressed more than any other.

The pattern which can be clearly seen in this conflict between traditionalism and modernism is thus the continuous affiliation to and disaffiliation from powerful social groupings which make total claims on the allegiance and support of their members. The clear loser in such a situation is the opposition. In crucial respects, therefore, countries like Ghana find that in attacking tradition and supporting modernity they become one-party systems. It is not that there is no opposition, but that or-

[13]In 1957 the NLM joined with other tribal parties like the *Ga Shiftimo Kpee* to become the United Party. The former leader of the party, Dr. K. A. Busia, is currently in Holland, Ghana's first real political exile.

ganized party opposition finds itself in difficult circumstances. Traditionalism, which serves the opposition as an effective rallying ground for popular support, is branded as subversive.[14] Indeed, at the Accra African Peoples' Conference in December, 1958, tribalism and religious separatism were defined as evil practices by Africa's leading nationalists. It was resolved that "those African traditional institutions whether political, social, or economic which have clearly shown their reactionary character and their sordid support for colonialism be condemned."[15]

What, then, has political modernization meant in Ghana? Attacking tradition has resulted in the development of an "organizational weapon" type of party which, constantly on the attack, probes for weaknesses in the system. It seeks to jostle the public into functionally useful roles for the pursuit of modernization. To prevent the loss of power, and to modernize as rapidly as possible, are the basic goals of those who have inherited the mantle of British power. Modernization has come to require a host of attitudes of mind and social organizations antithetical to traditional ways of doing things. Political modernization therefore attacks head-on traditional ways of believing and acting.

In these respects, the Ghana government has been unable to make use of traditionalism to support innovation. The past has become a dead weight on the present government, which by the use of inducements, and by occasional kicks and blows as well, seeks to drive people toward a new way of life. Because of the government's loss of support in the traditional sectors of society, the burdens of modernization on Ghana have become more intense. Unlike Senegal, where the blending of traditionalism and modernity has eased the transition to new political and economic forms, in Ghana traditionalism has not provided a genuine source of pride and inspiration. Unlike the French African concept of *negritude*, the slogan "African personality" has remained largely devoid of content.[16] Ghana,

[14]At the same time, the parliamentary opposition in Ghana has been effective on occasions. There are times when the CPP backbench threatens to bolt party whips and vote with the opposition. Such a threat has been a useful means of modifying the position of the government on several issues, not the least of which was modification of the Emergency Powers Bill, while the constitutional changes of early 1957 were incorporated under pressure from the opposition. Bitterly contested decisions which often resulted in suspensions of parliamentary sessions have been those involving basic liberties. Three such measures were the Ghana Nationality and Citizenship Bill, the Emergency Powers Bill, and the Deportation Bill. For an excellent study of Ghana's parliament, see D. G. Austin, "The Ghana Parliament's First Year," *Parliamentary Affairs*, XI, No. 3 (Summer 1958), 350–60.

[15]All-African Peoples' Conference, Resolution on Tribalism, Religious Separatism, and Traditional Institutions, *Conference Resolutions*, I, No. 4, issued by the Conference Secretariat, Accra, 1958.

[16]It is interesting to note that while the term "African personality" is widely attributed to Nkrumah, it is in Nigeria that an effort is being made to give it content. Examples of such efforts are the journals *Black Orpheus* and *Odú*, which, as cultural and literary journals, seek to give a philosophic and cultural significance to the term.

in assuming the heavy burdens of modernization without the supports of traditionalism, has become a relatively autocratic system.

Uganda shows a completely different political pattern. Unlike Ghana, which is a maritime nation, Uganda is situated inland on the shores of Lake Victoria.[17] It is roughly the same size as Ghana, with an area of 80,000 square miles and a population of approximately 6 millions.[18]

By virtue of its superior institutions and successful collaboration with the British, Buganda was made a privileged area. The Uganda Agreement of 1900 formally recognized these privileges, and elsewhere in the country the Kiganda pattern of territorial organization was established—a three-tiered system of local government, each with a chief and a council (*Lukiko*) and ranging in scope from the parish to the county. The British retained an appointive chieftaincy system, but one which followed the practice of a regular civil service, with chiefs being promoted, transferred, and retired. Theirs was the task of maintaining peace and good order, collecting taxes, and otherwise taking care of the areas under their jurisdiction. Buganda, as a province, formed the model for the other ethnic groups to follow in the districts. In more recent times the parliament of Buganda, the Great Lukiko, has been the model for the district councils, which have become the object of considerable tribal parochialism in the districts outside of Buganda.

The three races, African, Asian, and European, live in uneasy proximity. Asians are involved in petty commerce, and increasingly in larger commercial enterprises in urban centers such as Kampala, while Europeans generally remain in charge of major commercial operations. Few Europeans were successful in farming in Uganda, where a situation comparable to that of the white settlers in Kenya never developed. Asians and Europeans have always tended to collaborate in representing the commercial interests of the country.[19] Asians were represented on the Legislative Council along with Europeans from the very onset, after World War I. No Africans were represented on the Legislative Council, nor was it regarded as desirable that they should be, until after the Second World War. It was widely held that Buganda's own Lukiko served as her political outlet, and the same situation was thought to prevail in the districts. It was regarded as essential to the interests of Africans that the principle of trusteeship, the mainstay of administration

[17]Blessed with an exceedingly good climate and well-distributed rainfall, most of Uganda is fertile agricultural country. To supplement her two main crops, cotton and coffee, she needs more diverse export commodities, and copper and other raw materials are being successfully exploited on an increasing scale.

[18]See *Colonial Report* (Entebbe: Government Printer, 1959). Buganda represents approximately 20 per cent of the population of Uganda.

[19]The Indian Association and the Uganda Chamber of Commerce were instruments of that cooperation.

during the interwar period, should be maintained through the Governor and his staff.[20]

Until the present day, nationalism in Uganda was largely expressed through the Buganda government "establishment." There is now stirring the kind of "modern" nationalism which is increasingly inclined to limit the powers of the Kabaka and make of Uganda a united, self-governing nation. But modernism as an ideology is confined to a very few. Indeed, it has been largely pre-empted by the Buganda government. Let us examine the process by which this occurred.

Although the Baganda did not suffer national defeats as did the Ashanti, religious wars in the latter part of the nineteenth century resulted in the deposition and restoration of the Kabaka by Europeans on two occasions. The Baganda have never gotten over this. Given the special position of the Kabaka in the structure of Kiganda society, cavalier treatment of them on the part of the Europeans deeply wounded and aggrieved the Baganda. Even during the period of closest collaboration with the British (roughly from 1900 to 1926), such grievances were nursed. A singular touchiness has thus characterized relations between the British and the Baganda. Unlike the more typical case in the districts, changes in political organization have, if they originated with the Protectorate government, been stoutly resisted. The Kabaka as a symbol of modern nationalism has been continuously strengthened and now has more power than at any time since British control.

When the Agreement of 1900 was signed, the Lukiko, or African parliament, dominated by the chiefs, was empowered to distribute land on a freehold basis to the most important people in Buganda. The three chief ministers received the largest estates (with the exception of the Kabaka himself), while others were given land according to their chieftaincy rank, or their general status.[21] Few pagans received any land.

Since chieftaincies had been divided up according to religion, both Protestants and Catholics of wealth came to have considerable stake in the modified system. By fixing the proportions of chieftaincy along religious lines, family wealth and position were distributed in the same manner. Both Protestants and Catholics had some wealthy families in possession of land, and in important positions in the community. The Muslims suffered most of all the religious groups, while paganism quickly disappeared.

Those in the clan system who had been traditionally entitled to certain burial estates or clan lands, and who lost those lands during the parcel-

[20] For a discussion of this period, see K. Ingham, *The Making of Modern Uganda*, (London: George Allen & Unwin, Ltd., 1958), *passim*.

[21] Uganda Agreement of 1900, para. 15.

ing-out of freehold, became the first political force in Buganda. The clan system thus formed the "natural" opposition to a government of chiefs. This resulted in considerable internal dissension. Gradually the *bataka*, or clan groups, came to represent the *bakopi*, or peasantry. Land holding had become almost synonymous with prestige and social position.[22] Indeed, it appeared for a time that the system would become based on dynastic land-holding families, and the principle of easy access to political office and performance would be eliminated. Yet other innovations helped to prevent this. For example, the expanded educational system, which was enthusiastically supported by the Baganda, did not limit facilities to the children of chiefs, but included peasant children as well. Education was regarded as a major basis for entry into the political hierarchy (which remained the only major social organization throughout Buganda).

The instrumental values of the Baganda, colliding with a threatening monopoly of political roles by families of the senior chiefs who had received land, or by important Protestant and Catholic leaders, prevailed over both elites without altering the autocratic principle of hierarchical kingship. This allowed progressive modification of the Lukiko and greater opportunities to the public as a whole. Unlike the consummatory system of Ashanti, where individuals had virtually to withdraw from the traditional system in order to seek new careers and opportunities in a different kind of society, the Kiganda system was modified in practice, while posing few contradictions in principle.

Although the Buganda government was often in conflict with the peasantry, such conflicts appeared in the guise of government and its loyal opposition. The British, through a Resident, built up the influence of the chiefs and the ministers of the Buganda government, whom they regarded as modern because of the ease and alacrity with which they learned to collect taxes, adapted themselves to methods of bookkeeping, and were able to control the public.

Thus the autocratic principle has prevailed in Buganda until the present. Innovations, it is widely believed, have come not from an alien source, but through the Buganda government itself. With the country's leader able to maintain social discipline (because to act irresponsibly is to act against the Kabaka), a sense of awe and formality in social relations has helped retain public support. To keep the public "on the

[22]Important in preventing such dissension from assuming proportions of "class conflict" was the fact that peasants could, and did, buy freehold land. Moreover, no landless peasantry was created. Everyone could get a leasehold property at a nominal and fixed rental. This deterred migration to towns, and no urban-rural cleavage developed. Buganda remains a rural "suburbia." See A. W. Southall and P. C. W. Gutkind, *Townsmen in the Making*, East African Studies No. 9 (Kampala: East African Institute of Social Research, 1956), *passim.*

alert" and politically conscious, skirmishes against the intervention of the Residency are constantly fought.

As a result, the Baganda have regarded themselves as exceedingly blessed in a state of political autonomy. The Buganda government has been the most successful nationalist "party" in the country. Success in the economic field as well, particularly with the cotton and coffee crops, brought the Baganda considerable wealth as compared with the rest of Uganda. To add to their complacency, they had, by such visible indicators as tin roofs on their houses, number of bicycles, number of laborers from elsewhere working for them, and number of educated people, the highest standard of living in the Protectorate. They were able to absorb new forms of income, and to accept the standards of education, knowledge, skill, and training as requirements for a job such as chieftaincy, while retaining the essential character of their political system.

The freehold system, the chieftaincy system, the method of recruitment, the standards of selection, the acceptance of cash crops, all helped to make Buganda extremely modern in many ways. *But the prerequisite to accepting any modern feature on the political level was that some real or mythical traditional counterpart had to be found for it.* Hence, if the Lukiko was now a regular council with minutes, committees, and a budget, it was nevertheless regarded as an age-old institution. If chiefs were now almost invariably large landowners or related to the original holders of freehold, in custom those responsible for the control over "heads," i.e., over families and soldiers, were found to be the equivalent.

In 1955 several important measures were passed. In the districts, the District Councils Ordinance gave the councils both executive and legislative powers, enabling them to make bylaws on a wide range of subjects.[23] In Buganda, after the deportation of the Kabaka for refusing to co-operate with the Protectorate government (part of his effort to retain autonomy for Buganda), a new Agreement was signed which enhanced the powers of the Lukiko, made the Kabaka in effect a constitutional monarch, and gave the Baganda three new ministries—Health, Education, and Natural Resources—in addition to the three they already had (Prime Minister, Chief Justice, and Treasurer).[24] These reforms in effect gave to Buganda and to the district governments substantive warrants of authority and responsibility to attend to most of the economic and social schemes which are regarded as necessary to modernization. In Buganda the autocratic nature of the system has now come under attack—but the attack is still exceedingly mild. Elsewhere, in the districts, the effort to achieve local autonomy is regarded as the essence of political modernity.

What the system in Buganda cannot resolve are challenges to the prin-

[23]See *District Councils Ordinance, 1955* (Entebbe: Government Printer, 1955).
[24]See *Buganda Agreement of 1955* (Entebbe: Government Printer, 1955).

ciple of autocratic or hierarchical kingship. Resisting the first direct elections to be held in Buganda in 1958, the Baganda saw themselves threatened by devolution of authority to an African national government. Opposed to the nationalism of political parties, they regard representative government on an all-Uganda basis as tantamount to the destruction of their own society. In a pamphlet justifying the position of Buganda, the *Katikiro*, or Prime Minister, recently pointed out that the "peaceful growth of Western democracy in Buganda has been possible because the Baganda's customs and traditions are adaptable to new ideas which do not seek to uproot their fundamental political conceptions. . . ." Yet the pamphlet also warns that "The Baganda cannot exist as a people unless the Kabaka is the Head of the political structure in his Kingdom. Therefore, any constitution which envisages placing any other ruler or any foreign monarch in the position of the Kabaka of Buganda has no other intention but to cause the Baganda to cease to be a nation." More important, he concludes: "From time immemorial the Baganda have known no other ruler above their Kabaka in his Kingdom, and still they do not recognize any other person whose authority does not derive from the Kabaka and is exercised on his behalf."[25]

As a result of this position, it is the Protectorate government and British officials who are trying to build a modern national state in Uganda. How well they have succeeded is indicated by the fact that in the first direct elections in 1958, Buganda refused to participate, as did several other districts.[26]

Still more recently, a constitutional committee has recommended the establishment of responsible government at the center, with a legislature possessing 72 elected seats.[27] The Buganda government voiced its bitter opposition, but non-Baganda see in it the possibility of a political society not dominated by Buganda. With the Baganda anxious to secede from Uganda entirely if that is necessary to maintain the position of the Kabaka and the Buganda kingdom, there is bitter conflict between the Buganda government, on the one hand, and party politicians allied to British authorities, on the other.

There is now emerging among many Baganda an awareness that the absorptive capacity of the traditional system and its instrumental values has been reached. This is taken by the traditionalists to indicate a need for secession if the system is to be preserved. Younger groups are anxious to build a larger national society, a united Uganda. These are regarded

[25]M. Kintu, *Buganda's Position* (Information Department, Kabaka's Government; Kampala: Uganda Printing and Publishing Co., 1960), pp. 1–2.

[26]See C. P. S. Allen, *A Report on the First Direct Elections to the Legislative Council of the Uganda Protectorate* (Entebbe; Government Printer, 1959), Appendix J.

[27]See the Wild Report, *op.cit.*, which anxiously notes the need for political parties in order to create effective central government.

as traitors by the traditionalists. However, the traditionalists are not anti-modern. Quite the contrary, as we have seen, they have built up a modern if miniature state in Buganda and now that very modernity is used as a justification for autonomy.

The result is that political parties remain largely ineffective both in Buganda and in Uganda as a whole. Recently, in an effort to gain popular support, several parties induced anti-Asian riots aimed at reducing the economic and commercial power of Indians. But in spite of such efforts, political parties remain weak and the Buganda government continues to be the main source of parochial nationalism. Political party leaders hope that when responsible government develops at the center and the financial resources of the country are allocated on the basis of popular government, the strength of the Buganda government will be diminished. The struggle to obtain parliamentary institutions is less concerned with Britain or the colonial administration than was the case in Ghana. Rather, it is directed against the Buganda government because of its unwillingness to subordinate hierarchical authority to the principle of representative government. Thus the ethnic nationalism of Buganda remains the most important political obstacle to self-government and has crippled political party growth, rendering the political heart of the country virtually lifeless.[28]

As has been pointed out above, however, non-Baganda groups are developing a new political party that has been launched by recently elected African representatives of the Legislative Council. They seek to make the Legislative Council the crucial political organ in Uganda, and are reluctant to be tied to the tail of Kiganda parochialism. Thus the possibility presents itself that the central conciliar institutions of Uganda will now tend to favor the rest of the country. Grants in aid, development plans, and educational schemes can now become the target of competitive nationalism, fought out in the context of competing parochialisms. In that event, neither the traditional institutions nor their insularity will long be maintained.

Moreover, direct elections to the Buganda Lukiko will bring party politics strongly into the Buganda sphere.[29] It is possible that competitive nationalism can be transformed into federal government at the center.

[28]It must be pointed out, however, that in Uganda, unlike colonial Ghana, everyone knows that self-government is forthcoming. Lack of such certainty helped to develop an effective nationalist movement in Ghana, where to remain outside the party was tantamount to being pro-colonialist. In Uganda, all groups know that the country will eventually get self-government, and there is far more effort on the part of each of them to retain and expand their influence and power. Foreknowledge of self-government, in that sense, has helped to diminish the urgency of nationalism.

[29]Already in the new Lukiko, elected in 1959 (without direct election methods), five political parties are represented, a predominantly Catholic party supplying 80 per cent of all party representatives. The Buganda government has accepted the principle of direct elections but has steadfastly refused to implement it.

Federal government is a compromise system brought about by conflict among the constituent states, and conflict is necessary for its vitality. What is possible in the Uganda situation is political modernization in a federal system, in which the several traditional states will be allowed to modernize their institutions on their own terms. In the demand for federalism all groups see some hope for their survival. Federalism itself has come to mean political modernism.

CONCLUSION

In both Ghana and Uganda tribal or ethnic parochialism has persisted with widely varying results. Kiganda parochialism has itself been a form of modernism. Civil-service chieftaincy and bureaucratic norms have bolstered the kingdom. Indeed, the Buganda government is widely regarded as the most progressive force in the country. Hence, for the Baganda, to be modern is to be parochial.

In Ashanti, modernism clashed directly with traditionalism. The religious aspect of the traditional political and social structure was an important part of a network of suitable restraints on behavior. When these were disrupted by innovations in commercial enterprise and colonialism, traditional authority was quickly undermined. Yet because traditional authority was so much a part of daily life and custom, those who broke with tradition found themselves in drastic need of new and powerful social affiliations, for to break with tradition was to break with family, lineage, and ancestral fidelity.

In contrast to Ashanti, Buganda remains the most powerful solidary association possible. Social satisfactions are still achieved within Buganda and its government for all those who belong to the kingdom. In Ashanti the formation of a new political party was itself a process of forming new and powerful symbolic attachments. The Ashanti members of the CPP became fiercely devoted to the organization. The messianic role of the leader was based on the development of a new morality to supplant the old. Hence the deep cleavages in society which remained after self-government had been obtained posed the problem of nation-building after independence rather than before it.

We can summarize some of the more salient points of contrast between the two systems as follows:

1. *Absorption of innovation.* Ashanti, with its consummatory-pyramidal system, was unable to control the effects of innovation, and tended to shrink from contact with the modern world. Early missionaries were imprisoned. The Ashanti wars were efforts to expel the British, as a foreign body, from the body politic. The effects of contact loosened the hold of traditionalism, although it remained a powerful force.

Buganda was able to control innovation. The European presence was absorbed and rendered useful. By careful planning and the use of modernizing agencies, the Buganda government increased its autonomy and control as time went on, rather than suffering partial decay.

2. *Internal divisions and discontinuities.* What had hitherto been reinforcing social institutions of the consummatory system of Ashanti rapidly broke down into competing power groups and sources of internal antagonism and weakness. Thus the development of conflicts between youth and age, royals and non-royals, slaves and non-slaves, were all examples of conflict over the continuing strength of particularistic criteria which could be reconciled only so long as older religious and institutional checks were sustained. Such social controls were highly internalized, with authority variously distributed. As soon as the continuity of past and present was disrupted, the various groupings rapidly came to compete.

In Buganda the internal conflict continued, as in the period prior to contact, between clanship and chieftaincy—all, however, under the umbrella of the king as both Sabataka, head of all the clans, and Kabaka, or king. The advantages of appointive chieftaincy had long been apparent in the military undertakings of the kingdom and a secular tendency inherent in the system was simply reinforced by contact with the British. The system was able to modify itself to restrain the old conflicts sufficiently so that the principle of hierarchic kingship did not require substantial alteration. Allegiance did not become confused.

3. *Competition for affiliations.* Internal conflict in Ashanti produced widespread attitudes of guilt. Cleavages divided the extended and nuclear families. Social breaks which meant modifying one's religious practices and sundering ties with the past (and one's ancestors) led to migration of individuals to urban areas which supported very different patterns of social life. These created more fundamental differences in outlook between urban and rural groups who, within one generation, had grown apart but were still not socially distant. The Ashanti were able to retain affiliations among those who represented orthodoxy. However, breaking such affiliations could not be resolved by the simple acceptance of heterodoxy. Rather a new orthodoxy had to be posed against the old. Thus the new affiliations of the political party assumed the proportions of a militant church movement.

In Buganda, there was relatively easy adaptation of internal cleavage to serve the larger purposes of the state. As a result, no Baganda repudiated their chiefs or the Kabaka. The Buganda government was itself a source of modernism, and no incompatibility between modernism and traditionalism resulted in the enforced disaffiliation of discontented groups. No discontented urban groups emerged, anxiety-ridden and seeking drastic change.

4. *Legitimacy conflicts.* Just as innovation could not be controlled in Ashanti, so the secular authority of the colonial government was posed against the traditional authority of the chiefs. Immemorial prescriptive rights clashed with concepts of efficiency and performance as a basis of authority. In Buganda, the autocratic principle prevailed and two oligarchies, British and Baganda, worked alongside one another. They were in constant competition, but they did not challenge each other's legitimacy. Both were oriented to efficiency and performance.

In Ashanti almost any outside activity, by being resisted, posed an ultimate legitimacy problem. So closely interrelated were the elements of social life and belief that they conformed nicely to Durkheim's concept of a fragile and mechanical society. Ultimately all threats were threats against legitimacy. Hence not only was colonialism viewed as a threat to traditional legitimacy, but nationalism was even more so. The conflict between lineage and ancestral sanction (immemoriality) for current acts and secular forces was introduced by colonialism, and helped to produce the nationalism which then had to break the power of traditionalism and its residual hold upon the public. Thus modern nationalism in Ghana is essentially an effort to create a wider legitimacy which introduces some of the same instrumental characteristics which Buganda possessed traditionally. *The result is a growth of an autocratic principle of leadership in Ghana*—the organizational weapon serving as its own justification.

In contrast, in Buganda, the conflict over legitimacy never emerged in sharp form in the colonial-Buganda government relationship. Indeed, even when the Kabaka was exiled, early in the relationship, or more recently when the present Kabaka was deported, the principle of the Kabakaship was not questioned by the Protectorate government authorities.

However, now that the problem of building wider affiliations has been tackled effectively by the Protectorate government, political parties are challenging the principle of hierarchical authority. *They are seeking to supplant hierarchical authority with representative authority* as a means of building a modern nation. They do not, however, need to create attitudes of universalism and performance as the basis of political recruitment since these are already widespread and traditional.

Where the consummatory-pyramidal system prevailed, there developed fierce competition between traditional and secular leaders to monopolize allegiance. This was expressed by the latter in efforts to build overarching and autocratic institutions which by autocratic means fostered egalitarianism in political recruitment and the exercise of authority. The problem was to prevent social atomism while mobilizing those resources of the society which could capitalize on change itself. This put exceedingly heavy burdens on political nationalists, whose need for organizational control and support became all important.

In the instrumental-hierarchical system prevailing in Buganda, change has aided parochialism and modernism of a local sort, making political modernism of the national state more difficult to achieve. Where consummatory values prevail in the traditional sector, the political leaders lose the advantages of traditionalism. Their need is to find new ways and means of employing it to ease the burdens of political development. Where instrumental values prevail, the local and national forms of modernism need to be brought into some kind of useful identity, so that instrumental traditionalism can reinforce political modernization at the national level.

Ghana shows the effects of a single-party unitary government and its difficulties in modernization. Can a modernizing nation be created through a federal system of government in which the parts will reinforce the whole? In this respect, Uganda represents a potential alternative to the Ghana pattern. Out of regard for instrumental traditionalism, Uganda may find a political compromise proximate to the needs of the public, achieving modernity with both prudence and freedom.

Modernism and traditionalism have become key political issues. Buganda has retained both her tribalism and her separatism, penalizing the political advance of the country as a whole. Ashanti, the last stronghold of tribalism in Ghana, has been defeated by modernism in the form of nationalism. Buganda and Ashanti, Uganda and Ghana, both facing similar problems in different ways, shed some light on the politics of modernization in contemporary Africa.

The Politics of Solidarity in Ghana

Ghana has proceeded slowly and haltingly toward the single-party state. A substantial body of opinion in Ghana, by no means restricted to intellectuals, remains basically unsympathetic to the mobilization objectives of the regime. Ghana's political development illustrates the creation of a one-party mobilization system which is, in many ways, a compromise between the views of militants and moderates. A far cry from totalitarianism, it is nevertheless a genuinely new form of society which is being created under the auspices of the party. To study the Convention People's Party (CPP) is to study the design for the country. Moreover, as Ghana was the first country in colonial Tropical Africa to obtain independence, and the CPP was among the first parties to effect mass politics in Africa, we now have a history that enables some perspective on the role of political parties in new polities.

Material for this paper was obtained on a number of field trips to Ghana under various auspices. Previously unpublished data on the political opposition and the 1956 general election were gathered on a field trip undertaken in 1957 under the auspices of the West African Comparative Analysis Project under a grant from the Carnegie Corporation. More recent material was obtained during a visit in 1962 through the assistance of the University of California and the Institute of International Studies. In addition, funds made available by the Institute of Industrial Relations provided time for the writing of this article. I am grateful to each of these scholarly bodies for their assistance and hasten to add that they share no responsibility for the remarks made herein. I would like to acknowledge the assistance of Dr. David Brokensha of the Institute of International Studies, who read the manuscript and gave me many helpful comments.

This discussion is confined largely to the development of party politics in Ghana. A more detailed analysis of the constitutional structure and the wider political picture is to be found in the new edition of my book, *Ghana in Transition* (New York: Atheneum Press, 1963).

On the twelfth anniversary of the Convention People's Party in Ghana, Kwame Nkrumah made the following statement:

> This anniversary meets the Party and the nation with me as General Secretary of the Party and President of the Republic.
>
> This fact constitutes a remarkable historical landmark for our people, for it shows that, as I have often said, the party and the nation are one and the same, namely: the Convention People's Party is Ghana and Ghana is the Convention People's Party.
>
> Comrades, it is needless for me to ask you, therefore, to recognize this outstanding fact: that a very grave responsibility lies on the shoulders of us all, not only as Ghanaians, but also as members of the Convention People's Party which, no matter what may be said by our detractors, remains right in front of the struggle for the total liberation of Africa and the union of the independent African states.[1]

In addition to stating the key role of the party in the state, Nkrumah emphasized that the dangers of neocolonialism require vigilance, sacrifice, determination, and courage on the part of Ghanaians. He pointed to Ghana as an example of African self-government, neutralism, and nonalignment, and attacked Balkanization. Finally, Nkrumah said, "the Convention People's Party must mobilize our total manpower for the industrial, economic, technological and scientific reconstruction of Ghana, so that we can produce the necessary conditions which shall mean an abundance of every good thing for our people and the greatest welfare of the masses."[2]

This statement illustrates important characteristics which the CPP holds in common with several governing African parties today. One characteristic is, of course, reliance on the single-party pattern.[3] A second is emphasis on an internal organization that is capable of withstanding neoimperialism. African leaders maintain that colonialism does not end when independence is achieved, but merely takes new and subtle forms. A policy of neutralism (as in the early days of the American Republic) represents as much a moral rejection of the "older" world as it does a practical device for maintaining freedom of action. Other themes include sacrifice and self-improvement, hard work, and a commitment to society rather than to self, which are expressed in the requirements of party loyalty, collective responsibility, and mass solidarity. The party, vigilant against neoimperialism and dedicated to the safeguarding of neutralism and autonomy in international affairs, directs the energies of the public toward economic development.

[1]*The CPP Twelfth Anniversary: A Message by Osagyefo* (Accra: Government Printer, 1961).

[2]*Ibid.*

[3]Ghana is now a one-party state, and the CPP is the only constitutional party.

Ghana did not always follow this pattern. By what steps did she move in this direction, and why? To some extent Ghana shows the effects of a movement with a charismatic leader which transformed itself into a monopolistic party whose symbolic ritualization of leadership offset declining charisma and established legitimacy by subsuming the state under the party. But why was charisma possible in the first place? What has led to the present situation where opposition groups, voluntary associations, or ethnic groups can barely function in the political sphere without being branded as subversive? Can pluralism in the society be manifested within the party? Is there such a thing as one-party democracy?

FROM FACTION TO PARTY

The history of political parties in Ghana began with the early emergence of factions and "clubs." Indeed, the early stages recapitulated the development of political parties in the West. A morphology of political party development in Ghana might look something like this:

A. Ethnic factions and pressure groups, 1870–1940
  1. Ethnic associations, such as the Fanti Confederacy
  2. Protective associations, such as the Aborigines' Rights Protection Society (ARPS)
  3. Improvement associations and old boys' clubs, such as the Young Men's Free and Mutual Improvement Society
  4. Literary and discussion groups, such as the Achimota Conferences

B. Factional coalitions for political objectives, 1920–1950
  1. Local coalitions, such as the Ratepayers' Association
  2. National coalitions, such as the West African National Congress

C. Representational political parties, 1945–1956
  1. Conservative nationalist parties, such as the United Gold Coast Convention (UGCC)
  2. Radical nationalist parties, such as the Convention People's Party (CPP)

D. The party of solidarity (the CPP), 1957–1960

E. Factions within the monolith
  1. Conservative wing, including constituency and branch organs
  2. Radical wing, including auxiliary organs
  3. Intellectuals
     a) Socialist militants
     b) Socialist opportunists

These general categories overlap, both in chronology and in organizational relationships. The various factions correspond to a prepolitical phase in Ghana's history in which groups could pressure local administrative authorities, district commissioners, and the provincial and central governments. In some instances local pressure was contagious and larger coalitions took shape around specific issues such as opposition to the Crown Lands Bill of 1894 and the Forest Lands Bill of 1911, when deputations were sent to the British Parliament. From the first such deputation there developed the Aborigines' Rights Protection Society. Still other coalitions came into being, particularly after 1925, when direct elections on a limited franchise were held in the major coastal municipalities for seats in the Legislative Council. Factions at times fought with one another, and at times cooperated, as did political coalitions. The more stable and all-embracing coalitions after 1945 became representational political parties, and groups like the UGCC based their organization and practices on Western and parliamentary models. Indeed, in that instance, the party came in advance of the necessary parliamentary reforms that would have made it more fully like its British counterparts. Much of the nationalist agitation by the UGCC was directed not so much at self-government as toward establishing in the Gold Coast a parliamentary framework with all its ramifications.

Left to itself, the UGCC or its successor organizations might have been successful, if the CPP had not captured the imagination of the nascent Ghana society. Even the CPP was first a party of representation. It developed a form of leadership, however, which required the party to become more or less monopolistic, disciplining itself, abolishing its enemies, and generalizing itself into society, with the result that the representative parties disappeared as the CPP emerged victorious. The victory was not merely against other parties. It meant the triumph of a different party type: instead of the party of representation, the party of solidarity, which in turn altered the fundamental political outlines of the state.

The present stage of party development is interesting because there is a renewal of factionalism, but now it takes place within the context of the party of solidarity and the single-party system. When factionalism is excessive in the party of solidarity, however, what happens to solidarity itself? One answer is that the party becomes riddled with opportunists and sycophants. Another is that the leaders most relied on are the most loyal rather than the best suited for the job, with a resulting growth of political cynicism. This is one of the reasons that the party puts so much stress on the new generations. These are the ones the party must "socialize" and indoctrinate. It is in part a generational revolution that the party now seeks.

The Sources of Factions

The Gold Coast was, as its former name implies, a country whose seacoast was the scene of extensive trade. People lived mainly in hamlets and villages. Their social life was gregarious, centering on family and clan, with extensive internal pluralism and political diversity.[4] Wealth, originally derived from the slave trade and later from cash crops such as cocoa, permitted greater social and physical mobility. Towns grew and prospered. People moved easily between town and countryside. Yet the various groups composing the population preserved an atmosphere of intimacy and communication. Even today everyone knows the tribe, the family background, and the education of prominent men.

A limited but superior educational system was established relatively early in Ghana. In addition to primary schools, the Gold Coast had, by 1925, Achimota, Mfantsipim, Adisadel, and St. Augustine colleges, all of them excellent secondary schools whose instruction showed a strong classical bias. These institutions produced an elite from whom came the first impetus to a nationalism focusing upon legislative and social reform.[5]

Two types of nationalists emerged: the chiefs, and the newly educated elites. The nationalism of the chiefs was linked to their councils, which were given formal powers. Its electoral significance was expressed in provincial councils, composed largely of chiefs. Chiefs were often arrayed against the more urbanized middle-class nationalists, lawyers, and journalists from coastal towns who organized the Aborigines' Rights Protection Society and the West African National Congress. Some members of these associations were descended from old families of Creole origin, or were products of the extensive intermarriage that occurred in Cape Coast and Accra between Africans and Dutch, Danes, Germans, or English. These nationalities, in addition to introducing Western occupations, harbored traditions of education and values which helped set them apart from the chiefs.[6] Not only did they conflict with chiefs over purely political matters; they also differed on economic issues.

The Gold Coast economy, based on the single cash crop of cocoa, was hard hit by depression. Despite this, the intellectuals, encased in their literary societies in Cape Coast, Accra, and Saltpond, and associated with the Aborigines' Rights Protection Society, gave surprisingly scant attention to economic matters. Although at an early date they had been interested in forestry and land policy, and were certainly anxious to expand the number of trading and clerical posts open to Africans both in govern-

[4]In the Gold Coast the Ashantis, the most powerful ethnic group, fought the British and resisted education and other British efforts to modernize them. The southern part of the country, having long enjoyed trading and political relations with the West, became the center for a nontribal and urban elite. These southern elites often contended with the chiefs as well as with the British.

[5]See D. Kingsley Williams, *Achimota: The Early Years* (Accra: Longmans, Green & Company, Ltd., 1962), especially Chap. 7 and Appendices 1, 2 and 4.

[6]J. W. de Graft-Johnson, *Towards Nationhood in West Africa* (London: Headley Brothers, 1928), Chap. ix.

ment and elsewhere, their main concern was political. Preoccupied with widening the franchise and with constitutional reforms, they collided with the chiefs, who also sought wider representation in the enlarged legislative council system and wider participation in the affairs of the country, and with the administration, which regarded educated "natives" doubtfully, to say the least. By the 1930's the middle-class nationalists had lost interest in nonpolitical issues, but the chiefs remained directly involved in economic matters, and, through these, in politics. After having suffered an initial decline in prestige and support because of their somewhat slippery dealings with the British authorities, they now sought to regain their prominence by putting forward economic and social grievances through their state councils and the regional councils. The great "coacoa holdup," a voluntary trade boycott which in 1937 halted the sale of cocoa to the great European marketing firms, was in part facilitated by the chiefs.[7] Moreover, as chiefs, they had to be concerned with the indebtedness of farmers, maladjustments in tenure and occupancy of land, the control of immigrants and other newcomers in rural towns, and the administration of local justice, cooperating with local administrative officers in their districts. Their nationalism was that of the successful negotiator who enhances the well-being of his community by the shrewdness of his dealings with others.

It would be wrong to regard the chiefs and the middle-class lawyers as always opposed to each other. Not only were they brought together in court cases against the government or private firms, but the middle-class nationalists tried to explain matters of land and custom to British authorities, and, by so doing, safeguarded stool land and ameliorated the conditions of administration. Indeed, to this day some of the most able discussion of customary law and traditions is to be found in books and articles written by lawyers like John Mensah Sarbah, Joseph Casely Hayford, and J. W. de Graft-Johnson.[8] But it was the chiefs who remained closer to economic realities, as lawyers became more concerned with constitutional reform.[9]

These brief comments provide some background to an understanding

[7]W. K. Hancock, *Survey of British Commonwealth Affairs* (London: Oxford University Press, 1942), Vol. II, Part II, 207–31.

[8]John Mensah Sarbah, *Fanti Customary Laws* (London: William Clowes & Sons, 1904); J. Casely Hayford, *Gold Coast Land Tenure and the Forest Lands Bill, 1911* (London: Phillips, 1912), *Gold Coast Native Institutions* (London: Sweet & Maxwell, 1903), *The Truth about the West African Land Question* (London: Phillips, 1913), and *United West Africa* (London: Phillips, 1919); de Graft-Johnson, *op. cit.*

[9]One significant factor in the growth of Ghana politics was the absence of permanent European settlement. As the coastal elites were successful in enlarging their political roles and their participation in government, the devolution of authority could therefore not include European settlers, but, rather, was fought out between two African groups, the middle class and the chiefs.

of party growth and development in Ghana. The two forms of nationalism in the Gold Coast reflected a very different set of social and traditional patterns. Urbanization, education, long contact with the West, the nature of tradition, the lack of religious conflict, and the absence of settlers were some of the characteristics of the Gold Coast. In an atmosphere of intimacy, alternative forms of life were rural or urban, tribal or modern. There were also choices regarding values and society resulting in differing concerns about what constituted political advance and elite status, and indeed what it meant to be African. Increasingly, the middle class, and chiefly the nationalists, fought with one another to achieve political prominence in more or less "national" political institutions.

The cleavages produced by these conflicts were deep, and in the twenties, the thirties, and the forties led to ever-widening rifts between different groups in the population. In the Gold Coast what was needed to bring the people together was an all-embracing political movement containing within itself the vision of a new society. This was the circumstance that produced the CPP.[10]

The Nature of Factions

In the emerging pattern of politics, a range of organizations—some made up of chiefs and their representatives from various ethnic groups, others composed of tribal associations working for some particular aim or for the amelioration of local conditions and calling themselves committees or associations—wrote petitions, applied pressure, organized opinion, and made representations to authorities. Thus in 1871 the Fanti Confederacy, a grouping of the major Fanti states, put forward constitutional proposals to establish the confederation as a state with a president-king and a representative assembly. This led to the formation of the Aborigines' Rights Protection Society which, after successfully opposing land bills at the end of the nineteenth century, turned its attention to political participation in municipalities. Chiefs were active members of the Society, one of the first clearly political organizations in Tropical Africa. By 1912 the society had 100 members, mainly chiefs, lawyers, businessmen, and journalists.

After World War I, in 1920, the National Congress of British West Africa was established under the impetus of one of the leading members of the Society, Joseph Casely Hayford, a lawyer. Its objectives included

[10]Since this paper was completed, a detailed political history has appeared. David Kimble, *A Political History of Ghana, 1850–1928* (Oxford: The Clarendon Press, 1963), an extremely useful and exhaustive study, is essential for an understanding of this early period.

association with the Pan-Africanist movement founded in 1919 under the leadership of W. E. B. Du Bois. The Congress was a West African body established in Accra, and at its inception included representatives from Sierra Leone, Gambia, and Nigeria, as well as the Gold Coast. These three associations—the Fanti Confederacy, the Aborigines' Rights Protection Society, and the National Congress of British West Africa—were organized expressions of nationalism. The chiefs and the middle-class elite sometimes joined together, while at other times they were at odds.[11] We may call them the *progressive chiefs* and the *constitutional progressives*, respectively. They represented the two durable groups in Gold Coast politics which were prepared to put pressure upon colonial authorities and administrators in order to achieve reform, wider political participation, and more political responsibility for Africans.[12]

The progressive chiefs were the main beneficiaries of the early activities of both the society and the congress. British authorities, hostile to the intellectuals, were prepared to work with the chiefs.[13] Provincial councils, composed of paramount chiefs, were established in the Eastern, Western, and Central provinces. These councils became electoral colleges for six of the nine African elected seats on the Legislative Council, as provided in the 1925 Constitution. The other three seats were to be filled by a municipal electorate in the three coastal townships that possessed town councils. These reforms not only enhanced the significance of the chiefs in the political life of the colony (the coastal part of the Gold Coast), but they also turned the attention of the intelligentsia to municipal matters. Interest in nationalist politics was found only in literary societies, study groups, and cultural organizations, and among journalists. Because of this, new semipolitical groups manifested a rising sense of political consciousness (more or less antagonistic toward chiefs), but within the bounds of a colonial system. Such a "nationalism" was

[11] *Ibid.*, pp. 330–404.

[12] Not without interest are some of the achievements of these associations. The confederacy, influenced by a parliamentary select committee report of 1865 which argued for eventual self-government for British West Africa, organized itself in order to prepare for the event. But instead of granting self-government, the British consolidated their authority in the Gold Coast. Many of the chiefs then joined the society, and together with the able lawyers agitated successfully against the Forest Lands Bill, which would have converted unoccupied land into crown land. The result was the Concessions Ordinance whereby land could not be alienated without an elaborate legal procedure. Finally, the demands of the congress for widening the African membership of the Legislative Council resulted in the 1925 Constitution, which gave representation to the chiefs, the congress, and the society. This constitution, however, because it was weighted heavily in favor of the chiefs, led to a conflict between them and the intelligentsia.

[13] J. B. Danquah, *Liberty: A Page from the Life of J. B.* (Accra: H. K. Akyeampong, 1960), p. 29.

essentially reformist and intellectual.[14] In contrast, the progressive chiefs sought to widen their powers in the new political institutions established for the colony area, and subsequently for the country as a whole. The Joint Provincial Council, created in 1936 out of sixty-five paramount chieftaincies grouped into five confederacies, was an example of successful cooperation among chieftaincies for political ends in the colony area.

One reason for the political strength of the progressive chiefs was that they were less vulnerable to the impact of the depression in the 1930's than were the constitutional progressives. The depression was felt especially in the urban areas where the intelligentsia lived. Not only did the latter depend upon salaries, but they had developed a style of living which did not allow an easy return to the more rustic life of the villages. The depression sharpened their grievances, but robbed them of their resources. The West African National Congress declined in strength, and the Aborigines' Rights Protection Society suffered from lack of funds. The progressive chiefs were in a more secure position, and, after the provincial councils had been established, they reached the height of their political influence. Their counsel and guidance were not only accepted by the British authorities, but were actively solicited. The chiefs were extremely influential in the Legislative Council; for example, the Native Administration Bill of 1927 was largely drafted by Nana Sir Ofori Atta I. The Native Administration Treasury Ordinance of 1934, sponsored by the chiefs, gave them the power to impose taxes. Moreover, their skillful participation in the activities of the Executive Council helped to make them the dominant group in political life.[15]

The constitutional progressives, who played a limited role in the Legislative Council, tried to displace the chiefs in the legislature, and to enlarge the opportunities for Africans in administrative cadres. They also became involved in African international affairs.[16] Their support came

[14]Virtually all this activity was confined to the coastal area. Ashanti, having actively opposed British intervention, was not represented in the Legislative Council until the Burns Constitution of 1946. Between 1901 and 1934 the old Ashanti Confederacy had been abolished. Much of the nationalist activity among the Ashantis was directed toward the reconstitution of the confederacy. Some divisions, such as Techiman Wam Atabubu, Jaman, Abease, and Berekum (i.e., Brong areas), which in the past had been troublesome, were by no means anxious to be included in the restored confederacy. Today Brong has been set up as a separate region. See Eva Meyerowitz, *At the Court of an African King* (London: Faber and Faber, 1962), *passim.*

[15]The recent struggle against chieftaincy conducted by the Convention People's Party in Ghana is difficult to understand without knowledge of the central political role of the chiefs under British rule.

[16]In 1934, on political missions protesting certain laws in the Gold Coast, the chiefs represented the unofficial members of the Legislative Council and the intelligentsia represented the Aborigines' Rights Protection Society. The ARPS representatives helped to organize the International African Friends of Abyssinia after the attack by Italy.

largely from the Christian towns along the coast, where small political study groups were established which eventually formed two associations. One of these, organized by Dr. J. B. Danquah, was the Gold Coast Youth Conference. The other, launched by staff members of Achimota College, rapidly attracted a wide variety of participants concerned about the future of the Gold Coast. A political association, the Friends of African Freedom Society, and two political parties, the "radical" Mambii Party and the "conservative" Ratepayers' Association, were also organized.[17] Important newspapers of the period were, first, the *Times of West Africa*, edited by J. B. Danquah, and, later, the *African Sentinel*, edited by I. T. A. Wallace-Johnson, a Sierra Leonian who founded the Youth League, and the *Africa Morning Post*, under the aggressive editorship of Nnamdi Azikiwe. Azikiwe, after returning from his studies in America, was so dramatically outspoken in his editorials that he was imprisoned for sedition and libel in 1937.

Perhaps the most significant development was the series of conferences held by the Youth Conference. The first met at Achimota in 1930 to discuss progress and make plans. The second was held at Mfantsipim in 1938, and the third in Kumasi in 1939. There were two further conferences at Akropong and Sekondi. By careful organization, and with a continuation committee in office between conferences, the Youth Conference made strong efforts to bring together old boys from the major secondary schools, particularly Achimota and Mfantsipim, the Aborigines' Rights Protection Society, the intelligentsia, the chiefs, the Ashantis, and important groups in various cultural centers along the coast. The Youth Conference also published a number of pamphlets, one of the most noteworthy being *First Steps towards a National Fund*, edited by Danquah.[18]

Emergence of Political Parties

The efforts of the Gold Coast Youth Conference brought into being a loose network of political organizations which, emerging in the municipalities, soon spread to towns and villages, embracing chiefs, youth, and intelligentsia up and down the coast. Even Kumasi, the capital of Ashanti, hitherto more or less excluded from the political and social life of the country, now became more politically prominent. Achimota and Kumasi discussion groups continued the tradition of the Youth Conference during World War II, and helped to make a new generation politically sensitive.

[17]These parties and a few others, the Oman or National Party, for example, were primarily concerned with municipal matters. The conflict between the chiefs and the intelligentsia, however, centered in the municipalities. The Ratepayers' Association supported the intelligentsia, who in fact made up the membership. The Oman Party supported the elites.

[18]For further discussion of this period see Apter, *op. cit.*

A markedly different political climate began to prevail, particularly among the youth. Efforts to bring political parties together made for greater effectiveness. The Ratepayers' Association and the Mambii Party combined under Dr. F. V. Nanka-Bruce to form the National Democratic Party, which stood for the slow but solid achievement of self-government. Ultrarespectable, serious, and dull as some of these groups were, they nevertheless made political parties part of the Gold Coast scene. Out of these experiences were to come the United Gold Coast Convention and the Convention People's Party.

The interwar period was thus marked by a proliferation of voluntary associations which were the most significant single source of political socialization. Inevitably, as grievances remained unsatisfied, various groups cast about for ways and means to further their objectives. They sought analogies to their condition in the political history of England, and to some extent in history of other countries as well. At the outbreak of the war, their loyalty to the Empire evoked the promise of radical reform in the colonial sphere, but, when peace had returned, a new postwar constitution proved a disappointment. Africans then turned to amateur constitution writing, and confronted colonial authorities with draft constitutions, petitions, and memoranda demanding political reforms. Their political expectations, evolving slowly in the interwar period, now emerged sharply as they concentrated on specific grievances, asking for political power, postwar benefits, action to curb the postwar inflationary spiral, cognizance of the political ambitions of ex-servicemen, and, finally, definition of the role of the intelligentsia. As politics gathered momentum, the chiefs were left behind. Over the years many chiefs had once again fallen into disrepute. Malpractice was common. They seemed to lag behind the times, despite efforts to modernize their role and to adopt new practices. With their position worsening, ethnic nationalism declined in the Gold Coast, as conditions permitting a more truly national consciousness evolved.

Two aspects of the interwar period were extremely important in Ghana. The first was the growth of voluntary associations with an increasingly political focus. The second was the development of political elites whose concern was constitutional advance and self-government. In the postwar period two other factors entered into the picture. One was the development of a professional corps of political organizers, who might be called "political entrepreneurs"; the other was the effort to build movements rather than parties.

These two latter factors are related in meaningful ways. A politician whose job it is to engage in public life on a full-time basis requires a governmental framework within which to operate. The system within which he works must, however, specify his role, or at least demarcate the limits within which he may legitimately function. In any stable political system these two conditions are in harmony. In the postwar Gold Coast they were not. Hence the professional politician had to create an acceptable role for himself by changing the structure of government. In order to do so he had to destroy the legitimacy of colonial rule and establish both a new government and a new basis of authority. This process is one important feature of the ideologies of nationalism and revolution. Its moral dimension depends on its ability to provide a new basis of authority from which derives a more harmonious relationship between political roles and governmental structure. Indeed, in many ways nationalist and revolutionary ideologies depend on their moral dimension rather than on programmatic or specific goals.[19] The colonial systems had, of course, been changing in response to the pressures of new elites as well as to the growing demands by chiefs for more formal powers. Professional politicians therefore found it necessary to widen their attack against colonialism so as to include both chiefs and elites, and thus they acquired a radical and populist orientation.

The Professional Politicians

In the postwar period of the first two political groups, the nationalist-progressive chiefs and the constitutional progressives, were confronted with the emergence of a third group, composed of radical and populist nationalists. All three contended for greater authority. The first two believed that the devolution of authority to them by means of increasingly responsible government would allow a smooth and orderly transition to independence. Years of experience on legislative and provincial councils, not to speak of their positions of responsibility in the political and social structure of the country, gave sobriety and continuity to their demands. They could visualize their political roles as already fitted to the evolutionary structure of government.

In contrast, the group of radicals and populists had to destroy the position of prestige and dignity which the chiefs and the conservative elites commanded. Although each of the contending factions had a relatively stable following, the populists appealed especially to three classes in Ghana society: the growing intermediary group of partially educated, dissatisfied younger elements recently arrived in the urban areas; the small but articulate and status-conscious group of journalists, ex-servicemen, and teachers; and the rapidly growing number of semi-industrial workers who were excluded from the competition for urban status but were aware of their significance in the postwar climate of economic development.

[19] See the discussion of ideology and legitimacy in my introduction to *Ideology and Discontent* (New York: The Free Press, 1964).

These three groups were disliked both by the chiefs, who regarded them as upstarts, and by the conservative elites, who found them embarrassing. Anti-intellectuals living in slum or near-slum conditions, yet skilled in the ways of both town and bush and close to the economic realities of colonial society, became the backbone of the Convention People's Party. Among them were the professional CPP politicians—a hard-core group represented in all the main towns and villages—who were aggressive, militant, and quick to take offense, but remarkably hard-working and diligent.

UNITED GOLD COAST CONVENTION AND CONVENTION PEOPLE'S PARTY

By 1949 there were four main political groups in the Gold Coast: the chiefs, who played an extremely influential role in their state councils, in provincial councils, and in the Legislative Council; the urban business groups in the National Democratic Party, which carried on the conservative traditions of the old Ratepayers' Association; the United Gold Coast Convention, founded in 1947 by J. B. Danquah, a lawyer, George A. Grant, a businessman from Sekondi, Francis Awoonor Williams, and R. S. Blay; and the Convention People's Party, founded in June, 1949, and led by Kwame Nkrumah, the former general secretary of the UGCC.

The objective of the UGCC was "to ensure that the direction and control of government in the Gold Coast shall pass into the hands of the people and their Chiefs in the shortest possible time." The UGCC was organized around an executive committee, with major regional headquarters at Sekondi, Cape Coast, and Accra. It made little headway in Ashanti, and no attempt was made to organize the north. The Asante Youth Association, before going over to the CPP, was its strongest ally in Ashanti. Although the UGCC had no press, strictly speaking, it received intermittent support from the *Africa Morning Post*, the *Spectator Daily*, and the *Daily Echo*.

In both the UGCC and the CPP, actual organization departed substantially from the ideal. During the period (1948–1949) which gave rise to the split between Danquah and the UGCC executive on the one hand, and Nkrumah, who had become its secretary, on the other, the organization took advantage of the opportunities presented by the Burns Constitution of 1946 to press for a greater degree of self-government. Popular unrest, resulting in the riots of 1948, was largely ignored, and even after the riots an atmosphere of conciliation prevailed. A new governor set up the "Coussey" Commission on Constitutional Reform, a measure viewed by the UGCC executive as a token of success for the policy of moderation. It was perhaps this success that made the split with Nkrumah inevitable. Although Nkrumah's primary responsibility was to build up the party's organization, he was neither fully admitted into the elite nor given control over UGCC funds. Consequently he formed the Committee on Youth Organization within the UGCC, which then broke away from the parent body to establish the CPP. Organized primarily in the towns, the CPP, with the assistance of lorry and taxi drivers, railway workers, market women, teachers and "Standard VII" boys, shopkeepers, and others, spread into the villages. Party members, representing groups of townsmen in coastal towns and villages, moving easily between rural and urban life, and familiar with chieftaincy and tradition, were the brokers who stood between the elites, who were demanding recognition of their own status, and the wider range of associations—some traditional, some modern, some cultural, some economic—which had been formed in response to diverse pressures of social and political change. A newspaper was essential to publicize the activities of Nkrumah, K. A. Gbedemah, Kojo Botsio, James Markham, Kwame Afriyea, and Gamesu Amegbe; indeed, their organizational work centered on publication of the *Accra Evening News*, which had become the party's organizing instrument as well as an ordinary newspaper.

The UGCC, collaborating with the Coussey Commission, found itself working at cross-purposes with the Committee on Youth Organization (CYO). The UGCC called for a national constituent assembly to implement the Coussey report with certain amendments. It expanded its views, not to the public, but to the chiefs, telling them that "we desire to cooperate with you in your study of the proposals and recommendations of the Report, but as the time is short and we cannot visit every State or Divisional Council for this purpose, we submit the following views for your consideration."[20] Meanwhile the CYO, with Botsio as secretary, attacked the Coussey Commission root and branch: "As usual the appointment of the Coussey Commission to draw up a New Constitution smacks of the taint of out-moded imperialist Crown Colony system. . . . We unreservedly repudiate the idea of being 'trained' for Self-Government. Self Government is acquired by practice, not otherwise."[21] From that time on, party politics in the Gold Coast assumed a mass populist form. The clumsy efforts of urban conservatives, chiefs, and intellectuals to denigrate Nkrumah only helped to enhance his popularity. After January 8, 1950, the day when positive action was declared, the Convention People's Party became a social movement as well as a political force.

[20]*The Country's Demand*, United Gold Coast Convention (Accra: West African Graphic Ltd., 1950), p. 5.

[21]*The Ghana Youth Manifesto*, Committee on Youth Organization (Kumasi: Abura Printing Works, 1949), p. 5.

The history of the organization and the rise of the CPP is well known and need not be recounted here. In effect, Nkrumah achieved what the UGCC had been unable to accomplish. And the youth organizations antedating the UGCC, particularly the General Council of the Youth Conference, whose general secretary had been J. B. Danquah, were restricted to the "quality" elite among the youth who were to become the next generation of middle-class urban professionals. Nkrumah built upon a wider base. Moreover, by focusing on the middle group that was taking form between urban elites and rural traditionalists, Nkrumah made the values of each of the latter more proximate and less antagonistic. He reduced the importance of the urban professional and thus eliminated him from membership in a new *Stand* composed of relatively inaccessible roles.

The Convention People's Party consisted of a number of different elements: journalists working on Nkrumah's newspaper, the *Accra Evening News*, of whom the most prominent was Gbedemah; youth groups, including representatives of the Youth Study Group in Accra, whose president was Gbedemah; the Asante Youth Association, whose secretary in Kumasi was Krobo Edusei (this association later combined to form the Committee on Youth Organization with Nkrumah as "promoter" and Kojo Botsio as secretary); ex-servicemen under the leadership of Dzenkle Dzewu, a former sergeant major in the army and general president of the Ex-Servicemen's Union; the market women, represented by Mrs. Hannah Cudjoe; and the young urban radicals of the League of Ghana Patriots under the leadership of Kofi Baako, editor of the *Cape Coast Daily Mail*. In addition, many voluntary and youth associations, such as the Sekondi Ghana Youth Association, the Tamale Youth Movement, the New Era Club, the Manya Krobo State Improvement Association, the Mandated Togo Farmers' Association, and the Ada Youth Association, either by supporting the CPP or by taking a direct interest in its affairs, helped to expand its network of organization.

The CPP was organized in two stages. First, an effective executive, composed of Nkrumah's associates both within the UGCC and outside it, was established. This meant building upon the CYO and the group of journalists associated with the *Accra Evening News*. Kofi Baako became the director of information. The second phase was to fashion Nkrumah into the symbol of liberation. The First National Delegates' Conference, held at Saltpond, appointed a committee of eight to draft a party constitution. At a second conference, held at Ho in 1951, the constitution was presented and the political spirit of the party was defined. "We shall not tolerate factionalism in our Party," said Nkrumah, pursuing a line that has continued to this day. "We shall expel from our ranks those individuals and those little caucuses who meet in their little holes and conspire against the backs of the Party. If they have any grievances against the Party let them come out in the open and defend their position. This, Comrades, is democratic centralism."[22]

The constitution established a national executive committee, and a central committee to serve as its "directorate." The annual delegates' conferences were concerned with major policy objectives. Regional committees with a regional conference, constituency organizations, and party branches completed the organizational structure. In addition, there was a national secretariat with a general secretary, a propaganda secretary, and other officers in charge of the administration of the CPP. Committees of the national executive were responsible for ideology, education, international affairs, and other phases of party work.[23]

The three core organizational units were the national Executive Committee, the regional committees (for a time), and the party branches. By 1952 there were six regional committees, and at the end of a year 4,000 CPP branches had been established. A women's section was organized, and the Youth League, launched in 1951, had eighty-three branches by the end of 1952. Moreover, the National Association of Socialist Students' Organizations (NASSO) had begun the work of teaching socialism to study groups and classes, and had set up its own branches. By 1952 the combined registered membership of the CPP was 800,000.[24]

The fact that the CPP was able to contest elections from the very first contributed greatly to its organizational success. It won its first victories in municipal elections shortly after it came into existence as a political party, and these were soon followed by others. The Gold Coast Constitution of 1950 made provision for general elections on a wide franchise throughout the colony and Ashanti areas. Nkrumah's emphasis on effective party organization bore results in the first general election in the Gold Coast,[25] held while Nkrumah himself was in jail. The CPP won thirty-four of the thirty-eight municipal and rural seats, and its popular vote was roughly 59,000 against a combined opposition vote of 6,000. The UGCC obtained only two seats in the Legislative Assembly. Indeed, because of the mixed composition of the Assembly and the combination of direct and indirect methods of elections to it, it was the chiefs and their representatives who constituted the parliamentary opposition party. The CPP suddenly realized that its real rival was not the intelligentsia,

[22]Kwame Nkrumah, *The New Stage* (Accra: Nyaniba Press and Publishing Co., 1952), p. 4.

[23]*Constitution of the Convention People's Party*, 1st ed. (Accra: United Press, 1952).

[24]See "Freedom," *C.P.P. Monthly Magazine*, No. 1 (December, 1952). Kofi Baako was the editor of this journal.

[25]Indeed, the general election became identified with the CPP, even though it came about as a consequence of the constitutional recommendations of the Coussey Commission. The UGCC and the Coussey Commission were thus robbed of the fruits of their labors.

but rather the traditional leaders, secure in their native administrations and entrenched in their state councils. Thus the new CPP government directed its first attack against the progressive chiefs, with whom the defeated constitutional progressives now made common cause.

The CPP made three efforts in this direction. First, it launched an organized campaign which, following hard on the heels of the 1951 general election, was designed to set up a CPP branch in every village and town. Second, it enacted legislation which reformed the native authorities system so as to give power to elected local councils instead of to chiefs and their representatives. CPP organizational campaigns thus capitalized on local grievances against chiefs within each chieftaincy, and recruited many local party leaders on purely local grounds. Third, the CPP set out to change the country's constitution so that in the next general election all seats in the legislature would be based on single-member constituencies and direct elections under universal suffrage; this would eliminate the indirect systems which favored chiefs and their representatives.

All three of these objectives were realized. The Local Government Ordinance, passed in 1951 over the strenuous opposition of the chiefs, made district and local councils two-thirds elective. The "Nkrumah" Constitution of 1954 provided that all members of the Legislative Assembly be elected by direct vote from single-member constituencies, thus eliminating the political power of the chiefs. Finally, the irresistible power of the CPP made possible the organization of new party branches in all parts of the country.

Opposition to the CPP

Nevertheless, there was opposition to the CPP. Although the National Democratic Party disappeared in all but name and the UGCC had suffered a disaster from which it never recovered, it was not long before disaffected individuals such as Joe Appiah, Kwesi Lamptey, Dzenkle Dzewu, and others began to leave the ranks of the CPP. Some felt that they had been ignored by Nkrumah. Others disliked certain aspects of the party. Furthermore, older intellectuals of the Aborigines' Rights Protection Society, the National Democratic Party, and the UGCC now put an end to the years of strife with the chiefs; the latter, recognizing the seriousness of their conflict with Nkrumah, looked to the intellectual elites for leadership in a new kind of politics which left them with no direct political outlets.

Despite these efforts to organize against Nkrumah, however, the combined opposition refused to recognize the strength of populism and the effectiveness of the CPP organization. When attacked by local CPP politicians, the chiefs retired to sulk in their state councils, and one by one were eliminated by CPP adherents who helped destool them or otherwise render them impotent. The intellectuals issued manifestoes and argued with one another. They formed one group after another, but remained politically unsuccessful.

Opposition to the CPP took three forms. First, J. B. Danquah and others sought to show that the intellectuals and the chiefs had been the most active participants in the constitutional negotiations leading to the first African government in a colonial territory. It was they, not Nkrumah, who were the really effective nationalists of the country. Indeed, to underscore the point and to embarrass the new government, Danquah made a motion in the 1951 Assembly favoring the establishment of a constitutional committee. This proposal, which would have led to immediate self-government, the Nkrumah government had to turn down. In 1952 the UGCC issued a program for self-government and called for a national emergency council to declare the readiness of the Gold Coast for independence.[26]

Second, efforts were made to build a combined opposition to the CPP. A meeting of a committee for the formation of a united front held on April 6, 1952, "with a view to preventing the rise of dictatorship and also to establishing a stable and democratic government,"[27] was called by G. Ashie-Nikoi and Dzenkle Dzewu, both of whom had defected from the CPP. The committee included Ashie-Nikoi; Ako Adjei; Kwesi Lamptey; N. A. Ollennu, a prominent lawyer of the National Democratic Party; and two journalists, Henry B. Cole, a Liberian, and M. Therson-Cofie. Dr. Kofi A. Busia was later made a member. The committee proposed a loose association of all political parties and organizations to fight the CPP. Upon the committee's recommendation, the National Democratic Party and the UGCC did not merge, but were replaced by a new organization, the Ghana Congress Party (GCP). The word "Congress" was considered to be acceptable to the chiefs, and the name "Ghana" was taken to show that the party would have a nationalist outlook. Its program included general welfare measures of a reformist nature.

The GCP attempted to brand the CPP with corruption. It claimed that the government's plan for education was lowering standards. It wanted more fiscal austerity. In 1954 its slogan was: "Vote for the GCP—the party which will give the country real prosperity, peace and progress."[28] None of its proposals were likely to capture popular support. As the GCP was dedicated to fostering widespread disillusion with Nkrumah,

[26] *The "P" Plan: UGCC's Seven-Point Scheme for Gold Coast Liberation* (Accra: Iona Press, 1952).

[27] "Deliberations of the Committee on the Formation of a United Front for Political Action in This Country" (Accra: mimeographed, 1952).

[28] *Manifesto of the Ghana Congress Party* (Accra: West African Graphic Co., 1954).

it was never very successful. Busia, who became its leading figure, had trouble with older politicians like Lamptey and Danquah who resented one another. Danquah did not dissolve the UGCC for fear of being without a party of his own making. Instead of appearing as a reasonable alternative to the CPP, the GCP began to look more and more absurd. Despite the dignity of some of its leaders, it created the impression of being a carping, negativistic, and opportunistic set of dissidents. This in turn enhanced the prestige of the CPP.

Another attempt to form a combined opposition failed in 1954, when the Volta Charter was suggested. The language of the charter itself reveals the predicament of the opposition more effectively than any description:

> (1) We shall organize effectively on a common platform during the election campaign so as to sweep the polls at the forthcoming General Election. (2) The manifestoes already prepared by the various Parties shall be examined and embodied in one manifesto acceptable in principle by all the Allied Parties. (3) A Central Election and Finance Committee shall be set up. (4) A Central Co-ordinating Secretariat shall be set up in Accra with full-time staff to see to the successful running of the campaign. (5) In the event of our winning the election, which we pledge ourselves to help achieve, we shall form a National Coalition Government.[29]

The participating parties were the Togoland Congress, the Ghana Nationalist Party (founded by Obetsebi Lamptey after he was expelled from the GCP), the Ghana Action Party, the Gold Coast Muslim Association Party, the All-Ewe Conference, and the Ghana Congress Party. Because the representatives could not agree among themselves, the Volta Charter was never signed.

The third effort of the opposition was to collaborate with the chiefs. Here it came close to achieving its objective, particularly after the 1954 general election, when popular disaffection with Nkrumah was beginning to appear in parts of the north and in Ashanti. Indeed, the coalition between chiefs and certain of the GCP leaders was successful (particularly for Busia and Danquah, whose brother and cousin, respectively, were chiefs and members of royal families). A number of regional parties emerged, utilizing the only organizational device open to them—the traditional organization of the states. Robbed of their previous power, these traditional groups were ready for use as units of ethnic parties. In 1954 the National Liberation Movement (NLM) was formed in Ashanti under the patronage of the Asantehene (paramount chief of the Ashantis), and with the support of the Asanteman Council and the Ghana Congress

[29] *The Volta Charter* (n.p., 1954).

Party, particularly K. A. Busia. Bafour Osei Akoto, a prominent cocoa farmer in Ashanti and the Asantehene's chief linguist, was chairman. He proclaimed the NLM as a national movement of Ashantis rather than a political party, and it was frankly an organ of Ashanti nationalism, rallying around the Asanteman Council. Except in the coastal areas, where tribal feeling was weakest and urban population largest, ethnic and local forms of opposition became characteristic.

The new efforts of the opposition after 1954 were successful enough to attract much of the youth to its standard. Several factors helped to bring the Asante Youth Association over to the NLM, as well as to foster new anti-Nkrumah youth groups in the south. One was resentment over the stiffening of the policy of recruitment of young men eligible to promotion within the CPP, for by 1954 the party had filled most of its available administrative and governmental posts and would be unable to create additional positions until self-government was safely in its hands. In the resulting competition for CPP positions, the Accra and Kumasi youth who were unsuccessful became embittered. Another reason for the defection of young people from the CPP was the harsher party discipline imposed by Nkrumah. Youth groups were not disposed to take orders from the Nkrumah government or from the party. Thus the bitterly anti-Nkrumah Ghana Youth Federation, which collaborated closely with the NLM, was formed in the coastal area in 1954.

Though the opposition was poorly organized, it continued to grow in strength and reached the height of its effectiveness just before independence. It also gained the support of the chiefs, who, deprived of seats in the Legislative Assembly after 1954, allied themselves with political opposition groups. Some of them cooperated with the Muslim Association Party, organized primarily among Muslim groups in Accra.[30] But once again, as in the earlier days of the Coussey Commission, the prospect of success divided them. Splintering along tribal lines and plagued by personality conflicts, the opposition could find no broad base for unity even in coalition. More often than not, the older leaders looked back to the organizations they had sired as the proper progenitors of nationalism and independence, and bemoaned the fact that these had been usurped by Nkrumah and his upstarts. Others, having split off from the CPP, sought local strength in a combination of urban-ethnic minorities such as the Ga Shifimo Kpee movement which arose in Accra in 1957 to oppose Nkrumah in his own and adjacent constituencies. Such parties sprang into being, flared briefly, and extinguished themselves, but a spark always remained to smolder.

[30]The Muslim Association Party originally wanted to coöperate with the CPP. In 1951 it offered to support CPP candidates and asked to participate in joint nominations of candidates for both general elections and by-elections. The offer was refused by the CPP. See *Manifesto of the Muslim Association Party* (Accra: Iona Press, 1954).

These ephemeral opposition parties contained three elements which are illustrated by the Ga Shifimo Kpee (only one of many of its type). The first was Ga and Andangme traditionalists who sought to reassert the control of their people over land alienated to "foreigners" or to other ethnic groups. (The objective was to gain control over tribal lands now in the city of Accra.) The second element was young men who had hitherto formed the backbone of the CPP "strong-arm" groups: tough, poorly educated, truculent, and rootless Ga men who had received few benefits from the CPP. Their complaint that "everyone else was able to get off the veranda but them" referred to the term "veranda boys,"[31] which had once been contemptuously leveled at Nkrumah and his followers by the elites. The third group comprised earlier associates of Nkrumah, such as Dzenkle Dzewu and a former women's organizing secretary of the CPP who belonged to the Ga group; journalists, such as Henry Thompson, the West African editor of *Drum*, and his brother; older leaders of earlier parties, such as Obetsebi Lamptey; and, of course, most of the traditional leaders of the Ga peoples. Economic grievances, traditional issues, and disgruntlement over the lack of opportunities for advancement within the CPP formed the basis for the organization of an opposition party around a tribal group. Chiefs poured a libation in honor of young toughs whom they had only recently regarded with contempt. Young toughs identified themselves as members of Asafo companies (traditional warrior groups), and found a new organizational core from which to work. Old chiefs found their spokesmen in the intellectuals and journalists.

The Ga Shifimo Kpee movement, though highly localized, was one manifestation of dissastisfaction with the CPP, but the opposition groups could not combine successfully. Agreement upon issues could bring about unity among people only within the tribe, and could not phrase these issues in the universally ideological terms required if an opposition party was to succeed. Because the opposition was fragmented, local parties could be annihilated by the CPP one by one: by exploiting an existing conflict, as among Ga traditionalists; by eliminating a powerful chief, as with Nana Ofori Atta II, the former Omanhene of Akim Abuakwa, and ruler of the single most powerful anti-CPP state in Ghana; or through promises and benefits, like those extended to the paramount chiefs of Mamprusi and Dagomba who, before long, were soliciting subscriptions for the CPP treasuries.[32]

[31]The term is invidious, signifying people who slept on the veranda and had no home or room of their own.

[32]It is noteworthy that Ga opposition is still very strong. A large proportion of the CPP top officials presently in jail under preventive detention, such as Tawia Adamafio, Kofi Crabbe, Ako Adjei, and Boi Doku, are Ga.

Despite its difficulties, the opposition continued to strive for a more effective organization. With the NLM as its core, the United Party was formed in October, 1957, under the leadership of Busia. Not long after the party was founded, however, Busia became Ghana's first political exile. Leading Nigerian merchants who had contributed funds to the United Party were deported to their home country. The political activities of the Asantehene were investigated and many of the leading members of the party executive, particularly R. R. Amponsah, were accused of participating in a plot to assassinate President Nkrumah and were put in prison under preventive detention, one of a series of measures which the government took to ensure political control. The opposition was destroyed. In the process the CPP itself underwent fundamental changes. No longer a party of representation, it now became a party of solidarity, changing the basic quality of political life in Ghana.

Too late, the opposition was propelled toward a semblance of unity by the government in the summer of 1957, when the Avoidance of Discrimination Act made tribal and religious parties illegal. This forced the opposition groups—the National Liberation Movement, the Ga Shifimo Kpee, the Northern People's Party, the Togoland Congress, the Anlo Youth, and the Muslim Association Party—to come together in a better-organized body. But just as a loose unity seemed to obtain, the CPP eliminated by a variety of means the effective leadership of the United Party.

Opposition Ideologies

In his valuable discussion of the early relationship between the Working Committee of the United Gold Coast Convention and Kwame Nkrumah, Dennis Austin remarks:

> The broad nationalist front started under UGCC leadership fractured quickly along moderate versus radical lines—it is probably fair to add "along lines of economic and social interest" too. But the great advantage and the great strength of the political struggle in the Gold Coast at this time was the general agreement which existed between all sections of local society—the lawyers, the "young men," the farmers, even many of the chiefs (at least south of the Volta)—on the desirability of self-government. There were differences over methods and between leaders, but not on ends, not even—in 1949–50—on the form of self-government that the end should bring.[33]

To recapitulate, the expansion and the proliferation of political groups had begun in the twenties, and were accelerated in the thirties by the growth of cultural, youth, and old boys' associations. This led to a group

[33]Dennis Austin, "The Working Committee of the United Gold Coast Convention," *Journal of African History*, II, No. 2 (1961), 296–97.

division between constitutional progressives and progressive chiefs. The first group could be distinguished from the uneducated, and the second from the more old-fashioned traditionalists. Lawyers, journalists, and teachers, whose past associations were with the Aborigines' Rights Protection Society and the West African National Congress, composed the first group. Chiefs who had participated in the Legislative Council and had helped to frame reform legislation for local government formed the second group. Their past associations went back to the relationship between Nana Sir Ofori Atta I and Governor Sir Gordon Guggisberg, a relationship steadily reinforced by the political ideas that inspired indirect rule.[34] Indeed, the Gold Coast never had indirect rule in undiluted form, partly because the chiefs themselves were influential participants in central government affairs from 1925 onward.

We have already noted the rivalry that developed between the constitutional progressives and the progressive chiefs. Often their members came from the same families. Mainly drawn from the coast, the two groups were not a purely urban phenomenon. The constitutional progressives, for example, did not even have their headquarters in Accra. The ARPS had its office in Cape Coast. The office of the United Gold Coast Convention was at Saltpond, a small town on the coast. The chiefs had their headquarters at Dodowa, the site of the Joint Provincial Council. Leaders were scattered up and down the coast and inland by virtue of their professions or their state councils. There was little effective organization in the UGCC, despite wide sympathy from diverse associations and individuals. In contrast, local organization was strong among the chiefs through the modified structure of the state and provincial council system. Although never properly adapted for national political purposes, these councils participated increasingly in central government while carrying on local government.

The CPP was able to organize all those groups that, although peripheral to the constitutional progressives and the progressive chiefs, made up the bulk of the population. Younger groups were kept at arms length by the chiefs as well as by the elderly leaders of the UGCC, such as George "Pa" Grant. As Thomas Hodgkin put it after the CPP electoral victory in 1951, "The measure of social revolution involved in the CPP's victory at the recent elections can be realized from a study of the election results. In the constituency of Assin–Upper Denkyira (Rural Area), for example, Alfred Pobee Biney, former locomotive engineer (CPP) obtained 51 votes from the electoral college, as compared with 13 votes for

[34]Even anthropology played an important role in this relationship; if the general policy of indirect rule was often reinforced by the observations of anthropologists, a more direct sympathy between the British administration and the chiefs for the modification of traditional situations was provided by the writings of R. S. Rattray.

Nana Sir Tsibu Darku, Kt., O.B.E., Omanhene of Assin Attandansu. This defeat was typical of many."[35]

Local conflicts within state councils, however, created points of entry for CPP politics. Those in opposition to the chiefs, often because of local and family matters, were anxious for an alliance with outside forces. The most famous example occurred in the Brong areas of Ashanti. The Brongs had fought long and quite unsuccessfully against the Ashanti Confederacy (after its restoration in 1935). The CPP allied itself with the Brongs against Ashanti.[36] Today the Brong-Ahafo region is separate from and larger than the Ashanti region, and is as well one of the strongest CPP areas in the country. The CPP also intervened in disputes over stool lands and in problems involving the destooling of chiefs, protests against taxes, unpopular European commercial activities in rural areas, and other key issues concerning chiefs and their followers. What occurred then was a conflict between the African "establishment" and those who wanted to enter it.

Indeed it was rather a long time before issues polarized themselves into basic conflicts over ideologies and aims. From 1949 to 1954 both the CPP and the opposition groups remained essentially parties of representation. Their aims were to widen the franchise, organize for elections, enlarge the sphere of representative government, and thereby gain control of the society. Political coalitions seeking unity among diverse groups remained the basis of both government and opposition politics for a long time.[37]

Typical political demands of the constitutional progressives may be found in the pamphlet, *The Country's Demand*, which is written in the

[35]Thomas Hodgkin, *Freedom for the Gold Coast?* (London: Union of Democratic Control, 1951), p. 9.

[36]Meyerowitz, *op. cit., passim.*

[37]J. B. Danquah is an excellent symbol of the "coalitional nature" of the opposition, if only because he so clearly illustrates the qualities of its leadership and its pattern of activities.

His elder brother was Nana Sir Ofori Atta I. Danquah was well educated both in Ghana and London (second-class Honours B.A. in philosophy and a Ph.D. in ethics from London University). He became a lawyer, and helped found the Gold Coast Students' Association and the West African Students' Union in Great Britain. He belonged to various religious bodies; he worked both with chiefly bodies and with more urbanized political groups; he established the youth conferences in the thirties; he published the *Times of West Africa*, and wrote on Akan religion and Gold Coast politics; and he participated in the Joint Provincial Council, the Legislative Council, the legislature, and assemblies. Throughout his remarkable career his activities remained consistent with his belief in pluralism. His own party, the United Gold Coast Convention, was never more than a coalition, and his later participation in the Ghana Congress Party was based on the same principle. His later support of feudalism was a natural product of his belief in political pluralism.

There were many such figures in the opposition. Kofi A. Busia was another younger man who moved easily between the educated elite, of which he was a key member, and the progressive chiefs, of whom his brother was one. See Danquah, *op. cit.*

form of a "Letter to Nananom [Chiefs] in Council." It called for a two-chambered legislature with the upper house of chiefs composed predominantly of elders who would represent them. The traditional state councils were to retain their powers. In effect, chieftaincy and its particularly Ghanaian form of traditional "democracy" were to continue to provide the major link between the state councils and the central government, while popularly elected representatives in the lower house would provide representation for the population as a whole.[38]

Two years later the opposition stated its program in a pamphlet, *The "P" Plan.* The program called for a national emergency council to declare dominion status and establish an interim constituent assembly in which seats were to be distributed as follows: Convention People's Party, 5; Joint Provincial Council, 3; Asanteman Council, 3; Northern Territorial Council, 3; British Togoland Council, 1; United Gold Coast Convention, 4; People's Democratic Party, 1; and Aborigines' Rights Protection Society, 3. Delegations from political parties were to speak at territorial councils, the trade-union council, University College, the teachers' union, churches, chambers of mines and commerce, and farmers' associations. Hence the "convention" aspect of the opposition, which was also present in the early stages of the CPP, stressed a kind of loose coalitional unity.[39] Notably absent was a concern that the people of the country be granted broad political participation. The appeal was always to a coalition of organized groups and interests.

It was only when the Ghana Congress Party was formed in 1952 that emphasis was placed on the electorate and the public. Then, however, the main objective of the opposition was to capture support being given to the CPP. "The new Party should make no distinction between classes of people in our national community." But even this statement was diluted by a reference to chieftaincy: "Unlike the United Kingdom, the people and their Traditional Rulers *are one and the same people.*" In fact, the emphasis on chieftaincy soon became much stronger, partly because the structure of the Ghana Congress Party depended more and more on traditional organization and chieftaincy.[40] By 1956 it was chieftaincy that was keeping alive the most stubborn opposition. Rural groups, disenchanted with the government's cocoa policy and disturbed by the slow pace of development in the villages, rallied to the chiefs. This was particularly true in Ashanti.

The constitutional progressives, in keeping with their tradition of coalition, called for a federal union with an upper house composed of forty-

[38]George A. Grant, *The Country's Demand* (Saltpond: United Gold Coast Convention, 1950).

[39]*The "P" Plan.*

[40]"Deliberations of the Committee on the Formation of a United Front for Political Action in This Country." Italics added.

eight members: ten from each of four regions to be elected by the territorial council of the region, one from each region to be appointed by the "federal government," and one from each region to be appointed by the governor-general on the advice of a council of state. In addition to an elective lower house and a federal prime minister and cabinet, there would be a council of state, consisting of the governor-general, the heads of the regions, the federal prime minister, prime ministers from each region, and the federal ministers of defense and external affairs, the interior, and justice. Each region would also have upper and lower houses. The upper houses, to consist of chiefs and their representatives, would be built around the existing territorial councils; the lower houses would be elected by universal adult suffrage every four years. Enumerated powers for the federal government were to be relatively restricted, with residual powers remaining with the regional governments. The regional assemblies would play a key role in constitutional amendment.[41]

In summary, the constitutional progressives and the progressive chiefs had formed an alliance in defense of their interests. In this alliance the chiefs were in the ascendency, drawing a large part of their strength from their ability to modify age-old institutions so as to reinforce their claims on the traditional loyalties of the rural population. Conflicts with the CPP over local issues were transformed into matters of deep national interest. "Ethnic" parties thus used "traditional" organization as the basis for electoral combat. Political party struggles became conflicts over basic beliefs as to the nature of Ghana society and its future political organization. Violence, always a good index of such conflicts, increased sharply just before independence. A new and younger political leadership, made up of such men as Victor Owusu, R. R. Amponsah, Joe Appiah, and others who were untainted by the earlier failures of the constitutional progressives, came forward to work with the chiefs. As they breathed new life into the opposition, events began to move more rapidly. Indeed, two events brought the conflict to a head and almost precipitated a revolution. One, before independence, was the 1956 general election, which many thought at the time would be the last free election in the country. The other, after independence, was the establishment of the republic with Nkrumah as president in 1960. The period between these two events was marked by a struggle between government and opposition over the nature of the state.

In general, the loose coalitional approach favored by constitutional progressives and progressive chiefs began to consolidate after 1954 into a tighter organizational structure. By 1957 the opposition parties, with

[41]*Proposals for a Federal Constitution for an Independent Gold Coast and Togoland* (Kumasi: Ahma Printing Works, 1956); see also *Statement by the National Liberation Movement and Its Allies* (Kumasi: Ahma Printing Works, 1956).

their new leadership and their more popular appeal, had become one party of representation with real strength centered upon the institutions and the practices of traditional society. The proposals for federal forms of government represented the political stand of the progressive chiefs, the royalists who accepted innovation and were prepared to fight for it on the basis of pluralist democracy.

The CPP, originally a collection of diverse ethnic groups and associations balanced within a decentralized framework, also underwent changes. After coming into power in 1951, the party employed the full strength of government as well as the prestige of the civil service to enhance its power and consolidate its position. Conscious manipulation of Nkrumah's charisma was blended into the pursuit of economic development, the expansion of education, and the achievement of self-government and independence. The sheer proliferation of membership in the party, an increase in the range of its political activities, and the all-inclusive quality of its political ambition brought significant changes. From a loose alliance of youth, economic, and social associations, as well as ethnic groups, with a strong political nucleus at the center, the CPP had become both a political movement and a political party. As a political movement it appealed to the whole of society for independence, in the name of the leader. Radical in the speed with which it sought to achieve its political objectives and in the militancy it required of its members, it remained mainly middle class or rural in its following. Shortly after the CPP came to power, its leaders were "small middle-class people—petty traders, chemists, school teachers, farmers, journalists, etc. A few of them [came] from the Trade Union movement. There [were] also one or two lawyers among them. But the standard of living of most of them [was] not very far removed from that of the mass of the people."[42]

The CPP was a political party which more and more became a movement. As a movement, it claimed more than parties normally do. As a party, it remained a party of representation until independence. Better-organized than the opposition, it deliberately adopted policies designed to attract the support of diverse groups in the population on the basis of interests that were popularly generated or stimulated by its leaders. Inevitably, however, in the effort to please some, the party offended others. Indeed, just as the opposition forces were beginning to coalesce into a political party, the CPP was alienating increasingly large numbers of people. Ordinarily the two parties of representation would simply have competed for political power, but each drew its strength from completely contradictory sources of legitimacy. Behind the constitutional progressives were the chiefs and the manipulators of tradition, local, sectarian, and increasingly embittered. Behind the CPP as a party stood the CPP as a

[42]Hodgkin, *op. cit.*, p. 9.

movement, monopolistic, demanding total loyalty, and defining its friends and its enemies in terms of that loyalty. In the end the political movement won. The parties of representation disappeared. A new militancy replaced the old popular appeal—a militancy with a strong quality of coercion about it. The CPP had become a party of solidarity. It is in the light of these changes that the elections in Ghana will be examined.

ELECTIONS

There are several reasons for the transformation of the CPP from a party of representation into a party of solidarity. As a party of representation, it had to abide by certain principles of constitutional government. Moreover, its effectiveness in implementing programs depended upon substantial, if not overwhelming, electoral support. With major weaknesses in electoral strength, the CPP as a political movement remained unstable and vulnerable.

Before analyzing the general elections that have taken place since 1951, when the CPP came into power, it is vital to record some of the vast changes that occurred between 1951 and 1956 regarding the purposes and the composition of the legislature as well as the system of elections itself. Although the 1950 Constitution provided for a wider and more representative legislature than any previous colonial constitution, nonetheless it continued the representation of a number of significant political groups in the Gold Coast, particularly the chiefs and their representatives, and rural and urban groups. Rural members were indirectly elected, and the territorial councils elected representatives as well. The only direct elections were those in urban areas, based on a broad but by no means universal franchise. Moreover, a system of electoral colleges prevailed in the north. Not until 1954 did the legislature become a fully representative body with an assembly drawn from 104 single-member constituencies.[43] The change that occurred in 1954 was, therefore, almost as fundamental as that of 1950, when the nominated unofficials (mostly constitutional progressives), by providing for the direct election of urban members, occasioned their own removal from the Assembly. Some of them were then elected by territorial councils as representatives of the chiefs. But in 1954 the chiefs were unable to send representatives to the Assembly unless they were directly elected. This meant that mass organization throughout the country was the only effective means of ensuring parliamentary victory.

Despite the organizational weakness of the opposition, however, its

[43]In 1960, ten additional regional seats for women were added, bringing the total membership of the National Assembly to 114.

record in various elections shows how widespread was its support, a fact that the parliamentary successes of the CPP tend to disguise. In practice, the pluralities by which the CPP won most of its elections were not overwhelmingly larger than those usually found in stable two-party systems. In fact, before the CPP onslaught against all opposition groups, when it became abundantly clear to all that to vote for the opposition was idle or even dangerous, the opposition was more than holding its own. As the accompanying figure shows, in the period from 1954 to 1956 the presence of the British limited the use of political force by the CPP against the opposition. In the 1956 election, the "independence" election and presumably the particular inheritance of the CPP, the percentage of voting was highest where the opposition was strongest. In Ashanti, the

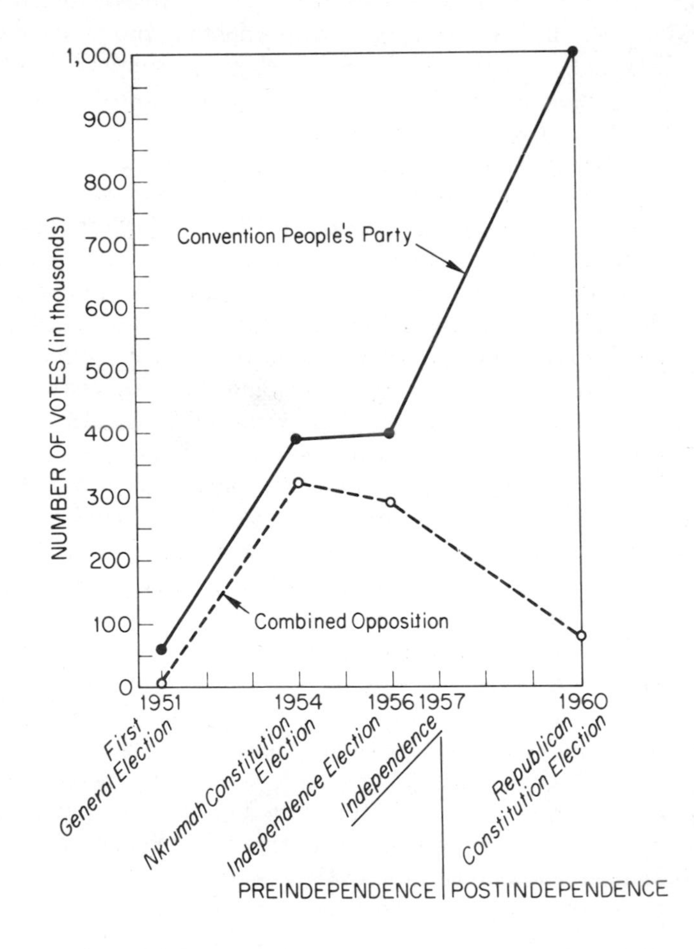

Figure 1. *Ghanaian Elections, 1951–1960.*

NLM stronghold, 57 per cent voted; in Transvolta-Togo, 51 per cent voted; and in the Gold Coast colony or coastal area, where Nkrumah was especially strong, 47.5 per cent voted.[44]

The 1954 general election was the first popular election in the country. The opposition popular vote was relatively strong, totaling 324,822; the popular vote for the CPP was 391,720, or 20 per cent more than that for the opposition, with 59 per cent of the eligible voters actually voting. Parliamentary representation, however, presented a very different picture:

Party	*Number of seats*
Convention People's Party	71
Independents	16
Northern People's Party	12
Togoland Congress	2
Ghana Congress Party	1
Muslim Association Party	1
Anlo Youth Organization	1

After the 1954 election the Ghana Congress Party began to disintegrate, as personal conflicts among its leaders became sharp. Relations among opposition leaders had never been too harmonious: Obetsebi Lamptey had broken away to form the Ghana Nationalist Party; Danquah had refused to acknowledge the leadership of Busia; and Dzenkle Dzewu had withdrawn in disgust after the failure of the combined opposition to sign the Volta Charter the February preceding the 1954 general election.

The poor parliamentary showing of the opposition in the 1954 election (many of the independents were in fact CPP "rebels" who rejoined the CPP once in the Assembly) stimulated organization along ethnic lines. The National Liberation Movement, formed shortly after this election, illustrated the trend (see p. 154, above). Despite the growth of ethnic nationalism, however, the CPP was able to increase its over-all voting strength in the general election of 1956. It received 398,141 votes, and the combined opposition received 299,116. Thus the CPP won 38 per cent more of the popular vote than the opposition, an increase of 18 per cent over its record in the 1954 election.[45]

These figures, however, are somewhat misleading. A more detailed analysis of the 1956 election statistics shows that the opposition vote was heavily concentrated in the hinterland. Moreover, in some areas where the CPP won, the turnout was relatively low. For example, in Accra Municipal, the center of CPP support, only 31,840 of the 86,603 registered voters actually voted. In Accra Central, Nkrumah's own constituency, registered voters totaled 32,944, but Nkrumah received only 11,119

[44] "Report on the General Election of 1956" (mimeographed).
[45] *Ibid.*

votes. His opponent, S. E. Odamtten, a constitutional progressive and a founding member of the Ghana Congress Party, received 1,865, and the turnout was only 39 per cent. This surprisingly low figure is subject to two interpretations, both of which are reasonable. One is that everyone knew that Nkrumah would win and therefore many did not bother to vote. The other is that in Accra Central, a strong Ga constituency, a quiet and unorganized opposition to Nkrumah was beginning to emerge, though it did not come into the open until several years later.[46]

In some areas where it had exploited traditional conflicts, the CPP gained its heaviest vote. For example, in the Brong area, where it had supported the Brongs against the Ashantis, not only was the vote large, but the CPP did exceptionally well, receiving 38,373 votes against 25,633 for the opposition. In Kumasi, where before 1954 the CPP had won overwhelmingly both in municipal elections and in the 1951 general election, the issues were bitterly disputed, and loyalties and rivalries had been deeply inflamed, particularly in non-Brong areas in Ashanti and in the north. Southern Ghana, for instance, gave only 42,602 votes to the opposition, or 16 percent of the votes cast, whereas the rest of the country gave it 256,514 votes, or 35 percent of the total vote. This opposition vote, without benefit of well-organized parties, was indeed remarkable, particularly after effective rule by the CPP, which was asking for a vote of confidence to bring the country to independence. In fact, the CPP did not increase its number of seats until after independence, when opposition members began to cross the floor and the opposition as such was finally abolished. A more detailed breakdown of the 1956 general election, in which 50 percent of the eligible voters went to the polls, is shown in Table 1.[47]

The elections held after the 1956 general election, including by-elections, are particularly significant because they illustrate some of the major conflicts that arose between the CPP and the opposition. They also illuminate the rise of the United Party, the attack upon it by the CPP, and the circumstances under which the CPP developed from a political movement and a party of representation into a party of solidarity in a single-party state.

Kumasi South, a critical Ashanti area, illustrates the fluctuations in popular support of the CPP and the fickleness of the public in four elections: the 1954 and 1956 general elections, a 1958 municipal election, and a 1959 by-election (see Table 2). This interesting constituency contained a relatively cosmopolitan but predominantly Ashanti population whose ties to the Asantehene were weakened by urbanization and by the

[46]*Ibid.*

[47]Dennis Austin and William Tordoff, "Voting in an African Town," *Political Studies*, VIII (June 1960), 130.

influx of relatively stable and commercially or professionally successful strangers (non-Ashanti), particularly from the south, who had intermarried and settled down in the constituency.

In other areas the decline of the opposition after 1956 was overwhelming. In Sekyere West, for example, in the 1959 by-election, the United Party lost the seat formerly held by its secretary-general, R. R. Amponsah (who had been put in jail for alleged participation in a plot against Nkrumah). The CPP candidate, Kwaku Bonsu, received 10,840 votes to 5,153 for the opposition candidate, Kwasi Agyarko. In another striking illustration, K. A. Busia, leader of the opposition and Ghana's first political exile, lost his seat to his long-time political enemy, C. E. Donkoh.[48] In the violent campaign preceding the election, fifty-eight people were arrested and two CPP supporters were killed. The result was never in doubt. The vote was 13,676 for the CPP and only 1,589 for the United Party.

Everywhere, from 1957 on, the constituency organizations of the opposition were attacked root and branch. The leaders of the United Party were subjected to abuse, and many of them were jailed and expelled from the National Assembly. Finally, in the spring of 1960, in the last major election held, the effects of this policy were amply displayed. J. B. Danquah, who stood for maintenance of the *status quo* with the prime minister continuing to be responsible to Parliament and the Queen, was soundly beaten by Kwame Nkrumah, who campaigned for a change to republican status with himself as president under a new constitution. The vote for the republic was 1,000,740 to 131,425 against. Nkrumah received 1,016,076 votes for president; Danquah, 124,623. The rout was complete. A year and a half later, Danquah, the leading symbol of opposition and the person most responsible for bringing Nkrumah back to the Gold Coast from the West African secretariat, joined his colleagues in prison under preventive detention.[49]

THE CPP AS A PARTY OF SOLIDARITY

The CPP electoral successes have virtually eliminated the opposition as an electoral threat to the government. However, the effect on the CPP itself requires comment. Three tendencies have become apparent since 1960. First, the CPP constituency and branch organizations have declined, not in number, but certainly in significance within the party.

[48]Busia's brother, the former chief of Wenchi who had been destooled, has also gone into exile.

[49]Danquah has since been released, and is currently president of the Ghana Bar Association.

TABLE 1

General Elections of 1956 in Ghana

Region	Number of registered voters	Number of votes cast	Opposition parties								Total opposition vote
			CPP[a]	*NLM*[b]	*NPP*[c]	*MAP*[d]	*FYO*[e]	*TC*[f]	*WYA*[g]	*IND*[h]	
Accra Municipal	86,603	31,840	27,076	2,950	. .	1,814	. .	. .	. .	. .	4,764
Western region	226,911	111,896	97,064	7,109	. .	. .	. .	. .	3,898	3,825	14,832
Eastern region	167,605	77,890	54,884	16,065	. .	. .	1,230	. .	. .	5,711	23,006
Transvolta-Togo	197,195	101,584	55,508	. .	. .	. .	5,617	20,352	. .	20,107	46,076
Ashanti	389,153	224,069	96,968	119,033	. .	7,565	. .	. .	. .	503	127,101
Northern territories	325,407	149,478	66,641	. .	72,440	1,732	. .	. .	. .	8,665	82,837
TOTAL	1,392,874	696,757	398,141	141,157	72,440	11,111	6,847	20,352	3,898	38,811	298,616

Representation in Legislature

Number of seats won	1,392,874	99[i]	66	12	15	1	1	2	. .	2	33[j]
Uncontested seats	66,869	5[k]	5	. .	. .	. .	. .	. .	. .	. .	. .
TOTAL	1,459,743	104[l]	71	12	15	1	1	2	. .	2	33[j]

[a] Convention People's Party.
[b] National Liberation Movement.
[c] Northern People's Party.
[d] Muslim Association Party.
[e] Federation of Youth Organizations.
[f] Togoland Congress.
[g] Wassaw Youth Association.
[h] Independents.
[i] Total number of seats won.
[j] Number of seats won by opposition parties.
[k] Total number of uncontested seats.
[l] Total number of seats in legislature.

SOURCE: "Report on the General Election of 1956" (mimeographed).

TABLE 2

Four Elections in Kumasi South, 1954–1959

Election	*Number of registered voters*	*Total votes cast*	*Per cent voting*	*Convention People's Party*		*Opposition*		*Independents*	
				Number of votes	*Per cent of votes cast*	*Number of votes*	*Per cent of votes cast*	*Number of votes*	*Per cent of votes cast*
General, 1954	23,926	13,499	56.4	11,232	82.3	2,104	15.6	163	1.2
General, 1956	32,860	19,622	59.7	7,740	39.4	11,882	60.6	[a]	. .
Municipal, 1958	38,890	26,741	68.2	14,849	55.5	11,687	43.7	205	0.8
By-election, 1959[b]	38,838	19,015	49.0	9,023	47.5	8,653	45.5	1,339	7.0

[a] No candidate.

[b] The 1959 by-election marks a change in the pattern. Owing to a split in the CPP branch, the extremely popular CPP candidate, B. E. Dwira, was ousted and therefore ran as an independent. He received 1,339 votes. The CPP candidate who replaced Dwira, Owusu-Afriyie, had the support of Nkrumah and of the party's Central Committee and won 9,023 votes. The opposition candidate, J. Fordwo of the United Party, received 8,653 votes. This by-election is particularly noteworthy because it shows that latent opposition continued to exist, and that interference from Accra, even in local CPP affairs, could cause the opposition vote to rise sharply. The significance lies in the facts that the opposition is thus more real than apparent, and that the electoral system may check the actions of CPP politicians. Source for the 1959 data was *West Africa*, April 25, 1959, p. 387; May 9, 1959, p. 449.

Second, the auxiliary and functional organizations of the party have become more important. These two tendencies have led to a third, the increase in internal factionalism, in competition for influence, and in inner party intrigue. This in turn has caused Nkrumah to tighten his authority over the entire party apparatus. These three changes have produced modifications in the organization of the party and its auxiliary agencies, which serve as quasi-public bodies.

The Decline in Significance of Constituency and Branch Organizations

The disintegration of the United Party as an electoral force created a new and unanticipated problem for the CPP. Branch leaders, no longer attacking opposition forces in the constituencies, began instead to patch up their differences with those they had vanquished. Efforts were made to recruit former rank-and-file United Party adherents into the CPP in order to swell the latter's membership, augment national and local treasuries, and build more effective solidarity for the local tasks confronting both the party and the local government authorities. Opposition assemblymen crossed the floor in large numbers. Local party officials tried to mend those ruptures in family and social life which had appeared at the height of constitutional conflict. A new *rapprochement* took place between chiefs, now overtly pro-CPP, and elders in the community.

As a result, many of the issues originally raised by the United Party were taken up by the branch and constituency organizations of the CPP. A new localism appeared. Branches were pitted against regions. At times both would unite against the national secretariat. Conflicts arose between them. Sometimes the Central Committee would oppose a constituency organization's choice of candidate to the National Assembly, as happened in Kumasi South. Other issues centered on demands for special funds for development, or stemmed from resentment against district commissioners, who were now political appointees. More frequently, resistance arose against manipulation of local constituencies by central bodies through the district commissioners, or by local representatives of the United Ghana Farmers' Council, the Trades Union Congress (TUC), and later the Young Pioneers. The constituency organizations, no longer required to fight hard to win by-elections, took on the political complexion of their erstwhile opponents, and, as loyal CPP members, argued vigorously for the issues formerly espoused by the United Party. Moreover, because they were inside the CPP, they could argue such causes much more convincingly than the United Party ever could. This posed severe discipline problems for both regional and central authorities in the CPP.

The Growth of Auxiliary and Functional Organizations

Partly as an answer to the growth of localism in the constituency parties, and partly as a basis for reorganizing society along lines of Nkrumaism and socialism, functional and auxiliary organizations were given much greater prominence than ever before. Under the general program of consolidating the revolution along the lines laid down by George Padmore in his *Pan-African Manifesto*, the two most important functional organizations so honored were the Trades Union Congress under its leader, John Tettegah, and the cooperatives. By the action of the government, which consolidated the trade-union movement and instituted an automatic checkoff system, and by the action of the party, which made Tettegah an ambassador extraordinary and minister plenipotentiary, with an office in the new CPP building in Accra, the TUC was transformed into a vanguard movement for the building of Nkrumaism.[50]

There was also a consolidation of the entire cooperative movement into a single organization. Among the reasons for this step was that more than a breath of scandal surrounded the operations of the Cocoa Marketing Board and the Cocoa Purchasing Commission, and local farmers' organizations were attacking the CPP for mismanagement and corruption. Indeed, one of the main grievances on which the opposition had been able to capitalize was the confused state of the various cooperative and marketing boards under CPP control.[51]

[50]The Trades Union Congress had been plagued by a series of internal conflicts between pro- and anti-CPP elements, and by a split within its own ranks. Moreover, a large number of strikes, not unrelated to political events, took place between 1956 and 1957. Pro-NLM labor leaders were gradually eliminated from the TUC, and the TUC was restructured by its General Council. As Tettegah said at the time, "We do not want to be bothered with Cambridge Essays on imaginary ILO standards, with undue emphasis on voluntary associations" (cited in L. Snowiss, "Democracy and Control in a Changing Society: The Case of Ghana" [unpublished M.A. thesis, University of Chicago, 1960]). Not only was the TUC made into an arm of the state and the party, but civil servants, who had been regarded as uncommitted to the CPP and often hostile to it, were now required to join the TUC as a form of "protection."

[51]A sample of the complaints is to be found in a petition of the National Liberation Movement: "The members of the Cocoa Marketing Board who are also Directors of the Cocoa Purchasing Company Limited are also the Leaders of the Convention Peoples Party and since its establishment in 1952 [*sic*] it has been taken for granted by the members of the Convention Peoples Party of which Dr. Kwame Nkrumah, [then] Prime Minister, is the Life Chairman, that the Cocoa Purchasing Company Limited, a Public Company run with public funds, is an organization affiliated with the Convention Peoples Party and a reservoir from which funds might be drawn to run the Convention Peoples Party. Indeed in a debate in the Assembly in 1954, Mr. Krobo Edusei, a member of the inner circle of the Convention Peoples Party, much to the embarrassment of the Ministers, unabashedly and shamelessly stated that the Cocoa Purchasing Company is the CPP and the CPP is the CPC, a

The CPP farmers' organization—the United Ghana Farmers' Council—virtually eliminated the opposition National Farmers' Union and, in the aftermath of the investigation of irregularities in the Cocoa Purchasing Commission and other marketing organization, became the nucleus of the new Ghana Cooperative Movement (GCM). Like the TUC, the GCM publishes its own newspaper (the *Co-operator*); the editor is Dorothy Padmore, widow of the late George Padmore. The leader of the movement is an ambassador extraordinary and minister plenipotentiary. Through its control of the entire cooperative movement, it implements the government's farm policies.[52]

In transforming the TUC and the cooperative movement into organs of party and state, the CPP had two objectives. First, it wanted to implement the new style of social and political life emerging in Ghana. The trade-union and cooperative movements both represent a type of organization or discipline through which each individual is linked to the state not only by the party, but by a voluntary association or an occupational grouping under party supervision. Participation in society extends beyond party membership to a relationship based on meaningful work in the significant areas of labor and agriculture. Second, these two organizations are functional, and cut across other forms of organization, such as ethnic and religious groups; thus they reduce the significance of the latter.

In order to make these movements effective, however, the CPP had to elevate the position of labor and agricultural organizations within the party. Nor were these the only groups to receive such attention. Postwar urban growth had been phenomenal.[53] A general movement from the villages to the towns had increased in tempo, because urban centers offered more skilled and semiskilled occupations and greater educational opportunities than rural areas. After independence, a sharp drop in cocoa prices helped encourage farm laborers to come to the towns, where they joined the ranks of the partially employed or the unemployed. Moreover, political conflict in the rural areas, often extremely bitter and intense,

---

statement not altogether unsupported by facts. For example, the week one Twumasi Ankrah, Regional Propaganda Secretary of the CPP Kumasi, went from Accra to Kumasi with fifty pounds of CPC money, he openly boasted he had come with orders to kill the Leaders of the NLM. Four days later he murdered E. Y. Baffoe, Secretary of the National Liberation Movement, for which he was duly convicted by the Kumasi Assizes" (see *Why CMB-CPC Probe*, Petitions Submitted by the Asanteman Council, Farmers, NLM and Allies, and the Opposition in the Legislative Assembly [Kumasi: Abura Printing Works, n.d.], pp. 1–2).

[52]The GCM emphasizes cooperative farming of various kinds, and has established the Kwame Nkrumah Cooperative College. See the *Co-operator*, I, No. 15 (September 1961), for a review of GCM activities by the chairman of the National Cooperative Council, Martin Appiah Danquah.

[53]See *1960 Population Census of Ghana* (Accra: Government Printer, 1962), compiled by the Central Bureau of Statistics.

aggravated the flow of disgruntled villagers into the towns. Finally, the ex-servicemen were restive, many of them being unemployed. The Ghana Legion replaced the former Ex-Servicemen's League with a central council, whose chairman was appointed by the minister of defense. Builders' Brigades (now Workers' Brigades) were established to provide work for the unemployed on rural development schemes, housing projects, and the like. These have had to be disciplined on several occasions, but they are given semimilitary training and indoctrination in Nkrumaism.

The same pattern held with respect to women's organizations and youth groups. All were abolished except the National Council of Ghana Women associated with the CPP. The Women's Organization Bureau was established at the highest echelons of the party, as was the Youth Bureau. The fluctuating loyalties of such organizations as the Asante Youth Association were no longer tolerated. The CPP made the National Association of Socialist Students' Organizations responsible for the ideological training of young people. It established a unit called the Vanguard Activists, whose members were to promote ideological devotion to the party, and the youth were organized in the Young Pioneers.

The effort by the CPP to penetrate every sector of organized life was by no means limited to the functional auxiliary bodies in Ghana. Various apostolic churches formed CPP branches within their congregations, as did the Anglican churches, with the full support of their bishops; some Presbyterian churches followed suit. Organizations such as the Kumasi Marketwomen's Association, which were affiliated with the National Council of Ghana Women (NCGW), also formed party units and CPP Study Groups. Instructions on forming party branches were published:

> And this is what the harmonial national pattern will look like. For all upper and primary schools we have the young pioneers (teachers who are party enthusiasts here to form party branches). For all secondary schools we have the Party's Young Peoples League—PYPL (teachers who are party enthusiasts here to form party branches). For all offices, workshops and farms party branches may be formed by at least two party members. In very large concerns or well organized offices, the ideal is to form party branches in every department of the same establishment each with only an elected secretary. And all these branches teaming up to form the main party branch in the office with only an elected secretary convener to connect them with the general secretary of the party. There shall be no Serinkin Zongos. The party shall henceforth deal directly with tribal heads of the communities concerned. Moslem and Christian, non-Christian and non-Moslem should also form party branches wherever they congregate.[54]

[54]*Evening News*, Oct. 26, 1961.

The result of all these activities has been to proliferate party branches into more but smaller units. Some large and powerful branches have been broken up by the organization of more atomistic smaller ones.

The auxiliary and subordinate arms of the party may be categorized as follows:

1. *Ideological and youth organizations.* These include the National Association of Socialist Students' Organizations, the Young Pioneers, the CPP Study Groups, the League of Ghana Patriots, and the Kwame Nkrumah Ideological Institute at Winneba. Recently, as a consequence of the rise in autonomy within the party of the militant left, the NASSO and the CPP Study Groups have been abolished.[55] Since then, the main burden of political action has devolved upon the Young Pioneers and the Kwame Nkrumah Ideological Institute. Because of the extraordinary importance assigned to ideological training, seminars and discussion sessions are held at the school to train youth leaders and Young Pioneer activists who return periodically for refresher courses. Moreover, Young Pioneer branches are being set up in all the schools.[56] Interestingly enough, there is considerable opposition to the Young Pioneers not only from teachers and headmasters, but from the students as well; this is clear evidence that more intensive ideological work is necessary. As the party sees it, the requirement is not simply indoctrination, but rather the political socialization of a whole new generation upon which will stand or fall the program of the CPP.

2. *Trade unions and cooperatives.* Originally the Trades Union Congress was independent of party politics. After a series of splits and maneuvers, it became an integral part of the CPP, and achieved an automatic checkoff system, a revised and more limited branch structure, and a senior position among party auxiliaries. Its president, John Tettegah, became an important party official. The right to strike is contingent on prior negotiation and government approval. The prevailing role of the TUC is perhaps best defined by Nkrumah himself:

> In the United Kingdom, I organized colored workers to combat the exploitation of their labor power. What is more, my whole philosophy is Marxian, a fact which ranges me immediately on the side of any or-

[55]"Other things being equal, the Central Committee considers that the NASSO and the Party Study Groups have done their work and done it very well. They have stirred up great enthusiasm in the field of Party education and their activities have led to the general raising of the standard of enlightenment among the rank and file of the Party. Nevertheless, the time has come when Party education should be carried forward to its final stage—the stage of mass Party education. General Party education must reach the masses at the base." Kwame Nkrumah, *Guide to Party Action* (Accra: Central Commiittee of the CPP, 1962), p. 3.

[56]The headmaster of Achimota College, Daniel Chapman, resisted the establishment of a Young Pioneer branch at Achimota and has resigned his position in order to take a post with the United Nations. The CPP has announced that a powerful Young Pioneer branch will soon be established at Achimota.

> ganization fighting to abolish the exploitation of man by man. I have actively encouraged since the beginning of our struggle, the building of a virile and responsible trade union movement because I believe that it is necessary to give correct leadership to the workers for the great exercise of the industrial and economic reconstruction of our country.
>
> The Government which is formed by the Convention People's Party is a people's Government—indeed a government of the people—free, strong and independent, pursuing a socialist pattern of reconstruction. The interest of workers is therefore well catered for by the State. The trade unions therefore have a different role from that of trade unions in a capitalist society.[57]

In May, 1961, the All-African Trade Union Federation (AATUF), with headquarters in Accra, was formed. It is the answer to international trade-union movements of both Western and Eastern countries: the International Confederation of Free Trade Unions and the World Federation of Trade Unions. The central roles of the TUC and the AATUF as militant instruments of party policy are clear enough.[58]

A key role has also been assigned to the United Ghana Farmers' Council. This organization was founded in 1953, when an earlier group, the Ghana Farmers' Congress (organized in 1950 by G. Ashie-Nikoi after his release from prison along with Nkrumah), bolted to the opposition. It also replaced older organizations of farmers, such as the Asante Farmers' Union, whose chief farmer and secretary had both joined the National Liberation Movement. Subsequently, the National Cooperative Council was established to supervise the cooperative movement. The United Ghana Farmers' Council was then given the main responsibility for running the cooperatives, as well as the new state farms that are being established under Israeli auspices. Martin Appiah Danquah was appointed general secretary of the United Ghana Farmers' Council, ambassador extraordinary and minister plenipotentiary, and chairman of the National Cooperative Council. Like the TUC, the United Ghana Farmers' Council is entrusted with the realization of important state objectives: "The United Ghana Farmers' Council has shown in many ways that it can be relied upon by the state to pursue vigorously the duties set before it."[59] And, like the AATUF, it has a Pan-African equivalent, the All-African Union of Farmers.

[57]*Speech by Osagyefo Dr. Kwame Nkrumah, President of the Republic of Ghana at the Opening of the First Biennial Conference of the Ghana TUC at Kumasi, 26th March, 1962* (Accra: Government Printer, 1962). See also Kwame Nkrumah, *Towards Colonial Freedom* (London: Heinemann, 1962), a pamphlet written in 1947 but not published until 1962. Nkrumah claims in the preface that his views have not changed.

[58]Tettega has been made secretary-general of the AATUF.

[59]*Inaugural Address by Osagyefo the President at the Ninth Annual National Delegates Conferences of the United Ghana Farmers' Council, Kumasi, 26th March, 1962* (Accra: Government Printer, 1962).

3. *Women's organizations.* Ghana women have always played an extraordinary part in nationalist politics. This has been manifested by their financial support of the party and by their role in trade boycotts and marketing. Women's organizations have a long traditional history, and include singing and dancing societies, market women's associations, and the like. One of the original members of the Committee on Youth Organizations, Mrs. Hannah Cudjoe, had long been in charge of womens' organizations in the CPP. The National Council of Ghana Women, established in 1960 as an integral part of the party, helps to select candidates for the ten regional parliamentary seats reserved for women, opens party branches within its own organization, and takes over other organizations of women. Just as the Young Pioneers have become the major youth organization (although the Boy Scouts continue to exist, with about 2,000 members), so the NCGW has superseded the YWCA and other women's organizations. Although many of these remain, they are slowly being weakened.

4. *Other organizations.* Other groups, such as the Workers' Brigades, the Central Organization of Sports, and the Ghana Legion, have been brought either directly under the party or into a quasi-official relationship with it. Among these organizations, the Bureau of African Affairs, under the leadership of Michael Dei-Anang, is particularly significant. The Bureau provides a liaison with other political parties in Africa, and helps to train party men from other countries at the Winneba Ideological School. It has been instrumental in setting up various Pan-African conferences, including the Ban the Bomb Conference in 1962. It is increasingly an organ of militant Nkrumaism, and in 1962 took a decisive step. After Nkrumah proposed a joint military command and an African army, navy, and air force, the Bureau rejected nonviolent resistance as the only means of political action against colonialism.

5. *The party press.* The party press is regarded as an instrument of ideology and training. The journalists who hold editorial positions are the most extreme party militants. They are on good terms with the militant left of the AATUF and the TUC, and were key figures in the party Study Groups before the latter were abolished.

Each major arm or auxiliary of the CPP has its own newspaper or journal. The most important papers are still the *Accra Evening News*, the *Ghanaian Times*, and *The Party*, which are controlled by persons at the ideological heart of the party. Recently a militant weekly, *The Spark* (taking its name from Lenin's newspaper, *Iskra*), has appeared. It is edited by Kofi Batsa, who also edits the *Voice of Africa*, organ of the Bureau of African Affairs. The Bureau also publishes pamphlets, and speeches on Pan-Africanism; its director is A. K. Barden, a member of the militant left. The TUC publishes *Labour* under the editorship of another militant socialist, J. P. Addei. An international journal, the *African*

Worker, is published in French and English by the AATUF. The *Cooperator* has already been mentioned.

There is at present no genuine opposition paper in Ghana, but the *Daily Graphic* has the distinction of not being a party newspaper. Formerly part of the *Daily Mirror* chain, it is now published by the Graphic Trust in Ghana. A former opposition paper, the *Ashanti Pioneer*, was made subject to censorship and eventually capitulated to the government.

Changes in Party Structure

A party reorganization that took place after 1959 was itself a product of the CPP's new role as a party of solidarity. In 1959 a new party structure was designed to consolidate changes in the party and articulate the goals of the new society. Not only was the party to protect the "revolution," but it was to create African socialism, establish the welfare state, and, through political means, bring about the economic and social reconstruction of the country. Under the new party structure, which came into effect simultaneously with the new constitution establishing the Republic of Ghana, Nkrumah became the first general secretary of the CPP. The Trades Union Congress, the United Ghana Farmers' Council, and the Cooperative Movement were given representation in the national executive with the right to send a specified number of delegates each to national delegates' conferences.

Under the new structure, the party modified its national secretariat. The secretariat presently consists of a general secretary, an administrative secretary, and a director of ideological studies; bureaus of information and publicity, organization, African and international affairs, local government, functions, education and anticorruption, national propaganda, finances, membership, youth, and women's organizations; a bureau for trade unions, cooperatives, and farmers; and a bureau of disciplinary control. The national secretariat, under the control of the Central Committee, is the key administrative organ of the party, linked closely with branches, constituencies, and regional executive committees and secretariats. Regional secretariat staff members are appointed by the Central Committee, and the broad mandate for the national Executive Committee of the Central Committee derives from the annual delegates' conference. Noticeable in the new national secretariat is the strong emphasis upon discipline, organization, and ideology.[60]

The branch executive committee remains the party's key organizational unit, and party branches are found in every village, ward, and rural area. Three key posts in the CPP are those of the secretary-general of the

[60]For a full discussion of the new structure, see Tawia Adamafio, "The New Party Structure," *The Party*, I (September 1960), 9–10.

TUC, the general secretary of the United Ghana Farmers' Council, and the general secretary of the party. Hence a dual organization prevails: the party branch with its executive, the constituency, and the regional organization with its executive and secretariat reach out into each area; the functional organizations, particularly union locals and cooperative associations, cut across the geographically based party units. In addition, youth organizations, women's organizations, and others are associated with their own ideological units in schools and party branches, both functional and geographical.

What effects did the new structure have upon the party? There are several that are worth particular mention. By elevating the functional organizations, the party created a dualism that was to have almost disastrous results. Excessive pressure brought to bear on local branches and regional groups, which had become extremely localized, parochialized, and even oppositionist, resulted in a disenchantment with the party in local areas. The functional groups, which provided a new power base against the constituency and local organizations, stimulated competition between the leaders of the functional and ideological groups and those of the constituency organizations. At the same time conflict was intensified between ethnic and regional branches, on the one hand, and newer and centrally controlled functional groups on the other. Such a situation would be difficult enough under ordinary circumstances, where the desire of local and regional groups to enlarge their autonomy creates antagonism between them and the central party organization. In Ghana it resulted in tension between functional and other party groups, between ethnic and national loyalties, and between secretariat and field organizations, all within the party itself.

Intrigue, sycophancy, and mistrust at the center, and cynicism in the rural areas, became more common. In 1961 Nkrumah tried first to eliminate the corrosion within the party by attacking the right wing, which had been the most opportunistic and around which had swirled rumors of "deals," "negotiations," and corruption.[61] All party officials, ministers, and ministerial secretaries were required to submit their financial records to a committee, listing houses, cars, and land owned by them.[62] The resignations of K. A. Gbedemah, Kojo Botsio, E. Ayeh-Kumi, E. D. Dadson, W. A. Wiafe, and S. W. Yeboah were demanded. Botsio was read out of the party.[63] Gbedemah fled the country. Others have come back

[61]See the Dawn Speech, *Broadcast to the Nation* (Accra: Ghana Information Services, 1961).

[62]*Statement by the President Concerning Properties and Business Connections of Ministers and Ministerial Secretaries* (Accra: Government Printer, 1961). The statement directed that no minister or ministerial secretary should own more than two houses with a combined value of £20,000, more than two motor cars, and plots of land in addition to the first category with a total value above £500.

[63]He has now been reinstated and is at present Ghana's foreign minister.

to positions of authority. Krobo Edusei was removed from office for a while and others were forced to relinquish property. In effect, this was a "purge" of the right wing. The militant left was jubilant. The party press singled out former old-guard party leaders for particular abuse.

After the purge, Nkrumah designated as the integral parts of the party the Trades Union Congress, the United Ghana Farmers' Council, the National Council of Ghana Women, the Ghana Young Pioneers, and the Cooperative Movement:

> All these bodies have their various functions in the particular aspect of our national life in which they operate, but there is one strain running through all of them, which is basic and fundamental, namely, the membership of the Convention People's Party. Whatever they do the character of the Convention People's Party must be clearly manifested for all to see. They all have a single guiding light, the guiding light of our Party ideology. This light must constantly be kept bright and full of luster and must on no account be allowed to dim, for, as soon as this happens, we are bound to find ourselves in difficulties.

The emphasis was to be on discipline:

> Why shouldn't the workers of the State, who are composed mainly of the laborer group, be put into uniform? It would give them an added incentive to serve the State, a reason to feel proud of their service and a sense of belonging. They can be employed on various national jobs by the State Construction Corporation. This will eliminate the present element of idleness which takes place when a particular job is completed and the workers await assignment of another job.
>
> The Asafo Companies also, the members of which are almost all members of the Party individually, will come within this category. They should be properly uniformed and perform their traditional role in a modern manner.
>
> Another group of workers whom we now call "Watchmen" will have a new orientation and come under this category. And why shouldn't they also be dressed in a smart uniform and be renamed "Civil Guards"?
>
> All this will lead to one useful result–discipline. The whole nation from the President downwards will form one regiment of disciplined citizens.[64]

This, then, was to be the basis for building a new social order. The general secretary of the party was Tawia Adamafio, also a minister plenipotentiary and ambassador extraordinary. At the same time, the "cult of personality" was deliberately encouraged. No other leader had a public building or street named after him except Nkrumah. There were the Kwame Nkrumah leaders' schools, the Kwame Nkrumah state farms, Kwame Nkrumah Avenue in Accra, the Kwame Nkrumah University in

[64]Nkrumah, *Guide to Party Action*, pp. 7–8.

Kumasi, and so forth. Hymns were sung in praise of Nkrumah, and Nkrumaism became the philosophy of the day.

This emphasis was a response to the various conflicts within the senior ranks of the party. Disciplining the complex party formations which had been built up, and which operated in local areas, both rural and urban, as well as at the center, required increasing obedience to Nkrumah himself. Coordination and control became a major problem. Indeed, the more powerful the auxiliary, the greater the momentum it acquired within the party, and the more dangerous it was to the party as a whole. There were references to Nkrumah as "the Old Man," and sidelong looks for a successor. Adamafio was a possibility. So was Tettegah, the young and able trade-union leader. But there was no effective party opposition, for virtually all the dissidents were in jail or out of the country. Opposition could come only from within the party itself. Moreover, "foreigners" began to play a role; refugees from other parts of Africa, particularly South Africa, moved into party circles in growing numbers. The result was confusion.

The socialist militants, so clearly in the ascendancy, pressed for greater autonomy and strength within the party. The party press became more and more extreme. When lower echelons in the party objected, as in the Sekondi-Takoradi strikes of 1961, party discipline was immediately imposed.[65] Harsh government actions and an inadequately presented, extremely unpopular budget also spurred on the efforts of the socialist militants to reorganize the society. Non-Ghanaians, such as Abdoulaye Diallo, Guinea's minister to Ghana, represented a more austere and pure form of Marxism beside which the Ghanaian form seemed shabby and confused; this contrast helped to encourage the socialist militants.

With the right wing effectively downgraded, ideological as well as personal differences emerged between two groups of socialist militants. One group might be called the *socialist puritans*; the other, *socialist opportunists*. The first was, on the whole, a studious and sincere group, not in the public eye, whose members were particularly interested in the study of Marxism and of Neo-Marxist thought. The second group consisted of slogan manipulators and emotional socialists in journalistic and party positions which brought their names before the public. Perhaps the largest group among the socialist militants fell between these two groups. But it was the socialist opportunists who contributed the most to building up Nkrumah, proclaiming their loyalty to him and arousing bitterness and cynicism in the party ranks. And it was they who established deifica-

[65]The strikes in the Sekondi-Takoradi area and elsewhere were a protest not only against government policy, but also against TUC leadership. Several of those put in jail under preventive detention were junior trade-union leaders, loyal party members who resented their own senior officials.

tion oaths for the Young Pioneers, according to which "Nkrumah will never die." Indeed, as cynicism within the party and among the public grew, as widespread rumblings from the constituency parties began to be heard, and as the ranks of the quietly disaffected expanded both inside and outside the party, a new emphasis on Nkrumaism was offered to the public.

Party Ideology

A rather bitter, though socialist, ex-CPP adherent who had quarreled with Nkrumah has described the ideology of the party as "Nkrumaism, the highest stage of opportunism." This is an unfair description, except in one sense. Nkrumaism is not so much a consistent ideology or dogma as it is a search for perspective in the African revolution, and for a sense of destiny and purpose by means of which attention will be focused on the most important and significant events within Ghana and abroad. That it leaves much to be desired as an ideology is perhaps its greatest advantage, for pragmatism thus remains a feature of the new ideological look.

The easiest way to describe Nkrumaism is perhaps through examples. In a recent issue of the *Co-operator* there is a discussion of farm cooperatives and what they mean. After describing the main types—service cooperatives, cooperative tenant farming societies, joint farming societies, and collective farms—the article concludes:

> Obviously each country must adopt the form or forms which are best suited to its environment, national or local customs and character. Farmers may find that a blend of types may be best suited or they may choose a particular form and adapt it to the local conditions. This should not affect the general nature of Co-operative Farming, which is that those who participate are rewarded in proportion to the amount of work they put in.[66]

Again, the secretary of the CPP Bureau of Information and Publicity, O. B. Amankwah, argued that Nkrumaism looks on scientific socialism as the "basis for correcting the inequitable distribution of food, shelter and clothing—the basic necessities of life which are the legitimate right of every human being." Nkrumaism is anticapitalist; it postulates the "vigorous but systematic elimination of capitalism from society taking into account the prevailing situation in a given country." It is based on the "projection of the African personality which is one of the tenets of Pan-Africanism," and its philosophy is "embodied in the life and teachings of Kwame Nkrumah."[67]

[66] *Co-operator*, I, No. 15 (September 1961).
[67] O. B. Amankwah, "What Is Nkrumaism?" *The Party*, I (September 1960), 12.

Through the CPP Study Groups, the NASSO, the Winneba Ideological School (now the Nkrumah Institute), and, more recently, the organizations of branch chairmen and Young Pioneers, Nkrumaism has been strongly urged on the people. Preceding a series of articles on Nkrumaism, this message appeared in the *Evening News*:

> Nkrumah is our Messiah. Whoever sees his brother's need and supplies it—not by casting off the discarded garment to him—but by giving him a moral and spiritual standard by which he shall live; that is the Messiah, the Saviour, the Christ.
>
> From time to time, individuals have caught glimpses of the Christ or the true idea of God, good. Long before Jesus, were men like Moses, Joshua, Elisha, etc. who demonstrated the true idea of sonship. This demonstration by no means ended with Jesus. Why! Karl Marx demonstrated the Christ, and so did Lenin of U.S.S.R., Ghandi of India, Moa [*sic*] of China and in our midst is Kwame Nkrumah.
>
> When our history is recorded the man Kwame Nkrumah will be written of as the liberator, the Messiah, the Christ of our day, whose great love for mankind wrought changes in Ghana, in Africa, and in the world at large.[68]

Couched in spiritual language, this is clearly an effort to personalize morality, and to provide a sense of social mission in both moral and political terms. An example may be found in the series on Nkrumaism offered by the *Evening News*: "Nkrumaism is the quest for African unity and independence, a way of life that ensures security, abundance and prosperity for all through brotherly love one for another based on work and happiness not for a few but for all." That is the theme. Afterward come the variations.

> Nkrumaism will introduce a society in which the exploitation of man by man has been abolished forever. A society in which the wealth and natural resources of the land belong to the people; a society in which there is no unemployment, a society in which there is no existence of economic crisis, a society where the standard of living of every individual citizen is appreciably high, a society that recognizes the creative ability of her citizens and pays them according to their production and standard of work, a society where neither tribalism nor race discrimination exist.[69]

In essence, this is a literature of morality. That there are doubters only increases the intensity and, at times, the shrillness of the CPP ideological drive. It ought not to be read in terms of its precision, its immediate content, or its prescriptive quality. Just as it venerates political good it castigates political evil, and particularly evildoers. The doubters and the antagonists are vilified and excoriated. For example, a once respected

[68]October 14, 1961.
[69]October 23, 1961.

opposition leader who had fled to Togo, a former associate of K. A. Busia's, was named in the press as follows:

> WANTED! OBETSEBI LAMPTEY [in banner headlines]! Description: Criminal, Scoundrel, Assassin, Coward, Nincompoop, Swindler and Desperate Political Lunatic!
>
> Bloodthirsty, Obdurate Fiend, Heartless Looking, Addicted to the Opium of Tribalism, Vain Boasting and often suffering from fits of mad yelling and screaming and using his fists on innocent people.
>
> REWARD: Any information leading to his immediate capture will be amply rewarded. Must be captured alive. Finder: hundred guineas.[70]

In another fall from grace, the once powerful minister of finance, K. A. Gbedemah, was dropped from his post; the bill of particulars included alleged irregularities in financial matters. The party press called him a "bloated vain frog." "We have a mission," the abusive article went on. "By your deeds you have given abundant evidence that you have no sympathy with the Party's missionary faith. And that is why you have been thrown out of the Party's high councils and indeed the Party itself if you continue to behave in the way you are doing at this moment."[71] Gbedemah found it expedient to leave the country to avoid possible imprisonment under preventive detention.

Exhortation, missionary work, equalitarianism, opportunism, Pan-Africanism—these are all key aspects of Nkrumaism. In short, it is a modern religious crusade, using political forms of religion.[72] Its critics complain about its fulsomeness, its inconsistency, and the poverty of its ideology. All these criticisms may be turned around. The fulsomeness of Nkrumaism must be taken as a language of morality and religion. Its inconsistency is a token of its lack of dogma and strictness. Its preaching, unlike the narrow dogmatism of modern Marxism-Leninism, does not drastically narrow the range of alternatives open to political leaders as they seek solutions to their problems. Its ideology is symbolic rather than precise, expressing commitment to honesty, to work, and to the community.

The language of Nkrumaism, although it grates on foreign ears, is perhaps less foreign than we may think. If one were to go back to the speeches from the pulpit, the exhortations by missionaries, the extravagant claims for Christian miracles, one would find a direct link between the religious language employed for a hundred years along the coast in Ghana, and the quasi-religious language of Nkrumaism today. Nor is the

[70] *Evening News*, Oct. 6, 1961. Lamptey returned secretly to Ghana and was arrested on preventive detention, and is presently in prison.

[71] *Ibid.*, Oct. 2, 1961.

[72] See my article, "Political Religion in the New Nations," in Clifford Geertz, ed., *Old Societies and New States* (New York: The Free Press, 1963). [Reprinted in this volume.]

language purely emotional. In part it is directed at stamping out widespread corruption, both in the local organizations of the party and at the highest levels. Although there were obviously many reasons for his dismissal, Gbedemah was removed from his post because of alleged irregularities. The same reason was given for the dismissal of Kojo Botsio, the long-time confidant of Nkrumah's. It was also the charge against Krobo Edusei. In his famous "dawn" broadcast, Nkrumah pointed to the deeper issue, the cynicism that was emerging in the party:

> Let me turn to some other causes which I consider plague Ghanaian society generally and militate against undisturbed progress. A great deal of rumor-mongering goes on all over the country. "Berko said that the Odikro informed Asamani that the Ohene said he paid a sum of money to a party official to become a paramount chief."
>
> "Kojo said that Mensah told him that Kweku took a bribe." "Abina stated that Edua said that Esi uses her relations with Kweku to get contracts through the District Commissioner with the support of the Regional Commissioner and the blessing of a minister in Accra."
>
> So, day after day, night after night, all types and manner of wild allegations and rumors are circulated and they are always well sprinkled with: They say, They say . . .[73]

It is against the background of cynicism, private self-seeking, and local plunder that the lofty expressions of political morality must be viewed. Moreover, such an ideology is capable of adapting to the vast changes in the government now under way, which have transformed the role of the president; he has become a ritualized leader, a "president-monarch" in whom the trappings of monarchy and the executive authority of the supreme party leader were merged. Nkrumaism is the projection of the African personality:

> The African personality to Nkrumah does not mean the policy of separatism or racial discrimination. Such ideas are a direct contradiction to the principles of communalism which is basic to African life. The projection of an African personality calls for a total integration of all that is best in Africa into all that is best from outside Africa. It demands a new way of thinking and a breakaway from former colonial dogmas under which we have existed so long. Having succeeded in decolonizing ourselves and gaining our sovereignty we have also to dementalize ourselves of the colonial mentality which shut our eyes against self-respect and dignity and took away from us a sense of objectivity and national pride.[74]

Finally, the meaning of Nkrumaism in economic and political terms, and its value to the CPP, have been stated in the party's program: "This program has been formulated in the conviction that Socialism implies

[73]Nkrumah, *Broadcast to the Nation.*

[74]Stephen Dzirasa, *The Political Thought of Dr. Kwame Nkrumah* (Accra: Guinea Press, 1962), p. 21.

central planning in order to ensure that the entire resources of the State, both human and material, are employed in the best interests of all the people." Five sectors of the economy are recognized: (1) state enterprises; (2) enterprises owned by foreign and private interests; (3) enterprises jointly owned by the state and foreign private interests; (4) cooperatives; and (5) small-scale Ghanaian private enterprises.[75]

If the philosophy of Nkrumaism is by no means organized or programmatic, it is clearly a language of socialism, progress, and development. Party and state are one. Despite internal conflicts the party of solidarity has shown the same buoyancy and optimism that characterized the social militants. By mid-1962 Ghana seemed well on the road toward building a popular one-party socialist state. In the context of national struggle, Pan-Africanist successes, and anti-imperialism, closer links were sought with socialist countries. The National Council of Ghana Women became associated with the Union of Mali Women and the Union of Senegalese Women, and, at the Conakry Conference of 1961, established links with the Women's International Democratic Federation Affiliates. The All-African Trade Union Federation secretariat consists of eight members, seven of them supported by the World Federation of Trade Unions. The Ghana Cooperative Movement, through the National Cooperative Council, maintains affiliations with cooperative organizations in the Soviet Union, the German Democratic Republic, Poland, Yugoslavia, Israel, Hungary, and Czechoslovakia. The council is a member of the International Federation of Agricultural Producers. All these are Communist-dominated international bodies.

Finally, on July 2, 1962, the *Evening News* reported: "This morning at the State House, Accra, the Nation's Founder and Fount of Honor, His High Dedication Osagyefo the President was presented with the 1961 Lenin Peace Prize." In the capitals of the West as well as in Ghana itself, observers wondered where it would end.

THE NEW FACTIONALISM

"The Convention People's Party is a powerful force, more powerful, indeed, than anything that has yet appeared in the history of Ghana. It is the uniting force that guides and pilots the nation, and is the nerve center of the positive operations in the struggle for African irredentism. Its supremacy cannot be challenged."[76]

On August 1, 1962, when Nkrumah was returning from talks with President Maurice Yameogo of Upper Volta, a bomb was thrown at him

[75] *For Work and Happiness*, Program of the Convention People's Party (Accra: Government Printer, 1962).

[76] Kwame Nkrumah, "What the Party Stands For," *The Party*, I, No. 1 (1960).

in the northern Ghanaian village of Kulungugu. Several people were killed and Nkrumah was injured. Shortly afterward, Tawia Adamafio, then minister of information and broadcasting, Ako Adjei, minister of foreign affairs, and several party leaders, Boi Doku, former propaganda secretary of the CPP, and Kofi Crabbe, were put in jail under preventive detention. Curfew was immediately established and road blocks were set up along roads leading into Accra.

Ghana was politically restless. Everyone wondered what would be the next step. Anti-CPP groups, consisting of exiles from the United Party and other defeated organizations, had been forming in Togoland. The Ghana Democratic Party under the leadership of John Alex-Hamah, formerly a regional ideological secretary in the TUC, had been established in London with West African headquarters in Nigeria. Alex-Hamah, who had been sent to Peking, Leipzig, and Moscow to get special training, broke with the TUC upon his return from one of his visits, remaining in London to organize anti-CPP students before going on to Nigeria. Gbedemah, still abroad, was active in building an anti-Ghanaian coalition, and hoped to gain support for his policies from American and British authorities.

Inside the party, those appointed to high political positions by Adamafio were quiet. No one was quite sure who was a socialist puritan and who a socialist opportunist. N. A. Welbeck, long a loyal supporter of Nkrumah's (he had been under a cloud for failures in two important posts, first as Ghana's minister to Guinea and then as Ghana's ambassador to the Congo during the period of the Lumumba crisis), was made acting general secretary and then executive secretary. Krobo Edusei came back as minister of agriculture, and Kofi Baako, the originator of Nkrumaism, became minister of defense. Kojo Botsio returned as foreign Minister.

More bombs were thrown, this time at a demonstration of public thanks that Nkrumah had not been killed in the August episode. An additional wall was put up around the President's residence, Flagstaff House. Rarely did the President venture forth from his home. In a speech to the Assembly, he declared:

> We must tighten our ranks ever closer. We must work as an organic whole, not only to hold our own against the onslaughts of those who desire our downfall, but to further that second revolution on which we embarked when we took the road of independent nationhood. . . . For this a revolutionary outlook is necessary in our thinking and actions which will engender absolute loyalty, absolute honesty, and absolute sincerity. The country must be cleaned forever of corruption and nepotism. . . . The security of the State is not a matter for the police alone. It is the concern of every one of us. With vigilance on the part of us all, it should be impossible for anyone to set up within the Party, cells which are inimical to the safety and the welfare of our nation and our people.[77]

[77] *Ghanaian Times*, October 3, 1962.

There exists today a new quiet in Ghana. The police are much in evidence. A guard stands behind the statue of the President in front of Parliament House. Police lines have been set up outside Flagstaff House. Yet it is the old group that is in power, however uneasily. Welbeck's links have always been with the constituency organizations of the party and the local branches, where he knew everyone. For the time being the party is trying to repair the organizational damage that resulted from the strengthening of the functional auxiliaries. John Tettegah, picked up by the police for questioning and newly chastened, is head of the AATUF; in that post he is more remote from direct contact with the rank and file of the TUC. Not only are the moderates in power and the militants under a cloud, but the Soviet Cultural Center has been closed. A new emphasis is being placed on *African* socialism by several leaders: "Nkrumah is like a chief. His linguists are the key members of the Cabinet and the Party."

The Deputy Minister of Foreign Affairs put it another way. African politics remain in the context of clan and chief. Chieftaincy is the essence of the African personality. Duty is to the state because the state is the family and the clan, and any individual derives from a clan. African socialism implies that use rights may be allocated, but property belongs to the state as in traditional land tenure. There is personal property and there is property of the society. Anyone who uses the property of the society must pay for the privilege. One should not enrich one's personal property from excessive use of state property. Hence the high taxes on expatriate firms. If personal property becomes excessive it sets people apart from one another, destroys the basic unity of African life, and violates custom. Elections are simply a way of emphasizing that unity and of according recognition to a chief. Western elections are different.[78]

Hence there is a renewed effort to give meaning to the term "African socialism." There is greater caution in dealing with the Soviet Union. The socialist opportunists were the ones who were jailed, and the lesson is not lost on the socialist puritans. The CPP is undergoing a stocktaking and realignment of factions. The socialist puritans play an important role in Pan-African affairs and the press. They scrutinize the civil servants, the African socialists, the expatriates, and the rest.

CONCLUSION

We have seen a series of radical transformations in the life of political parties in Ghana. Political factions in the early days of nationalist activity helped stimulate political awareness and participation. As these factions

[78]Interviews with the Reverend Stephen Dzirasa in December 1962.

attempted to coalesce, major groupings appeared—the progressive chiefs and the progressive constitutionalists. Gradually the latter helped to form the first parties of representation. The Convention People's Party, itself a mixture of faction, party, and movement, developed steadily toward the latter, and attempted to blend party, state, and society in a single community, organically tied together through the various instruments of the party and sharing in a common loyalty to Nkrumah.

The opposition parties of representation disappeared. Opposition appeared within the CPP: constituency organization against auxiliary, old guard against young militant, socialist puritan against right-wing and socialist opportunist. Around the President politics swirled as in the court of a king. Extravagant titles and praise disguised the intrigue. Disenchantment became more widespread.

Perhaps the wheel has come full circle. The party is not the monolithic organization it has often been portrayed. The politics of faction, which predate political parties in Ghana, are now inside the CPP. Nor is tradition destroyed. Chiefs will never recover their position, but perhaps chieftaincy already has. Clearly Nkrumah is more than ever like a chief. The drums beat when he makes his appearance; libation is poured. These are not empty symbols. The traditionalization of authority has begun. Under the socialist slogans are the thousands of practical translations that ordinary people make in ordinary ways in terms familiar and comfortable. It is with these ordinary people and their ideas that the CPP and its leadership must make their peace.

POSTSCRIPT

On December 31, 1963, Nkrumah announced that a constitutional referendum would be held which would formally make Ghana a one-party state and give the President the right to dismiss judges of the Supreme Court and the High Court at any time. The news followed in the wake of the trial in which Ako Adjei and Tawiah Adamafio were acquitted of the charges of conspiring to commit treason. (Two other men were sentenced to death.) The acquitted were retained in custody. Sir Arku Korsah, the chief justice (once acting governor-general of Ghana), and the other judges were dismissed. In explaining the dismissal, Nkrumah said:

> The Judges of the special court by their failure to take me into their confidence meant to create discontent and terror throughout the country. You, the people of Ghana, have made me the conscience of the nation. My duty is not only to govern but to ease the conscience of the people by giving them peace of mind and tranquility. A nation cannot tolerate a

> dishonest and corrupt judiciary. I want to assure you all that there is the possibility of a retrial of the persons involved in this particular case, depending on the results of certain investigations now in progress.

Accordingly, the desired amendments to the constitution would "invest the President with 'power in his discretion to remove a Judge of the Supreme Court or a Judge of the High Court at any time for reasons which appear to him sufficient.'" As well to ensure a wider unity in the country, the amendments would also provide that "in conformity with the interests, welfare, and aspirations of the people and to 'develop the organizational initiative and political activity of the people, there shall be one national party in Ghana.' This party would be the 'vanguard of our people in their struggle to build a socialist society and the leading core of all organizations of the people.'"[79] For such changes Nkrumah wanted an unequivocal mandate for what is now called Marxist-Nkrumaism, to allow the party to "combat" all forms of "hostile ideology and propaganda emanating from Western imperialist countries, and at all times expose the total hollowness, corrupting influence, and decadent nature of capitalist-imperialist culture." In its broadest terms, then, the referendum was to be ideological: Marxist-Nkrumaism versus capitalist-imperialism.

The mass media were utilized to the fullest extent to mobilize a huge affirmative vote. Owners of motor vehicles were directed to report to the regional commissioner's office, or some other appropriate place, to obtain "Vote Yes on the Referendum" stickers to display on their automobiles. The result of the referendum was overwhelmingly in favor of the single-party state, with 2,773,920 affirmative and 2,454 negative votes;[80] there were charges that in several areas the number of "Yes" votes exceeded the number of voters. The poll itself included 95 per cent of the eligible voters.

Shortly thereafter, amid anti-American rioting (which ended with the expulsion of several American staff members of the university, as well as the temporary detention of others), it was announced that for "pur-

[79] *Times* (London), January 1, 1964.

[80] The over-all results of the national referendum in each of the eight regions of the country and the Accra District were officially given as follows:

	Yes	*No*
Upper Region	325,859	186
Northern Region	201,781	30
Brong-Ahafo	368,369	—
Ashanti Region	425,022	—
Western Region	217,947	—
Central Region	441,041	—
Eastern Region	390,938	—
Volta Region	261,393	677
Accra District	141,570	1,559

poses of our revolution, the hallmark of good conduct in our universities should be close identification with the spirit and objects of the Party." The party suggested that the universities be "brought to heel."[81] At the same time a new seven-year plan was announced and five administrative committees were set up, the most important being a national planning committee, which is to be responsible for over-all planning. There will also be a state planning committee under the chairmanship of the President.

These events, representing a further stage in the development of political life in Ghana, are worthy of serious attention because they show the emergence of two major tendencies which until now have been latent in the political situation. The first of these involves the militant Left; the second, the administrative structure.

The militant Left, until now, derived its power largely from Nkrumah himself. Its adherents were concentrated mainly in the press, the Bureau of African Affairs, and, to some extent, the Young Pioneers. These groups have been given a much more central role in the party. In an effort to bypass the political generation that emerged just after independence—it might be called the Adamafio generation—the younger and more militant Left has acquired a mass following. What has emerged is a pattern of party control of the youth, the future cadres of Ghanaians. Despite the obvious reluctance of headmasters and teachers to attach much importance to the militant Left and the Young Pioneers, a strong effort will be made to build loyalty and conformity through the school system. The same reasoning guided the effort to take over the university (which has remained largely anti-CPP). Dubious about the brand of knowledge represented by the university, the socialist puritans hold as their ideal a working university with a much stronger emphasis on technical subjects and with humanistic subjects linked closely to the building of Ghanaian socialism. The socialist puritans will attempt to build a new party through the Young Pioneers, whose "inspiration" comes from a 1948 comment by Nkrumah: "Place the young at the head of the awakened masses. You do not know what strength, what magic influence the voice of the young have on the crowd. You will find in them apostles of the new social order. But youth lives on movement, grows great by example and emulation. Speak to them of country, of glory, of great Memories."

Equally important is the new administrative structure, which will downgrade the largely hostile and increasingly opportunistic civil service. What began as a career service in the British pattern has long been regarded by the socialist puritans as a stumbling block to the achievement of socialism. Well educated and, in living habits, residence, and traditions very much in the British expatriate tradition, the civil servants have always taken a rather dim view of the CPP. Yet their standards of work

[81] *Ghanaian Times*, February 6, 1964.

and efficiency have been crucial to carrying out government policies. Now they are under direct attack. As the *Evening News* put it, the "appointment of anti-Party, anti-Socialist rascals on the basis of bourgeois qualifications alone leaves open the possibilities of creating so many agents of neo-colonialism in a State administration."[82] Calling civil servants "intellectual spivs" and the Civil Service Commission "semi-colonial," the party will establish planning bodies in the President's office which will become, along with the Ghana Bank, the critical administrative organs of the state.

Youth and administration, then, are the key concerns of the new Ghana. Party criticism will be allowed. Parliament will continue as a forum of debate. The Ghana flag will be the CPP flag with a black star added to it. The party is the guardian of the state. As Nkrumah's speech after the referendum made clear, the

> Party is the rallying point of our political activity. Without the Party there would be no force through which to focus the needs and desires of the people. The Convention People's Party is this force. The Party, therefore, is the hard core of those who are so dedicated to its ideology and program, that they make their membership the most serious business of their lives. The Party is nothing but the vanguard of the people, the active organ of the people, working at all times in the service of the people.
>
> All of us are now one in the acceptance of a One-Party State. Our task is to plan for progress in the interests of the whole people. To carry out this work of service to the people, the Party needs the assistance of everybody, even those who are not members. . . .
>
> As long as we carry out these obligations, we can rest assured that we are doing the right thing and that no one can interfere with us. For we shall be interpreting the constitutional rights and duties vested in us as the source of power and the guardian of the State.[83]

This most recent stage in the evolution of the Convention People's Party is in some respects the most important of the long series of developments described in this essay. Whether or not the socialist puritans will succeed in transforming the political style of Ghanaian political life remains to be seen. One thing is clear. The alternatives in Ghana are rapidly shrinking. The billiard game of politics is being played on a table that constantly grows smaller. Ghana has been steadily using up her supply of political capital. Punishing her friends, she has chosen a lonely course. The job of building a new Ghana will now be more difficult. Even the party anticipates that it will operate in an atmosphere of suspicion

[82]See the *Evening News*, February 4, 1964, for a discussion of changes in the Civil Service Commission.

[83]*Ibid.*

and fear. "The Party must establish as a matter of urgency an anti-Rumor Squad to augment the Security Machinery of the Nation," says the referendum commentary in the *Evening News*. "Ghana lives. Osagyefo, the Generalissimo and Conqueror of Imperialism is determined with the Party to lead our people to Socialism and the rumor-mongers will be ashamed of themselves. Listen to the Leader's word this morning as he met with high Party officials: 'We are not joking. We are moving forward.' "[84]

[84] *Ibid.*

Political Religion in the New Nations

I

Today it is virtually impossible to read a scholarly journal in the social sciences without somewhere encountering the terms "development," "modernization," "industrialization," or "Westernization." The meanings of these words ordinarily overlap, but they do share two main emphases. One is that the poorer nations are interested in increasing their wealth by enlarging their own productive capacities. A second, related to the first, involves increasing differentiation and complexity in available roles in developing societies.

An increase in productive capacities can proceed along several lines, of which industrialization is the most striking. Recognized models for successful industrialization are Japan, which became a traditionalistic society adapted to an economy based on industrial enterprise, the Soviet Union, which achieved the same goal swiftly by drastically altering the pre-existing social framework, and the Western complex of nations, where the process occurred more or less piecemeal and over a long period of time. Much scholarly enterprise has gone into efforts to determine the relevance of these experiences for the new nations.

I would like to record my indebtedness to the Institute of Industrial Relations and the Comparative Development Group of the University of California, Berkeley, for their assistance and support while writing this paper. I would also like to thank Professor Neil J. Smelser for reading and commenting on the manuscript. The original stimulus in developing these ideas came from my colleagues on the Committee for the Comparative Study of New Nations at the University of Chicago, particularly Professors Edward Shils, Lloyd Fallers, and Clifford Geertz.

In this enterprise some scholars have attempted to ascertain the character of those roles necessary for industrial societies. Notwithstanding these efforts at understanding, many unsolved and pressing problems remain—the relations between new élites, administrators, and professional men and traditional roles, the social tensions arising from the increase of wealth and the reorganization of roles, and the political problems emanating from these tensions.[1] Taken together, the problems of increased productivity and material welfare, as well as role alteration and integration, identify crucial areas of social tension and political sensitivity around which a large number of other, more secondary political problems arrange themselves.

Efforts to understand these matters have naturally led to the examination of countries where successful modernization has occurred. The political needs and urgencies of new nations has led us to look for historic parallels elsewhere. Examples most commonly referred to are the Soviet Union and the Western democracies. Among the new nations of greatest concern, precisely because they use the language of militant socialism and an almost Leninist reliance on control of the state by a single political party, are those countries that have set out to modernize at a very rapid rate, with particular emphasis on industrialization.

Among these are nations disinclined to handle development problems in terms of democracy, pluralism, and individualism, even though in practice, to draw a clear line between these and other new nations is more difficult than it sounds. States with autocracy, monolithic structure, and community imperatives are not wholly different from the others. All face the complexities resulting from increased productive capacities. All are troubled by the same need to create, fit, adjust, and integrate new role systems.

States with monolithic structure, autocratic government, and a wide range of community imperatives face a particular political problem. This problem stems from the fact that productivity and role integration become primary concerns of government, with the result that all social life becomes politicized in some degree. When social life is heavily politicized, government requires exceptional authority. Such authority tends to be monopolistic. Monopolistic authority needs to replace older belief about other forms of allegiance. New political forms are developed that have the effect of providing for the continuity, meaning, and purpose of an individual's actions. The result is a political doctrine that is in effect a political religion.

The effects of political religion are such that they strengthen authority in the state and weaken the flexibility of the society. Hence it becomes

[1]See Kingsley Davis and Wilbert E. Moore, "Some Principles of Stratification," *American Sociological Review*, X (April, 1945).

difficult to change from autocratic to more democratic and secular patterns of political organization and social belief.

My conclusion is that the combination of autocratic-structural arrangements and reliance on political-religious authority in several of the new nations creates latent instabilities in the development process that, once they become apparent, cannot be resolved either by democracy or totalitarianism but by something different from either. Political "solutions" will take the form of new theocracies partly because of the failure to achieve massive industrialization as a means of raising productivity, and partly so that new and modernized roles can be regulated and integrated by central values expressed as political religion. Older and newer roles will be blended in the context of a modernizing autocracy.

The states with which I am immediately concerned include Guinea, Ghana, Mali, China, and Indonesia. Other examples could be cited, but these are most relevant to our discussion. I should like to show that in the beginning of the modernization process these seem closer to the Soviet or even to the Japanese examples. The important point is, however, that no matter which model they resemble, none will evolve in the western pattern.

Hence we can distinguish between those new nations that accept autocratic solutions to the problem of rapid change from those preferring democratic ones, even if the lines of demarcation are blurred in practice. The new nations indicated above are more autocratic in political structure and authority than Nigeria, India, Senegal, and the Federation of Malaya.

However, even the most autocratic of the new nations differ from the Japanese and Soviet patterns in one very important respect. Few of them can modernize through massive industrialization because only one or two have the potentialities for large-scale industrial enterprise. *Modernization* and *industrialization* are not the same. Failure to recognize their differences is a common weakness among many contemporary political leaders, who see the need to restructure roles primarily as these are functional to the industrialization of society. By viewing productive capacity in industrial terms, they discipline the population to achieve the unachievable. The resulting internal problems are met by stringent political methods increasingly backed up by a new moral code expressed in religious terms.

Thus, while both the Soviet Union and Japan dealt vigorously with the problems of social discontinuities produced through the unevenness by which institutions and values were adapted to the development of industry, they were at least engaged in the actual process of industrializing. Managerial and fiscal changes no doubt worked hardships on prevailing habits of savings and investments and on patterns of organization and control of commercial and social life and, as well, on belief systems, but these were rendered compatible with industrial techniques.

The Soviet Union, beginning in revolution, developed a particularly stringent system of political control that was bolstered in great measure by political beliefs devoted to the worship of science and technology. In Japan, incompatibilities resulting from industrialization resulted in a more gradual harmonizing of discontinuities accomplished by increasing the veneration for the emperor and meanwhile militarizing crucial sections of the community.[2]

These forced-draft methods of modernization are attractive to political leaders in several of the new nations. That is why in some of them virtually all aspects of social life are political. However, under such conditions, the tasks of government become extremely burdensome. Certainly government is more complicated than during the colonial period. Discontinuities appear in the sphere of values and beliefs during a period of modernization, and also appear to threaten government. This is because most of the governments of the new nations are weakly legitimized in the first place. Government is not fitted into that range of cherished objects included in the central values of a changing community. As a result, political leaders tend to use force to retain authority and to instill in the citizens attitudes of respect and devotion to the regime. Such a tendency to use force drives a wedge between government and the people.

What bridges the gap between ruler and ruled, individual and society? Not the actualities of industrialization and a restructuring of social life on an industrial basis. Rather, government puts forward an ideological position that identifies the individual with the state. Modern political leaders come to recognize quickly, however, that no ordinary ideology can prevail for long in the face of obvious discrepancies between theory and practice. A more powerful symbolic force, less rational, although it may include rational ends, seems necessary to them. This force is what I shall call political religion. It feeds its own categorial imperatives into authoritarian political structure on the one hand, and on the other, as we shall indicate, it affects the most fundamental needs of individuals by specifying through the state religion the permissible definitions of individual continuity, meaning, and identity.

In this sense the Soviet and Japanese patterns are different from those of the new nations insofar as they successfully industrialized, and similar mainly insofar as the former used political religion and the latter religion politically to support authority. The Soviet experience is more relevant on the organizational side, since most of the more autocratic new nations use a Leninist party and governmental structure as well as the language of socialism. However, they will become more similar to the Japanese as they develop in a theocratic direction.

[2]Indeed, the "military" solution is one of the characteristic ways in which traditionalism and innovation can be conveniently blended to restructure social life.

Although most of the new nations will not industrialize, they will continue to modernize. Internal markets and resources are too poor and limited in size for rapid industrialization. The new nations are short of capital and skills. Although their infrastructures can be improved to handle commercial and extractive enterprise, it will be a very long time before they can anticipate deriving the major part of their gross national product from industry. Hence, they cannot ultimately use the industrialization process to resolve role discontinuity or increase material welfare, the two key political objectives.

Modernization is possible. At a minimum, modernization means that two conditions are present, neither of which is limited to industrial societies: a social system that can constantly innovate without falling apart, including in innovation beliefs about the acceptability of change and, as well, social structures so differentiated as not to be inflexible; and second, a social framework that can provide the skills and knowledge necessary for living in a technologically advanced world, including the ability to communicate in terms of the technology. These are what I shall regard as the minimal attributes of modernity.

A lack of understanding about modernity, reflected in the belief widely held by leaders of new nations that only industrialization can bring modernity, means that the discontinuities in the modernization process cannot be appraised realistically by many political leaders. This is why I have said that solutions to the problems of weak legitimacy, excessive politicization, and lack of industrial opportunities are sought in the state as a moral and regenerative force, a force that has independent validity and that, requiring discipline and obligation on the part of the citizens, will in turn give them both new dignity and new religion. In this way political religion becomes a form of modernization with or without other forms. It is indeed this aspect of modernization that makes the Soviet Union significant to the developing areas, rather than its successes in industrialization. Moreover, a political religion that can universalize values linked to the widespread desire for better material conditions stimulates modernization by raising material and mundane ends to the level of the sacred.

Having sketched in the nature of the problem, I shall illustrate my remarks first by showing the nature of theocratic rule, and second by indicating how this differs from more secular pluralistic systems, although the latter evolved from theocracy. Finally, I shall indicate the role of political religion in some of the more autocratic countries, particularly as this relates on the one hand to the structure of authority and to the structure of personality needs of individuals on the other.

My point of departure is J. L. Talmon's interesting book *The Origins of Totalitarian Democracy*. More clearly than any other contemporary theorist, Talmon has pointed to certain contrasts and tendencies in Western political practice that I believe have been given fresh relevance in some of the new nations. Specifically, I have in mind Talmon's notion of totalitarian-democratic practices, practices that have a strong appeal in the new nations.

The term "totalitarian democracy" is an invidious one. It stresses a particular theory of popular autocracy implicit in the notion of extreme popular sovereignty. As such, I do not think it entirely appropriate for an analysis of the new nations, and I shall employ a somewhat different set of terms. However, many of the qualities that are found in the notion of totalitarian democracy are also to be found in systems that I shall call "mobilization systems," that is, those systems that are profoundly concerned with transforming the social and spiritual life of a people by rapid and organized methods.[3] Talmon describes the totalitarian-democratic school as one based upon the assumption of a sole and exclusive truth in politics. It may be called political messianism in the sense that it postulates a pre-ordained, harmonious, and perfect scheme of things, to which men are irresistibly drawn, and at which they are bound to arrive. It recognizes ultimately only one plane of existence, the political. It widens the scope of politics to embrace the whole of human existence.[4]

This "school," Talmon claims, began in the French Revolution, although it was implicit at an earlier time in the thought of the French *philosophes.* It forms a continuous tradition of Jacobinism, emerging in modern times around the twin problems of political freedom and social revolution. Modern Jacobins in Africa and Asia have been stimulated by these two problems to create new communities whose political philosophies can be blended with militant organization for a moral purpose. The result is a mystique that has a compassionate concern for men, while at the same time acting in a ruthless manner against the enemies of the "cause."

The contemporary Jacobins of the mobilization systems follow a classical pattern of leadership. They unite practice and philosophy in a conscious synthesis. They are doers who are writers, and shapers who are thinkers. They wish to make their mark not only upon their countries but also in the realm of political ideas. They are practical prophets rather than idealistic reformers.

[3]The typology used here was developed in collaboration with my colleague Carl Rosberg, and first published in our joint article "Nationalism and Models of Political Change in Africa," in *The Political Economy of Contemporary Africa*, ed. D. P. Ray (Washington, D.C.: The National Institute of Social and Behavioral Science, 1959). Subsequently, I altered the terminology somewhat by replacing the concept of "consociational" with "reconciliation," the term used here.

[4]J. L. Talmon, *The Origins of Totalitarian Democracy* (London: Secker and Warburg, 1955), p. 2.

In contrast to these, Talmon offers the liberal democratic pattern. The latter, he says, assumes "politics to be a matter of trial and error, and regards political systems as pragmatic contrivances of human ingenuity and spontaneity."[5] Here Talmon's point is similar to one made by Popper.[6] It offers a more piecemeal solution to problems of social change.

Talmon's formulation of liberal democracy requires a further structural element, that is, that such systems are organized pluralistically and have diverse centers of power that must be reconciled when basic decisions are made. I prefer to call this a "reconciliation" system, to denote its organizational structure. Ideologically it conforms to Talmon's description.

These two systems challenge each other even when they have certain ultimate ends in common. In the reconciliation system the Jacobin tradition is checked by a plurality of ideas that are entertained by diverse effective power groups. Alternatively, it is not possible for the mobilization system to adhere to basically liberal attitudes. To do so would limit the power of the state and undermine its effective freedom of action vis-à-vis the citizens. However, the mobilization system makes certain of the liberal values into a religious support for the state. By doing so, it introduces a new element into the state, the definition of individuality in purely social and corporate terms.

II

One difference between religion and other forms of thought is that religion has more power. So fundamental is its power that one cannot examine individual conduct or desires without reference to it. In that sense religion cuts into human personality in a way in which ordinary ideological thought rarely does.

One can see this in two systems already discussed. In the reconciliation system, society is conceived of as a summation of individual values held together by a framework of law that is itself highly valued. The mobilization system is represented by valued goals laid down by higher authority and regarded as a sacrosanct. There is a difference between the two systems in the way they approach change and consider history.[7]

[5] *Ibid.*, p. 1.

[6] K. R. Popper, *The Open Society and Its Enemies* (London: Routledge and Kegan Paul, Ltd., 1945), *passim.*

[7] The one is flexible in its ends but is conservative in many ways, and concerned especially with individual rights. The other is more doctrinaire in its commitment to certain ultimate values, while remaining tactically more supple. The classic Leninist formulation of theory and practice, strategy and tactics, is the clearest expression of the latter's code.

Talmon points out that despite their differences both have their common origins in modern western political thought. He turns to the French Revolution and its immediate antecedents in search of the origins of those ideas that are steppingstones to the totalitarian-democratic pattern. This is a familiar technique in political theory, and is certainly valid and useful. My approach, however, is to look at the development of new societies. As their own internal dynamics become more clear, we can see what aspects of political belief are more in harmony with their own internal needs. Indeed, it is the fate of many of the political ideas of the past, including those that provide a common fund of political values, to become altered and twisted in application.

The point is that when political religion becomes a key feature of the polity of a new nation, its likely outlet is a mobilization system of some kind. These mainly fall into the radical and populist tradition of political religion, but it is not inevitable that they should do so. Consider, for example, South Africa, which has elevated the doctrine of the Dutch Reformed Church into political virtue, and by so doing has changed what was a reconciliation system (at least for the European community) into what is increasingly a mobilization system. It has done so despite the fact this entails great risk. South Africa steadfastly is cutting its ties with the West, the Commonwealth, and even the United Nations in preference to losing its political religion. It has refused to follow along these lines of more pragmatic change that a reconciliation system would require.

To include South Africa in our analysis confuses the issue somewhat and certainly extends Talmon's notion beyond his intent. Nevertheless it is important to do so because it raises the question of relationships between concrete structure and belief, between political form and religion. It becomes necessary to examine the relationship of religion to politics, at least in summary fashion, before going on to the specific subject of political religion in the new states.

Political religion begins in man's religious views of the human community. Most ancient societies, and most primitive societies as well, were theocratic. It was the unique achievement of the West to alter hitherto theocratic forms of polity. A number of factors account for this—Christianity for one, the growth of rationalism for another—resulting in the secular polis with its emphasis on the separation between church and state. In turn this nourished the ideal of a common collectivity that raised the political ends of society to a new prominence and, indeed, elevated them to a sacred level. Jumping to modern times, we can view colonialism as merely the overseas extension of conflict between traditional theocracy and secularism as it was embodied in alien political rule. Anticolonialism and movements concerned with independence and development are the contemporary aspects of the conflict between the secular colonial system and the new political religions.[8]

Secularization involved a genuine liberation from the stuffy closets of theocratic traditionalism. In this sense, nationalist movements evolved in a very Western pattern. On racial, political, and economic grounds they embodied the Jacobin demands for equality and opportunity. As well, they argued for participation by Asians and Africans in government. This at least was the first stage—a stage in which individualism was advanced as a prerequisite to political independence. Examples of this initial process of secularization in the political field were to be found in both the Indian National Congress and the Moslem League in British India, in the West African National Congress, in the Aborigines' Rights Protection Society in Ghana and Sarekat Islam in Indonesia. All these sought greater political advance and, with this, education and opportunity as the basis for political progress. After independence the situation changes radically. Not individualism but mass participation through community action becomes the condition of national success. The ends of the state become elevated to virtually a sacred level. "Human investment," originally a Communist Chinese doctrine, finds its counterparts in Guinea and Ghana. Indeed, the older political programs become identified with conservatism and neo-colonialism, while in many of the new states "guided democracy" and the single-party system emphasize an imposed unity that, by raising the political ends of the society to a sacred level, also serve to define and justify authority.

This pattern is in sharp contrast to much of western practice, but it is no less modern. Nor is modernization brought about only through mobilization of the community. Arguments over which form of system will more quickly bring about modernization tend to be rather sterile, but one point is clear. Different programs of modernization exact different penalties. In the reconciliation type there may be more personal disillusion, petty politicking, frustration at the inability to solve problems, and the waning of idealism to such an extent that the springs of effective action and responsibility are dried up and society becomes an object of plunder by political elites. In the mobilization type, which is burdened by self-imposed obstacles and excessive politicization, failures in planning and organization and a measure of ruthlessness and coercion create almost pathological conditions of fear, mistrust, and duplicity, coupled with re-

[8]Not that this implies a pattern of inevitable historical evolution. There are theocracies today, such as Pakistan, among the new states. There are successful newly independent nations without political religion, such as Nigeria. There are others where the separation of church and state exists within a context of national solidarity and highly valued political ends. Egypt today is an example of a consciously Moslem country with a strong penchant for sacred political ends.

prisals and oppression if public sentiment gives these voice. It is a sad commentary on Ghana's government today that, amid bomb throwing and large-scale detentions, the President lives surrounded by security measures that no British governor before him ever considered necessary. It is one thing to define the ends of the state as sacred. It is another to translate that definition into an acceptable pattern of belief.

The mobilization is quite unlike the reconciliation system, where secular ends can never really become sacred. In the western pattern, with the early separation of church and state, the role of the state was to devise better ways through which individual fulfillment could occur. Eventually what emerged was a compromise between religious tolerance and political freedom, a mutually congenial arrangement that resulted in a sharing of responsibility for the running of social life between church and state, and between private and public authorities. Pluralism was thus built into the conception of political democracy.

But, it may be asked, how did this pattern emerge in the first instance? By what fortuitous circumstances did the separation of church and state occur? The answers to this are shrouded in a still earlier western tradition, a theocratic one. It was a Christian innovation to make the distinction between the sacred and the secular spheres by challenging the state religion of Rome. To that extent the church as a political movement, which would have preferred its own theocracy to any form of secular government, nevertheless created the ideal of temporal rule when it could not substitute its own power for state power. Religion and politics became two separate ideologies that were in competition but continued to coexist, each representing powerful institutional forces.

It can be readily seen that there is a good deal of relevance to these historical situations when we begin to examine modernization in the new states. Theocratic elements, secularization, and political forms all jostle one another and compete for prominence. Each has a significant part to play. If purely traditional theocratic elements have their way, the problem posed is one of resistance to innovation. Most traditionalists tend to see changes as undermining their power. They cannot support the secular outlook because the religious basis of the state would be swept away, and with it the theocracy. Secular systems that welcome innovation provide little in the way of organization and belief. The problem of alienation to society becomes profound, and the unevenness of modernization causes conflict resulting in political instability and chronic dissatisfaction. Where political religion is established, alienation disappears, at least overtly, but oppression obliterates freedom, fear replaces spontaneity, and everything is politicized, from family and kinship to voluntary associations. One has only to encounter the Brigades de Vigilance in Mali, whose task it is to root out "subversion" in the home, the clan, and the state, to recognize what this means.

It becomes clear that these three historical types of political experience still exist in the new states. The theocratic type exists in the traditional systems of most of the new nations—traditions that are by no means ended. The reconciliation pattern has been experienced by most new nations, and indeed its values were at one time regarded as the essence of modernity and democracy. The mobilization pattern is a more recent development that for a variety of reasons has come to prominence. Not only are these patterns to be found in the array of new states; their proponents are present in each country.

So far we have merely presented an overview of some of the key problems with which we shall be concerned. These are secularization, innovation, and authority, with respect to the modernization process. Modernization not only involves all three but also arranges them differently in three types of political arrangements: the theocratic, the reconciliation, and the mobilization systems. These three respond differently to the modernization process, particularly with respect to public reactions. In theocracies change must be filtered through traditionalizing instruments; in reconciliation systems it produces alienation and often corruption. The mobilization system has emerged prominently as an alternative to both. A key feature of the mobilization system is political religion. Proponents of the mobilization system argue that such a system is a transitional phenomenon to more democratic practices once modernization has occurred. Political religion may express this millennial view of the political kingdom.

That in sum is the argument. I have deliberately used terms rather loosely to convey a kind of historical sweep in my argument. The processes of modernization now under way have their counterparts in earlier movements. In our discovery of relevant problems in the new nations we ought not to forget that. Indeed, Tocqueville's words about parliament in prerevolutionary France would sound familiar in Sudan, Pakistan, Guinea, Ghana, Indonesia, and several other new nations after the defeat of colonialism:

> But when absolute power had been definitely defeated and the nation felt assured that she could defend her rights alone, the parliaments at once became again what they were before: a decrepit, deformed, and discredited institution, a legacy of the Middle Ages, again exposed to the full tide of public aversion. To destroy it all the King had to do was to let it triumph for a day.[9]

[9]See Alexis de Tocqueville, *The European Revolution* (New York: Doubleday & Company, Inc., 1959), p. 68.

It is now essential to examine these ideas more carefully and to show the relationships between religion and politics in the differing systems outlined above.

The Theocratic System

I cite the case of classic Greece as a theocracy. Barker comments that in the Greek polis "the state exists for the moral development and perfection of its individual members." It is "the fulfillment and perfection of the individual which means—and is the only thing which means—the perfection of the state."

He points out that "a state which is meant for the moral perfection of its members will be an educational institution. 'Its laws will serve to make men good.'" Thus its offices ideally will belong to "the men of virtue who have moral discernment. Its chief activity will be that of training and sustaining the mature in the way of righteousness. That is why we may speak of such a state as really a church: like Calvin's church it exercises a "holy discipline." Political philosophy thus becomes a sort of "moral theology."[10]

There is much in common between Barker's view of the Greek state and the aspirations of several of the new nations of the world, as well as some of the militantly Marxist ones such as China and the U.S.S.R. True, the specifically religious content that was so much a part of the antique world has been downgraded and regarded as prescientific. Nevertheless, the state provides images of virtue and purpose. The individual's will is bent to serve what the state decides is important. Nor is this done in a spirit of autocracy. Rather, there is an ideal of moral and material uplift that, having as its apotheosis some visible form of political order, presumably will secure human happiness.

In theocracies, political and religious associations are one and the same. Some specialization of political roles is possible, but these have their significance in a religious system of ideas. A king is a spiritual counselor as well as a warrior. He is the classic defender of the faith in addition to being a lawgiver. Justice is tempered with divine guidance. The great difficulty that theocracies faced centered mainly upon the control of despotic and corrupt kings and priests, whose transgressions of law offended human society and natural society.

Theocracies had a system of authority in government that shared power with the wider authority of the gods. Revolutions, changes in regime, tyrannicide, and other instabilities were regarded in the same manner as storms, earthquakes, and other natural catastrophes. There

[10]See E. Barker, *The Politics of Aristotle* (Oxford: The Clarendon Press, 1948). See also the discussion in his book *Social and Political Thought in Byzantium* (Oxford: The Clarendon Press, 1957), pp. 6–7.

was a blending of the sacred and the secular, but the sacred was not debased by the secular.

Theocratic societies did not question the larger order within which they found themselves. Suffering was religiously meaningful. Kings or priests were the interpreters and lawgivers in the name of a wider context of religious practice. Among the ancient Jews we find a very clear conception of theocratic politics:

> Israel's monarchy is grounded not in the priesthood, but in apostolic prophecy. Israelite kings had the right to perform altar service and were charged with the maintenance of altars and temples. But they never bore the official title "priest"; their priestly function was but a by-role. The Israelite king succeeded to the task of the prophet-judge, not of the priest; the latter never bore secular authority in Israel. The ideal king of the future is a just judge, God-fearing and mighty; he has no priestly features. Modeled after the apostolic prophet-judge, the king is the elect of God. He does not incorporate any divine essence; he does not control the destiny of the cosmos through the cult; he is but the bearer of God's grace, appointed to office by his messenger-prophet. The king is thus another embodiment of the idea that it is God's will that rules on earth.[11]

Similarly in the case of China and Japan. In the Confucian tradition of government, political order was the creation of the early kings. "The early kings, by virtue of their high intelligence and perspicacity, revived the mandate of Heaven and ruled over the world. They were of one mind in making it their duty to bring peace and contentment to the world."[12]

If the king is the elect of God, human society is part of His universe, to be governed in accordance with His laws. This did not mean that kings, even despotic ones, had an easy time of it. Their responsibilities, while including human affairs, often transcended the world of man and spilled over into the world of nature. In many African kingdoms, for example, kings were held responsible for food supplies, rain, and other important natural phenomena. In the early Semitic kingdoms there were many cases of rulers being regarded as responsible for the deity in the coming of rains, for bad crops, and other natural disasters. "In Babylonia in some prehistoric period there existed a belief that the king was responsible for the state of agricultural land, and for the time occurrence of seasonal phenomena, and that belief exists sporadically today over the East."[13]

What are some of the general characteristics of theocracies? They have

[11]Yehezkel Kaufmann, *The Religion of Israel* (Chicago: The University of Chicago Press, 1960), p. 266.

[12]Ogyu Sorai, "The Confucian Way as a Way of Government," in *Sources of the Japanese Tradition*, ed. William Theodore de Bary (New York: Columbia University Press, 1958), p. 424.

[13]S. H. Hooke, *Myth, Ritual, and Kingship* (Oxford: The Clarendon Press, 1958), p. 28.

a system of kingship or priesthood, although leadership may be shared jointly. Many forms of leadership are thus possible, but leaders have two major qualities. First, they are in roles that are both personalized and institutionalized. Second, they are representatives of the deity. Their authority derives from that even if they are selected by the public at large.[14]

Theocracies are communities that are part of a natural and wider order both of nature and transcendence. There is thus no sharp distinction between the natural universe and the state, nor is there a sharp dividing line between the living and the dead, nor the real state and the transcendent state, that is, between the kingdom of man and the kingdom of God.

Laws tend to be linked to custom, ritual, and other religious practices, having their origins in prophecy, whether oracular or personal, or by decree. Changes come about in the effort to conserve and strengthen the existing system rather than in attempting to transform it.

An important part of the sacred element in the community is maintained by religious practices and special classes of individuals who cater to ritual and custom in efforts to maintain the purity of the society and prevent the defilement of the sacred by the secular.

These characteritics should be sufficient to indicate the nature of theocracy. Most societies of the ancient world, including those of Greece and Rome, were theocratic, as more recently have been African political communities and those in the Middle East and Asia. What revolutions they had were to change regimes rather than fundamentally to alter the conception of authority and community. Their problems were related to the cosmos, and thus were no more disturbing than the larger mystery of life and the gods themselves.

Systems with political religion elevate the secular to the level of the sacred, and incorporate theocratic elements. They make the universe subservient to and an extension of man and his society. If in the theocra-

[14]R. Caillois puts it as follows: "Power like the sacred, seems to be an external sign of grace, of which the individual is the temporary abode. It is obtained through investiture, initiation, or consecration. It is lost through degradation, indignity, or abuse. It benefits from the support of the entire society which consitutes its depository. The king wears the crown, scepter, and purple reserved for the Gods. He has guards to protect him. He executes all types of coercion capable of forcing the rebellious to submit. But it must be pointed out that these means do not explain as much as they demonstrate the efficacy of power. To the degree to which people regard them as powerful, or consider them able to subjugate, or reveal reasons for being afraid, it is unnecessary to explain the motives for complaisance and docility. . . .

"Every king is God, descended from God, or ruler by the grace of God. He is a sacred personage. It is consequently necessary to isolate him and to construct watertight compartments between him and the profane. His person harbors a holy force that creates prosperity and maintains the order of the universe. He assures the regularity of the seasons, the fertility of the soil and women. . . ." See Roger Caillois, *Man and the Sacred* (New York: The Free Press, 1959), pp. 90–91.

cies, the cosmos and nature are not divorced from the state, they are larger than the state, and control it. In systems with political religion, man is the center of the universe. It is the reconciliation system that is the obverse of theocracy, not the mobilization type, although the latter contains elements of both.

The Reconciliation System

What I mean by a reconciliation system is most aptly expressed in the phrase "a government of laws and not of men." By this statement, which is the foundation stone of constitutional democracy, it is meant not only that men are required to obey laws, a characteristic of all communities, but rather that law has a wider wisdom than any individual man. As such, its status is venerated for its own sake. Through laws, prudently known, man perfects his individuality and protects others from it. Although Plato does not consider law in *The Republic*, his concept of truth and harmony is itself a notion of an abstract law to be known through reason, that is, knowledge of the good. Insofar as law is a standard as well as a framework, Plato begins the tradition of natural law in the western world.

From then on, law is the constant preoccupation of secular theorists. How to shape it to human needs without destroying its insulation from the ordinary whim and fancy of men gave rise to great commentaries on law that are still the cultural tradition of the West—Justinian's and Gaius's Institutes, the works of the Glossators and the Commentators, Blackstone, Maine, Maitland, and Vinogradoff. Law as a framework embodying wisdom has been a constant object of study. The effort to resolve some of the paradoxes between an objective plane of law, at one with the rest of the universe, and with the ordinary and day-to-day laws made for the governance of the minutiae of daily life is a never ending dialogue over where natural law leaves off and positive law begins. It is a dialogue that in the medieval period came to include another division, between divine law and canon law, all of which needed to be sorted out in the respective spheres where their authority would be particular and useful.

This preoccupation with law in the West was one of the important ingredients for the development of a community that regarded the framework of law itself as the sole and ultimate commitment by which the community lived, breathed, and prospered. But it was not the only factor relevant to the development of a reconciliation system. The second was the separation of church and state. I shall try to show that the separation of church and state was in fact an essential element in developing such a system and, as well, how the notion of law was a necessary ingredient. This point cannot be emphasized too strongly, because I believe that the separation of church and state without a strong belief in the objective quality of law is in fact one basis for the growth of political religion. In the latter case (a government of men and not of laws), the legitimacy of the sovereign is substituted for the legitimacy of the law, with the result that politics becomes endowed with sacral characteristics. However, such matters will be examined when we discuss political religion. For the moment, we can explore more deeply the separation of church and state.

This doctrine itself is a curious one, and peculiarly Christian. Whatever the historical reasons, and I am sure there are many, Christianity, which originated in a condition of political subservience, saw its status enhanced by winning tolerance for itself. Not that it was content with mere tolerance and would not have transformed the community into a theocracy if it could have done so, but by and large it could be content with tolerance and live in a relatively harmonious relationship with secular authorities. Divine law and natural law were never quite the same, but were regarded as complementary. Revealed truth and rationality were not opposites but rather different sides of the same coin. The great achievement of St. Thomas was in effect the strengthening of the accord between church and state and providing it with an intellectual synthesis.

St. Thomas gave Christianity a profounder basis for what had already been established in principle, in the Pauline doctrine of rendering unto Caesar the things that are Caesar's. It was Pope Gelasius who made a fundamental point of this at the end of the fifth century:

> The Emperor, is the son of the Church, not its director. In matters of religion it is his to learn and not to teach. He has the privileges of his power which he has obtained by the will of God for the sake of public administration. . . .
>
> Before the time of Christ, some did have the offices of both king and priest, and in heathen times the devil copied this and the pagan emperors held the office of Pontifex Maximum. But Christ who was both king and priest never entrusted both powers to the same hands, but separated the two offices and the functions and dignities proper to each, and therefore, as Christian emperors stand in need of priests for eternal life, so the priests for the course of temporal things employ the directions of emperors.
>
> There are two authorities by which principally this world is ruled, the sacred authority of the bishops, and the royal power. . . .[15]

The most important consequence of this doctrine, which was reinforced rather than weakened by the historic battles men fought over it, was the conflict between church and state—the separation of temporal and

[15]Quoted in Charles Howard McIlwain, *The Growth of Political Thought in the West* (New York: The Macmillan Company, 1932), pp. 164–65.

spiritual jurisdictions. The fortunes of the one could, and did, vary independently of the other. No matter how religious a monarch, not even during the height of the doctrine of the divine right of kings was the principle undermined.

What was significant about this? It provided a philosophical basis for limiting the power of the executive. For the concept of checks and balances implies a faith that such a system helps to restore the governance of men to a natural harmony in which the individual's true nature is one of freedom within civil society. Civil society ruled by law is in turn reinforced by spiritual sanction on an individual basis. Indeed, Protestantism helped to reinforce this doctrine so that right conduct, guided by a Christian ethic, and individual freedom, tempered by representative government, were mutually reinforcing elements. The result was a high degree of self-restraint in behavior—such self-restraint being the essence of the liberal democratic polity.

Even now, when religion itself has declined and the burdens of civil society are immense, the concept of limited government has remained in the West. Such is the fear of arbitrary power in government that the idea of parliament and law, as well as a belief in constitutions and social compacts, becomes the sole symbolic instrument of civic rule. What there is of the sacred in Western secular government is in the framework itself. All other ideologies have declined. A constitutional framework, although it cannot be heroic, gives men the opportunity to make of their society what they will, within the framework of law. Law through representative government is to an important extent the political content of our civilization. It is the means by which we amend our way of life, without abdicating individual rights. It is necessarily undramatic, and to a large extent without glamour. As well, change under such circumstances is slow. The competition of individuals and groups, a pluralistic universe with relativistic values, is its main characteristic. Indeed, all values can change except two. One is the dignity of the individual, which can only be preserved through the dignity of law. The second is the principle of representative government.

What are some of the more practical virtues of such a system? Perhaps two are the most important. A government of laws allows that amendment that enhances law by tempering and ameliorating the difficulties its citizens face. In that respect, when it functions well it has resolved the twin problems of stable society and succession in public office. As well, it allows for secular value germane to industrialization. Having been established, the framework can persist even though the sacred "sword," as distinct from the secular one, has declined. However, it has not accomplished this without difficulty. The decline of religion has imposed on the Western democratic polity the singular problem of how to provide alternative sources of meaning, faith, and spiritual sustenance that all men need in some degree. Our crisis can thus be seen as arising out of unsatisfied moral ambitions. And our political framework mirrors faithfully this weakness. Precisely because our problems lie in the moral sphere, those new nations that have developed a system of political religion now appear to be morally less ambiguous than we are. Even though the political religions in the new nations have not reemerged in the classic form of theocracies, but in the form of secular beliefs, they define political and moral aims as one and the same. What loses is the idea of individualism. The peculiar genius of our civilization, that is, the relationship between individualism and law, is viewed as imprisoning, reactionary, and parochial—a western notion.

At stake, then, is the survival of democracy itself. Reconciliation systems are undergoing a crisis intensified by the secularization of the religious sphere. The logic of this argument would be a return to religious belief as the way out of our difficulty. Whatever the merits and logic of this course of action, it is highly unlikely that it will come about. New solutions must be found. The resulting internal danger is that reconciliation systems might turn to political religions to reinforce their own position or in an illusory effort to eradicate enemies both within and without.

The Mobilization System

Political religion that arose in the West is itself a response to the loss of faith that characterizes present reconciliation systems. What I have been suggesting can be rephrased as follows: By placing no reliance on church religion, one of the stabilizing elements that originally supported the political framework in reconciliation systems, the sacred, is employed in many new nations to develop a system of political legitimacy and to aid in mobilizing the community for secular ends. Thus constitutional democracy becomes irrelevant to their experience. Having made political doctrine into political belief, efforts are made to formalize that faith as a means by which to achieve major aims.[16] In none of the new nations has this entirely succeeded, but particularly in Ghana, Mali, Guinea, Egypt, and Indonesia efforts at formalization have been made.

[16]But if the aims were achieved, they would lose their significance. So it is that political religions need to have aims not all of which can be achieved. One such aim is the transformation of human beings into some higher order of being. The Soviet argument is that capitalism is in the long run a corrupting element in human society, and individuals who show capitalistic vestiges are to that extent corrupt. New nations tend to have similar views with regard to tribal societies. The latter, having fallen from grace by being corrupted by colonialism, remain corrupt.

The mobilization system contains an implicit assumption: That which divides men from one another is due to unnatural causes—colonialism, neocolonialism, classes which derive their differences from hostile relationships centering around property. Men must be freed from these unnatural differences by both acts of leadership and exceptional public will. Harmony in the political sphere derives from the messianic leader who points out the dangers and noxious poisons of faction. Many such leaders are charismatic who represent the "one." They personify the monistic quality of the system.

To achieve such oneness, mobilization systems begin by politicizing all political life. As a result, politics as such disappears. This is in keeping with monistic political belief. Conflict is not only bad but also counterrevolutionary. It runs counter to the natural evolution of human society, and ideas of opposition downgrade and confuse the power of positive thinking. Ideas not only are dangerous, challenging the legitimacy of the regime or the charisma of the leader, but they also represent an unscientific vestige wherever they run counter to those of the regime. Hence the most counterrevolutionary groups of all are dissident intellectuals.

Mobilization systems are characterized by what Durkheim called repressive law. Punitive and symbolic, it is political crimes which are punished with great severity. Such regimes are humorless. Their model of society is an organic one. Although it does not always fit exactly, Marxism or some variant thereof is appealing because it satisfies these conditions theoretically and Leninism supports them organizationally. Such systems represent the new puritanism. Progress is its faith. Industrialization is its vision. Harmony is its goal. These are the factors that lie behind modern political religion.[17]

The new nations with political religion regard themselves as being without sin. The idea of sinlessness stems from the notion of rebirth, that is, the rise of new political units from colonial status, with all the purity of the newly born. Their objects are regeneration and emancipation of the citizenry from backwardness and other handicaps, such as racial discrimination. Rebirth lends itself to messianic government, which makes a rule of law and not of men virtually impossible. Regeneration regards individualism as backward-looking and restrictive, and this makes public checks on political authority extremely difficult.

In perhaps the best description of what I have been trying to convey, Talmon points out that

> the decline of religious authority implied the liberation of man's conscience, but it also implied something else. Religious ethics had to be

[17]See Edward Shils, "The Concentration and Dispersion of Charisma: Their Bearing on Economic Policy in Underdeveloped Countries," *World Politics*, XI (1958).

> speedily replaced by secular, social morality. With the rejection of the Church, and of transcendental justice, the State remained the sole source and sanction of morality.[18]

The original impulse of political messianism was ethical, not economic. In the new nations today it becomes ethical, but is now expressed in economic objectives. In his distinction between liberal and totalitarian democracy, Talmon suggests that both traditions

> affirm the supreme value of liberty. But whereas one finds the essence of freedom in spontaneity and the absence of coercion, the other believes it to be realized only in the pursuit and attainment of an absolute collective purpose. It is outside our scope to decide whether liberal democracy has the faith that totalitarian democracy claims to have in final aims. What is beyond dispute is that the final aims of liberal democracy have not the same concrete character. They are conceived in rather negative terms, and the use of force for their realization is considered as an evil. Liberal democratics believe that in the absence of coercion men and society may one day reach through a process of trial and error a state of ideal harmony. In the case of totalitarian democracy, this state is precisely defined, and is treated as a matter of immediate urgency, a challenge for direct action, an imminent event.[19]

The reasons for the rise of political religions among the new nations are not hard to find. Faith is a source of authority. The new nations face the problem involved in the creation of over-arching loyalties that transcend the more primordial ones of ethnic membership, religious affiliation, linguistic identification. That such loyalties are stubborn and not easily replaceable can easily be demonstrated in such new countries as India, Indonesia, and Nigeria. Where hitherto racially compartmentalized groups are to be found, the problem is immeasurably more difficult, as in the Federation of Rhodesia and Nyasaland.

Nor are such loyalties blind and unreasoning. Race, ethnicity, religion, and language are the means whereby people identify themselves, organize their community, find meaning for their sentiments, and express their beliefs. All the critical elements of man in society appear to be touched in some important manner by each of these matters. If such affiliations are to be increasingly less significant, a public must find itself linked up by a common interest in the wider polity through which their identity, their sentiments, and their beliefs are enlarged and strengthened rather than minimized and destroyed. The point is that political religion seeks to do these things and render massive change heroic and joyful, infectious and liberating. But this is by no means simple to do, and in the development of a political religion conflicts are

[18]Talmon, *op. cit.*, p. 4.
[19]*Ibid.*, p. 2.

engendered that can be as fierce and time-consuming as the religious wars of the past, even if they are less dramatic.

The task, therefore, of building the polity is a difficult one, and one of the functions of political religion is to supply meaning and purpose to what might otherwise become a void. One cannot simply destroy primordial attachments and replace them with nothing.

Another major problem facing the new nations, in addition to breaking down parochial attachments (and it is closely related to that), is the problem of constituting authority. A system that enjoys a constitutional framework can achieve this only after a certain consensus about primordial loyalties has already gained acceptance in the wider community. Without such consensus political authority remains the most sensitive political problem in the new nations. Some older countries have never been able to overcome these difficulties. France never institutionalized her constitutional order sufficiently. Primordial loyalties still flourish. Political authority, never fully integrated within the framework of law, demeaned the framework itself in spite of the very elaborate legal structure of France as a modern state.

In the new nations, political leaders now in power have only recently been in the business of challenging colonial authority and weakening men's obedience to political rule. To some extent, when popular enthusiasm and revolutionary ardor began to wane, these political leaders inherit an instability of regime and authority that is partly of their own making. Endowing their roles with sacred elements makes their authority stronger and the regime more secure. Moreover, since everything is known about the leaders, their past, their family, their daily routine, they can hardly be remote and distant. Quite the contrary, they characteristically remain friendly and fraternal. If such familiarity is not, however, to result in disrespect for authority, the sacred role needs to utilize familiarity and turn it about. The public comes to be grateful for the spreading of the sacred largesse. They are purified by the divine. They see that the "Man of the People" remains with the people, but they never confuse him with ordinary men. Authority then becomes stabilized in the role of the Leader and his manipulation of power, and friendliness is a token of majesty.

Still another major problem which the people of new nations face is the material development of their country. Everyone desires the things of this world, and a political religion can survive on austerity only up to a point. It must have its practical consequences. Here political religion is always less powerful than church religion because the former promises a different type of reward than the latter. Political religion says that the political kingdom will provide abundance in material things—things, moreover, that have an immediate feel about them, such as cars, houses, food, clothes, television sets, transistor radios. Church religion, by promising more intangible rewards, has a better time of it in this respect.

The political religion thus requires a more specific ideological component than church religion, and it has built into it a particular kind of rationality as well—the rationality of economic life. This is both its handicap and its advantage. It is a handicap insofar as political religion will rarely have the same extrarational pull on a long-term basis that church religion does. It does not have the same sticking power. It is an advantage inasmuch as it turns men's minds to practical tasks, with the rationality necessary to achieve them. To the extent that development becomes successful, it becomes possible to consider the decline of political religion and in its place the rise of a constitutional order. That is the great hope the West retains about the U.S.S.R. It is also the hope we bear for the new nations.

Political religion in new nations then comes to center upon three main objects: the development of a single system of central authority, the material development of the country, and the institutionalization of rationalistic values. All three are intimately connected as processes. All can be aided in important ways by political religion.

We can now consider the substance of political religion. What are its characteristics? How can it be recognized? How does it become transformed into something else? I shall try to show some specific examples of what I call political religion, and indicate how it functions. We can then see why political religion has the capacity for carrying out these functions.

III

I suggest the general characteristics of political religion as follows. First, the state and the regime take on sacred characteristics. The sacred even extends to ordinary laws. What I mean can best be described in terms of Durkheim's distinction between repressive and restitutive law, as I have already suggested. Repressive law punishes on a symbolic level. The sacred quality of the community, having been violated, must be revenged. Death for treason is an example of repressive law. In communities with a small degree of political religion, it is hard to find cases of men being put to death for theft. In communities with a large degree of political religion, death for theft is not uncommon.[20]

Second, the sacred characteristic becomes essential to maintaining solidarity in the community. This has the effect of giving sacrosanct

[20]Sekou Touré's comment is a good example:

"If you like, we may say that the Party is the brain of our society, while the State is the executive part of it, the part which works according to the spirit and the intentions of the Party.

"The State settles the great problems of a social, economic, financial, or adminis-

qualities to the new state. From this, in turn, a regime derives its legitimacy which is reinforced in a variety of ways. One way is characterized by a renewed interest in a semimythical past, to produce antecedents for the regime. Another is a persistent attack on a particular enemy. For example, the attack on colonialism is enlarged to include neocolonialism, which becomes a higher form of villainy against which political religions in new nations must be ever vigilant.

The mythical past, in addition to stressing continuity between an earlier period and the present, also serves to "periodize" a time of disgrace and misfortune. In new nations this is the period of colonialism. Both the new era and the golden past serve as reminders of the suffering and degradation through which the public passed, and stress the achievement of independence. The "birth" of the nation is thus a religious event, forming a fund of political grace that can be dispensed over the years.

The agent of rebirth is normally an individual—an Nkrumah, a Touré who, as the leader of the political movement, is midwife to the birth of the nation. Sometimes this is expressed in songs and chants and at other times in political prayers.[21]

---

trative character, in the light of the objectives which the Party has decided to attain.

"It is thus that the Party, which has decided to create a new society for the greatest happiness of man, comes up presently against several difficulties. In the present society there are thieves, murderers through social imprudence. The thief and the murderer constitute a social danger. They make the members of the society feel worried and unsafe; they injure the property and the life of other people. Neither of them concerns himself in any way with the properties and the lives around him; they feel no respect for the social surroundings in which they live and operate, they have no sense of solidarity with all the men who make up society. The role of the State is to protect society from the evil deeds of such men.

In our eyes, the thief is an evil being. Whether he steals several millions or only a pin, his behavior comes from a mentality which we intend to destroy. Whoever he may be, whatever the conditions in which his theft has been committed, we shall punish him with the utmost severity. No one will be excepted." See *Towards Full Re-Africanization* (Paris: *Présence Africaine*, 1959), p. 46.

"That is why, at the suggestion of the Party, the Government has decided to deal with them with the utmost severity. In future, no pity will be shown to thieves. We shall impose extreme penalties on them. We have said that, if you caught a thief in the act of breaking open your door you could shoot him.

[21] "Sekou Touré
Grand-Merci à toi, Touré
La libération de la Guinée
Ne nous surprend guerre
L'affame ne sent-il pas de loin
Le fumet du plat salutaire
Sekou Touré
O don Divin à la Guinée
Salut à toi, soit beni
O toi, bienfaiteur de la Guinée
Apôtre de la bonne cause
O l'enfant prodigue."

From the poem "Independance," by Diely Mamoudou Kande, printed in *Présence Africaine* (December 1959–January 1960), p. 95.

Political leadership centers upon the individual with characteristics of revealed truth. From leader to party to state is a single line embodied in the twin notions of personal authority and collective responsibility. The goals of the society are demanding, and are laid down from above. By achieving them, men become honorable and moral, reborn, and closer to perfection. Sometimes this is considered to extend beyond a country's own borders. The former chairman of the Convention People's Party, and Minister of Presidential Affairs, in an officially distributed pamphlet wrote:

> Today . . . barely three years after the birth of Ghana, to millions of people living both inside and outside the continent of Africa, Kwame Nkrumah is Africa and Africa is Kwame Nkrumah. When the question is asked: "What is going to happen to Africa?" it is to one man that everyone looks for the answer: Kwame Nkrumah. To the imperialists and colonialists his name is a curse on their lips; to the settlers his name is a warning that the good old days at the expense of the Africans are coming to an end; to Africans suffering under foreign domination, his name is a breath of hope and means freedom, brotherhood and racial equality; to us, his people, Kwame Nkrumah is our father, teacher, our our brother, our friend, indeed our very lives, for without him we would no doubt have existed, but we would not have lived; there would have been no hope of a cure for our sick souls, no taste of glorious victory after a life-time of suffering. What we owe him is greater even than the air we breathe, for he made us as surely as he made Ghana.[22]

As well, the party is the state. Those who do not accept this unity are suspect. Nkrumah himself has written:

> The Convention People's Party is Ghana and Ghana is the Convention People's Party. There are some people who not only choose to forget this, but who go out of their way to teach others to forget also. There are some persons, both staff and students [of the University College of Ghana], who mistakenly believe that the words "academic freedom" carry with them a spirit of hostility to our Party and the Government, the same Party of the workers and the farmers, and the same Government whose money founded the University and maintains it and who provides them with their education in the hope that they will one day repay their countrymen by giving loyal and devoted service to the Government of the People.
>
> The Convention People's Party cannot allow this confusion of academic freedom with disloyalty and anti-Government ideas.
>
> In the future we shall attach the greatest importance to the ideological education of the youth. The establishment of the Young Pioneers will be a step further in this direction. The Youth Section of the Party will be

[22]Tawia Adamafio, *A Portrait of the Osagyefo Dr. Kwame Nkrumah* (Accra: Government Printer, 1960), p. 95.

fully mobilized under the close guidance of the Youth Bureau of the National Secretariat. We shall make our party ideology fully understood in every section of the community.

We must regard it as an honor to belong to the Convention People's Party. And I repeat we must work loyally and with singleness of purpose for that is the essence of the true Party spirit, the spirit that routed imperialism from our soil and the spirit which we must recapture for the struggle that lies ahead.[23]

The party contains an elect. Control is centralized. There is purification in belonging, comfort in comradeship, democracy in loyalty, brotherhood in membership.[24]

Similarly in the case of Guinea. There the structure of the party extends into each village. There is a hierarchy of councils. At the top:

. . . Le Parti assume le rôle dirigeant dans la vie de la nation qu'il dispose de tous les pouvoirs de la nation: les pouvoirs politique, judiciare, administratif, économique et technique sont entre les mains du Parti Démocratique de Guinée. C'est donne lui qui désigné le Chef de l'État par la voie du souffrage universel direct.[25]

Or, again, Sekou Touré:

We have often said that, in our eyes, there are no soldiers, no civil servants, no intellectuals; there are only supporters of the Party. It is among the supporters of the Party that the standards of the value, of faithful-

[23]Kwame Nkrumah, "What the Party Stands For," in *The Party*, C.P.P. Monthly Journal, I, No. 1 (September 1960).

[24]The messiah-like qualities of the president have been to some extent ritualized and made more permanent, both in ceremony and in thought, than was true in the past. Religion itself has not confronted this development, but has more or less found a different level in those interstices between the metaphysics of national philosophy and the transcendental and personal beliefs of individuals.

The case of Mali is quite similar. However, a very high proportion of the population is Moslem. There is an acceptance of Islam by the government, and traditional religious and social beliefs are modified through deliberate government policy. Recently I attended a wedding in Mali that illustrates this point. The traditional extended clan unit had been recognized by the government, although the chief was, as was the case with most traditional chiefs who had previously worked with the French, removed from office. A very old man from a royal lineage was elected in his place. He carried the ceremonial sword, and all groups gave respect to it. The actual leader of the ceremony was an important government official very high in the party, the Union Soudanaise. The various traditional sections of the clan, women, elders, children, men, danced and participated in the ceremony not only in their traditional role but, as well, as members of the clan women's brigade, the youth organizations, the party section, as the case might be. The blessings invoked were to fall on the marriage partners, but also on the clan, and also on the party and the state, simultaneously. Here, then, is an example of the blending of old and new, church and political religions within the context of older cultural and social groups.

[25]Sekou Touré, *Cinquième Congrès National du Parti Démocratique de Guinée*, Rapport de Doctrine et de Politique Général (Conakry: Imprimerie Nationale, 1959), p. 38.

> ness, of course, of unselfishness are. It will be the supporters who establish [*sic*] make possible the prosperity of Guinea, as they made possible its independence. *If the Party wants the State to run as it desires, it should fortify its basic organization and ensure that democracy remains the essential and permanent principle of its activity.*[26]

Spreading the political religions abroad has also been attempted. The effort to establish a mobilization system failed in the Congo, but in that tragedy there are revealed some of the relationships between political coreligionists. In one of his famous "Dear Patrice" letters to Lumumba, Nkrumah wrote that

> in any crisis I will mobilize the Afro-Asian *bloc* and other friendly nations as in the present attempt to *dethrone* you. Whenever in doubt consult me. Brother, we have been in the game for some time now and we know how to handle the imperialists and the colonialists. The only colonialist or imperialist I trust is a dead one. If you do not want to bring the Congo to ruin, follow the advice I have given.[27]

These represent examples of the development of political religion through the single-party democracy emerging in Guinea and Ghana. There are, of course, many other examples to be found elsewhere, Indonesia, China, Mali, to mention only a few. China is, of course, exceptional. But so, in degree at least, are her problems. For the most part the mobilization systems are not communist. The failure to distinguish between the more general phenomenon of political religion in the mobilization system and the particular brand of political religion and structural form of Soviet or Chinese communism often leads Americans to broad errors of judgment about the new mobilization system.

The characteristics of political religion in mobilization systems can be summarized as follows. There are similarities between political religions and church religions. In the former as well as the latter there are saints and villains, prophets and missionaries. Where there is political religion the possibility of a political calling replaces for each individual the possibility of a religious calling; there is mysticism and authority. The real question, however, is whether or not the similarities mentioned above (and many others could be found) are nevertheless sufficient to establish political religion as an equivalent to church religion. Are the resemblances between the two only superficial? Is it not a mistake to consider the artifacts of ritual and symbolic manipulation as the substance of religion itself, resulting in a misunderstanding of both religion and politics? One could argue indeed that this view debases the first and glorifies the second.

[26]*Ibid.*, p. 89. Italics added.

[27]Quoted in Colin Legum, *Congo Disaster* (Baltimore: Penguin Books, 1961), p. 154. Italics added.

This may be correct, and I have, of course, considered this question in developing my analysis. What it raises, of course, is a larger view of religion. I should like to show that both church and politics can be seen as agents of the same fundamental phenomenon and that religion lies behind both churches and regimes.

IV

To consider the question of religion further requires a short digression, as well as a restatement of some of the arguments put forward so far.

As I am using the term, religion is that which is concerned with the sacred, that is, special ideas and objects that, socially understood, are exceptionally venerated.[28] Although it is mysterious, all men are privileged to share in it.

I said earlier that the oldest and most familiar system is the theocracy where leadership and authority are part of the seamless web of both politics and religion. There, the transcendental values expressed through the deity are transmitted by a king. Such a king is both ecclesiastical and secular simultaneously—so much so that it is impossible to separate, in any given act, the one aspect from the other. Many traditional African systems were like this, which is one of the reasons that many observers have commented on the profoundly religious nature of African societies. So, to some extent, was prewar Japan. Nor was Czarist Russia entirely different in this respect. All such systems had powerful secular

[28]A fuller definition of religion, to which I subscribe, is found in Bellah:

"By religion I mean, following Paul Tillich, man's attitudes and actions with respect to his ultimate concern. This ultimate concern has to do with what is ultimately valuable and meaningful, what we might call ultimate value; and the ultimate threats to value and meaning, what we might call ultimate frustration. It is one of the social functions of religion to provide a meaningful set of ultimate values on which the morality of a society can be based. Such values when institutionalized can be spoken of as the central values of a society.

"The other aspect of ultimate concern is ultimate frustration. As long as frustrations are seen as caused by determinate factors such as moral breach, the normal person can deal with them as they arise and they have no character of ultimacy. However, those frustrations which are inherent in the human situation, but which are not manageable or morally meaningful, of which death is the type case, may be called ultimate frustrations. The second function of religion is to provide an adequate explanation for these ultimate frustrations so that the individual or group which has undergone them can accept them without having core values rendered meaningless, and can carry on life in society in the face of these frustrations. This is done through some form of assertion that the ultimate values are greater than, can overcome, the ultimate frustrations and is symbolized in many ways—as the victory of God over death, or Eros over Thanatos, of Truth over illusion.

"The 'object' of ultimate concern, namely that which is the source of ultimate value and ultimate frustration must be symbolized if it is to be thought about at all. We may speak of these symbols as denoting the 'sacred' or the 'divine.'" See Robert N. Bellah, *Tokugawa Religion* (New York: The Free Press, 1957), pp. 6–7.

elements within them. So does any organized church. But the distinction between sacred and secular was not always meaningful within these societies themselves.

The origins of theocratic systems are necessarily complex, but there is a good reason why they emerge out of mobilization systems and take the form of autocracy which I call a modernizing autocracy. The reason is that messianic or charismatic leadership in the mobilization system remains shaky, despite manifest popularity of political leaders. The leader never fully legitimizes his regime. The regime never is entirely successful in consolidating the authority of the leader. Over time, charisma turns into something else, as Weber originally pointed out. To control the transformation of charisma with all its attendant dangers is to ritualize it and, by doing so, to institutionalize both the role of the leader and the political habits required of the public.[29]

States created through nationalism have taken a form not dissimilar to theocracies in that they attempt to create new systems of transcendental values which have the twin effects of establishing legitimacy for the state and the moral underpinnings for those roles necessary to political objectives. "Religiosity" in the political sphere is used, however, to create a system of instrumental means and secular objectives rather than theocratic ones. In this respect political religion is at least partly employed for nonreligious objectives.

The symbolism of birth, regeneration, the personalization of leadership, as well as many other characteristics to be found in the formation of religious movement have the effect of casting out defilement and shame. The question still remains, however—to what extent are political religions in actual fact religions?

The discussion that follows turns on the following premises: There are certain fundamental needs of individuals that can be met only by their acceptance of transcendental beliefs. The needs, as I see them, are three: (1) the necessity of accepting death; (2) the necessity of establishing individual personality; and (3) the necessity of identifying objectives. The classic puzzle posed by these three needs results from their paradoxical relationship. If we are all doomed, as it were, as individuals, why the necessity to find purpose in living? Why the passionate commitment to life? Why the importance of knowing who and what we are?

These are the problems to which religion addresses itself. It is obvious that our commitments to life are not nullified by the inevitability of our death. Religion provides us with some form of immortality through a transcendental haven for souls. Political religion accomplishes the same end through the continuity of present society with the past and a secure

[29]For further observation on the ritualization of charisma see my book *Ghana in Transition* (New York: Atheneum Press, 1963), Chap. 15.

political future. Individuals in a political community are made to feel that their lives are a product of lives lived before them within the context of the nation. This belief in turn is translated into family and kinship commitment as secured in the state. This is one of the reasons why family and kinship systems remain the building blocks of all political systems and, equally, why the state takes precedence over any family. The search for immortality, then, is expressed in both church religions and political religion. Both provide a means of triumphing over death in the face of its inevitability.

With respect to our second and third needs, it is a function of religion to provide identity and purpose to individuals. Identity is a reference point by means of which individuals relate to one another. This is closely connected to purpose. All religions try to explain why we exist, establish a standard of right and justice, and score inequity and human cupidity as well. If anguish, hardship, and suffering are all part of life, religion shows that justice and meaning are positive corollaries of these.

In the case of political religion, identity is to be found in citizenship, and meaning in justice. Plato's answer to Job's question is political, and in its own curious way, empirical. It is to be found in those arrangements of the human conscience that postulate justice not only as a highest good but also as a practical expression of the state.

This is why the state as a legal expression is not merely that of society in legal terms. It is also the basis for requiring obligation to the community. Meaning is thus political in relation to identity. The society gives purpose to the individual. The individual relates himself to others in a societal context. The state bases itself on a higher right to express that purpose and exact from its citizens those obligations necessary to ensure success. It may do so in a variety of ways, some of which appear indeed to obliterate the individual. Identity, then, through citizenship, locates the individual in relation to his obligations.

Obligation is related to our third factor, that is, purpose. Where church religion expresses moral purpose in right conduct and worthy objectives —aims that cleanse, purify, and promote in the individual a personal sense of worth—so too with political religion. It combines both the ultimate and intermediate aims of individuals in a morally acceptable blend. Theocracy does this when the ultimate ends of the state and the moral aims are one and the same because of the specific content of theocratic beliefs. Political religions introduce change in the normative order and require individuals to change their moral personalities. Thus in the U.S.S.R. the political religion requires a new type of individual. Motivation must be altered as egotism is denied. Selflessness and equalitarianism within the society are the moral imperatives. These are then translated into work discipline and, through alteration of the individual's motivational structure, efficiency. A given technological end thus coincides with the moral end, to create a new political puritanism. This is a particularly attractive aspect of political religion to leaders in those new nations with mobilization systems.[30]

Political religions, although similar to theocracies, go further. In contrast to mobilization systems, for example, a theocratic country like Pakistan sets more modest economic and moral goals for itself, demanding fewer role alterations from the population than is the usual case in mobilization systems. The sense of urgency is less, the concept of historical time more archaic.

More particularly, political religion in mobilization systems fits individual moral purposes and life chances to technological dynamism. Individual roles are acceptable only insofar as they enlarge that dynamism and share in it. Hence the roles that an individual plays are both morally and technologically functional. By this means, individual purpose and national purpose are the same, a situation that does not normally apply in anything like the same degree in theocracies. Older roles are either objectionable, defining their occupants as enemies, or they become sentimentalized, relegated to a pleasant museum along with old costumes, antique artifacts, and other symbols of the past. Indeed, by becoming sentimental they may become functionally serviceable.

Immortality, identity, meaning, and purpose are among the profound individual needs that both church religion and political religion satisfy. By satisfying them, sometimes in the same context, and sometimes in different spheres, they make possible purpose in the face of death and promote solidarity and cooperation.

If these elements do what we say they do, then both church religion and political religion should have similarities of both spirit and form. By satisfying such needs they provide the ultimate basis for authority. Both serve to demarcate groups of men, one from the other, along a significant criterion of membership. Both demand allegiance as a condition of membership. Both provide the main routes of escape from death and oblivion.

There is, however, an important difference between the two that requires further comment. Church religious belief is more universalistic than political belief. Church religion seeks a widening affiliation through universal human values. Politics tends to be limited by the state. This is a threat to political religions, and one they readily recognize. Hence political religions seek universal formulas that have as their object the

[30]For a brief discussion of the "new puritanism of socialism" see my article "Political Organization and Ideology" in *Labor Commitment and Social Change in Developing Areas*, eds. Moore and Feldman, (New York: Social Science Research Council, 1960).

breaking down of national boundaries. The kingdoms of man must be one. This is one reason for the Communist commitment to completing the revolution. It cannot rest until it has universalized itself empirically so as to realize itself religiously.

If political religions are to satisfy the needs of individuals as I have defined them, what are the means open to them? First, prophets are needed. These interpret immortality, identity, and purpose through their own personal gifts of grace. They need to be father and teacher as well as founder of the community. They are the present equivalent of ancestral gods in theocracies or those mythological figures associated with the founding of older societies.

Such prophets need to light a tinder of hope in the ordinary day-to-day level of human demands. In new nations this is provided by creating something new, a new polity for future generations. Hence, political religions are for the young and are interested in the future. They provide hope and a belief in progress. To create hope and progress is to reinforce the immortality gained through family, kinship, and society itself.

By following the prophet one joins a select group. Identity and comradeship, human relationships and group functions are then combined, and each person finds his place in the scheme of development.

Finally, purpose and individual dignity, useful roles and satisfying work are enhanced by the link they provide with the messianic leader. Roles become more than functionally satisfying; they also partake of grace.

However, to achieve this requires more than a prophet. It requires effective organization. Indeed, a prophet without an organized militant following is poorer than without honor—he is unsuccessful. In mobilization systems the political religion is turned into an ideology expressed through the mechanism of the single party. We have seen that leader, party, and the state become one and the same. The community is organized according to the translation of political values, by means of the leader, into a popular but controlled system of roles.

We can now begin to draw together some of the threads of this discussion. If we contrast Ghana, Guinea, Mali, China, or Indonesia—that is to say, mobilization systems with political religion—with India and the Philippines—reconciliation systems without it—we find that in all of these, personality counts for much. Nehru, for example, occupied an exceptional place in his country's politics. The difference is that in both India and the Philippines, the quality of religious intensity is lacking *in* politics, although church religion remains certainly a factor *of* politics. No country is without some personal quality in its leadership. But the practice of catering to immortality, meaning identity and purpose and thereby justice, through prophetic leadership is more pervasive in Guinea, Ghana, and Mali, or China.

Here, then, we have one difference among the new nations. Several consequences follow. Those that center religiosity in politics ordinarily regard church religion as archaic. Justice is phrased less in terms of equity than in terms of purpose, with purpose directed toward collective ends. The search for meaning and identity results in such concepts as "African personality," Nkrumaism, or Sukarno's five principles. An earnest effort is made to ascribe new meaning to group life.

Ultimate ends are bound up directly with the state. It is the state that will fulfill the psychological and social needs that lie behind religions, not the church. The means include modernity and development, industrialization and science. These in turn are elevated to the status of transcendental beliefs. There a difficulty arises because they in fact are not transcendental but concrete, and as such exert a secularizing influence upon the social body. Such a difficulty is ordinarily kept in check by identifying concrete ends with "science." Modernity and technology become the prevailing "laws" of human schemes.[31]

This is, of course, in sharp contrast to the system built around a constitutional framework. The latter posits ends beyond the state itself, more universal, indeed derivative from church religion. The state is merely an organized means for reconciling the multiplicity of objectives among the members. In this the state cannot provide identity but only membership. It cannot provide meaning, for its policy is an amalgam of many group and individual purposes. Purpose is left to individuals, to seek it out as they can. There is a separate role for church religions as such.

In reconciliation systems justice and political morality are more largely a matter of individual and social conscience. Things as they are are often the measure of things as they should be.

Hence, one conclusion I draw from this discussion is that what divides new nations is less a matter of formal politics than it is a difference between the countries with political religion and the countries without it. The latter have a constitutional framework providing for what individuals press as their own objectives. If these objectives are cheap and demeaning, so will the society appear cheap and demeaned. If the citizenry has some loftier conception of its values, these too will be mirrored in its activities. For a constitutional framework is just that. It is a mirror held up to the working community, and in a very real sense it is what democracy is all about. Leaders in countries with political religion have a great deal of difficulty understanding this, or if they do, accepting it, for it requires patience both with one's self and one's fellows.

[31]In many mobilization systems the leaders are supporters of church religions as well, that is, of nonpolitical religious groups and beliefs. They may be hostile to specific churches, however. In other words, political prophets can be religious men in the usual sense of the term.

In the terms laid out above, political religion qualifies for the title of "religion." I said earlier that I believe church religion to be more ethically powerful than political religion. However, in mobilization systems the decline of church religion gives to political religion a singular opportunity to fill those spiritual lacunae that, arising from the basic needs of individuals to find immortality, define identity, and determine their fate, can no longer be satisfied in more ordinary ways.

With respect to political communities, the single-party system with a prophetic leader at its head who is the repository of final authority expresses itself in mobilizing the resources of the community to suit the ideological and organizational needs of newly developing countries. Bringing wide participation in social and material life together with militantly disciplined political control, it enhances stability and organization in the name of sacrifice and lofty objectives.

Can mobilization systems with their political religions transform themselves into reconciliation systems whose commitment is to a liberal framework of law? This is a question of great concern to the West. One tendency in favor of transformation to a reconciliation system lies in the fact that a mobilization system successful in promoting economic development must eventually confront its own successes. It will need to decentralize authority and increase its economic efficiency. This could have the effect of reducing the prophetic element and, as well, diffusing and spreading authority. One might even see the beginnings of this process in the Soviet Union. Evidence, admittedly slender, and subject as well to less sanguine explanations, can be found in Khrushchev's Twentieth and Twenty-second Congress speeches. Even if one grants this tendency, however, the question remains whether or not political religions themselves possess sufficient flexibility to tolerate structural changes from one type of system to another.

Another possible factor favorable to the decline of political religions is that they are successful only in so far as ultimate ends and material ends are considered synonymous. This is possible only when what might be called the "aspirational gap" between material ends and genuine potentialities is extremely wide. Material ends appear to embody happiness, prosperity, well-being, dignity, and achievement, and similar venerated ultimate ends. It is, of course, the wisdom of the rich to know that material ends embody nothing of the sort. True, an industrial society has some pride of achievement and a sense of technological and political superiority that rankles those who are poorer. But evidence in the West shows that in a society in which there is a decline in church religion, the public has been left emotionally starved and dangerously anomic, despite the high rate of material achievement. We therefore might expect that an increase in material prosperity will increase secularization and weaken both the organizational and the ideological strengths of political religion itself.

Another factor that can contribute to the decline of political religion is a generational one. Once a revolution has been consolidated, its revolutionary achievements become remote to the next generation. Only if its prophets are made to appear larger than life size can the religious aspect be institutionalized. If this is not successful, the revolutionaries may become less than folk heroes, and even comic and absurd. Prophetic statements lose the power of prophecy, and "young pioneers" are simply trying to get ahead like everyone else. Does political religion lose its creativity through the mere erosion of time and generation? This is one possibility, since it is an integral part of the mechanism of government. Beliefs may themselves become tarnished if the state becomes a center of antagonism. If revolt against church religion is iconoclastic, the revolt against political religion tends to be cynical.

Despite these possibilities, however, it still appears extremely unlikely that mobilization systems with political religion can become changed into reconciliation systems without it. For one thing, the pace of economic growth would need to be great enough so that contradictions between the sacred and the secular could not be resolved by other means more appropriate to maintaining autocratic rule and monolithic structure. Moreover, even if decentralization of authority occurred, one would need to find other factors germane to reconciliation systems that I have already discussed, particularly a growth in individualism, competitiveness, and values about a framework of representative government as exemplified in new political roles.

Mobilization systems are understandable responses to pressures upon political leaders from their followers. They define a range of problems as political that in both theocratic and reconciliation systems are mainly handled apart from government. They chip away at the entire tradition of individual liberty—a tradition that in many new nations is probably stronger than we ordinarily think. They pose the problem of modernization in terms of an organizational rather than an industrial revolution; and, in order to achieve modernization by organizational means, political religion stresses the values that will both have organizational value and, as well, institutionalize new roles more fitting to modern life. In order to be effective, such political religion makes monopolistic claims of authority and prescience. The difficulty with it lies in the fact that, once having become significant as the key to both modernization and authority, factors other than political religion (including pluralism in political beliefs, factionalism in parties and government, and the veneration of law as a framework for political life) are all conspicuously absent.

If the possibility of change to a reconciliation system is small, what other alternatives present themselves? One can consider here the possibility of a frank and open totalitarianism. In that case, even if cynicism and disbelief occur, no one dares speak of these, and indeed a kind of inverted realism emerges. This was most dramatically exhibited in the Moscow trials. The dependence on the state for immortality, identity, and purpose was complete because individuals had no recognized existence apart from the state. One needs only to look at the final statement of Bukharin at the Moscow trials to see the apotheosis of the state-awarded personality. However, this alternative probably sounds more likely than it really is. One factor militating against it in new nations is that totalitarianism there cannot be quite so efficiently organized as in western totalitarianisms. That kind of organization takes considerable technology. Much more likely as a prospect is the growth of new theocracies in which the state and the political religion become ends in themselves. Whereas the political religion of the U.S.S.R. seeks to express itself in values that, even if unfilled, nevertheless are universal in their relation to both the wider religious systems of the West and are integrated with the actualities of industrialization, it is possible that we shall see in some of the new nations a parochial blending of religion and state not entirely dissimilar to the traditional societies that preceded them. Here, then, is a third and most likely possibility: the emergence of new theocracies. Present leaders who, children of the West as much as of their own traditions, can in time be elevated to a pantheon of their own creation. A reinterpretation of political religion will absorb its modernizing significance by expressing modernization in traditional theocratic terms. We can expect, then, ritual and dogma to increase as political religion declines.

Such matters are not to be ignored, despite the rhetoric of modernizing nationalists. To return to the point I raised at the beginning of this discussion, one could assume that the new nations would be able to industrialize rapidly; we might argue in favor of the effects of industrializing that such a mixture of roles and functions would be produced in which all industrial countries might eventually come to look more and more alike. This argument does not apply to most of the new nations, however, because, as we have said, industrialization is not readily achievable in the foreseeable future. Possibly the only major exception to this statement will be India, and even there the picture is by no means clear. Hence a form of neotraditionalism, expressed in modern theocracies, can utilize modern techniques of government and administration, and regard the state as an educative body instilling right principles of conduct and outlook. Particular values embodying political obligation and community, presently associated with a dominant party and leader, may also provide the basis for both prophet and scripture. The very real possibility exists that mobilization systems can be transformed into neotraditionalistic theocracies in which both traditional theocratic religions and modern political ones combine.

Our conclusion, then, points to the following three possibilities: First, for reasons intrinsic to the nature of political religion, mobilization systems among the new nations will be unstable in the long run. Second, few mobilization systems will be transformed into either reconciliation or totalitarian types. Third, there is a real possibility that they will be changed into *modernizing autocracies* within the framework of neotraditionalism, using ritual to institutionalize political religion.

If we can expect the ritualization of political religion within a new form of theocratic state as a most likely prospect in many of the new nations, it would be interesting to speculate on some of the probable characteristics of potential modern theocracies. Tendencies can already be identified. Formal monarchies are not apt to be established, associated as they are with pre-emancipation and with ethnic and premodern local groups against which the new state is often in conflict. More than likely are presidential systems, or, more accurately, "presidential monarchies," with nondynastic aspects of presidential systems combined with the dynastic aspects of ceremonial and ritual functions associated with kingship. A presidential monarch can play an active political role utilizing concentrated power, and a ritualized religious role as well, representative of the symbolic qualities of the entire nation.

The nationalist single party comes to form the new group of guardians and warriors of the state. These carry on the modern functions of entrepreneurship through state enterprise and leadership. Composed of an elect, they are the purveyors of ritual. Among them are those whose job it is to interpret and explain matters of dogma and ritual to the public. If not high priests, they are nevertheless appointed keepers of the sacred texts.

The texts themselves are a blend of ideology and theology. Mixtures of mysticism and pragmatism, they tend to be nonprogrammatic so that innovation will not be offended by any strict doctrine. However, they provide guides to moral conduct and help define individual relationships to the state and the leader as well. Beyond ordinary ideology, they strive to enhance individual immortality by linking it to the leader who is founder of the state, provide purpose by defining it, and indicate a hopeful future state of affairs to be achieved through the political kingdom. One would expect that the norms of egalitarianism, mass participation in social life, opportunity, abundance, that is, the values expressed in the totalitarian-democratic tradition of which Talmon speaks, will all be expressed. The language of these texts, some of which already exist and are mainly written by the leaders themselves, follow the terminology of socialism in an extremely wide and loose sense. Evidence is already available about these texts and the expressions they possess. For example, in the African case, we can cite two main types. One consists of the writings of the President of Guinea, whose militant socialist version of *negritude* has blended the communal and esthetic properties of African traditional life with modern socialist values and practices. Another is the effort in Ghana to establish Nkrumaism as a philosophical system combining aspects of socialism, with an emphasis on the African personality and certain traditional customs and social forms. Notably absent are concerns with two central features of socialist doctrine: property and class.

The enemies include capitalism (as distinct from investment capital), neocolonialism or neoimperialism, racial discrimination, traditionalism, and those individuals or groups that show antagonism to the leader, regime, or political religion. The notion of evil can also be extended to include those roles that are not functional to the performance of modernized social and political activities that the state supports. In this respect the political religion helps to distinguish "good" and "bad" roles and to tie them to the needs of the modernizing state.

It is, of course, impossible to do more than briefly sketch in some possible characteristics of the new theocracies. Not all the new states will follow this pattern. That should go without saying. Those that do will show widely differing practices. For example, they may vary in the degree in which all significant groups come under the religious umbrella. Particularly in the case of the civil servants, a kind of "positive neutralism" within the state may surround the bureaucratic role, with the effect of exempting them from ritualized practices and religious observances. The same may also hold true for groups representing church religions. The monopolistic quality of political religion does not always need to be directed against church practices and beliefs. Indeed, it is more likely to direct itself against other political religions instead (unless the church religion becomes an inhibiting influence in the state).

Political ritualization can help to blend the new roles of leader, priest, elect, into an effective system, surrounded by a religious doctrine that is itself a mixture of modernizing values (as in socialism) and unique traditions (as in *negritude*). These stress change with continuity, and form the basis of authority in the society. The ritualization of these values is therefore one way to institutionalize new roles of the polity, and most particularly that of the "Presidential monarch."[32]

The importance of political religion lies precisely in the barriers it places in the way of smooth transition from societies in which politics is sacred to those in which it is not, and, correspondingly, in the change

[32]For a detailed analysis of a modernizing autocracy, see my book *The Political Kingdom of Uganda: A Study in Bureaucratic Nationalism* (Princeton: Princeton University Press, 1961), *passim.*

from mobilization systems to reconciliation types. Despite the forces working to erode political religion, it is clear that, once authority is in some measure dependent on it, its decline becomes a political problem because it affects the basic stability of the society and the legitimization of authority embodied in a particular regime. Hence mobilization systems tend to fight secularization whether it derives from the ultimate incompatibilities posed by elevating material ends to sacred rank, or from the growth of disillusionment and cynicism.

Perhaps we have been somewhat misled by certain of the tendencies toward wider association between peoples and nations, which is itself an important and obvious consequence of the decline of colonialism. I say "misled" because within the universalizing and fraternizing relations of the new nation-states there is also to be found a new parochialism. Under certain circumstances such a perfectly respectable doctrine as neutralism may turn out to be a disguised way of withdrawing from more widely accepted responsibilities. If the values of the political religion become less than universal, and if the level of political life in the mobilization system becomes a source of shame and embarrassment to political leaders, then the iron-curtain phenomenon could appear in those new nations that desire an exemption from ordinary standards of judgment applied to them in other parts of the world. In other words, if a new nation should exhibit a second-rate countenance to the world, it may also find it necessary to invert the criteria of second-rateness. Disguised in the doctrine of each nation's finding its "own way" in wrestling with internal problems is the danger of self-delusion. Political religion does, after all, deal in illusions.

If these assumptions are correct, the likely possibility of change will become centered upon ritualization, a circumstance that limits the functional consequences of religion without destroying its relation to authority. Political leadership will derive from strongly ritualistic roles. Exactly what the the specifications of these roles will be it is impossible to predict, but they would certainly have strong traditionalistic features at least superficially attached to them. We can see this occurring already in the titles taken by Nkrumah in Ghana, which include a number of traditional forms in addition to "Osagyefo" (Military Savior).

V

Obviously the analysis we have sketched in above has proceeded on several levels. The difficulty has been how to weave together the relationship between those fundamental needs both religion and politics can satisfy in ordinary human beings while relating them to the dynamic properties of different structural types. Properly, then, this discussion ought to be regarded as the beginning of a study rather than as the end of it. There is no doubt in my mind that political religion is one way of assisting polities to define their aims and establish their priorities while allowing political leaders to remain exempt from ordinary criticisms and errors. That this is dangerous goes without saying. As well, such a process might have the effect of stifling creative thought and daring among those who have been brought up in the faith. Nevertheless, if this is an age in which religious faith has been sharply restricted as a guide to men's actions and purposes, it cannot be too surprising if the state steps in to fill the void—especially when there are so many other compelling reasons for the state to do so.

What should be clear about political religion is that it is an unsettling factor in a state—at least in the long run. Political religions are subject to even more severe and cynical disenchantment by their adherents than church religions. For the latter, in addition to their more transcendental concerns, are also a code for expressing individual terrors and moralities. True, not all religions deal specifically with moral questions. Ultimately, however, they express individual continuity, individual identity, and individual purpose.

Our hopes for democracy in the new nations are based on unreliable notions that man will eventually assert his personality against restrictive governments no matter what the odds against him. That in the long run no matter how abjectly a man is made to crawl before the state he will in the end assert himself against it. This is a comforting notion. It is lent some substance because in new nations it is difficult to insulate even relatively distant and faraway peoples from the echoes of liberal beliefs and from democratic and libertarian events. Perhaps if educational programs emphasize something more than a combination of technical information and ideological indoctrination (a growing trend), there will be resistance to the decretals put forward by political religionists.

What is more likely, however, is that real modernization will begin in most of the new nations when the political religions are turned in upon themselves and when the insularities and exemptions from judgment that so many political leaders demand are ended in a new round of secular questioning. This will take time. Meanwhile, Tocqueville's words on the French Revolution are relevant:

> They will say that a country governed by an absolute ruler is a *democracy* because he governs by such laws and maintains such institutions as are favorable to the great mass of the people. Such a government, it will be said, is *democratic*, a *democratic monarchy*.
>
> But *democratic government, democratic monarchy* can only mean one thing in the true sense of these words: a government where the people

> more or less participate in their government. Its sense is intimately bound to the idea of political liberty. To give the democratic epithet to a government where there is no political liberty is a palpable absurdity, since this departs from the natural meaning of these words.
>
> Such false or obscure expressions are adopted: (*a*) because of the wish to give the masses illusions, for the expression "democratic government" will always evoke a certain degree of appeal; (*b*) because of the embarrassing difficulty in finding a single term which would explain the complex system of an absolute government where the people do not all participate in public affairs but where the upper classes have no privileges either and where legislation aims to provide as much material welfare as possible.[33]

The phenomenon of which Tocqueville speaks is not entirely dissimilar to the mobilization systems among the new states. They are "presidential monarchies," and rather aristocratic ones. Their political religions express liberty in corporate discipline. Through corporate discipline the state provides immortality, meaning, and purpose. But even when such political religions are compelling for other reasons, they are less profound than church religions. The intermingling of the sacred and the secular makes the former more mundane. Political religions rarely incorporate the spirit and the wider meanings of human life, although they may make explicit and even ennoble the narrower meanings of social life. They cannot contemplate the concept of fate itself, even though determining the career and opportunities for an individual. They cannot give immortality even when they perpetuate the race, provide for the protection of the incumbents, and seek to provide for family and society.

Talmon argues that the

> reign of the exclusive yet all-solving doctrine of totalitarian democracy runs counter to the lessons of nature and history. Nature and history show civilization as the evolution of historically and pragmatically formed clusters of social existence and social endeavor, and not as the achievement of abstract man on a single level of existence.[34]

I hope that he is right. But nature shows such multiplicity and diversity that claims in its name can give false comfort. More likely we shall witness pragmatically formed clusters of social belief, political practices, and patterns of leadership more in keeping with the undigested practices of uneven modernization. Here the problems of political ritualization, manipulation of symbols, and new theocracies are equally plausible solutions to problems of political religion, authority, and modernization.

[33]See Tocqueville, *op. cit.*, pp. 102–103.
[34]Talmon, *op. cit.*, p. 254.

Ideology and Discontent

INTRODUCTION

In this essay I intend to pursue several themes that are to be found elsewhere in the book but in an almost muttering kind of way, picking up an idea, putting it down again, returning to it as the mood strikes me. I have done so deliberately, in order to establish an attitude of mind, as it were, about so trying a subject. For ideology has no specific referent, although, despite its elusiveness, it remains powerful, meshing as it does at so many different points in our organized lives and intimate selves. While there are, therefore, main themes here—the role of ideology in society, in personality, in new nations as well as in old ones—there is also a random quality to these remarks, which are designed to explore the outermost limits of the significance of the subject.

Perhaps the main reason for studying ideology is its mirror-like quality, reflecting the moral and material aspects of our understanding. These aspects become intensely interesting, especially in an age of science when they can no longer be rooted in faith. For all their sturdy tenure together, reason and morality have remained uneasy partners. In his book, *The Logic of Liberty*, Michael Polanyi has commented that science is in a paradoxical condition that reflects the modern mind: "A new destructive scepticism is linked here to a new passionate social conscience; an utter disbelief in the spirit of man is coupled with extravagant moral demands. We see at work here the form of action which has already dealt so many shattering blows to the modern world: the chisel of scepticism driven by the hammer of social passion."[1]

[1]Michael Polanyi, *The Logic of Liberty* (Chicago: The University of Chicago Press, 1951), p. 4.

This paradox is to be found in all modern societies; those in the first stages of their development (where the freshness of self-discovery gives way to the dicipline of organized power), as well as those which have gone through earlier upheavals in the effort to transform themselves. At a time when the Russians have conquered space, their new writers and poets, Voznesensky, Yevtushenko, Tertz, and others revolt against, rather than exult in, the achievements of science. Their counterparts can be found in the West.

We have refined our moral sensibilities along with our skepticism. At no time in history has the world been so sensitive to moral subtleties and more likely to take its transgressions seriously. This sensitivity is expressed in many ways, among the developing nations in a search for new political forms, among the older ones in a public desire for reform. In both, there is a new willingness to apply scientific research to human problems. Yet experience tells us that the more we desire to ameliorate our ills, the more they crowd in upon us. Each fresh solution uncovers more problems. The truth is that men at work on these matters are troubled men.

This "Polanyi paradox" is reflected in our attitudes to modern ideologies. None seems able to capture the public imagination either programmatically or morally. This observation is true of the developing areas as well as of our own. In the former, it is the heroic individual or leader, more than the content of his ideas, around which the many rally in order to organize themselves. In their eyes, leadership and progress go together. It is more complex than that in the highly developed countries, where offended morality leads to outrage. We still do not know where outrage will lead.

One clue is offered by the study of ideologies. Ideology and outrage have affinities, which reflect something of what men claim to strive for even when their thinking is contrived and dull. The vaguest of ideologies can be made to shine in the reflected glow of moral indignation.

Why is that? Because ideology is not quite like other subjects. It reflects the presuppositions of its observers. The study of ideologies soon draws one into the analysis of social science itself, into meta-analysis, with all its peculiarities and its uniqueness. Weber and Mannheim after him pointed out this fact because they were struck by the capacity of social scientists to understand the meaning of events from the inside, as it were. One cannot comprehend the motives of stars because they do not have motives. The inner life is the unique quality of living man. Furthermore, each place has its own mood and its own special problems which are expressed in ideologies. That is why the subject remains important. Our assumption here is that, if we examine ideology contextually and comparatively, we shall learn something about the coherence and intellectual cultures of modern nations and their degrees of integration.

This book is concerned with various ideological formulae some of which have arisen in response to the problems of development. Development is not an ideology, but it embodies hope and a positive notion of the future (even though it may reveal, at any moment, consequences so negative that they are blinding). The ideologies employed in development seek to transcend negativism and to define hope in programmatic terms. Of the many ideologies we could discuss, three are of interest because of their general acceptance. The first is the ideology of socialism. The second is the ideology of nationalism. The third, which is presently evolving in modern development systems, results from the adaptation of the scientific spirit to social science. We can properly refer to it as a social-science ideology and discuss its conditions and consequences.

Ideology Defined

Before going on to these matters, however, some definition of ideology is essential. "Ideology" refers to more than doctrine. It links particular actions and mundane practices with a wider set of meanings and, by doing so, lends a more honorable and dignified complexion to social conduct. This view is, of course, a generous one. From another vantage point, ideology may be viewed as a cloak for shabby motives and appearances. The more generous version lays emphasis on the behavior of individuals in a setting of action-in-relation-to-principle.

"Ideology" is a generic term applied to general ideas potent in specific situations of conduct: for example, not *any* ideals—only political ones; not *any* values—only those specifying a given set of preferences; not *any* beliefs—only those governing particular modes of thought. Because it is the link between action and fundamental belief, ideology helps to make more explicit the moral basis of action. It is not a vulgar description of something more noble and sacred than itself, like a cartoon of a stained glass window.

Furthermore, ideology is not philosophy. It is in the curious position of an abstraction that is less abstract than the abstractions contained within it. Powerful ideologies and creative ideologists (like religious ideas and innovative clerics) do much to enlarge the role of the individual. That is why the role of ideology is central to the thinking of revolutionaries. Working out an ideology is for them a way of stipulating the moral superiority of new ideas.

Political ideology is an application of particular moral prescriptions to collectivities. Any ideology can become political. Hegelianism became the "ideological" justification for the Prussian state. Marxism-Leninism is the "ideology" of Communist societies. Both claims to superiority lie in a presumed relationship between higher human consciousness and more evolved forms of material relationship. The ideologist is the one who makes the intellectual and moral leap forward; by virtue of his superior knowledge, his view ought to prevail.[2]

In the Western world, ideology has changed considerably from the more dogmatic statements that periodically in the eighteenth and nineteenth centuries heralded total solutions to world problems. Today our ideologies are disguised. Their language has changed. The utopian element has disappeared. One might say that our own society holds some vague belief in democratic progress through the application of science to human affairs, and that in recent times this belief has come to include social science. The special application of science in social affairs represents our commitment to the rational improvement of our society. Not only does this application fall within our definition of ideology, but, as applied to collectivities, it is increasingly political. This way of putting things is no doubt somewhat troublesome because it extends our ordinary notions of ideology into new areas. But if these notions have any merit, then the subject of ideology is more important to study than ever before.

Why? Perhaps not much more need be said in answer than it is hard to understand the meaning of human conduct without some knowledge of it. As Inkeles remarked in his book on the Soviet Union, "Certainly a knowledge of their fundamental beliefs is hardly sufficient for the explanation of men's actions in the real world. But insofar as these actions reflect a mutual adjustment between ideology and social realities, an understanding of ideology becomes a necessary condition for an understanding of the action."[3] As I have already suggested furthermore, the study of ideology reveals the "scientific" status of social science more clearly than does any other subject. To study *about* ideology (as distinct from examining specific ideologies) raises issues about the scientific quality of social science methods. These issues are: the role of the observer—aloof social scientist or passionate but reflective participant; the degree to which we can assume the motivations and attitudes of others by "empathizing" with their roles or playing similar ones; the degree to which we can separate observer roles from previous ideological commitment, or put more generally, the problem of bias in research; and the nature of prediction.

Such matters have become more pressing as the social sciences have become more interested in precision. A science is, in the long run, evaluated on the basis of the useful predictions it can make, and these pre-

[2]George Lichtheim, *Marxism: An Historical and Critical Study* (London: Routledge & Kegan Paul, Ltd., 1961), Parts I and II.

[3]Alex Inkeles, *Public Opinion in Soviet Russia: A Study in Mass Persuasion* (Cambridge: Harvard University Press, 1950), p. 21.

dictions depend in turn on the power of the independent variables used in analysis. Ready or not, social scientists are being asked to do research leading to policy formation. What happened first in the natural and physical sciences is now beginning in the social sciences—that is the modification of change through the application of planning and control. Some years ago, Bertrand Russell made a comment about the role of science that is increasingly applicable to social science as well. "Science used to be valued as a means of getting to *know* the world; now, owing to the triumphs of technique, it is conceived as showing how to *change* the world."[4]

These themes then serve as the underlying rationale for this view. Methodologically, the commentary ranges from the broadly structural to the more precise and behavioral. The units of analysis are nations because the roles and contents of their ideologies seem particularly interesting. We have included older development communities of the West and some newer ones in other areas. We have excluded the Soviet system largely because the changes going on there are so great and wrapped in so much conjecture that they require a separate treatment.

A FUNCTIONAL APPROACH

I am inclined to the view that ideology helps to perform two main functions: one directly social, binding the community together, and the other individual, organizing the role personalities of the maturing individual.

These functions combine to legitimize authority. It is the relation to authority that gives ideology its political significance. In "early-stage" development communities, authority becomes legitimized on the basis of those ideologies that lay claim to superior planning and rationality and that provide moral bases for social manipulation for development purposes. Such authority is supported by large bodies of technicians, economists, administrative specialists, and fiscal experts. In short, ideology helps to support an elite and to justify the exercise of power. This observation is no less true for highly developed societies, even though in them the position of ideology is shakier, with corresponding weaknesses in social solidarity and individual identity. It is the curious mood of our time that the rise of unlimited opportunities in the development sphere, through the applications of social science to modern problems, is accompanied by much ideological restlessness.

[4]Bertrand Russell, *The Impact of Science on Society* (New York: Columbia University Press, 1951), p. 45.

The Solidarity Aspect

The solidarity aspect of ideology was first made explicit by Marx. His views can be briefly summarized as follows. Change in the material conditions of life is expressed in two forms: the intensification of class struggle resulting in the emergence of different kinds of systems and the evolution of a higher form of consciousness that coincides with the evolutionary pattern of system growth.[5]

Less clear is the degree of determinism Marx attributed to productive relations. This vagueness in the Marxian theory has, of course, been the basis for a great deal of debate. If productive relations determined all, then it ought to be unnecessary to study ideology. Yet ideology is very much a concern of the Marxians.

Lenin, the ideologue of Marxism, reinforced his polemics with claims to superior wisdom. From analysis of "material conditions," the ideologue can lay down a "correct" political line for the public to follow. Superior wisdom is equated with ideological authority by means of which the public is converted to the political line.[6] Indeed, ideological purity be-

[5]Lichtheim points out that there is a conflict here, which Marxists in their "objectivism" do not like to admit. Although it is "in accordance with Marx's own manner to take a historical view of his work, such an approach presupposes a vantage-point made available by developments beyond the stage reflected in the Marxian system. In other words, it assumes that the Marxian categories are no longer quite applicable to current history. For obvious reasons, this is an admission which orthodox Marxists find hard to make, while others may wonder why this particular scruple should arise in the first place. Its emergence is due to the fact that Hegel and following him, Marx, took a view of history which is not the familiar positivist one. They saw history as a process whose meaning reveals itself by stages, the succession of the latter reflecting man's growing awareness of his role in creating the historical world. To comprehend its past, mankind must raise itself to a higher level; hence, our ability to understand our predecessors suggests that we have reached a new altitude." Lichtheim, *op. cit.*, p. xv.

It was this problem that concerned Mannheim. Although Marxism supported the objectivist school of thought, the consequences of his theories were to produce the neo-Marxian subjectivist school of the sociology of knowledge. Mannheim and his followers, however, cannot avoid the same criticism to which Marx was subject.

[6]This view is nicely brought out in the conflict between the "Economists" and Lenin. Consider, for example, the criticisms leveled against *Iskra*, Lenin's newspaper, and Lenin's reply. The criticism: "*Iskra's* excessive predilection for controversy is due primarily to its exaggerated idea of the role of 'ideology' (programs, theories . . .) in the movement, and is partly an echo of the internecine squabbles that have flared up among Russian emigrants in Western Europe, of which they have hastened to inform the world in a number of polemical pamphlets and articles. In our opinion, these disagreements exercise almost no influence upon the actual progress of the Russian Social-Democratic movement except perhaps to damage it by introducing an undesirable schism among the comrades working in Russia. For that reason we cannot but express our disapproval of *Iskra's* polemical zeal, particularly when it exceeds the bounds of decency." Lenin's reply was characteristic. He flayed the "Economists" for not staying ahead of the revolutionary consciousness of the people. He charged

comes the rock against which waves of deviationism must be dashed unless they submerge the promontories of revolution.[7]

Lenin made ideology into a form of philosophical propaganda. He was both ideologue and ideologist. In his hand, communism became a revolutionary dogma: not a philosophy—it contained one; not an epistemology—it prescribed one; not a system of values—it was a program for achieving one. But he did not transform ideology into much more than propaganda. It is Sorel, rather than Lenin, who spins out the implications of solidarity to the fullest and "completes" Marx "instead of making commentaries on his text as his unfortunate disciples have done for so long."[8]

The feature of Sorel's work that makes explicit the solidarity function of ideology is the role of myth—more particularly the myth of the general strike. Myth is the social equivalent of metaphor, or, to put it another way, myth is to solidarity what metaphor is to identity. It is a way of binding the individual and the social together. For such myths to be useful, Sorel argues, they must be in tune with the worthier moral tendencies. It is on a moral basis that ideologies must be evaluated rather than on vague belief in dialectical progress. He taxes Marxians for failing to recognize that old myths can be revived in order to modify the historical processes, thus leading to reactionary revolutions: "Marx does not seem

---

that the authors of the attack "fail to understand that an 'ideologist' is worthy of that name only when he marches ahead of the 'spontaneous movement,' points out the road, and when he is able, ahead of all others, to solve all the theoretical, political, tactical and organizational questions which the 'material elements' of the movement spontaneously encounter. In order to give 'consideration to the material elements of the movement' it is necessary to be critical of it, to point out its dangers and defects, and aspire to elevate spontaneity to consciousness. To say, however, that ideologists (i.e., conscious leaders) cannot divert the movement created by the interaction of environment and elements from its path is to ignore the elementary truth that consciousness participates in this interaction and creation."

Lenin equates ideology with more than the simple manipulation of ideas. Rather, it is created by those who share a higher consciousness and a more informed intelligence about social matters. He calls ideological "elements" those "conscious elements [who] operate according to plan." Nicolai Lenin, "A Conversation with Defenders of Economism," in *Collected Works of Lenin*, IV, ed. Alexander Trachtenberg (New York: International Publishers Co., Inc., 1929), Book II: "The Iskra Period," 66–67.

[7]This aspect of ideology, building solidarity within confusion and vulnerability without, is one of the reasons why Marxism as an ideology is attractive to many youthful leaders of new states. Marx considers ideology to be those ideas that represent a particular mode of social organization. "To consider ideology as a set of ruling ideas which have been separated from the ruling individuals and given an independent force, an element of creativity in social affairs," he considers nonsense. The real basis of ideology, he points out, is in the material conditions of life, particularly in social relationships, division of labor, and productive power. Ideology is thus a screen for reality, a cloak. Karl Marx, *The German Ideology* (New York: International Publishers Co., Inc., 1939) pp. 41, 42, 43; see also Karl Mannheim, *Ideology and Utopia* (New York, Harcourt, Brace, and Co., 1946), p. 110.

[8]Georges Sorel, *Reflections on Violence* (New York: The Free Press, 1950), p. 59.

to have asked himself what would happen if the economic system were on the downgrade; he never dreamt of the possibility of a revolution which would take a return to the past, or even social conservation as its ideal. . . .

"These are dreams which Marx looked upon as reactionary, and consequently negligible, because it seemed to him that capitalism was embarked on an irresistible progress; but nowadays we see considerable forces grouped together in the endeavor to reform the capitalist economic system by bringing it, with the aid of laws, nearer to the medieval ideal. Parliamentary Socialism would like to combine with the moralists, the Church, and the democracy, with the common aim of impeding the capitalist movement; and, in view of middle-class cowardice, that would not perhaps be impossible."[9]

The myths and the utopias provide each great event with its moral dimension. Sorel asks, "what remains of the Revolution when we have taken away the epic of the wars against the coalition, and of that of the victories of the populace? What remains is not very savoury: police operations, proscriptions, and sittings of servile courts of law."[10]

For Sorel it is the myth of the proletarian general strike that activates the class struggle and carries it forward. In this sense, we can say that he carries Marx to an ideological conclusion, for without the ideology of the general strike, regardless of the full weight of material development or the evolutionary emphasis in dialectical materialism, the revolution may fail or become reactionary. Ideology is a necessary ingredient of progress.[11]

What makes Sorel interesting to us, however, is not his doctrine of the proletarian general strike or his justification of violence. It is, rather the claim he makes for ideology. Its role is to build solidarity, and solidarity is the moral basis of society. Solidarity is for Sorel a moral system based on class and held together by myths. It is the foundation of change. Solidarity-producing myths are "good" when they lead to a higher morality. His plea for solidarity is thus also a plea for a more social personality and a superior human community.

This connection between solidarity and morality is the essence of authority, a fact well recognized by leaders of new nations. Solidarity and myth as expressed in ideology are commonly manipulated in order to supply a moral dimension to political forms. In this sense, the creation of

[9] *Ibid.*, p. 107.

[10] *Ibid.*, p. 119.

[11] Sorel, although an admirer of Marx, is by no means dazzled by his doctrine. He quotes with relish a "learned exponent of Socialism" who said that "the art of reconciling opposites by means of nonsense is the most obvious result which he had got from the study of the works of Marx." *Ibid.*, p. 138. See also Ernest Cassirer, *The Myth of the State* (New Haven: Yale University Press, 1946), Part 1.

myth, the moral solidarity of the community, and its authority are intimately linked.

The Identity Aspect

Sorel helped to clarify the function of ideology for society in building its bonds of affect, social commitment, and historical perspective. The natural outcome of his analysis centers attention less on the particular polemics of his own ideology than on the diverse but concrete manifestations of solidarity in ideological form. These manifestations include the use of historical myths, the rewriting of history, the search for a golden age—all ingredients that serve to promote the ends of a political community. So far, ideology in society has been our point of reference. But ideology, like language and dreams, is related to morphologies of behavior by universal psychobiological variables. Balance, mastery, and control are the desired results of ideological behavior. Ideas help men to control and change their environment. Such ideas arise out of action rather than out of pure speculation. Such was Freud's view. He wrote "It must not be assumed that mankind came to create its first world system through a purely speculative thirst for knowledge. The practical need of mastering the world must have contributed to this effort."[12] These views of Freud's would apply to all forms of belief, including animism, magic, taboos, and presumably political beliefs.[13]

For Freud, ideology is a form of personal *rationalization*. (In this view, he might have agreed with Marx.) Both he and Marx saw ideas as a cloak behind which "reality" hides, although, of course, each had a different idea of reality. For Freud ideologies are elaborate mental fictions, which the observer must penetrate in order to understand personality. Ideology in his view is uniquely personal. The scholar who seeks to understand ideology is the psychotherapist who unravels the mental rationalizations of his patients. It is hard to say whether or not this attitude defined ideology as a pathological condition for Freud. Certainly he would consider political extremists emotionally suspect. He did not have much taste for the bizarre, despite the novelty of his views.

[12]A. A. Brill, ed., *The Basic Writings of Sigmund Freud* (New York: Modern Library, Inc., 1938), p. 867.

[13]Perhaps Freud's most direct concern with ideology is his analysis of the "chosen people" myth. Freud's transposition of the Moses legend is remarkable for its imaginative skill. More to the point, Freud argues that "the human intellect has not shown itself elsewhere to be endowed with a very good scent for truth, nor has the human mind displayed any readiness to accept truth. On the contrary, it is the general experience that the human intellect errs very easily without our suspecting it at all, and that nothing is more readily believed that what—regardless of the truth—meets our wishes and illusions half-way." Sigmund Freud, *Moses and Monotheism* (New York: Alfred A. Knopf, Inc., 1939), p. 204.

Yet Erikson, who recently became concerned with such matters, does not do too great violence to the ideas of Freud when, in his study of Luther, he emphasizes the forbidding emotional complex that led to greatness. His concern with the conditions leading to the formation of creative personalities leads him to both the study of ideology and its role in personality. In psycho-history more than in any other form of social analysis, the observer relies on unorthodox sensitivities as he sniffs for evidence, clues, and data, much of which has barely been touched by previous analysts. He is more on his own in social analysis than either the ordinary historian or the social scientist. Erikson's point is that, since he observes ideology in the context of personality, the psychotherapist *cum* social-science observer can contribute a great deal to the understanding of why individuals are so receptive to ideology. Erikson establishes a theory of personality formation based on that aspect of maturation he calls the search for identity. Because identity search coincides with role search, youth (as well as others who have never quite "found" themselves, as the vernacular goes) is particularly vulnerable to ideologies. This point adds another aspect of the study of ideology to the one offered by the Marxians, motivation. None of the Marxians can explain why class interest ought to *be*, and they are confused enough to deny the universality of the proposition by showing how it is possible for some individuals to emancipate themselves from that class interest. This contradiction is an important weakness in Marxian theory, for, much as Marx would have liked to deny the independent validity of ideas for action, he had to leave some loopholes for the gratuitous entry of nonworking-class Marxian ideas. The link between material conditions and class behavior cannot therefore be axiomatic. The result is an incomplete and inconclusive treatment of ideology. Erikson defines ideology as "an unconscious tendency underlying religious and scientific as well as political thought: the tendency at a given time to make facts amenable to ideas, and ideas to facts, in order to create a world image convincing enough to support the collective and the individual sense of identity. Far from being arbitrary or consciously manageable (although it is as exploitable as all of man's unconscious strivings), the total perspective created by ideological simplification reveals its strength by the dominance it exerts on the seeming logic of historical events, and by its influence on the identity formation of individuals (and thus on their 'ego-strength')."[14]

This formulation helps us understand why individuals are receptive to ideology, by showing how ideology satisfies the identity function. It also helps us to realize how it is that the creative ideologist is formed. By

[14]Erik H. Erikson, *Young Man Luther: A Study in Psychoanalysis and History* (New York: W. W. Norton & Company, Inc., 1958), p. 20. He goes on to describe his book as a study of "identity and ideology."

relating identity to maturation—by defining it as a critical problem for youth—Erikson suggests why it is that ideology has a particular attractiveness to youth. The first point provides some insight into the conditions of personal conflict that lead to the acceptance or rejection of ideologies. The second helps to explain prophets, charismatic leaders, and manipulators of ideology. The third is of particular relevance to new-development communities, where the emphasis on youth raises it to a particularly high level of prominence in society at the precise time when the search for identity is at its most critical stage.[15]

IDEOLOGY IN THE DEVELOPING AREAS

So far we have been exploring the significance of solidarity and identity as laid down by social theorists who have had something appropriate to say about them.[16]

In this section, we shall discuss these matters with respect to both new and old nations. Rightly or wrongly, I visualize developing communities as if they were strung on a continuum. The new developing communities are trying to sort out certain problems that the older ones have more or less resolved, although not in all cases. These problems involve the more "primordial" sentiments based on race, language, tribe, or other factors, which, although not relevant to the development process, may be relevant to the maintenance of solidarity or identity. What I call "nationalism" is the ideology that embodies these primordial sentiments. It is well to bear this special meaning in mind as we discuss the relationship between nationalism and socialism. In the highly developed communities, such primordial sentiments are less a problem than are confusion, irresponsibility, withdrawal, and cynicism. Here we can find conditions pointing to what

[15]"Youth stands between the past and the future, both in individual life and in society. It also stands between alternate ways of life. . . . Ideologies offer to the members of this age-group overly simplified and yet determined answers to exactly those vague inner states and those urgent questions which arise in consequence of identity conflict. Ideologies serve to channel youth's forceful earnestness and sincere asceticism as well as its search for excitement and its eager indignation toward that social frontier where the struggle between conservatism and radicalism is most alive. On that frontier, fanatic ideologists do their busy work and psychopathic leaders their dirty work; but there, also, true leaders create significant solidarities." *Ibid.*, pp. 38–39.

[16]"Solidarity" is a highly abstract term for the bonds that hold individuals together through shared emotions about the same highly valued ideas and objects. Ideology cannot therefore be other than significant in solidarity. Identity is the self-definition of individuals with reference to their roles and the roles of others. Ideology cannot help but suggest guidelines to the self-definition process. It is also the case, however, that ideology responds differently to different demands made upon it in both the solidarity and identity spheres. In addition, the relationship between solidarity and identity deeply affects the appropriateness of particular ideologies.

Durkheim called *anomie*. More common is something like Scheler's *ressentiment*. Generally there is a feeling of fear and disappointment in the consequences of development. Boundless confidence in the benefits it will bring (common in new nations) is not very widespread in the older nations.

Countries that are neither new nor old in this process include Japan and the U.S.S.R. We shall briefly mention the former because in Japan nationalism has played a crucial part in relating solidarity, identity, and development to one another. The Soviet system we shall not discuss—partly because there is insufficient data. We do not know the role of ideology there at the moment; nor is it clear what ideologies are prevalent. If we can consider the ideology of the Soviet Union conservative, embodying as it does principles that are to be realized through the Soviet state, it is also true that we cannot evaluate its role without comparing it to an ideology of rebellion. The only hints we have are in the poems, plays, and novels of the angry young Soviet men. As the U.S.S.R. moves toward the highly developed end of the continuum, we may expect that a new language and a new ideology will emerge. But such a time is in the rather distant future.

What we are suggesting then is that the role of ideology in the new developing communities is to promote authority. In the middle of the continuum it maintains authority. In the older societies, ideologies compete, weakening solidarity and identity with the resulting danger of alienation. Paradoxically, however, consensus varies in the opposite direction. In the new developing areas consensus is low, primordial loyalties high. Ideology blends them. In the old developing areas, consensus is high and primordial loyalties low. Ideology makes minor differences important. Correspondingly, the identity problem in the new development communities is to achieve a political consensus—the problem of political socialization and indoctrination—while in the older ones it is private, associated with a lengthy period of role search. Let us explore these propositions a bit further.

Almost all communities at the beginning stages of their development are seriously handicapped by various antipathetic cultural strains. Ideology, often consciously manipulated for the purpose of building authority, helps to minimize the consequences of such strain. That is how ideology performs its solidarity function. Similarly, in the case of identity, competing socialization processes, new and traditional, make the identity problem a complex one; ideology is employed to introduce greater coherence.

Two contrasting cases come to mind from Africa: Mali and Nigeria. In Mali, cultural discontinuities are being made to give way before new political arrangements in society represented in a Malian version of Marxism. In Nigeria, no single ideology defines political orthodoxy, and instead there is a host of competing traditions and ideas.[17] The young are enthusiastic supporters of the regime in Mali. In Nigeria, youth is estranged from the leadership, and no ideology has caught on. In Mali, solidarity is brought about by the conscious manipulation of ideology.

Socialism as an Ideology

Most of the political leaders in the developing areas profess to be socialists. This ideology enables them to repudiate prevailing hierarchies of power and prestige associated with traditionalism or colonialism. Furthermore, socialism helps to define as "temporary" (as a phase in economic growth) the commercial "market place" or "bazaar" economy.[18] Socialism, while it accepts the secularism of the market place, rejects the form; that is, roles associated with the market place are minimized.

In this sense, socialism has a very special meaning. It becomes the ethic for a system of political discipline leading to an emphasis on "science"—science for its own sake as a symbol of progress and as a form of political wisdom. In keeping with this aim, it offers a set of unified developmental goals that stress roles functional to the achievement of a workmanlike, rational society in which people extend helping hands to one another because they value highly the process of industrialization through community effort.

Such forms of socialism have very little to say about property or religion. Indeed they are largely silent on the subject of class antagonism. They are vague about the role of property, a factor central in Western ideas of socialism. The African variety, for example, prefers at present to delineate core values appropriate to modernization rather than to limit itself prematurely to particular economic forms.

In this sense, African socialism, like its counterparts in other developing areas, tends to look backward and forward at the same time. Although they may speak in the name of "revolution," in most cases political leaders are forced to make changes slowly by opening up the system to

[17]These problems take a different form in highly developed societies. Where the society is extremely complex, piecemeal legislation never quite solves problems to anyone's satisfaction. The individual feels lost. He is made trivial in a system, the magnitude of which dwarfs him. The result is a frustrating and continuous search for identity by the members of the society and a lack of solidarity among them.

[18]For a discussion of the "bazaar economy," see D. E. Apter, "Political Organization and Ideology," in *Labor Commitment and Social Change in Developing Areas*, eds. Moore and Feldman, (New York: Social Science Research Council, 1960), p. 337; see also D. E. Apter, *The Politics of Modernization* (Chicago: University of Chicago Press, 1965).

modernized roles. The result is that quite often what is called "socialism" is merely another name for "nationalism."[19]

What the various forms of socialism have in common, irrespective of their other ingredients, is an emphasis on development goals, for which individuals must sacrifice. Government is seen as a main source of development. Unity, represented in national citizenship, is the critical form of allegiance, with no other loyalties taking precedence over the state itself. Behind unity is the concept of society as a natural and organic body in which all the parts have their appointed functions, especially those linked to the development process.

Socialism is viewed as more rational than capitalism because of its emphasis on planning—more scientific, more secular, and more in keeping with the need to fit together and develop functionally modern roles. Socialism then has two aspects. In the content of its ideology, it defines modernity. In the application of its ideology, it defines social discipline manifested in solidarity groupings whose *raison d'être* is functionally for development. This functionality in turn lays down the terms of individual identity and establishes a new system of motivation that emphasizes achievement.[20]

Nationalism and Ideology—The Japanese Illustration

Quite often socialism, no matter how vaguely defined, breaks down into a number of competing dogmas that have the effects of weakening solidarity and confusing identity. When this danger arises, political leaders may opt for nationalism as the dominant ideology in new development communities. Nationalism incorporates primordial loyalties in a readily understandable synthesis, taking up the "slack" in identity and solidarity where socialism fails. Diffuse enough to encompass all specific forms of loyalty and tradition, it elevates them to a national inheritance. The value of nationalism lies in its functional flexibility.[21]

As Herskovits has pointed out, "African leaders faced with the challenge of economic growth and the need to establish higher living stand-

[19]Nationalism may be a revolutionary ideology vis-à-vis colonialism, but it is not normally so with respect to other aspects of social life. It is largely silent on the forms of economic organization.

[20]See David C. McClelland, "The Achievement Motive in Economic Growth," in *Industrialization and Society*, eds. Bert F. Hoselitz and Wilbert E. Moore (The Hague: Mouton & Co., N.V., Publishers, 1963), p. 74. McClelland points out that such achievement motivation becomes linked with identity because it is a desire to do well not for the sake of social recognition or prestige but "to attain an inner feeling of personal accomplishment." Ultimately, socialism as an egalitarian system is an effort to induce such achievement motivation.

[21]See, for example, Janheinz Jahn, *Muntu: An Outline of Neo-African Culture* (New York: Grove Press, 1961), *passim.*

ards began to re-examine traditional communal patterns with the objective of shaping them to fit the requirements of a new economic order. This re-examination occurred both where patterns of individual effort had become established and where socialistically oriented plans sought to use traditional communalism as an instrument to make the new system function." In this process, certain older values had to give way—the emphasis on age, hereditary status, kinship, and chieftaincy, for example. Once these values have given way, the remaining aspects of traditional life can be translated into more modern circumstances.[22]

Then nationalism takes on a more explicitly ideological complexion. Perhaps the best example, and certainly the best studied, is Japan. What made the Japanese case so interesting was the ability of the country to develop rapidly within the shell of traditional culture. Existing social beliefs mainly of an instrumental nature, allowed a bending and shaping of well-understood institutions, which, despite their alteration, provided a public sense of continuity. Some of these beliefs were represented in an emphasis on education for instrumental ends. Bellah points out that, in Japan, learning for its own sake "tends to be despised. The merely erudite man is not worthy of respect. Rather, learning should eventuate in practice. A truly learned man will be a truly loyal and filial man."[23]

The same considerations held for Japanese religion. "It was seen almost as a system of training which aided in the self-abnegating performance of actions expressing loyalty to one's lord."[24]

Religion and education, community and family, found their natural and practical expression in the state, which could therefore contemplate change while continuing to hold the loyalties of its members. (We have in mind the massive alterations occurring when Tokugawa evolved into Meiji Japan.) The primacy of political values and the emphasis on the polity allowed modification in social institutions, particularly economic ones, without dramatically rupturing the values and social beliefs of the Japanese.

It is not our concern, nor are we qualified, to discuss the many factors relevant to this process. Even in the Japanese case, however, the accumulated changes could not all be absorbed by the nationalist ideology and political framework. The result can be seen in the growth of Japanese militarism from 1900 onward. If the Meiji government represented a "logical fulfillment of a conception of the polity which already existed in the Tokugawa Period," as Bellah indicates, militarism was a natural outgrowth of both, to the extent that it combined instrumentalism in

[22]M. J. Herskovits, *The Human Factor in Changing Africa* (New York: Alfred A. Knopf, Inc., 1962), p. 467.
[23]Robert N. Bellah, *Tokugawa Religion* (New York: The Free Press, 1957), p. 16.
[24]*Ibid.*, p. 17.

the economic sphere with nationalism in the political.[25] Militarism was the imperial answer to the rise of trade unions, liberal and left-wing political thought, and advocacy of genuine parliamentary government.

As a result, education, religion, and the polity were brought together in an explicit orthodoxy, perhaps most clearly stated in the Japanese document, *Kokutai No Hongi* or *Cardinal Principles of the National Entity of Japan*. This document illustrates the uses of ideology in building and maintaining solidarity and identity in Japan. (It also illustrates how ideology as an instrument of solidarity can be applied through education.) As the editor points out in his introduction to *Kokutai No Hongi*, it is "primarily an educational book written for educators."[26] Hardly a pamphlet or tract in the ordinary sense, it is rather a religious document, which links together mythical history ("The great august Will of the Emperor in the administration of the nation is constantly clearly reflected in our history"), the role of the emperor in religious ceremony ("The Emperor, venerating in person the divine spirits of the Imperial Ancestors, increasingly becomes one in essence with Imperial Ancestry"), loyalty ("Loyalty means to reverence the Emperor as our pivot and to follow him implicitly"), and familial and national harmony ("In order to bring national harmony to fruition there is no way but for every person in the nation to do his allotted duty and to exalt it"). The nation then is like the family, the emperor like the father, and in the cultivation of both, people venerate themselves and realize higher purposes.

What makes this document so interesting is its explicit rejection of occidental individualism and liberalism. War is regarded as an expression of development, leading to great harmony. The martial spirit is sacred.[27] Life and death are basically one. "The monistic truth is found where life and death are transcended. Through this is life, and through this is death. However, to treat life and death as two opposites and to hate death and to seek life is to be taken up with one's own interests, and is a thing of which warriors are ashamed. To fulfill the Way of loyalty, counting life and death as one, is Bushido."[28]

Here we have a striking emphasis on loyalty and filial bonds that extends the notion of sacrifice and service further than in any Western ideology. At the same time, the primacy of national solidarity is linked to specific institutions, which trace their lineage to antiquity. The most immediate effects of modernization and industrialization are thereby deflected without hindering the modernization process in its economic

[25]*Ibid.*, p. 20.
[26]Robert King Hall, ed., *Kokutai No Hongi, Cardinal Principles of the National Entity of Japan* (Cambridge: Harvard University Press, 1949), p. 30.
[27]*Ibid.*, p. 94.
[28]*Ibid.*, p. 145.

sphere. Rather, education, industrial employment, and the enlargement of urban life help to reinforce rather than destroy the organic conception of society. Individual identity is found in service to the state and the emperor. Solidarity is expressed through the network of familial obligations, which includes the royal house. What are thus normally, in other systems, sources of tension, dislocation, and cultural strain are in the Japanese case twisted the other way around. Theirs is an explicitly traditionalist ideology, embodying instrumental ends, that was deliberately employed to make the identity and solidarity problems simpler. (Witness, for example, the unbelievable expansion of the educational system in the nineteenth century.) Nationalism in Japan was able to do what socialism in the developing areas could not do: to serve its functional purposes while transmitting a scientific temper.

Some Relationships between Nationalism and Socialism

"The process of shaping new principles or changing old ones is not without its tensions. One could almost say that there is a kind of 'dialectical' relationship between an ideologically oriented party and reality. The ideological party attempts to change reality and, in this way, is a revolutionary force; the new changed reality for a while corresponds to the ideology even while gradually changing itself; in time the ideology may become a conservative force; a new adjustment is eventually forced, and the ideology may then again become a revolutionary force."[29] In the new development communities, this "dialectic" takes place between nationalism and socialism. Each of these ideological forces emphasizes different attachments, meanings, and evaluations of solidarity, identity, and motivation.[30] Socialism is more universalistic and secular in tendency. Nationalism incorporates specific elements of tradition and employs them to bring meaning to the establishment of a solidly rooted sense of identity and solidarity.

In countries moving from dependent to independent status, the periods of nationalism build up slowly. At first there is emphasis on common citizenship, leading to more effective participation in agencies of rule and to greater educational opportunities. Nationalism also allows primordial loyalties to serve as the basis of the society's uniqueness. This attitude promotes pride in identity. In the period of nationalism, therefore, the main structure of society is accepted as it stands while greater

[29] A. K. Brzezinski, *Ideology and Power in Soviet Politics* (New York: Frederick A. Praeger, Publisher, Inc., 1962), p. 115.

[30] For a fuller discussion of this aspect of ideology, see D. E. Apter, "Political Religion in the New Nations," in *Old Societies and New States*, ed. Clifford Geertz (New York: The Free Press, 1963). [Reprinted in this volume.]

opportunities are sought. It is "radical" in only one political context, colonialism.

Quite often a nationalist movement takes a leftward turn during the last phase of a people's struggle for independence. The "radicalization of nationalism" results from a changed political emphasis. Independence is no longer the issue. The act of transferring authority from outside to inside turns out to be less simple than it had appeared. The radicalization of nationalism therefore employs socialism as a developmental ideology. A secular system of loyalties replaces more traditional forms. One effect of this radicalization is to add a sense of community to the earlier nationalist emphasis on common membership in the national state. Egalitarianism and a sense of shared purpose in the scientific evolution of the society are aspects of this sense of community.

A second effect of this radicalization is more individual. For those who have been involved in nationalism, identity is bound up with roles of daring innovation, often involving personal risk—"Robin Hood roles."[31] Many nationalist leaders have had no regular occupations other than political life, and they thrive on uncertainty. Once the nationalist period has achieved its main objectives, the socialist period takes over—different from the earlier ones because it involves leaders in a coldly calculated priorities system. For a few, possibilities open up for pioneering in new political and economic forms, rejection of approved and well tried formulae of political practice, and the search for new forms related to the special conditions of the country. Whatever the political form adopted, however, society now becomes bureaucratized. In a bureaucratic state, legitimacy is based on a system of roles functional to the development of the society.[32] Under such circumstances, the Robin Hood role is replaced by a bureaucratic one. But the continuation of these two role tendencies is a chronic problem.

Perhaps a diagram will summarize more adequately this relationship between socialism and nationalism.

At point A, we have the drawing together of a variety of social groups, which become increasingly "politicized" in a national sense, seeking a sharper definition of national society in political terms. At point B, a socialist "revolutionary" theme usually coincides with the appearance of a new group of political entrepreneurs, who take power away from the older and perhaps more "establishment"-minded members of the community. At this point, there is an emphasis on corporate community and functionally significant roles. Just after independence, nationalism goes through its apotheosis, and parochial and personal interests pale before the accomplishment of independence. Here solidarity and identity are

[31]For a discussion of "Robin Hood roles," see D. E. Apter, *The Politics of Modernization.*

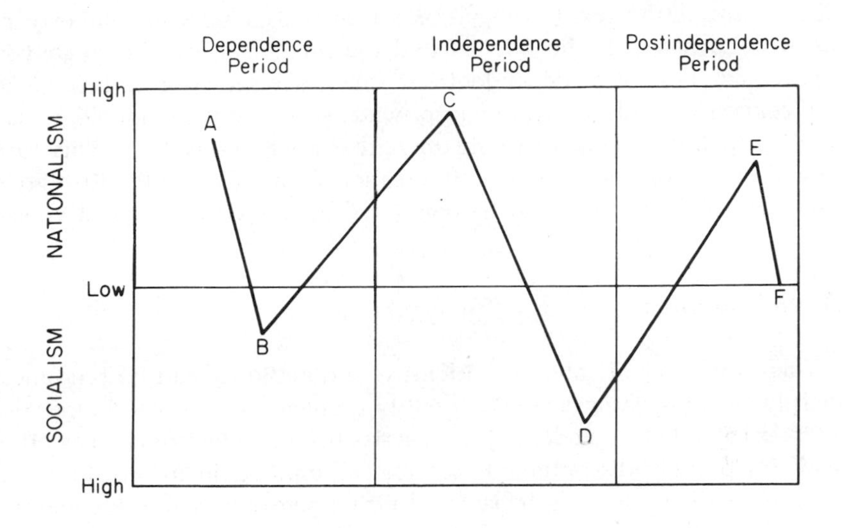

Figure 1. *Relationship between Socialism and Nationalism.*

linked with achievement. Old institutions become honorable and new ones exciting. At point D, the contradictions in culture, in social groups, and in solidarity and identity have resulted in a sweeping re-evaluation of society in the name of progress. It is the high point of socialism. Point D is the major ideological crisis point in the political life of a country, because it is at this point that the country becomes either a militant socialist state, or choosing moderately socialist ideas, turns accommodationist. In the case of Africa, this turning point pinpoints the dialogue between proponents of the more revolutionary view of socialism and of the more moderate African socialism—a dialogue affecting not only competition among leaders but policy toward education and indoctrination, or what is more broadly known as political socialization. When point F is reached, neither nationalism nor socialism is particularly relevant. At that point, what we have called the ideology of social science takes over. To achieve that point, however, involves not only a long period of time but a very complex process as well.

Changes among the four main variables we have been discussing form one basis for evaluating the tendency described. For example, the conditions of solidarity and identity change when nationalism is weakened and socialism strengthened. From a different angle, the need for nation-

[32]This bureaucratism is another reason for the high emphasis on technical training as preparation for economically significant but politically subordinate positions in the society. The functional roles are open to participants in development. In effect, we have a system in which the hierarchy of roles is functionally validated by the ethics of equality, that is, by socialism.

alism or socialism may be viewed as a result of changes in solidarity or identity. Each set, the ideological and the functional, can be treated in turn as independent or dependent variables for research purposes.

Weakness in solidarity and identity when socialism is the ideology may result in political leaders turning toward greater nationalism. This turn may have the unwanted effect of creating a provincial identity and a parochial solidarity that must be countered by the more universal appeal of socialism.[33]

Youth and Identity

These problems of solidarity, identity, and authority can be seen most sharply among a nation's youth. Identity problems among youth are very often exaggerated in modernizing societies because identity choices often lead to culturally discontinuous sequences resulting in inconsistent and often mutually misleading behavior. Furthermore, the search for identity coincides with a period of relative social freedom—the period of role search—when role testing and observation are at the maximum. Role search leads to anxiety over premature identity choices, such anxiety being a crucial element in the searching process. This anxiety can lead in its turn to temporary alienation from society. There have always been angry young men. In new nations, which rely heavily on youth as the backbone of society, identity problems can seriously undermine solidarity. This situation leads to serious political difficulties.

Resentful of the anxieties that result from role search, youth in new nations characteristically seeks its identity through revolt against the system. Socialism (among the young) may result in an attack on nationalism and an urge toward universality, while "socialists" who have come to power through *nationalism* respond by becoming more nationalist than socialist. The long-term trend is the nationalization of socialism. For example, Sékou Touré, once the exponent of the militant left in Africa, is widely regarded as a right-wing "deviationist" by members of the Federation of African Students in France.[34]

Furthermore, this anti-authority reflex can be demarcated generationally. A political generation in a developing society is quite often short (perhaps only four or five years), during which time a new group makes its claim to political power. This group consists of the angry young men of the post-revolutionary period who have no other direction than the political in which to direct their energies. The generational variable thus

[33]Other examples of interesting hypothetical conditions could be offered to show the dynamic relationships possible between the two sets of factors discussed so far, ideological and functional.

[34]See, for example, the study by J. P. N'Diaye, *Enquête sur les étudiants noirs en France* (Paris: Éditions Réalités Africaines, 1962).

links up with the larger problem of role search, alienation, and irresponsibility, which is centered largely on the identity problem. And where development depends heavily on the training and commitment of youth (both politically and technically), a group of alienated counterelites commonly emerges. They develop their own ideologies and identities through solidarity in a subgroup based on deviance from society. Indeed, if one treats solidarity and identity as independent variables, it is quite often the youth group with a high-deviance solidarity potential that triggers the ideological shift from socialism to nationalism, in order to achieve wider solidarity in the development community. Political parties take social pains to prevent this occurrence. As Eisenstadt has put it, "Almost all such modern movements have developed a special 'youth ideology.' The essence of these ideologies (from the point of view of our analysis) is that the changes which they advocate and struggle for are more or less synonymous with rebellion against the 'old' order and generation—a rebellion of youth, a manifestation of the rejuvenation of national social spirit."[35]

In the developing areas, youth cultures continue to be at variance with the regimes except during the short honeymoon periods after the success of national-liberation or revolutionary movements. Nor can the problems be solved simply by putting the young into uniforms and transforming them into obedient wards of the state. In many of the developing areas, each youth group brought under such "control" becomes a new center of local resistance within the existing party or other control group.

When is it likely that a transition will take place from both nationalism and socialism to a "higher" ideology of science associated with roles functional to the development community itself? It is hard to say. When nationalism can secure some honorific and traditional ideological inheritance and make it useful for maintaining solidarity and identity purposes and when socialism becomes a name for the values of science—then both will have lost their significance.

We have stressed the backward and forward movement between socialism and nationalism for two reasons. The first is that, in themselves, each represents the classic use of ideology in binding loyalties around major themes of political life and providing more than purely rational satisfactions from political activity. Second, an emphasis on functional skills in both socialism and nationalism places the technician and the scientist in an important political position, though clearly subordinate to the topmost level of leadership. This latter level is reserved for those who embody more than science and who do all the nonempirical things required of leadership, including supplying those meanings and identities

[35] S. N. Eisenstadt, *From Generation to Generation* (New York: The Free Press, 1956), p. 311.

that are central to the cultural hunger of a world in extreme transition. Such are the usual uses of ideology that have reached their greatest significance today in the developing areas of the world. Indeed, at times they take on the proportions of a political religion.[36]

In the developed areas (where it is commonly thought that ideology has disappeared), however, we find that it is only this "vulgar" aspect of ideology that is disappearing. Gone are the rather simple-minded explanatory notions of ideology (wrapped up in simplistic dogmas) that attribute behavior to explicit motives like desire for wealth or power. But if the new ideology is more sophisticated than the old, it is no less significant. Indeed it buttresses the authority of politicians with a universal appeal to scientific reason. Where the scientist or technician is frequently used as a basis for the legitimacy of political acts, whether the issue is development or civil rights, the Common Market or nuclear disarmament, legitimate action depends for its legitimacy on the advice of professionals. The battle of the politicians is in some measure enlarged to include charge and refutation by opposing experts employed by novices. In the West, the war had a great deal to do with stimulating this new ideology. It also fits into our traditions that the appeal to reason requires the competitive play of ideas in order to maximize information, which leads to the correct course of action. In the new societies, the professional becomes the symbol of progress. He is the "establishment" employed by the politicians. The social-science ideology, then, embodies a new form of solidarity and identity based on professional status. The appeal to science is an appeal to authority. The scientific establishment is itself based on a natural hierarchy of talent in which equal opportunities become the means to unequal political significance. We can conclude our discussion of modern ideology with examination of two conditions common in highly developed societies.

SCIENCE AND IDEOLOGY IN HIGHLY DEVELOPED COMMUNITIES

We have said that developing countries are engaged in the process of rationalizing all aspects of social life. There is another aspect to this process; the corresponding erosion of durable beliefs and traditions. Increasing complexity leads to less sure guides to social and political practice than those to which people have been habituated.

In highly advanced development communities, ideology takes its most elaborate and complex form when the following conditions are present: There is general acceptance of common membership in the society, so that nationalism has become internalized and implicit; sufficient development has already occurred so that social dislocations require fine adjust-

[36]This aspect is treated in my article in Geertz, *op. cit.*

ments rather than gross "solutions"; consensus prevails about which roles are functional to the continuous process of development. Advanced development communities are no longer in the process of changing from traditional to modern forms of social life. As a consequence, they look beyond programmatic ideologies with their simplified remedial suggestions. One of the outstanding characteristics of such communities is broad agreement on fundamentals and corresponding magnification of minor issues. In highly developed areas, these problems come to a head in what is called status competition. As a result of increasing differentiation in the economic sphere, neither class nor caste is so significant as status, with its gradations extending indefinitely up and down the hierarchy scale. Some individuals strive for status differentiation, while others work consistently to undermine status distinctions. The result is an elusive power and prestige system which provides only temporary advantages for those who achieve high status. Only the professional role, based on skill, is durable. This distinction reflects itself more and more in a division between a scientific elite and the rest of the community.

Bifurcation in the Community

This phenomenon helps to explain a peculiar lack of personal constraint in performance among many occupants of high-status positions. Knowing their status tenure is temporary, they do not have the same sense of obligation or duty to the community that a more permanent high-status group might develop. When status competition is a motivational system, the result is grave weakness in solidarity and an agonizing search for identity.[37] The reasons for this weakness are not hard to find. Functional hierarchies allow equality of access to unequally distributed sets of roles. One result is that the lower the position he occupies on the scale, the more fundamentally incapacitated, incapable, and unrewarded a person feels. Functional hierarchy (based on achievement) intensifies the hostility and personal anguish of those on the bottom of the hierarchy. No one can draw satisfaction from lower-status roles. The prospect now facing the highly developed communities is a large proportion of functionally superfluous people, particularly in unskilled occupations, and by that I mean those who are largely unemployable.[38]

How does a democratic society come to rationalize this bifurcation of

[37]See S. M. Lipset, "The Sources of the 'Radical Right'—1955," in *The Radical Right*, ed. Daniel Bell (Garden City: Doubleday & Company, Inc., 1963), pp. 260–64.

[38]These conditions, increasingly a part of modern life in highly developed communities, did not always prevail. The earlier "technological revolution" was associated with the belief that representative government (the equivalent of consumer's choice in politics) was coterminous with free enterprise. Industrialization was its "natural" product. Such an ideology was remarkable for its consistency and coherence.

the community into members of the "establishment" and the functionally superfluous, the responsible and the nonresponsible, the scientifically literate and the scientifically illiterate? Any major political issue serves to illustrate how. Any political conflict quickly becomes a problem of evaluating evidence. Each interested body employs its own experts to bring in findings in conformity with its own views. Laymen must decide which expert advice to accept. But the expert has been involved in the decision-making process. What happens to the nonexpert? Too often he cannot follow the debate. He withdraws, and the resulting bifurcation is more complete than one might ordinarily imagine. Modern society then is composed of a small but powerful group of intellectually participant citizens, trained, educated, and sophisticated, while all others are reduced in stature if they are scientifically illiterate.

In practice, of course, there is no single professional group. It is possible to be scientifically intelligent about some subjects and a complete fool in others. The dividing line between the "establishment" and the "disestablished" is therefore not sharp. There is a full-time and a part-time "establishment," and people with very little training may belong to the latter. But their participation in political problems and their interest in the community is largely limited to their fields of expertise. The result is, for them, a decline in their civic responsibilities and obligations.

One consequence of this decline in democratic societies is that government is almost always ahead of the public on most issues, in the sense that it is more progressive. Oil men interested in concessions, tide lands, and real estate are concerned with atomic disarmament only as it affects power resources and prices. We could cite other examples. Each particular interest group forces government to pay some attention to it, and to yield some special concessions. Each group is then partially satisfied in its functional interest, while bored with, alienated by, or positively opposed to government actions directed toward satisfying other functional interest groups.

Of course, this process can also work the other way around. A good illustration is the slow but increasingly steady intervention of government on the side of Negroes in the matter of race relations. The majority of the white population remains opposed to major change in the *status quo.* (Most whites would prefer to hide such opposition in vague sentiments of liberalism and moderate good works.) How do we attempt to quiet white objections? By bringing in the experts. Science is equated with democracy. The primacy of equalitarian values is asserted in the name of science which asserts that there can be no genuine equality between races until all sorts of special programs are put into practice: training schools for Negroes, special fellowships, the breaking up of neighborhood patterns, and so forth. Research on this problem, the results of which are widely distributed through the public press and the mass media, points the way to a "political" solution. Making the problem "scientific" makes it somewhat more manageable.

The case of race relations in the United States is a particularly interesting one, bringing into play as it does a number of competing social norms affecting solidarity and identity in the face of ingrained prejudice. I would argue, however, that this problem is much smaller (and will be more easily solved) than the one that lies ahead: the problem of inequality on the basis of differences in ability. Sicence can help to resolve all problems other than that one, for it is science itself that sets the conditions of that kind of unequal society.

Alienation and the Ideology of Science

Democracy is a system of government that requires a high level of self-restraint. Where this self-restraint does not prevail, democracy rapidly degenerates into a system of plunder, restricted only by the mutual check of hostile and antagonistic groups in the society. Social reforms become bargaining points—by-products of political life. Under such circumstances, democratic reform "does not have any unifying appeal, nor does it give a younger generation the outlet for 'self-expression' and 'self-definition' that it wants."[39]

Perhaps such alienation is a permanent feature of democratic society.[40] Even the "establishment" feels it, particularly if its members have well-developed sensitivities. Not easily corrupted by power, the new "establishment" can easily feel compromised by it. The scientific personality is, on the whole, a modest one, especially at the top. (Technicians are less so.) It can become alienated by its own successes. It does not like to be a pawn in the politician's game. One illustration of the "establishment's" ambiguous attitude can be found in its distaste for politics at the same time that it participates in politics—evident among scientists all over the world. There is, furthermore, a universality in the scientific ideology and role. Soviet scientists too are likely to push political matters aside in order to maintain a certain scientific chastity unviolated by political dogma. Despite noticeable lapses, especially in the biological field, they wear their professional status like a caste mark.

The ideology of science has very peculiar and diverse effects. On the one hand, it serves to identify a group of people who are themselves important and significant because they can manipulate the scientific culture.

[39]See Daniel Bell's interesting collection of essays, *The End of Ideology* (New York: The Free Press, 1960), p. 375.

[40]Marx's concept of alienation emerged from his analysis of nineteenth century England at a time when the "British way of life" appeared to outdistance all others in industry and entrepreneurial daring—resulting in a general Victorian smugness.

On the other, it casts out of the charmed circle those who are hopelessly incapable of understanding it.

But it is not science itself that causes alienation. This phenomenon arises when boundless hope becomes tempered with realization of the limits of one's abilities. This realization causes considerable bitterness against the system, if only because the alternative to alienation is self-hatred. Modern societies harbor large proportions of people with extraordinary degrees of self-hatred and self-doubt.

Some Consequences of Bifurcation

Our society is subject to a dangerous bifurcation, the "establishment" versus the "disestablished." The latter, in turn, is divided into the functionally useful (but with lower status) and the superfluous. The "establishment" derives its power from the expertise embodied in advisory and appointive posts; the middle from electional strength; and the bottom from threat of local violence. Opportunities to move from the bottom to the top exist, but they are rare, as with Negro members of the "establishment" (the extreme case, showing the great obstacles to be overcome). The middle group tries to restrict mobility from the bottom into the middle and to restrict the growing "establishment" (growing both in proportion and significance). Squeezed by the new "establishment" and the functionally superfluous, the disestablished middle fights back either by attacking the social-science and scientific ideologies or by attempting to ensure entry into the "establishment" for its children.

The search for talent begins at an early age—witness the eleven-plus examination in England, aptitude tests and intelligence tests in American elementary schools. Parents who want their children to be members of the new "establishment" try to instill in them the proper desire for study and work. Solidarity, centered around the "establishment," makes non-establishment people increasingly superfluous. Functional roles are those relevant to planning, policy, and research. The new "ideology" is increas-

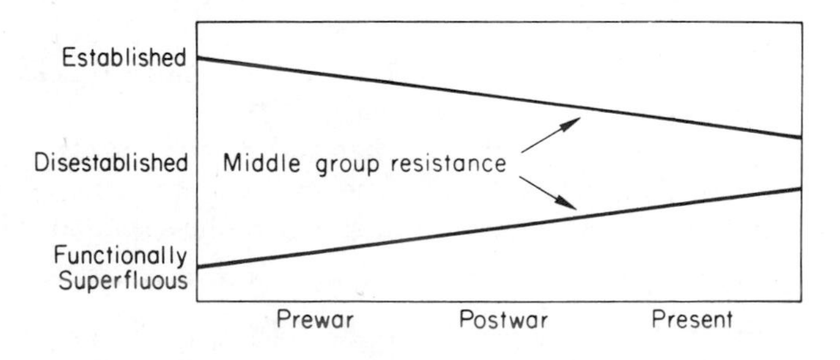

Figure 2. *Division in the Community.*

ingly rooted in a professional cadre of highly trained men. Solidarity within—alienation without; identity within—lack of identity without. What Weiss and Riesman have suggested holds true for the working class is increasingly true of all nonprofessionals in Western society. They point out that one of the things wrong with the working-class job is simply that it is a working-class job. "In a culture where the worth of a man is measured by how far he has gotten, the unskilled laborer or service worker, despite the pieties that may be uttered periodically about the dignity of labor, knows that he has not gotten very far."[41]

Technological superfluousness leads to social superfluousness. Nor is this matter simply a technological one. The alleviation of distress and the requirements for planning and calculation involved in modern politics, whether in urban planning or overseas aid, have helped to create a revolution in social science. The businessman, once the heroic figure of Western society, is increasingly an administrator. The old-fashioned ideal of capitalism, particularly in its more rural forms, becomes the ideological defense of the business and older professional groups against their own social displacement. It is no wonder that social science is so often identified with socialism and regarded as the enemy.[42]

In each of the three groups, solidarity and identity are different. Solidarity in the "establishment" centers around high-status *esprit* and a desire for more effective communications between disciplines and specialists. The recent discussion of C. P. Snow's Rede Lectures can be seen as an exhortation to solidarity between literary intellectuals and scientists. His concern over possible differences in their points of view presumes, on his part, a more fundamental identity of outlook.[43] Solidarity involves greater intellectual breadth and a shared appreciation of the values of the modern scientific community. Identity derives from the significance of the work engaged in by the individual, whose own personal satisfactions are in some measure a reflection of the recognition he receives within the "establishment."

For the disestablished, the situation is different. Their solidarity and identity have in the past been associated with the business community and territorially localized in villages, towns, and cities throughout the country. The "establishment" is a national elite. The disestablished have

[41]Robert S. Weiss and David Riesman, "Social Problems and Disorganization in the World of Work," in *Contemporary Social Problems*, eds. Robert Merton and Robert Nisbet (New York: Harcourt, Brace & World, Inc., 1961), pp. 484–85.

[42]One interesting role that combines valuations of superfluousness with an ambiguous but real functional value is that of the salesman. It is recognized that the salesman plays a key role in the success of modern business enterprise, but he is associated with deceit, lack of dignity, and doubtful utility.

[43]C. P. Snow, *The Two Cultures and the Scientific Revolution* (New York: Cambridge University Press, 1959); see also D. E. Apter, "New Nations and the Scientific Revolution," *Bulletin of the Atomic Scientists*, XVII, No. 2 (February 1961).

been a localized elite, their solidarity centered around churches, voluntary associations, and similar bodies.[44] These bodies have become increasingly parochialized and no longer provide solidarity satisfactions. The result among some of the disestablished is an increase in the significance of patriotic organizations associated with the radical right. Such solidarity groupings try to link the local with the national and to embody a new unity by means of which the disestablished would become powerful. On the other hand, the disestablished are losing the identities provided by middle-class business values and, in suffering this loss, are left bewildered and insecure.

The functionally superfluous have virtually no solidarity and are extremely difficult to organize, for their lives are preoccupied not only with basic poverty and all its consequences but in some measure also, in an affluent society, with escape. For them there are very few permanent identity symbols but only shifting popular ones, with resultant behavior divided between apathy and hysteria. For these people, the present situation is critical and utterly devastating.

SCIENCE AND DEMOCRACY

Rather deliberately the concept of ideology has been thrust to the center of the stage, making it a point of entry for the discussion of many problems, both methodological and substantive. So far, I have tried to show the significance of ideology for society, for personality, and for authority, first in the context of the problems of developing areas and now those of developed ones. In the process, both the virtues and the deficiencies of ideology as a theoretical interest are easily demonstrated. Touching on problems of a very diverse sort, it also exaggerates them and casts them bolder than life itself. So, it might be argued, the use of ideology as a category of analysis is itself a distortion of reality. Does it not do violence to the actual role of the scientist or social scientist and give him too prominent a place in modern society? Even worse, to consider ideas about science in the context of ideology does not make ideology scientific—but science ideological.

I think the answer is yes. As a category of analysis it does exaggerate, but it does so usefully. If the problems of solidarity and identity, for example, are real ones, then the answers to them will have a special ethno-and ego-centeredness about them. That is why they become matters of dogma and passion, relevant to ideology. Furthermore, the argument I have made about the bifurcation of culture in modern society between the educated and the uneducated is surely exaggerated. But if it has any

[44]See Bryan R. Wilson, "An Analysis of Sect Development," *American Sociological Review*, XXIV (February 1959).

merit, we should be able to find the instruments of bifurcation empirically. And we do. The schools reflect the differentiation of the public into the disestablished and the established. Fifteen or twenty major universities provide professional education and postgraduate training. A number of small and high-quality colleges derive their status as feeder institutions, providing a high proportion of those students who go on to the postgraduate programs. A somewhat wider group of universities is anxious to move into this "academic establishment." Then suddenly the dividing line sharpens. Below the line is the main bulk of our universities and colleges, representing education by the disestablished for the disestablished.

These institutions incorporate all the exaggerated socializing functions of college life, with few of its compensating intellectual advantages. And, as with the disestablished generally, the faculty members of these institutions—and the students too—are embarrassed and harassed by the identities created. Critical of one another, and divided, they work at cross purposes.

I cite the case of educational institutions because they, more than any other institutions in our culture, frankly adopt the natural hierarchy of ability and talent as an adjustment to inequality. Each institution recruits in its own image of ability, with minor variations. The norm of quality is accepted by all, but the functions of each set are different. With society too, the norm of quality is accepted by all, but the functional definition of it is different. So too with science, and increasingly with social science as well. Indeed, the norms of science are rooted in our ideas of education, and they are the standards on which a scientific ideology is based.[45] Furthermore, the hierarchy of educational establishments intensifies bifurcation. The schools, colleges, and universities are becoming a major screening device. Theirs is a monitor role, instilling the values of democracy in the elect, while to the nonelect democracy becomes an overpowering burden. This observation is true of Europe as well as of the United States.

In politics, social science assumes a new force. Its ideology differs in outward appearance from other forms. It is not polemical. On the contrary, its practitioners embody the norm of "scientific" modesty. Social scientists are the first to warn of the inadequacies of their disciplines when applied to social problems.[46]

[45]Norman Jacobson has argued that American versions of the democratic ideal embodied this norm from the start. See "Political Science and Political Education," *American Political Science Review*, LVII, No. 3 (September 1963).

[46]S. M. Lipset has bemoaned the fact that "the very growth of sociology as an intellectual force outside the academy in many western nations is a tribute, not primarily to the power of sociological analysis of politics but to the loss of interest in political inquiry," and he ends his sociological analysis of politics with a note of concern about this trend, since he feels "there is still a real need for political analysis, ideology, and controversy. . . ." S. M. Lipset, *Political Man: The Social Bases of Politics* (Garden City: Doubleday & Company, Inc., 1960), p. 415. More recently, he has also pointed to the application of science to political matters as one of the sources of the "decline of ideologies." *Daedalus*, 93 (Winter 1964), p. 273.

Underneath the modesty, however, is a lively belief in the norms and values associated with science and the useful potentialities of social science in political life. Special studies on every subject imaginable, from race relations to nuclear disarmament, represent the application of social-science techniques to problems of everyday life. Training, specialization, and research are the basis of knowledge, which is why, as we suggested earlier, the public is increasingly divided into the expert in social-science matters and the layman. The layman, as a citizen, does not have the facts. Nor does he have the ability to make important decisions. He may be irritated in the face of such expertise, but it is difficult for him to contradict it. Indeed, one token of the rising significance of the social scientist as a member of the political "establishment" is the attacks against him, particularly from members of the "old establishments," namely law and medicine. Lawyers are, by definition, manipulators of custom, that is, of laws. A developing community is less constrained by law than are more stable systems. It cannot wait for law to catch up with its own needs for development. In the field of medicine, emphasis is increasingly on the medical theorist or scientist rather than on the practitioner. The latter is being reduced to the status occupied by the pharmacist of two or three generations ago.

Another characteristic of the modern development community is the primacy of the political. Social welfare, development, reform, and revolution all place new responsibilities on governments. In order to live up to these responsibilities, governments seek advice. Authority is enlarged as responsibilities become more complex. The exercise of power is justified by the prospect of endless political reform through technical expertise.

This whole process has the effect of polarizing identities and undermining solidarities. Lacking a heroic dimension and requiring a wide range of intellectual discrimination, it imposes the burden of natural inequality upon the members of a single community. Superfluousness is not an article of faith in the social-science ideology, but an unfortunate consequence of science in an industrial age, punctuated by a growing gulf between those with status and those without. But those who represent the social-science ideology in the community come to represent, for the disestablished, a threat to the solidarity of the society and a deforming identity. Those inside the "establishment" are profoundly convinced, not only that it is highly desirable and a force for good, but also that their role within it is the critical one. Those outside the "establishment" become the ideologues of the extreme left or the extreme right, sniping at the "establishment" and increasingly frustrated by its imperviousness.

We have suggested so far that ideology helps to establish solidarity for society and identity for individuals within it. We have indicated that, in the development of new societies, socialist ideology is relevant in bringing about integration in the system and programmatic guides to functional roles, while nationalist ideology helps to promote solidarity and identity. We have also suggested that the political leaders in developing areas find sanction for authority in the claims of socialism to be scientific —but that these socialist ideologies do not belong in the same intellectual class with nineteenth century socialism or, for that matter, Marxism. Claiming the heritage of "socialism" enables political leaders in developing areas to make some wider connection with the philosophical heritage of Marxism without necessarily applying it.[47]

The West has gone beyond this stage. "Socialism has become an unthought-out assumption, a collection of economic recipes, and a nagging critique, from a distance, of existing institutions. The fresh self-confidence, the wonderful feeling of relevant discovery, the convincing air of ethical righteousness, and the vibrant expectation of a total—and significant—transformation of the entire life of society have nearly disappeared from the socialist movement and from socialist thought since the mid-twenties. The belief that socialist aims enabled one to see reality more realistically and fruitfully, the belief that socialism was a 'way of life' and not just a scheme for operating factories and wholesale enterprises has in the main evaporated."[48]

The New American Dilemma

The United States has clearly opted for science, and precisely because it has done so it must take the consequences. One of these consequences is that power and prestige will be based on functional roles germane to modern industrial society, in which science and efficiency go hand in hand. Equality of opportunity means that social life is a continuous screening process that begins with education. Parental status is no guarantee of future success. Ours is a system of downward, as well as of upward mobility—but a special kind of downward mobility. The "downwardness" is a measure of inability, while "upwardness" is a measure of ability and proficiency. The criteria are based on natural talent.

This phenomenon is as yet only dimly understood and only beginning

[47]By no stretch of the imagination could one find the opening of a major discourse on revolution by Marx, Lenin, or Sorel, beginning with the words used by Nasser: "Before proceeding with this discourse I would like to pause at the word 'philosophy'. It looks big and sounds grand." Nor would they be able to write, "I do not pretend to be a professor of history. This is the last thing my imagination may entertain. Nevertheless, if I were to attempt to study the story of our struggle like a schoolboy, I would say, for instance, that the revolution of July 23 is the realization of a hope that the people of Egypt, in modern times, have aspired to since they began to think of governing themselves and since they decided to be masters of their fate." See Gamal Nasser, *The Philosophy of the Revolution* (Buffalo: Smith, Keynes & Marshall, Book Publishers, 1959), p. 25.

[48]See Edward Shils's introduction to Georges Sorel, *Reflections on Violence* (New York: The Free Press, 1950), p. 14.

to emerge in our society. Luck, fortune, special advantages—these excuses could always be used to explain personal failure or success. Increasingly they cannot and an individual of the future will have to confront himself with some agonizing questions. Can the less gifted accept the fact? We have developed an elaborate rhetoric to disguise low status and to give it false dignity through titles, euphemistic job descriptions, and other accommodations that the "establishment" uses to salve its conscience. This rhetoric does not help to prepare us for the bifurcation that is occurring in our country—in which society divides into two mutually antagonistic and, in many ways, lonely groups. One is composed of ideologues who devoutly defend unreason because they are afraid that, in the face of reason, their orientation to the world around them will fall apart and that in the process their world will disappear. Ideology becomes a protection for people alienated from their society—a protection against the final alienation. They therefore stubbornly hang on to their ideologies in the hope that, by sheer persistence, they will prevail against other ideologies or even against reason itself. They represent the "disestablishment."

The second group is also alienated. Theirs is an alienation brought about by "superior wisdom," that is, by the ability to penetrate the ideologies of others and thereby to emancipate themselves. In this group is the social scientist, who is the objective observer. He penetrates all the disguises created by the untrained mind or the ideological mind and attaches himself to the image of the wise. He represents the "establishment."

The social scientist and the ideologue represent two increasingly antagonistic roles in modern society. The antagonism is all the sharper because, in an age of science, the nonrationality of the ideologue only makes him more defensive about his beliefs. More and more the social scientist is at the center of the society, and his probing and inevitably remorseless search for deeper levels of reality confuse the ideologue. The latter, more alienated, is therefore likely to engage in bold behavior calculated to inhibit the scientist and cause him to refrain from probing too deeply. To the disestablished, the language of social science is obscure and dangerous. The levels of reality probed by the social scientist are only dimly understood, if at all. Meanwhile, the universities controlled by the established set higher and higher standards of "quality." The insurance salesman, the bank clerk, the businessman, the retired army officer, and the other nonprofessional representatives of the middle class most often in possession of university degrees become the most concerned. They cannot find their places in the functionally unequal society.

The pattern of mutual alienation between these two groups is only intensified by the spread of quality education. With the increased dependence of the population on educational qualifications for positions that a generation ago did not require the same knowledge, the social scientist controls many of the main routes to power and prestige. The only recourse of the ideologue is intimidation of the social scientist by arousing the public against unorthodox or heretical views. And, episodically, he does so. So well entrenched are the universities, however, and so widely accepted is the norm of academic freedom that the ideologues as a group are rarely very successful, although individual ideologues may successfully enhance their personal careers by becoming professional witch-hunters.

Today's American ideologue is a middle-class man who objects to his dependence on science even when he accepts its norms. He is resentful of the superiority of the educated and antagonistic to knowledge. His ideology is more than likely not of the left but of the right. It is, in extreme cases, of the radical right, looking back to a more bucolic age of individuality and localism, in which parochial qualities of mind were precisely those most esteemed—to a simple democracy, in fact. Robbed of its individuality, the middle-class "disestablishment" forms loose associations with others who are escaping from the fate of superfluousness. Social hatred is directed against the Negro, the black enemy who can destroy the disestablished, and against the Negro's protector, the establishment man whose belief in rationality and equal opportunity has altered the system of power and prestige so that it is based on universalistic selection and talent. *Today, the radical right fights against the bifurcation of society on the basis of talent.* It is the resistance ideology of all those who hitherto were the *Stand* figures of our society in an earlier day; the models of once sober, industrious, and responsible citizens.

For the truly superfluous men, there is no ideology, only generalized hatred. Speed, violence, a frenetic round of petulant actions, or perhaps more simply despair, characterize these groups, which have been largely ignored by a prosperous society. Black or white, they are an embarrassment to the "establishment," which would like to take drastic remedial action—action that they find consistently blocked by the disestablished majority, which on the contrary, tries to preserve its superiority over those beneath it. And in the process, the disestablished look more and more alike. Violence, militancy, activism, in the name of radicalism or conservatism for which, especially in the United States, we have no traditional rhetoric—the result is seen in comical but dangerous extremist groups, which by their activities give to a nebulous ideology greater appeal and mystique.

CONCLUSION

Mannheim argues that the discovery that much thought is ideological challenges the validity of thought itself: "Man's thought had from time immemorial appeared to him as a segment of his spiritual existence and not simply as a discrete objective fact. Reorientation had in the past frequently meant a change in man himself. In these earlier periods it was mostly a case of slow shifts in values and norms, of a gradual transformation of the frame of reference from which men's actions derived their ultimate orientation. But in modern times it is a much more profoundly disorganizing affair. The resort to the unconscious tended to dig up the soil out of which the varying points of view emerged. The roots from which human thought had hitherto derived its nourishment were exposed. Gradually it becomes clear to all of us that we cannot go on living in the same way once we know about our unconscious motives as we did when we were ignorant of them. What we now experience is more than a new idea, and the questions we raise constitute more than a new problem. What we are concerned with here is the elemental perplexity of our time, which can be epitomized in the symptomatic question, 'How is it possible for man to continue to think and live in a time when the problems of ideology and utopia are being radically raised and thought through in all their implications?' "[49]

To expose the ideological aspects of human thinking does not, however, make ideological thought impossible. It divides it into new forms. One is that of dogma, which easily leads to violence and dissension. Those who see the world in stereotypes seek to protect their beliefs from those who would undermine them.

The more hopeful alternative is the spread of social science. It is in this sense that we can say that social science has become the ultimate ideology and science the ultimate talisman against cynicism. It defines its own purposes through the logic of enquiry. Some years ago, Michael Polanyi pointed out this process very clearly. What he said then of scientists in general applies more and more to the *social* scientist today: "Professional scientists form a very small minority in the community, perhaps one in ten thousand. The ideas and opinions of so small a group can be of importance only by virtue of the response which they evoke from the general public. This response is indispensable to science, which depends on it for the money to pay the costs of research and for recruits to replenish the ranks of the profession. Why do people decide to accept science as valid? Can they not see the limitations of scientific demonstrations—in the pre-selected evidence, the preconceived theories, the always basically deficient documentation? They may see these shortcomings, or at least they may be made to see them. The fact remains that they must make up their minds about their material surroundings in one way or another. Men must form ideas about the material universe and must embrace definite convictions on the subject. No part of the human race has ever been known to exist without a system of such convictions,

[49]Mannheim, *op. cit.*, p. 38.

and it is clear that their absence would mean intellectual annihilation. The public must choose, therefore, either to believe in science or else in Aristotle, the Bible, Astrology or Magic. Of all such alternatives, the public of our times has, in its majority, chosen science."[50] But the "Polanyi choice" (like the "Polanyi paradox" with which we began this essay) embodies some very troubling and universal problems. His statement shows a certain comfortableness about the majority choice. But what happens if, having chosen, the majority does not follow through on its choice and indeed rejects many aspects of it? What is the effect, too, upon the minority that has not made this choice—and by effect I mean particularly political consequences? Perhaps one illustration of what occurs is to be found in the United States at the present time.

What is happening in the United States may well be typical of other highly developed societies. In a functional and rationalistic universe, the scientists and social scientists are accorded an increasing monitor role in political life—though not because they possess a kind of Platonic predisposition that prepares them for the role of leaders. Quite the contrary, they share all the ambiguity about their roles that their fellow citizens have. By gaining a superior insight into the conduct of their fellows, however, they create a new role and an ideology that follows from it, a hierarchy of power and prestige based on intellectual ability, which, in its extreme form, is what Michael Young called the "meritocracy." Once the social scientists discovered that there is a discrepancy between behavior observed and behavior felt, between the act and the rationalization, between the conscious and the subconscious, and between virtue and conduct, he fashioned a new role for himself—the theoretically omniscient observer. Human mysteries have become technical problems. In the modern development communities, he is asked to apply his knowledge. He displaces the physician as a new symbol of aloofness. (The professional intellect is antiseptic.) He regards the layman as irresponsible or, at best, uninformed. It is therefore not surprising that the recourse of the disestablished is intimidation of the social scientist by arousing the public against unorthodox or heretical views.

The major propositions that emerge from this brief examination can now be indicated: (1) Science is a well defined ideology possessing norms of empiricism, predictability, and rationality as guides to conduct. (2) Social science is becoming accepted as scientific, and scientific norms are increasingly accepted as guides to social conduct. (3) There is a universal trend toward planning, calculation, and rationalistic goals concerned with the future in both the developing and developed areas. (4) In the developing areas, vulgar ideologies express the urge to science in some form of socialism associated with national independence move-

[50]Polanyi, *op. cit.*, pp. 57–58.

ments (African socialism, Egyptian socialism, Indonesian socialism). (5) In the developed areas, the new ideology expresses itself in the "meritocracy." Recruitment of talent is on the basis of competitive school and university examinations, with increasingly close links between the educational "establishment" and the bureaucratic "establishment."

Durkheim remarked about the pioneering role of economics that "for two centuries economic life has taken on an expansion it never knew before. From being a secondary function, despised and left to inferior classes, it passed on to one of the first rank. We see the military, governmental and religious functions falling back more and more in the face of it. The scientific functions alone are in a position to dispute its ground . . ."[51]

What was true for economics is increasingly true for the other social sciences. Both science and technology are, in application, intertwined with the social sciences. In modern scientific communities, governments are the greatest single consumers of social science. They not only stimulate policy research but consume the product as well.[52]

It is in the political sphere that the battle between social scientists and ideologues will be the most intense. More and more political leaders rely on the social scientists, as we have suggested. This reliance is growing both in the early- and later-stage development communities. As long as social science cannot perform functions of identity and solidarity, recourse will be had to ideology in its more dogmatic forms. Certainly there will be antiscientific ideologies. Political leaders will need to learn how to tread lightly between the alienated ideologues and the desire to apply science to human affairs.

We have suggested earlier that the dialogue in the developing areas is between nationalism and socialism. In the more developed countries, it will be between social science and nonrational vulgar ideologies. The ideologue will manipulate the slogans. The social scientist will ignore him. Political leaders will learn to rely on the latter without unduly arousing the former. Perhaps the long-run trend in both types of development community is a drawing of the lines between idiocy and intellectual merit more sharply until the ideologues fall of their own weight. But this end is too much to hope for.

What is the antidote? We need to understand problems of solidarity and identity more clearly. A kind of settling-down process is in order. With respect to ideology, social science differs from all others in one

[51]E. Durkheim, *Professional Ethics and Civic Morals* (New York: The Free Press, 1958), p. 11.

[52]One finds evidence for this increasing consumption in the mounting financial support given to universities for social science research and to other bodies. Increasingly, of course, government is undertaking its own research through such organizations as the RAND Corporation for example.

respect. The only antidote for it is more of it, addressed to solidarity and identity problems. Both new and highly developed communities need to accept the openness of spirit, the attitudes of questioning that probe the innermost secrets of social and political life (without feeling threatened). Such a spirit, essential to democracy, will perhaps have a destructive effect on all other ideologies.

We need, too, to pay more attention to the total educational system. I do not mean simply to refer to education in a pious way and to argue that modifying it will solve all our problems when obviously it cannot. But more social science education, the early development of a questioning attitude toward human affairs, and attention to discovery as a means of identifying the self, will help to break down the growing dichotomy between layman and specialist. That this process will take place has always been part of our liberal faith. It will not occur, however, through the trickling-down of jargon and a few manipulative ideas (as advertising executives, for example, pick up psychological jargon). What is needed, in addition to the modesty and propriety inherent in the scientific enterprise, is an understanding of relevant criteria for the evaluation of conduct, our own as well as others'.

We have suggested that the main uses of ideology in the developing areas are to promote solidarity and identity. The one represents the linking up of institutions, some of which are old, some new, and most of which emerge at the interstices between them. The other is the assertion of self (identity) through the marking out of new roles and the fulfillment of personality through such roles. The survival of "vulgar" ideologies, which are programmatic and explanatory, depends on the effectiveness with which they perform these two functions.

The scientific ideology can do little to promote solidarity and identity. The obligations implied in either are not very relevant, and a scientific ideology tends to downgrade the beliefs and intimacies that the vulgar ideologies promote. On the other hand, the scientific ideology handles these matters through professionality. The key to the "establishment" is its professional status. Its authority derives from superior knowledge. It has a code of ethics that enshrines integrity. The integrity of the research worker is only slightly less entrenched than the code from which it derives, academic freedom. This code, in turn, is linked with the concept of free enquiry. And, in an area where free enquiry produces a superior range of technological social alternatives for decision-makers, its concrete advantages become manifest.

Professionalization creates a sense of obligation among individuals, which by becoming moral is therefore much more significant than a simple contract and more reliable. A feeling of custodianship derives from this professional form of obligation, for it is the profession, the body of theory, the set of ideas that contain universals and represent the human intellectual inheritance that need to be enlarged by the incumbents of professional roles. Older professional roles that cannot make this kind of contribution become more mechanical rather than professional; become trades rather than professions. A move into the "establishment" begins when a particular group adopts a code of ethics and tries to establish some theory for its work, some transmittable body of ideas that can be called "scientific." The public relations experts who run polls, do sample studies for private firms on a contract basis, and function between the universities proper and corporate business are an example. The Bureau of Applied Social Research at Columbia University, the National Opinion Research Center at the University of Chicago, and the Stanford Research Associates are other examples of bodies that, although clearly professional, are doing contract work. The next step is for the large-scale private firms to claim the same professional status, followed by the more skilled advertising technicians. By this means, relating the needed skills to transmittable theory and the theory to some opinion—professionalization occurs.

Professionalization then gives identity to the role and solidarity to the organization. Such organizational identity and solidarity link the professional to the "establishment." Once in the "establishment," the individual has "arrived."

In this respect, the long-term aspects of ideology in the developing areas are the same as for the developed countries. Subordinate but senior roles on the basis of technical ability are already associated with civil-service positions, planning positions, and fiscal and other technical roles associated with development in the new nations. The occupants of such roles are like their counterparts from abroad. They have been trained in more or less the same institutions, and similar professional standards obtain. To this degree, the vulgar ideologies decline, and the scientific ideology takes over. Perhaps the long-run basis of association between new nations and old ones will take place largely between members of the professional establishments; for the sense of shared solidarity and identity, like the canons of science themselves, are more or less universal for professionals.

What we have been saying has, of course, been said before—and better. I know of no more adequate summary of these remarks than Werner Jaeger's introductory paragraph in *Paideia*. "Every nation which has reached a certain stage of development is instinctively impelled to practice education. Education is the process by which a community preserves and transmits its physical and intellectual character. For the individual passes away, but the main type remains. The natural process of transmission from one generation to another ensures the perpetuation of the physical characteristics of animals and men; but men can transmit their social and intellectual nature only by exercising the qualities through which they created it—reason and conscious will. Through the exercise of these qualities man commands a freedom of development which is impossible to other living creatures . . ."[53]

It is in this spirit that we examine ideology and discontent.

[53]Werner Jaeger, *Paideia: The Ideas of Greek Culture*, 2nd ed., Gilbert Highet, ed. (New York: Oxford University Press, 1945), p. xiii.

System, Process, and the Politics of Economic Development

THE APPROACH TO THE PROBLEM

Economic development and technological change are among the most desired goals of political leaders in contemporary new nations. Countries which have achieved independence from colonial status since 1945—and it is to these nations that this analysis is addressed—share urgent needs in both areas. The new nations have embarked on programs which they hope will help them to ameliorate their material standards. As a result, the relationship of political development to economic development in these nations is extremely relevant. What political forms are best suited to economic growth?

Of course, the role of the government varies considerably from one new nation to another. Depending on the role of the specific government, one nation's approach to technological change and economic growth will also vary from another's. The practitioner of economic aid must have a fuller understanding of the nature of the political systems emerging in new nations, if he is to understand—and, indeed, to anticipate—the probable uses and abuses to which economic aid will be put. Nor are such matters purely practical. Scholars, too, need to give special attention to the relationship between government and economic growth, if they are to understand both normative and analytical theories applicable to new nations.

I hope to show the relationship between politics and economics in new nations by exploring some of the properties of systems and processes at work, so that applications of policy and ideas of politics about new nations can be seen more realistically. My focal problem centers around the political strategies used to induce technological change and economic development. I have deliberately omitted any discussion of programs of investment and capital formation, technical training, or utilization of economic and technical elites. Nor have I discussed the adaptations of outlook and ideas that are necessary for technological change and innovation. I am aware of these factors, as is everyone involved in research concerning new nations—indeed, the immensity of these problems is blinding. This makes it imperative to attempt to build new theories, ones with a general design but admitting of specific applications.

Many choices in theoretical approach are available to the observer of development in new nations. One approach can appropriately be called "behavioral." The behavioral approach examines several variables to infer, from their relationships, an explanation of individual actions, motivations, and perceptions. Principles are established determining significant roles, their allocations and linkages. However, the larger context within which action occurs is not satisfactorily dealt with.

A second common approach is *ad hoc* analysis. In the problem of development, we can assess levels of growth, especially from a comparative point of view, if we introduce three useful factors of development: (1) the goals of economic and social development set by political leaders and others significant in the system; (2) the state of technology or resources and skills available for achieving those goals; and (3) the degree of outside support available. This suggestive and stimulating approach is, essentially, that of W. W. Rostow, as distinct from that of W. Arthur Lewis, in discussing economic growth.[1] By determining the nature of economic growth—or insisting on a standard of goals—and evaluating the resources, human and material, made possible by the state of technology, as well as the external contributions in investment funds and technical assistance, we are enabled to indicate conditions necessary for self-sustained growth and rapid economic development.

For our inquiry, which focuses on the relationship between government and economics, neither the behavioral nor the *ad hoc* approach is entirely satisfactory. In attempting to evaluate patterns of change through examining the phenomena of development, they fail to account for the "system" needs of governments. However, these system needs are in urgent need of analysis. This is illustrated by the fact that new nations are not very stable entities, and, second, that their governments are rarely effectively institutionalized in relation to the society at large.

The alternative approach I am suggesting here is structural analysis

[1]See W. W. Rostow, *The Politics of Economic Growth* (New York: W. W. Norton & Company, Inc., 1952); and W. Arthur Lewis, *The Theory of Economic Growth* (London: Richard D. Irwin, Inc., 1955).

utilizing comparative method. The concrete units of analysis are society and government. Economic development is a problem both of government and of members of society. To deal with these units in interaction, with respect to technological change and economic development, we want a theory which indicates the *properties* of the system that form the basis of the relationship between the two units. Moreover we want to indicate the processes which will result from action between systems when confronted with the problems of economic development and technological change.

I have written this long preamble because I wish to lay the foundation for what may appear an obscure way of dealing with readily discernible problems. The behavioral and the *ad hoc* approaches lend themselves to *probabilistic* theories, the third, to *systemic* theories. Each has its respective emphasis. The first two lead to an evaluation of behavior and efficiency in the development process. The structural analysis approach, as used here, leads to a theory of "properties" and relationships deriving from the needs of government—these needs having profound effects on the course of technological change. The specification of relationships is, thus, the purpose of this paper; and the problems of economic development and technological change are treated as of strategic importance for governments of new nations.

I propose to deal with these problems in two steps. First, we must specify from the range of characteristics distributed among the rapidly growing number of new nations the differences in the natures of political systems. Second, we must investigate the kinds of response to the problems of technological innovation that these differing systems evoke. Some of the immediate problems are (1) whether the role of political entrepreneurship is greater or smaller; (2) the degree to which reliance will be placed on state enterprise for economic development; and (3) the extent to which talents will accumulate in the central organs of government or will become dispersed and decentralized throughout the system. If this form of analysis proves useful—and, for the present, it must remain experimental—it should provide a more systematic basis for the three problems of growth mentioned above, namely, setting realistic goals, technology and its application, and the use of outside aid.

This discussion brings together two dimensions of analysis which have been developed elsewhere and used independently of one another.[2] The first dimension concerns the natures of the various authority systems that have emerged in the new nations. Of these, three developmental types have appeared. Each type manifests character mechanisms for de-

[2]David E. Apter and Carl Rosberg, "Some Models of Political Change in Contemporary Africa," in *The Political Economy of Contemporary Africa*, ed. D. P. Ray (Washington, D.C.: The National Institute of Social and Behavioral Science, 1959); and David E. Apter, "Political Development and Tension in New Nations" (unpublished background paper for the Conference on World Tensions, Chicago, 1960).

termining goals and for applying and using available technological and other resources. I have used such types because, while many of the acts and activities in which new nations engage are ostensibly common to many or all of them—and, indeed, many of the instrumentalities and mechanisms of political and economic development are essentially similar —nevertheless, their implications for a given society differ markedly, depending upon the type of political system that is predominant. Hence, if we can specify a useful set of systemic properties for political systems, we shall be better able to predict the preferences of political leaders for types of entrepreneurship and economic growth. In addition, more formally, the meaning and social implications of these mechanisms will become more apparent. Our first concern, then, is to define the properties of developmental types that are sufficiently differentiated to illustrate the vast differences in the approaches to economic development in the new nations.

The second dimension concerns the processes of change within each of these types of systems. Having enlarged on the qualities of each of the types, we determine which processes are characteristic in each.

The two dimensions are structural and dynamic. The models presented here are not complete, since extremely important elements are not within the scope of this discussion. Much material has, therefore, been excluded from this paper, because the integration of the dimensions of social analysis in a larger systematic theory must always be coupled with practical field work and research—if not, it is likely to become a sterile and arid system of formal theory-building. Moreover, the integration of dimensions of social analysis inevitably results in considerable overlapping and duplication. Therefore, I believe that the process of building a general theory should consist of taking a limited series of steps, which enable us to piece together theoretical statements and propositions in a careful but necessarily tentative manner.

I should like to emphasize a point I made earlier, namely, that the new nations are different from older and more stable ones in at least one way. One distinguishing characteristic of the former is that the rules of politics and the actions of governments take place in a less institutionalized framework than in the latter. Political leaders, however popular, are acutely aware of the fact that when the institutionalization of governmental structures remains weak, they are particularly vulnerable to public whim and fancy. Hence it is useful to have a dynamic approach to the relationship of government to society.[3] This form of structural analysis has many merits. First, general technological change can be

[3]By "government," I mean here the most generalized membership unit possessing (1) defined responsibilities for the maintenance of the system of which it is a part; and (2) a practical monopoly of coercive powers. By "political system," I mean society (or other unit whose government conforms to the definition above) viewed in terms of government.

considered in relation to its effects on political organization and on the needs and structure of governments in new nations. In addition, it enables us to indicate the role that government is likely to play in technological change, in terms of reliance on political entrepreneurship and government intervention in the economic process. By examining some of the characteristics of governments in new countries, we can provide a framework for determining the levels of development goals that decision-makers will choose, the uses and applications they will make of technology, and the terms under which they will seek and apply outside aid. In other words, I am attempting here, though dealing with the fundamental system properties of governments in developing areas, to establish general guides for the analysis of more immediate empirical phenomena. We shall now turn to structural types. First I shall indicate their properties, before going on to discuss process variables and relationships.

THE DEVELOPMENTAL TYPES

Three developmental types have been considered here. Each represents a form of regime. We are defining them in order to examine dynamically the relationship of government to society. The critical question centers around the capacity of each type to absorb change and generate further innovation. All three types have emerged with lightning speed as a result of the extension of political freedom to Asia and Africa.

These types are, of course, analytical, deriving from a larger structural system of variables. They are "constructions" from typical clusterings of variables which appear frequently in the empirical universe. In that limited sense, they may be regarded as developmental profiles. They were developed primarily with respect to emerging African systems, although it is my contention that they can be applied to the governments of other new nations.[4] They are intended to be similar to Lasswell's "developmental types," the most celebrated of which was "the garrison state." Unlike Lasswell's types, which are not rooted in a wider structural base, these are derived empirically by means of a more elaborate comparative scheme.[5]

Our investigations centered around the observation that each new country in Africa faces a series of choices; in making its choices, it de-

[4]The initial effort to develop these types was made in an earlier monograph, written with Professor Carl Rosberg of the University of California at Berkeley. While we share the responsibility for the development of these types, he is not responsible for their application here. See Apter and Rosberg, *op. cit.*

[5]See D. E. Apter, "A Comparative Method for the Study of Politics," *American Journal of Sociology*, (November 1958). [Reprinted in this volume.]

fines its political machinery. Some countries, e.g., Mali, Guinea, and Ghana, have chosen to mobilize their political energies and resources for a grand assault on poverty, ignorance, and backwardness. Others, like Nigeria, have tended toward some union of important constituent parts, seeking in political unity a common denominator to serve all the main groups within the country. Still others, e.g., Ethiopia and Uganda, represent something perhaps more rare. In these nations, change is filtered through the medium of traditional institutions—i.e., innovation itself is traditionalized and rendered compatible with traditional institutions.

The first type we have called a *mobilization system*, the second, a *reconciliation system*, and the third, a *modernizing autocracy*. Examples of the mobilization system include Guinea and Ghana, and, in a more extreme form, the Soviet Union and Communist China. The reconciliation system is operative in Nigeria; it has also been characteristic of the United States and other federal systems. The third, the modernizing autocracy type, may be found in Buganda, Morocco, Ethiopia, and, in its sharpest form, in Japan, particularly after the Meiji Restoration.

Each type comprises five categories: (1) patterns of legitimacy; (2) loyalty; (3) decisional autonomy; (4) distribution of authority; and (5) ideological expression.[6] We can now indicate how each of the three types of regime reflects these categories. Each is an effort to examine structurally the consequences of actual political arrangements in the politics of new nations. The crucial point on which we are examining each type is whether or not it has the capacity to absorb technological change, and, in addition, to generate new political forms.

Let me now consider the types of political systems in more detail. The mobilization system is most clearly described in Selznick's description of an "organizational weapon."[7] Characteristically, mobilization systems try to rebuild society in such a way that both the instrumentalities of government and the values associated with change are remarkably altered. In Africa, countries whose regimes are of this type incline toward the belief that, to produce "the new Africa," the structural precedents of African society must be altered, and a new system of loyalties and ideas must be created, focused around the concept that economic progress is the basis for modern society.

The characteristics of a mobilization system are as follows: (1) hierarchical authority; (2) total allegiance; (3) tactical flexibility; (4) uni-

[6]I am indebted to the participants of an informal seminar at the University of Chicago who helped derive these categories. They are Rodger Masters, Aristede Zolberg, Leo Snowiss, and Louis Cantori. Their perceptive comments were very useful during the preparation of this manuscript.

[7]Philip Selznick, *The Organizational Weapon: A Study of Bolshevik Strategy and Tactics* (New York: McGraw-Hill Book Company, 1952), p. 2.

tarism; and (5) ideological specialization.[8] Party or government becomes the central instrument of change.

The reconciliation system is considerably harder to define than the first. Its outstanding characteristic is the high value it places on compromises between groups which express prevailing political objectives and views. As we are using the term, a reconciliation system evolves with the formation of a simple political unit from constituent political units which do not lose their political identity on uniting. In practical terms, reconciliation systems can include relatively loose confederations which have recognized structure or highly organized parliamentary regimes. The reconciliation system is characterized by (1) pyramidal authority; (2) multiple loyalties; (3) necessity for compromise; (4) pluralism; and (5) ideological diffuseness.[9]

The third type of system is the modernizing autocracy, where hierarchical authority is buttressed by traditional concepts of legitimacy. One crucial typical feature of the modernizing autocracy is its ability to absorb change as long as the system of authority is not affected by it. For example, in Uganda, the Buganda Kingdom can employ new skills, modernize the school system, and expand social-welfare activities; a civil service has replaced the patrimonial bureaucratic system while retaining intact its traditional modes of authority. The modernizing autocracy manifests a profound internal solidarity based on ethnicity or religion, by means of which support is retained for the political leaders or king who makes claims on the members of the system and controls them. Its characteristics are: (1) hierarchical authority; (2) exclusivism; (3) strategic flexibility; (4) unitarism; and (5) neo-traditionalism.

I shall further discuss these types before going on to the second stage of this analysis, in which I shall include the consequences of economic development in each system-type. As I have said, the role of the government in a country's economic development varies in terms of goals of development, the level of technology and available resources, and the degree of outside support which the country is both willing and able to enlist. The way in which these aspects of economic development are handled depends largely on the nature of the political system in the given

[8]Although mobilization systems tend to have very pronounced ideological views on the main issues of development, in a peculiar sense such a system is less ideological than utopian—to use Mannheim's distinction between ideological and utopian thinking. In fact, in mobilization systems the party or the state will act on grounds of expediency and necessity, using ideology to give perspective and justify what appears necessary. It can be argued that opportunism remains more compelling than ideology. The most overwhelming commitment is either to the party or to the state. See Karl Mannheim, *Ideology and Utopia* (New York: Harcourt, Brace, and Co., 1946), pp. 49–93.

[9]See P. T. Bauer and B. S. Yamey, *The Economics of Underdeveloped Countries* (London: Cambridge University Press, 1957), Chaps. xi and xii.

country. The three forms of political structure of new states are alternative types of systems that are different in the ways in which they cope with these facets of economic growth.

If we examine the functioning of new nations in terms of these types, the following characteristics are discernible. In mobilization systems, the goals of economic growth are very important. They also tend to be unrealistic, as many of them are just beyond the normal capacities of technology and resources. Consequently, the effort to achieve them requires considerable discipline. New institutions must be created for the purpose of removing all social institutions which restrict the processes of economic development. Typically, mobilization systems are inclined toward the ideology of socialism as a contemporary expression of Puritanism. They emphasize discipline and hard work for the attainment of economic goals. This emphasis implies that economic development will re-structure society so that those roles and tasks which are functional to the establishment of a modern economic order will become dominant, while older roles will be obliterated. This is why the mobilization system places great stress on militancy and party organization. Governmental enterprise becomes the major mechanism for economic growth. Correspondingly, high investments are made in education and social welfare, on the grounds that an efficient labor force is the *sine qua non* of economic development. Such systems need a powerful organizational nucleus which takes the major responsibility for the establishment and achievement of goals. They are usually "autocratic" in an organizational sense.[10]

In the reconciliation system, economic growth is more diffuse. Just as political authority is widely dispersed, so there is greater reliance on private entrepreneurship than there is in the mobilization system. Political and economic decision-making is more widespread throughout the society. For example, government shares of the gross domestic product of Nigeria represent roughly only ten per cent, compared to the government shares of Ghana, which are almost twenty-four per cent and rapidly rising. Politically, the reconciliation system pays far more respect to cultural separatism and local parochialism than does the mobilization system. Insofar as the reconciliation type is limited in its decision-making processes by the need to find some "lowest common denominator" which will appeal to its constituent units, its progress toward goals of economic development, and the goals themselves, tend to be very moderate. The relationship between internal resources and the state of technology is closer than in the mobilization type. In the mobilization system, an effort is made to effect the quickest and closest approximation of the material

[10]The term "autocracy" is somewhat misleading. Such systems can be firmly "populist" and popular. See Donald G. MacRae, "Totalitarian Democracy," *The Political Quarterly*, XXXI, No. 4 (October-December 1960).

cultures of the technologically advanced nations of the world. Goals are thus endowed with a symbolic quality which is lacking in both the reconciliation or modernizing autocracy systems. Contrasting examples which illustrate the differences between a reconciliation and a mobilization system (where both are concerned with economic growth) are India and Communist China. The respective strategies of development, and their consequences for the people, are vastly different in the two.[11]

The modernizing autocracy exhibits structural similarities to the mobilization type, but it is distinguished by its stability within the context of rapid economic growth. Economic goals are usually more restricted and less symbolic than those of the mobilization system. Also, they must not be insuperable obstacles to the maintenance of crucial traditional institutions. For example, in a modernizing autocracy, it may be possible to change a patrimonial chieftaincy system under a king into a more rationalized civil service system; however, it would be considerably more difficult to absorb an emerging system of party politics—especially when the latter would alter the patterns of recruitment to posts of political power. Strong restraints are usually placed on changes that might lead to party politics. The modernizing autocracy may inhibit certain activities of economic development if they seem threatening to the autocratic principle of rule. In Uganda, the government of Buganda is willing to restrict foreign capital investment in commercial establishments when it feels that certain of its traditional institutions would thereby be altered. In other words, the goals of economic development are filtered through the screen of traditional institutions. To be accepted, economic goals must show some positive relationship to the existing system of authority. However, this does not prevent a great deal of modernization from taking place.[12] From this point of view, one of the intriguing aspects of Japan and Morocco—two traditional modernizing autocracies—is the alacrity with which they respond to the objectives of economic development.

Although the mechanisms of political and economic growth may seem very similar in all three types, each shows a different focus and emphasis. In the mobilization system, the problem of control is central; in its effort to transform society in order to attain economic objectives, it drives opposition underground. Local separatist tendencies must be smashed. Symbolic loyalties to the political leaders and to the state must take precedence over any others. Political leaders find that they are the managers

[11]See the brief discussion by C. Bettelheim, "Les exigences fondamentales d'une croissance accélérée de l'économie africaine," *Présence africaine* (June-September 1960).

[12]See David E. Apter, *The Political Kingdom in Uganda: A Study in Bureaucratic Nationalism* (Princeton, N.J.: Princeton University Press, 1961); and D. Anthony Low and R. Cranford Pratt, *Buganda and British Overrule* (London: Oxford University Press, 1960). See also the effects of modernization in Japan, as described in the introduction to *Kokutai No Hongi*, ed. Robert King Hall, (Cambridge: Harvard University Press, 1949).

of a society in transition and must take steps to safeguard their tenure and efficiency. Policy derives from finding a balance between the need to insure managerial success and the maintenance of political rule, on the one hand, and the actual achievement of economic goals, on the other. Such a situation is characteristic in the mobilization system. Usually, there is a government or party representative on all local development projects. He is there not only to initiate and stimulate local spontaneity but also to safeguard government or party control over the group. Local groupings must not become sources of opposition.

In contrast, the spontaneous development of new groups is an important feature of the reconciliation system. The new groups may or may not contribute to the efficient achievement of economic goals; they do enlarge the degree of pluralism in the system. In the mobilization type, much of the spontaneity of local and rural development is eventually lost, because every new center of organization is usually controlled by government. Reconciliation systems not only accept opposition; in addition, the government, by catering to opposition and separatist points of view, is profoundly affected and shaped in its goals and in the methods of fulfilling those goals. In the mobilization system, potential sources of opposition are immediately attacked and either eliminated or effectively silenced. In the reconciliation system, local development retains its vitality more easily. This has important implications both for national development and for democracy.[13]

The reconciliation systems are immediately concerned with the mechanics of establishing useful and acceptable economic priorities and with the means of achieving them in conformity with existing political practices. In this sense, they are far less flexible tactically than mobilization systems, while also being less doctrinaire. In reconciliation systems, the problem is to bring the goals advanced by the government into accord with public desires. Both the consent and the support of the constituents of the national society are required. This is one reason that reconciliation systems rely heavily on outside sources of assistance. A government in such a system also prefers talent to be dispersed rather than concentrated at the center. Reconciliation systems in new nations are usually moderately socialist, and consequently extensive planning agencies are part of their governments. Nevertheless, planning is essentially of the "enabling" variety, i.e., it provides opportunities for private enterprise and local self-help by manipulating strategic sectors of the economy.[14]

[13]For a discussion of these problems in Guinea, see "Democracy in Guinea," *The Economist* (November 14, 1959).

[14]This is particularly true in those ex-colonial territories where the colonial civil service or administration had been both the planning and the administrative arm; and traditions of service and skill reside in the bureaucracy. See Ignacy Sachs, "Patterns of Public Sectors in Under-developed Economies," *The Indian Economic Review*, IV, No. 3.

In the modernizing autocracy, as we have indicated, considerable political stability is likely throughout the process of change. Less reliance on control and coercion is evident than in the mobilization system, while more efficient means of achieving goals are available than in the reconciliation system. Traditional values are not destroyed; rather, they are modified and extended. Typically, the modernizing autocracy is bureaucratic. Traditional loyalties and the bureaucracy coincide. In the modernization system, on the other hand, the civil service bureaucracy is in conflict with the party bureaucracy which, having captured the organs of state power, is inclined to consider the internal needs of the party above all others. Party eventually comes to represent the state.[15]

In each type of system, the most important issue is economic development. It is economic development which either becomes the means to rapid change or else presents the greatest threat to the prevailing system. In most new nations, there are mixed feelings about the consequences of economic development. While few disagree with the material benefits of a rising standard of living, many are bitter about the organizational consequences and the demands upon individuals that such a process involves. The mobilization system is clearly willing to ride roughshod over more parochial interests. Economic development then attains the same symbolic meaning as a national goal that freedom and independence had during the nation's colonial period. Under the banners of "freedom from want" and "increased opportunity," the population can be "mobilized" for change.

The modernizing autocracy may proceed in great leaps toward modernization. However, its periods of rapid advance must be followed by periods of digestion during which the changes effected may be absorbed into the traditional political framework.

Thus economic development produces different problems, depending upon the nature and needs of the political systems. We can now extend our analysis and attempt to indicate some of the underlying factors which determine political responses to economic change. We are concerned not only with the degree to which each of the three systems responds to the achievement of economic development, but also with the consequences of such development for the future of each system itself.

Summary

All three types of systems discussed here have certain characteristics in common. Their political leaders are trying to achieve some balance between a desired level of public satisfaction, the attainment of goals

[15]In the reconciliation type, the bureaucracy is normally subordinate to the political arm and does not pose this problem. See D. Apter and R. Lystad, "Bureaucracy, Party, and Constitutional Democracy," in *Transition in Africa*, eds. G. M. Carter and W. Brown (Boston: Boston University Press, 1958). [Reprinted in this volume.]

of development, and the strengthening of political power. One important difference among the three types is the degree to which, in each, public satisfaction can be achieved immediately or must be postponed—a factor which has a great effect on the selection of goals. The mobilization system operates on the principle that immediate satisfaction must be sacrificed for the sake of future fulfillment. In such a system, there is a concept of forced saving in the most real sense of the term—i.e., the immediate benefits to which people aspire become limited, while postponed real gratifications through economic development become the goal of government. As a consequence, a system of government is produced in which savings for investment, in the widest sociological sense, become possible. Other things being equal, we would, therefore, expect the most rapid economic growth to occur in the mobilization system.

In the reconciliation system, goals must be moderated to conform to current demands, and the degree of forced saving is also more moderate. The degree of change is dictated chiefly by the availability of talents and resources that are widely dispersed throughout the system. If rapid technological change and economic change are to proceed, nonpolitical means must be used to fulfill the same objectives which, in the mobilization system, are maximized through political entrepreneurship and state enterprise.

In the modernizing autocracy, it may be possible to achieve greater forced savings if the government chooses to do so. On the other hand, private sources of investment and public enterprise are likely to collaborate effectively in a close-knit relationship. Control is the main concern.

However, each type of system manifests internal conflicts and contradictions in connection with the variables listed. To determine why each type responds in the ways generally described so far, we require a set of variables which can show the process consequences of system. Otherwise, discussion will remain at the phenomenological level, and information will be illustrative rather than explanatory. In the next section of this paper, we shall consider some process variables which apply to all three of the developmental types discussed.

In our remarks, the idea is implicit that all of the types exhibit two characteristic decisional outputs. One comprises developmental decisions; the other comprises system-maintenance decisions. Analysis of these outputs necessitates a discussion of process, and it is to the process variables that we turn for further investigation.

THE PROCESS VARIABLES

Having described the characteristics of the three developmental types of systems in new nations, we can now undertake an analysis of the political processes characteristic of each type.

Four variables are used in this analysis. They are (1) *goals*, defined as operative purposes of government including economic and social development;[16] (2) *costs*, which are the allocations of real income which must be made with respect to the achievement of such goals: (3) *coercion*, or government actions to insure some specific level of conformity; and (4) *information*, or the knowledge available to decision-makers, on the basis of which future decisions may be made.

These process variables can now be linked to our developmental types. Then we can determine, on the basis of empirical data, the political consequences of technological change and economic development that seem characteristic.

Process in the Mobilization Type of System

A mobilization system involves government in active intervention in technological change and economic development. The organizational characteristics of government become a central feature of its activities. Organization qua organization is always somewhat autocratic; and the organizational work of the government becomes pervasive, extending over wide ranges of the social and economic life of a new nation. As a result, people are "acted upon" by an "outside" system, i.e., government. In turn, this leads to a strengthening of the hierarchical and ideological facets of control over society at large. Leadership and the state tend toward identity. Goals assume the characteristics of (1) inviolability, and (2) satisfaction postponed to a future period. Goals are thus profoundly evolutionary and often symbolic.

Hence we can assume that increasing organizational control, for the purposes of mobilization and goal achievement, inevitably runs into public conservatism. A manifestation of increasing control is reliance on coercion to reach objectives that are established for the system. Coercion requires ideological justification. Technological change and economic development become symbolically important because they emphasize future social benefits. If developmental goals are very unrealistic, they may strain the available resources and technology within a new nation so much that mobilization systems may rely on external means to attain them —seeking to maximize their goals by political bargaining with industrialized powers or by acts of territorial expansion. The new nations have not yet indulged in the latter enterprise; but there are signs, in some mobilization systems, that agitation for territorial aggrandizement is beginning.

Third, we can assume that, as coercion increases, there is a correspond-

[16]An extremely difficult but important factor in goals is creativity. Although discussion of creativity is beyond the scope of this paper, a case can be made for greater creativity in the mobilization type than in the other two.

ing decline in free information—or, in other words, in the information about public support and interests that is readily available to government. When coercion is increasing, the public tend to supply government with information that will please it. This decreases the reliability of information on which action may be based. It also makes it difficult for government to create sub-goals proximate to public needs. Government then acts in an atmosphere of greater uncertainty. To compensate for this, government leaders are inclined to increase coercion still more to insure compliance; and a new cycle of reactions is introduced.

Such a pattern has a number of effects on economic development. First, government becomes progressively more enmeshed in investment and in seeking to control its side-effects in the society. Furthermore, the costs of coercion result in the diversion of revenue, hitherto available for investment, into military and police activities and other punitive institutions. Third, bargaining in external relations intensifies the need for stronger standing armies and better military technology, since in any bargaining relationship between independent nations, threats to one another are inherent in any interactions. Consequently, the costs of government rise continuously, and difficulties in spending investment funds for the expansion of government enterprise are met by raising public revenues and by the intensification of the mobilization process. Simultaneously, an increasing proportion of revenue is diverted to non-productive enterprise, i.e., to system-maintenance rather than to development.

In the mobilization system, the need for increasing governmental supervision and the effort to eliminate sources of major opposition result in a decline of cheap and valid information available to decision-makers. As this information declines, decision-makers find it more difficult to predict accurately the degree of public support that they have and the relationship of economic goals to public desires. To bridge the growing gap between the government and the people, there is an emphasis on ideological conformity. In order to insure the allegiance of the people, the highly centralized system of authority relies more and more on coercion. All voluntary organizations, trade unions, the military, and the bureaucracy must be increasingly devoted to the political leaders. The consequence is an even greater loss of free or inexpensive information, and, in extreme cases, the press and other media of public expression are controlled by the government.[17] The costs of coercion rise, and resources available for development are diverted, in part, to pay the rising expenses for the military and police. The optimal balance between economic

[17]For example, in Mali, the two newspapers are owned and controlled by the government and regarded as party instructional and informational sheets. The single party, the Union Soudanaise, considers the newspapers as agents of ideological communication to the local party cadres.

growth and public desire becomes more and more determined by the actions necessary to secure the positions of the government. In order to compensate for the diversion of funds which would ordinarily have been used for development, there is a tendency to use raw labor and "volunteer" labor for primary development. Talent accumulates at the center. The processes of administration are closely linked to the political control over economic development. Political leaders of the second rank and administrators are fearful of being posted far from the centers of power and intrigue.

Most new mobilization systems are autocratic rather than dictatorial. For one thing, dictatorship is inefficient without a substantial technology. In addition, dictatorship produces a control problem—not only are economic resources diverted, but, more important, many of the scarce managerial skills are consumed by the military and police. Most of the new nations of Africa and Asia, however, are more concerned with utilizing these scarce talents to attain economic and social goals. Therefore, typically there is a relatively mild autocracy, in which, frequently, nominal opposition or opposition within a single party remains possible. Thus, fairly inexpensive information is available to the political leaders. They can retain a closer relationship to the public and to public needs than would be possible in a totalitarian system. A mild autocracy becomes a relatively efficient means of implementing economic development and socio-political control simultaneously, by achieving equilibrium between high goal achievement, moderate coercion, and quite cheap information. This is possible in so far as the leaders are willing to modify goals in the light of information. If leaders are fanatical or inflexible about their objectives, they rely on coercion. The optimal balance of our four variables is upset; development becomes very expensive and totalitarian. Hence autocratic mobilization systems can be regarded as more efficient than totalitarian mobilization systems.

Process in the Reconciliation Type of System

In both the reconciliation system and the modernizing autocracy, the leaders are more willing to accommodate goals to public demands than are the leaders in the mobilization system. In trying to effect economic development, the mobilization system seeks to overhaul society in general through technological change. Precisely because of the ideological needs incurred by that process, the mobilization system attaches great symbolic meaning to such general goals, which become the moral basis of coercive politics.

Neither the reconciliation system nor the modernizing autocracy faces this difficulty. The modernizing autocracy derives its "morality" from tradition. The reconciliation system, when defining its objectives, is immediately concerned with gaining some agreement among its constituent units. I shall discuss this before examining process in the modernizing autocracies.

We have made several assumptions about reconciliation systems. First, in such a system, goals are based on information rather than on an image of the future. Then, too, they are high-information systems. Inexpensive information is made available to decision-makers by the variety of interest groups, voluntary associations, and political parties that express their demands to government. Third, reconciliation systems are low-coercion systems. Goals are in closer relation to resources and public desires, and government has less need to rely extensively on coercive techniques. In addition, since reconciliation systems are based upon the restrictions on government power inherent in this structural form, the government can rarely gain sufficient political consensus to enact coercive measures. Fourth, reconciliation systems cannot easily act autocratically except under very extreme circumstances, such as war.

Information is cheap in a reconciliation system because any efforts to use coercive measures would call forth expensive and strenuous opposition by local and non-governmental groups. Acting on the basis of information rather than through coercion, the government must evolve flexible strategies that enable it to win compliance. A high proportion of available resources can be utilized for economic development. However, there is one practical limitation inherent in the situation: A high rate of forced savings is politically impossible. The rate of capital investment is lower than in the mobilization system. The government's efforts take the form of stimulating non-governmental development or local entrepreneurship. This may be done by providing sources of credit for private entrepreneurs, by expanding the possibilities of joint government and private enterprise by industrial development corporations and similar projects, and by encouraging outside investment.

The role of government is not organizational. The government's need is to reconcile diverse interests; it is mediating, integrating, and, above all, coordinating, rather than organizing and mobilizing. The mobilizational system fights society; the reconciliation system is a prisoner of society. Government may show that goals required by public expectations cannot, in the absence of forced measures, be achieved. The public are unwilling to sacrifice current consumption for the sake of future consumption and otherwise to modify their behavior in order to attain these goals. For this reason, while the government may be democratic, it may also break down in unfulfillment, corruption, and compromise. Thus the degree of economic development in a reconciliation system depends on the steadfast motives of the top political leaders, and on the public's determination to enforce self-discipline and to insure, through local participation in economic enterprise, a high level of development. When there are lags in the acceptance of economic goals or voluntary means of achieving them (and where, also, great cultural discontinuities may persist long after a new government has established itself), governments of the reconciliation type may be condemned to slower economic progress than would a mobilization system—at least in the short run;[18] the long-run prospects may, of course, be vastly different.

The reconciliation system must make constant efforts to find local sources of talent and engage them in the development process. When technical elites are being trained, for example, there must be a concomitant effort to maximize their services in a decentralized manner. Thus the processes of economic growth are dispersed, not only between the private and the public sectors of the economy, but also in the provinces as well as in the main center. Local decision-making and local capital investment mean a great dependence on village and local communities. Hence, rapid economic growth is possible in a reconciliation system if and only if there are extensive self-discipline, popular participation, and great civic devotion. These preconditions occur only very rarely in new nations.[19]

Process in the Modernizing Autocracy Type of System

The modernizing autocracy presents a curious balance between the positions in the mobilization and reconciliation systems. First, the modernizing autocracy is able to modify its goal more easily than the mobilization system. In addition, modernizing autocracies have open to them certain coercive techniques, by traditional means, that do not result in restrictions on the flow of information.[20] Third, in so far as modernizing autocracies are autocratic, the coercive techniques available to political decision-makers have had a long tradition and are thoroughly understood by the public. Regularized means of public expression persist because, typically, modernizing autocracies have traditional limits placed on the power of decision-makers by custom and belief. Finally, the public have means for expressing their preferences about actions of government. These means are sufficiently institutionalized not to appear to government as dangerous forms of opposition within the society. The difficulty that the modernizing autocracy confronts is the possibility that changes ef-

[18]One need only compare India and China in this regard. See the discussion of economic growth and planning in the *Report of the Commission of Enquiry on Emoluments and Conditions of Service of Central Government Employees, 1957–9* (Delhi: 1959), pp. 35–45.

[19]See the excellent discussion of this problem in Edward Shils's "Political Development in the New States," *Comparative Studies in Society and History*, II (1960), Part II.

[20]i.e., through religious, clan, familial, and other pressures.

fected in the economic sphere may eventually threaten the principle of hierarchical authority, with consequent demands for the substantial alteration of the system.

Normally, modernizing autocracies are monarchical or bureaucratic systems of rule. The symbolic position of the ruler is heavily emphasized. Opportunities for patrimony are available to him. As economic development proceeds, larger numbers of educated and technically trained personnel are absorbed into the traditional hierarchy. Those who express the desire for greater participation in the decision-making process pose the major problem. The political, rather than the economic, consequences of technological change and development create the most serious difficulties for the modernizing autocracy.

The most important feature of the modernizing autocracy is that it is a low-cost coercion system. Precedent, custom, and traditional behavioral prescriptions, having persisted through time, are central mechanisms of control over both leaders and led. At the same time, the principle of hierarchical authority and autocracy makes leaders relatively less accountable to the public than they are in the reconciliation system. Hence the leaders play an important role in innovation. Modernizing autocracies can advance technological change and require public acceptance precisely because such assertions from government are validated in the traditional patterns of authority. In so far as the government sets realistic economic goals, considerable compliance and acceptance can be assured without increasing coercive costs and, equally important, without losing cheap information. It is interesting to speculate on the reasons for this.

The typical modernizing traditional autocracy centers around a monarch with two characteristics. He embodies complete and awesome power; he is the state personified; he is the personal lord of every citizen —the relationship between king and subject is direct and immediate. From this relationship, two contrasting forms of behavior can ensue. First, the use of authority is itself acceptable. Second, it is possible for the subject to feel that he can personally lay his complaints at the feet of his king and expect remedial action in his favor. This is the reason that modernizing autocracies are low-cost information systems, whereas in all other circumstances coercion and information have an inverse relationship to one another.[21]

One consequence of this set of circumstances is that modernizing autocracies can experiment with goals without paying the penalties of immediate instability. The modernizing autocracies, in contrast to the mo-

[21]Both the mobilization system and the modernizing autocracy tend toward "personal" government. In the former, ideologized justifications cover up capriciousness; in the latter, custom restrains it. See Thomas Hodgkin, *Nationalism in Colonial Africa* (London: Frederick Muller, Ltd., 1956), Chap. v. See also William Kornhauser, *The Politics of Mass Society* (Glencoe, Ill.: The Free Press, 1959), Chap. iii.

bilization and reconciliation systems, have well-institutionalized regimes. In this, they show the greatest parallel to the historical experience of Western Europe, where, particularly in England, vast changes in economic and technological development during the nineteenth century were in accord with modifications in the political sector. Despite the magnitude of the changes, England was able to retain great stability—a factor not unrelated to the economy's ability to expand as rapidly as it did. Economic development also enabled England to change from a modernizing autocracy to a parliamentary unitary reconciliation type of system. Other examples, however, show a different pattern. Tsarist Russia was clearly a modernizing autocracy, at least after the emancipation of the serfs in 1861. But the excesses of the bureaucracy, and corruption, war, and poverty required more effective and drastic structural reorganization than the government could provide. The Russian case can be regarded as a shift from a modernizing autocracy to a mobilization system. However, as a modernizing autocracy it sought economic development through war and expansion, as did Japan and Prussia. In these respects, the modernizing autocracies of Russia, Japan, and Germany at the turn of the century have many features in common.

The modernizing autocracies in the new nations are subject to tendencies similar to those operative in the examples given above. They can promote economic development along with stability only in the short run, because they cannot absorb the new elites sufficiently into the traditional hierarchy. The new elites become the spearhead of political reform, a situation which the modernizing autocracy can suffer only on a limited scale. (The rare exception, England, transformed the practice while retaining the form.)[22]

CONCLUSIONS

In our earlier remarks, we indicated that economic development and technological change could be viewed as a relationship between goals,

[22]Thus the prognosis in a modernizing autocracy is political trouble. In the short run, it is a stable system. In the long run, its success in the economic field creates elites who prefer either a reconciliation or a mobilization alternative. When this occurs, economic goals may be restricted by the monarch to prevent change which he cannot control; opposing groups can easily charge the system with being feudal and archaic. Political difficulties are inherent in the system. Turkey remains one of the most interesting examples to study. There the shift to Kemalism can be described as one from a modernizing autocracy of the traditional variety to a mobilization system after the downfall of the Ottoman Empire, with a move toward a reconciliation system in the decades since the war. This has now reversed itself in an abrupt transition back to a modernizing autocracy of the secular variety. See T. Feyzioglu, "Les partis politiques en Turquie," *Revue Française de science politique*, I, No. 1 (January-March 1954).

resources, and outside aid. Although we did not analyze our material in terms of these three factors, they are obviously of central importance to the problem we are discussing. We must now draw them into our analysis, in order to specify the theoretical relationships which have been elicited here. The three factors can be distributed by means of a variety of institutional variables which, in effect, compose the inheritance of each new nation. Such institutional variables could be extended further, but we shall incorporate the following as most relevant: (1) administration; (2) technology; (3) per capita income; and (4) entrepreneurship. These affect the nature of political goals. They also indicate the possibilities for development that derive from the given state of available resources and skills and the degree of structural flexibility which a new nation inherits upon independence. Although I have not discussed these factors, they are crucial as independent variables. Moreover, they are germane to any discussion of the origins of the development types. They must therefore be added to the system under discussion. If they are considered as independent variables, the theoretical system appears as follows:

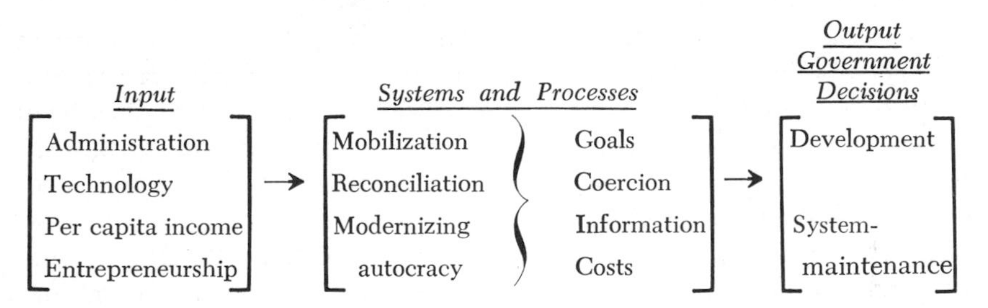

We would, of course, indicate a large number of possible situations which, logically derived from the model, have their counterparts in reality. We could also consider a set time period for a country, in which we evaluated the inputs, the operations of the system and process variables, and the decisional outputs, for their effect on the institutional inputs in a succeeding time period. Systemic analysis could then serve as a basis for probabilistic theories.

Limitations of space, however, preclude a more extensive discussion of this model. Nonetheless, it should now be clear that the heart of this analysis lies with the relationship between system-maintenance (politics) and development (economics). If politics is a conserving and protecting force, development must somehow strengthen and conserve the system. Hence the best test of development is a system-maintenance test.

We can now recapitulate some of the essentials of this discussion.

1. The mobilization system must find the optimal balance between the achievement of forward-looking goals and the allocation of real income between coercion and information. The degree of coercion is re-

stricted by its cost to the process of economic growth.[23] In the mobilization system, hierarchical authority seeks not only to maintain itself but to intervene in all aspects of social life. Economic development becomes the rationale for demanding total allegiance. Tactical flexibility is essential for assuring the immediate control over problems which may emerge in the economic process; its chief characteristic is that it requires a minimum amount of public accountability.

2. The reconciliation system must rely heavily on information when it defines its goals and the means of achieving them. It cannot utilize much coercion—if it does, it will be transformed into a mobilization type of system. Its distinguishing features are its participation in different aspects of group life and its stimulation of the public to participate more fully in economic processes.

In the reconciliation system, collective legitimacy results from a representative principle shared by the entire collectivity. However, the danger of separatism, and even secession, by one or more of the constituents imposes a real limitation upon the degree of freedom the political leaders have. Since multiple loyalties exist, economic development is by no means seen in terms of the state. Instead, its perspectives tend to be transformed into special interests. Developments must be diffused widely throughout the system. For example, in India, the political demands of various local interests made it necessary to construct an oil refinery in a less advantageous part of the country in order to build a refinery in the most economically desired location.

Since compromise is innate in a reconciliation system, the pace of development is determined by the willingness of the political leaders and of the public to follow a policy of the central government. The pace of growth is never more dramatic than that which the public is prepared to accept, since policy must agree with public desires. Frequently, the result is a greater degree of superficial instability in the system, with much spontaneous conflict and expressions of bitterness among the parts. In spite of this, coercive techniques remain at a minimum; and it can be argued that the strength of the reconciliation system lies, in some measure, in the perpetuation of the conflicts themselves. Each group finds a loyalty to the system determined by parochial interests and hopes to satisfy such interests. The hypotheses of both Simmel and Gluckmann concerning the social utility of conflict are relevant here. Conflict is not necessarily destructive of the social fabric.[24] On the contrary, under a reconciliation

[23]If this situation persists so that coercion becomes the primary means of assuring compliance, then there may be a change from a mobilization system employing a mild autocracy to a mobilization system employing more totalitarian methods. Should this occur, then for all practical purposes coercion and information coincide, and the perfect information system is the perfect coercive system.

[24]See George Simmel, *Conflict* (Glencoe, Ill.: The Free Press, 1955); and Max Gluckman, *Custom and Conflict in Africa* (Glencoe, Ill.: The Free Press, 1955).

system, conflict gives people a vested interest in the system as a whole.

3. Modernizing autocracies are suspicious of advanced, dramatic programs for economic development. However, they tend to isolate those aspects of economic reforms that seem capable of being absorbed without causing too many authority problems.

In the modernizing autocracy, goals are restricted by the implications they have for the system of hierarchical authority. Those which seem to entail substantial alterations of the political framework of the society are necessarily abhorred by the government. Others, which allow the system to continue while at the same time satisfying the public—particularly with respect to expanding material standards and raising income levels—are adopted.

At the beginning of this discussion, we pointed out that many of the mechanisms of development are often similar in each of the three types. In the same sense, certain processes in the modern business enterprise in the United States and in the Soviet Union are similar. The problem of economic growth, however, poses very different problems for each kind of political system. In some, the goals of economic and technological growth become a rationale for mobilizing an entire society, and coercion is heavily used to implement mobilization. The optimal level of mobilization is reached when the costs of coercion appreciably limit the achievement of goals. The reconciliation system decides on those goals for which there is already considerable public support, so that it need employ a minimum of coercion. However, in a reconciliation government the large amount of available information may inhibit decision-makers from attaining economic growth. In the last analysis, the determination of goals, and their achievement, depend on the public willingness to work on a spontaneous and decentralized basis.[25]

The mobilization system can be efficient if it does not need to divert a large proportion of its revenues and talents to the system-maintenance sphere instead of the development sphere. In so far as it is successful in concentrating on development, it feeds out satisfactions in the social structure at large that have system-maintenance consequences. Its ability to do this is partially dependent on the urgency with which political leaders seek to develop the country and on the time which they allow for the process. If these leaders are flexible and not quick to fall back on coercive measures, they probably represent the most efficient means of creating political stability and the most rapid possible economic growth.

[25]An important task for the government is the crystallization of economic goals—presenting them to the public in such a way that the people respond enthusiastically to the difficulties inevitable in economic development.

There is, of course, a different but related problem of information. If information is to be effective, it must be translated into goals by efficient decision making. If so much information is available that it cannot be "processed," decision-making suffers and the system becomes "inefficient."

In some mobilization systems, outside development aid may result in larger allocations of internal resources being made to system-maintenance. The dangers of this are obvious. On the other hand, suitable outside aid may effect non-coercive goal achievement without causing grave system-maintenance problems. Under such circumstances, outside aid may ultimately be the decisive factor in whether a mobilization system becomes totalitarian or democratic.[26]

An equally interesting situation occurs when the system-maintenance decisions of a modernizing autocracy become enlarged precisely because of the political problems posed by development achievements. As a rule, in such cases one can predict great instability for the regime, foreshadowing its change from a modernizing autocracy to one of the alternative types. Essentially, these conditions obtained in Iraq prior to the Iraqi revolution. Under such circumstances, outside developmental aid to the regime can only intensify the internal difficulties and is, therefore, ill advised.

Similar conditions obtain in a reconciliation system. If system-maintenance decisions become the major decisional burden of the government, this is a manifestation of an exceedingly unhealthy internal state; in addition it would hardly be likely that developmental decisions would help the situation. Under such circumstances, one can anticipate that, in a reconciliation type of system, there will be an increase in public expectations that is far beyond the capacity of the regime. Reconciliation systems are particularly vulnerable to this problem.

Each type of system under discussion represents a different set of relationships between goals, costs, coercion, and information. The evaluation of data about these variables should indicate the limits within which economic development and technological change can occur in each nation. Consideration of these variables should elicit the preferences which decision-makers will demonstrate by virtue of the system variables within which they must operate. It should indicate the effects that economic development will have on the systems themselves—including the transformation of one type into another.

To conclude: By means of systematic analysis of structure and process, I have attempted to provide a framework in which the study of technological innovation and economic development can be related to the politics of the developing areas. In addition, it should make it possible to draw inferences about the prospects of democracy in the context of social change.

[26]See Charles Wolf, Jr., *Foreign Aid: Theory and Practice in Southern Asia* (Princeton: Princeton University Press, 1960), Chap. viii. It can be maintained that the dilemma posed by the Lumumba government in the Congo about outside aid was of this nature.

Notes for a Theory of Non-Democratic Representation

INTRODUCTION

These notes are preliminary to a theory of non-democratic representation. Need for such a theory has been apparent for some time, particularly in relation to the processes of development, which change the context in which we are accustomed to consider representative institutions and their functions. In my view, most (although not all) non-democratic representation is better seen as "pre-democratic," rather than as alternative or hostile to democracy. Such representation is also functionally varied, depending for its relevance on the stage of development obtained and the prevailing type of political system. Indeed, different political systems stress forms of political participation relevant to the immediate context of their social situations. Since a political type is a means to solve problems, each system type has its advantages and disadvantages. None is permanent any more than the context of social life is permanent. Representation is a variable thing, and its forms and consequences are different in each type of political system. I offer these remarks to challenge the more commonly accepted view which evaluates all representation as it approximates our own western experience or some ideal type of it.

Our analysis begins with an effort to describe the changing character of social life by focusing on the special relationship between government and society formed through some form of representation. Three main

This article was written under the auspices of the Politics of Modernization Project of the Institute of International Studies, University of California, Berkeley.

types of representation are emphasized: *popular*, as associated with "one man-one vote" and a conciliar form of decision-making; *interest*, as associated with special corporate groupings seeking special and parochial attention; and *functional*, as associated with technicians, planners, civil servants, and the like. Each type represents a moral claim, so to speak. Popular representation is based on the rights of *citizenship*.[1] Interest representation is based on some presumed social significance or contribution to society from a particular type of group, primarily *occupational*, e.g., trade unions or business, or professional organizations. Functional representation is based on presumed or recognized expertise useful to society, primarily *professional*.[2]

The framework just indicated implies some main lines for analysis: (1) a developmental social context imposing conditions within which representation occurs; (2) a set of political types, each of which emphasizes alternative modes of representation; (3) a competitive relationship between each type of representation—popular, interest, and functional—in terms of a set of functions which we call the functions of representation; and (4) the functions themselves, which are *goal specification, institutional coherence, and central control*. (We assume that representation has these three functions as a significant minimum.) Hence two models emerge. The first, a general model, specifies the relationship between society and government in terms of stratification and political systems-type variables. The second, a model of representation, is based on types of claim to access and functions of a representational elite. This representational model is an intervening variable in the general model.

Although the concepts employed can be applied to any concrete system, our concern here is to elaborate them in the special context of predemocratic, developmental politics. We will attempt to illustrate their use in a series of short synoptic descriptions, which are intended to be sug-

[1]Although there is an elaborate numbers game which can be played with representation, particularly the form known as electoral geometry, we incorporate in this notion two main types of popular representation which may or may not involve electoral machinery. The first is direct representation, where citizenship becomes a shared condition or a common property of the members of a community with defined obligations and rights requiring direct participation on a Rousseauean standard. Where because of size, numbers, and complexity, direct democracy is impossible, and citizens cannot participate directly in the decision-making process, some "representative" must do the job. Representation in this sense requires a manageable elite speaking on behalf of a wider public. This second form of popular representation is most common, and it is the latter situation which primarily concerns us.

[2]Functional representation derives from the more technical aspects of social life, opening up special access to decision-making on the basis of a particular utility. Administrators and civil servants, governors and soldiers, specialists of various kinds in public works, such as irrigation, public health, and even religious or ideological matters, gain key access in proportion to the need for their skills by government. See Harold Wilenski, *Organizational Intelligence* (New York: Basic Books Inc., Publishers, 1967), pp. 94–129.

gestive of some possible future lines of application. Although these illustrations are purely descriptive and impressionistic, it is possible to operationalize the entire approach by identifying the main groupings of social actors (clustered in the present stratification categories) and determining empirically and over time their type of claim to representation (popular, interest, and functional), the "weight" of that claim, and the elite functions they perform (goal specification, central control, and institutional coherence).[3]

ON THE CONCEPT OF "NON-DEMOCRATIC"

As already indicated these comments are designed to refer to predemocratic, rather than "anti-" democratic, systems. Special attention is warranted because the association of representation with democracy is so close that to speak of non-democratic forms of representation seems somehow a travesty. Certainly there is an "incompleteness" about predemocratic representation, as if somehow it waits for "fulfillment." This is because our western conception of government implies an integrated political system in which needs (motives), access (participation), and goals (purposes) are balanced through representatives popularly elected and brought together in a conciliar decision-making body.

But pre-democratic forms of government are not simply imperfect forms of democracy. They imply a different form of integration, perhaps more coercive, in which needs are more arbitrarily defined, access is restricted, and goal priorities are realized within a public context. Public and private tend to be the same. However, representation exists here too, as we shall see. To discuss it, however, we are required to assess both the political form of government and the general underlying complexity and structural characteristics of society by identifying groups which demand government recognition in many ways: by expressing needs, demanding access, and identifying goals which governments may or may not acknowledge.

In general we can say that representation implies a permanent relationship between a government and its society. The limits of authority each can impose on the other change, however. Since these limits are in some measure determined by "social capabilities," they are best evaluated in a context of development and modernization. Analysis of the evolving bases of social life leads to identification of the particular representational claims which form that tension between society and government

[3]Empirical work of this kind on Argentina, Chile, and Peru is presently underway in collaboration with Torcuato di Tella under the auspices of the Politics of Modernization Project of the Institute of International Studies, Berkeley.

common in all systems and which are ultimately manifested in a changing equilibrium between discipline and freedom as follows:

Concretely, in order to identify the group representational basis of society in a developmental context, I use certain stratification categories which seem to correspond to a particular developmental stage. These categories are pre-class, e.g., caste and ethnicity; class in the sense of the formation of occupationally based classes; class in the sense of the emergence of multi-bonded forms of class; and finally, post-class, e.g., the growth of specialized functional status groupings. Generalizing from these categories gives a picture of the developmental process in which multiple and overlapping claims to representation result from a mixture of traditional social clusters and contemporary innovative ones introduced from industrialized systems.[4]

Analytically, the relationship between discipline and freedom provides a more directly political concern. It makes a difference whether society is the independent variable and government is dependent, or government is the independent variable and society is dependent. In the first instance, the claims of the society become the boundaries within which a government needs to act; in the second, society is to be moulded and changed by governmental decision. To handle this set of political problems we have developed four types of political systems: two in which government is the independent variable, the *mobilization system* and the *bureaucratic system*, and two in which society is the independent variable, the *theocratic system* and the *reconciliation system*. None of these systems needs to be "democratic" in the sense of western representative government, which is, in fact, being excluded from this discussion.[5]

It should be clear from the discussion so far that the representational variables which link stratification to political system are central to this analysis. We are able to treat the relationships between society and government in terms of those elite formations which compete for priority performance of three main functions: *goal specification, central control*, and *institutional coherence*. If the general proposition which emerges is that where society is the dependent variable and government the independent one, these three functions are more likely to be performed by government-sponsored elite formations, such as party leaders in a single-party system. In contrast, where society is the independent variable, com-

[4]Interesting combinations of roles result, which affect permissible behavior, such as a Latin American economist (functional status membership) living in an upper middle-class community (multi-bonded class) descended from an aristocratic family of landowners (caste origin changed into occupational class). Such a role is likely to be linked with planners and economists from the United Nations and other international bodies, yet it is associated, in a reasonably comfortable manner, with all other social groups in the system.

[5]For a more detailed discussion of these types see my book, *The Politics of Modernization* (Chicago: The University of Chicago Press, 1965).

petition between private and public bodies for the performance of these functions is likely. In both cases, however, the ability of particular groups to take a priority position vis-à-vis these functions will be seen to depend upon the stage of development in terms of the group structure which prevails. How these elite functions are distributed determines the participant basis of the society. Today, when these functions are seen in the context of modernization and development, we describe the result as a "participation explosion." This "explosion" includes greater access to roles in the modernized sectors of society as well as the spread of such roles in the society itself. Hence the wheel comes full circle. Greater proliferation in the modernized role sector means more modernization, which, in turn, changes the pattern of prevailing needs in the system.

THE DEVELOPMENT PROCESS AND THE GENESIS OF NEEDS

So far we have referred to the concept of *need* derivatively in terms of modernization and as made visible in the form of political demands. It is obvious that needs in traditional societies will differ in many important respects from those in industrial societies. During modernization, however, old needs will continue long after new ones appear. Need seen in developmental terms becomes progressively more complex. It has two aspects: the concrete demands produced, and the mechanisms by which these demands are represented. The first is a series of events of a day to day sort. The second is a set of institutional arrangements. The latter aspect concerns us at the moment.

Representative institutions are based on claims to representation by interest, functional utility, or equality of right. They derive their complexity from the overlapping qualities of traditionalism, modernism, and industrialism.[6] To diagram these we can describe the systemic aspects of development in terms of the following continuum (Figure 1).

Each general stage of development corresponds to a particular cluster of defined needs arising from social displacement and the formation of new tasks and objectives in the society, in combination with an overlay of "obsolete" ones. The result is cumulative and affects whichever roles

[6]The contrast between modernizing and industrializing in social terms is that modernization is a process in which roles appropriate to (integrated with) an industrial society are established in the absence of an industrial infrastructure. Industrialization, on the other hand, means that the economy has passed beyond the stage where resources are used directly to produce technically simple products for export or direct consumption and has reached a stage of complex application of resources and technology—all within "a pattern of inter-sectoral flows involving capital and intermediate products." See R. H. Green's review of Szereszewski's "Structural Changes in the Economy of Ghana, 1891–1911," *The Journal of Modern African Studies*, IV, No. 1 (May 1966), 126.

CLAIMS TO REPRESENTATION	Traditionalism	Modernization	Industrialization
	interest	interest	interest
	function	function	function
	right	right	right

Figure 1. *Developmental Continuum and Representation.*[7]

are appropriate. However, a set of roles appropriate to one developmental stage is never completely abandoned. It continues to remain significant in the next stage, sometimes serving a useful purpose and sometimes producing negative consequences. More important, the combination of need with role creates an integrative problem of the greatest importance, both in terms of the stratification system and of effective decision-making as well. If the institutional arrangements for linking need and role are visible in the particular combination of representational claims prevailing in the society in question, then the opportunities these provide for competitive elites to perform elite functions become a central empirical concern; such competition creates information for government, and more generally results in participation in decision-making precisely in the most sensitive areas of developmental change, e.g., the alteration in the hierarchy of power and prestige in a system. We can now turn from the concept of need to the analysis of stratification.

THE STRATIFICATION CATEGORIES

Each stage of development has been described in terms of social mobility. The most limited pre-class case is caste (or caste-like), in which portions of a population are separated into distinct and separate groupings (whether religious, ethnic, or racial). Boundaries here emphasize primordial attachments or an exclusivism which goes beyond ordinary prejudice.[8]

More complex stages of development enlarge *class* access. Mobility here is greater than with caste but is still clearly bounded (as in a Marx-

[7]The continuum is a common one. It is often used in comparing modernizing countries. However, there are some special problems here. If we set the continuum on an axis, we find that while traditionalism can give way to modernization, it is a contradiction in terms to say that modernization gives way to industrialization. The point is that modernization does not end in industrialization but is, rather, continuously defined by it.

[8]Such exclusivism extends this concept well beyond its ordinary usage in India so as to include ethnic and all other exclusivist boundaries difficult to penetrate except through kinship. Hence intra-tribal relationships in Africa, even in the same contemporary political framework, can be regarded as a form of caste relationship

ian sense). It includes a subjective awareness of membership in a semi-permeable group, the life chances of whose members are similar and primarily determined by occupation. This notion (similar also to the one held by Weber) makes class dependent on the relation to the means of production. Much less restrictive than caste, it is not "primordial" in identification, although it tends to transform its class interests into general values for a whole society. Its boundaries are fixed when opportunities for occupational mobility are limited. With this type of class one can also speak of the formation of class "consciousness." Demands for class representation here include seeking redress for grievances arising from limited access to mobility. We will refer to this class as type *A*.

At a more advanced stage of development, class is a more multi-bonded affair, and attributes of membership derive from many factors: religion, occupation, income, residence, family background, style of leisure, etc. Class in this more Marshallian sense, which we refer to as type *B*, puts forward claims which, also based on interests, *transform issues of value into negotiable interests*. The result is the opposite of Class type *A* —it breaks up rather than creates solidarity.[9]

Finally, we have post-class status differentiation based on types of status clusters, particularly those associated with industrial skills and embodying a degree of professionality. These create claims for functional representation and include private as well as public bureaucratic status groups and technocratic groups. The latter are specially characteristic of highly industrialized countries.

We can restate the argument so far by combing the developmental and stratification variables in the following structural model:

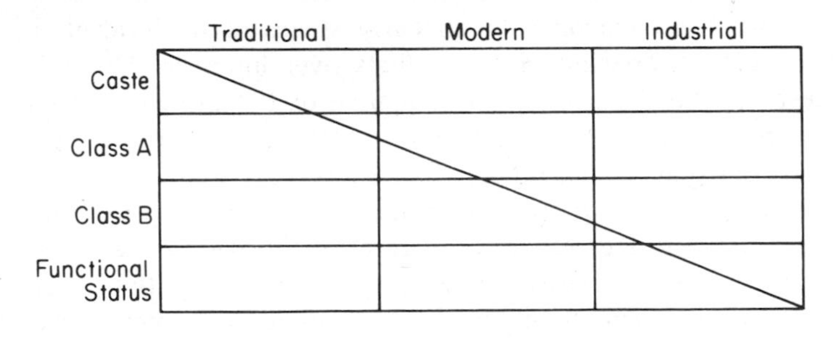

Figure 2. *Development Sequence.*

as the term is employed here. Caste may, of course, vary independently of hierarchy. See Clifford Geertz, "The Integrative Revolution," in *Old Societies and New States*, ed. by Clifford Geertz (New York: The Free Press, 1967) for a discussion of "primordial" attachments.

[9]See T. H. Marshall, *Class, Citizenship, and Social Development* (New York: Doubleday & Company, Inc., 1964), pp. 138–43.

During industrialization not only does the multi-bonded class type (Class *B*) come to predominate, but also the new types of status elites based on a functional role in industrialization or its related activities. These groups form an organizational elite. Using highly germane functional criteria (education, training, professional skill), such groups represent an intellectual "class" in the limited sense that they create information and knowledge which becomes the basis for innovation within industrial societies. Innovating status groups are found not only in industrialized societies, where they occupy central power and prestige roles, but, more derivatively, they are also established in late-stage modernizing societies. Indeed, such groups are part of the modernizing process, linked, too, to their counterparts in industrial systems. *Hence while we speak of development as a process along a continuum from traditionalism to industrialization (from left to right), in practice modernization is a process which moves from right to left, i.e., from roles originating in an industrial society, which we recreate in a non-industrial setting.* The consequence of this "reverse" overlapping of roles leads to the "embourgeoisement" hypothesis.

THE "EMBOURGEOISEMENT" HYPOTHESIS

If our analysis is correct, this reverse formation of roles (reverse in an historical sense) describes both a process and a tendency, which at the most general level can be called the "production of pluralism." By the "production of pluralism" I mean the proliferation of roles and role sets organized around primarily instrumental ends. Class *B* and status relationships are thus common even in early stages of modernization, converting conflicts over values into conflicts over interests. This allows us to suggest that the behavorial consequence of the growth of functional representation is the instrumentalization of need, which results in preferences for immediate gains rather than postponed gratifications. Such a consequence produces a predicament in non-democratic systems precisely because, in varying degrees, they operate on the basis of a higher component of "postponed" satisfactions than do representative democratic systems. Modernization, then, produces "embourgeoisement," which in turn creates a plurality of instrumental ends located unevenly in the stratification system and creating a tug-of-war between popular, interest, and functional claims.

This situation leads to a central proposition underlying the present analysis. We have already suggested that the greater the degree of modernization, the more the modernized roles in the society gain predominance, proliferate, and expand. These roles are predominantly instrumentalistic in consequence. In the absence of an industrial infrastructure, however, such roles are not integrated around a central allocating focus;

hence they create a severe "management" problem for government. The reason follows from the explanation suggested above, e.g., that while representation on the basis of modernized roles may take the form of demands for popular representation, remnants of traditional roles may outnumber them.

Popular representation then leads to a struggle for power. Those leading demands for a genuine popular representational system are the traditionals or near traditionals, while the modernized section supports a doctrine of the "weightier part." More often, "populism" is the result, with popular participation channelled into purely formal conciliar bodies lacking functional substance, as in most "single-party" systems. Claims may be made on the basis of interest groups formed in the modern sector. Functional claims may also arise. Whatever the form of representational need, however, the proliferation of modernized roles creates such ambiguity, coalitional possibilities, and competition between principles of representation by various elites that not only does the management problem become great, but the possibilities for both conflict and stagnation also tend to grow. The greater the problem of such role conflict, the likelier is a drastic non-democratic political solution. *Hence, the greater the degree of modernization, the greater the possibility of multiple claims to representation, and the greater the possibility of restrictive and authoritarian political solutions.* We can explore this proposition a bit more fully.

In the period of traditionalism (despite the variation in political types), the relationships between systems were both horizontal and vertical caste, or caste-like (ethnic), in the sense of a high degree of exclusiveness. In Africa, Europeans were at first virtually a caste group (cultural, racial, and religious primacy) imposed vertically on hitherto horizontally related ethnic caste groups (tribes). Subsequently, in most territories, the Europeans became a class group. In Latin America, vertical caste-caste relationships tended to harden in terms of Spaniards and Indians. In the African case, the dominant caste-status group was expatriate; in Latin America, it was first Spanish, then Creole, and eventually aristocratic and nationalistic. In the latter case, the typical form of caste-caste relationship was the patron-client relationship to sustain rural power. (Conflicts over federal or unitarian rule commonly erupted with this relationship.) Methods of cutting across such exclusiveness could also be found. Empire was one practical way whereby a dominant ethnic group could create political links and, by imposing hegemony, change caste into status, i.e., slave, warrior, etc. Perhaps the most common links which in varying degrees reflected traditional social organization were based on kinship.[10]

[10]Tribal or ethnic-ethnic forms of caste, as in pre-contact Africa, can be described as horizontal linkages. Caste in terms of political and culturally defined groups can be described as a form of vertical linkage.

In the early stage of the transition from traditionalism to modernization these caste-class or caste-status relations change. Caste tends to remain primarily in rural areas (especially in the form of patron-client relationships, as with the haciendados and campesinos in Peru or Chile), while in urban areas a "middle class" of the *A* type emerges, sandwiched in between the caste or caste-like status groups. (Such a middle class also represents the commercial and mercantile development characteristic of modernization.)

This stage two phenomenon shows similar characteristics in many parts of the world. In Africa it included occupational groups, such as clerks, teachers, and others related particularly to commercial life. At this point political factions representing class interests arise. Caste and status groups may also form into factions with restrictive but primordial ideologies of primitive nationalism. (In Africa these were usually concerned with widening the possibilities of representation in local and, more particularly, municipal councils.)

At a still more advanced stage of development, status groups may survive as a sector of an aristocratic class. The most rapidly growing group is a middle class of the multi-bonded type, lacking class consciousness, but aware of the self-rewarding characteristics of modernization, and very much preoccupied with social mobility.[11]

Finally during the transition to industrialization, this multi-bonded class begins to draw in both upper and lower class groups of the *A* type (as when campesinos move towards and into barriadas to become lower-middle-class groups).[12] Toward the end of the modernization period the *A* type class disappears. Modernization thus favors a class structure which is similar to urban middle-class life in industrial societies, the characteristics of which are increasingly accessible to all. In addition, because modernization today takes place through links with highly industrialized societies, the transportation of key roles creates salient points for the spread of "middle-classness." Hence modernization brings about the "embourgeoisement" of developing societies.

This "embourgoisement" accounts for the fact that even under conditions of high modernization with extreme inequality, as in Latin America, there is little radical working-class activity of the Class *A* variety.

[11]This is essentially what has already happened in Latin America. The broad public remained a residual caste (for example, Indians in Peru) or a peasant class. In Africa, on the other hand, in few areas has an aristocracy emerged. The old caste (ethnic) groupings have been rendered increasingly obsolete. No status elite has emerged aristocratic in quality, but rather a new type of elite, based on universalistic criteria: civil servant, technocrat, i.e., professional, trained abroad, but with strong middle-class associations.

[12]The aristocratic class becomes obsolete, with some of its members becoming members of the technocratic elite and others gradually becoming submerged in the elite section of the middle class.

Even peasant movements succumb to the lure of the cities. The multi-bonded notion of class does not lead to polarization of groups into ideological extremes showing ideological propensities. Instead, issues of values are translated into issues of interest. Issues of interest result in demands for representation on the basis of corporate groupings, including well-entrenched interest groups which can function best within the context of the formal pattern of one man-one vote while using special advantages to rig elections and sustain group representation. True, frustrations of some of the middle class of the type *B* variety, especially the intellectuals, may take the form of a radicalization, especially among youth or university students, but it is the middle class which shows these radical offshoots, not the working class.[13] Indeed, a country reaching the final stage of advanced industrialization is characterized by such a proliferation of multi-bonded class roles that it is difficult to speak about class at all; it is preferable to refer to interest groups and competing status roles, i.e., popular and functional.

Our point is that if we see development in structural terms, we can define a functional pattern of increasing need differentiation. The "embourgeoisement" phenomenon changes the demand for access from collective caste or class claims to personal status advantages by means of multiple organizational groupings. Thus conditions are created for competitive elites which cater to increasingly fractionalized interests.

As suggested earlier, each stratification category—caste, Class *A*, Class *B*, and functional status—indicates a type of need and demand. We have emphasized the point that these needs and demands will overlap and reinforce each other, just as the different stratification groups themselves will overlap. Hence the "symposium of needs" and the coalitional linkages possible in the society, which become more complex and differentiated as a society moves from a more traditional to a more industrial footing, create the "pluralistic" problem for government. The key question about representation for non-democratic governments is how they will confront and manage this problem.

POLITICAL SYSTEMS TYPES AND THE FORMS OF ACCESS

We have discussed public need in terms of developmental patterns of stratification. Before going on to a discussion of representation itself, we must first examine the problem of *access*. We see access as a function of

[13]Some of the late stage countries in Latin America have more in common with the highest stage of industrialized countries than with early stage industrializing ones, with this exception: many of the former tend to have the atmosphere of industrial societies during depression. Of primary concern in both is distribution in the face of frustrated production.

the political system. The political system as used here is formed as the result of a relationship between the norms of a society and the prevailing patterns of authority. On the first axis, norms may be expressed symbolically in ideological or religious terms, in ethical precepts, or in terms of concrete goals of society. The most effective political systems combine in a linked system both intermediate and ultimate ends, such as was the case with Calvinism in the seventeenth and eighteenth centuries or with socialism in modern China, with powerful motivational results. On the second axis of the relationship defining a political system, authority, we refer to the degree of accountability of leaders to those led. *In theory, perfect accountability would exist where there was perfect representation.* Both sets of variables define four possible political types, each involving different types of access. Systems emphasizing ethical (consummatory) values and hierarchical authority result in "mobilization" systems. Those emphasizing concrete (instrumental) values and pyramidal authority are "reconciliation" systems. Systems with instrumental values and hierarchical authority can be called "bureaucratic" systems. Those with consummatory values and pyramidal authority can be called "theocratic" systems. We can diagram these as follows:

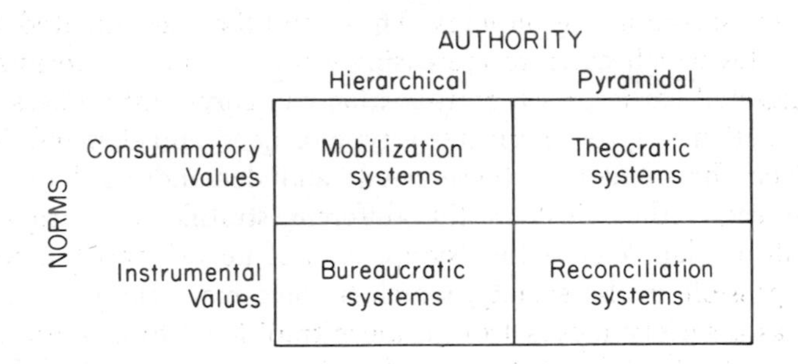

***Figure* 3.** *Political Systems.*

Concrete applications of each type are as follows:

1. *Mobilization systems*, such as Communist China, have a universalizing political ideology in which issues of interest are concerted into issues of value. A command system of control comes closest to the pure type.[14]

[14]Mobilization systems do not need to be of the "left"; they may be of any political persuasion. Peron's Argentina began with an effort to create a mobilization system combining both "left" and "right" characteristics. It failed, especially in the second half of its tenure. Guinea, Ghana, and Mali attempted to establish mobilization systems around a universalized political ethic (African socialism), but they had limited developmental capacities. Characteristics of a mobilization system include a charismatic or prophetic leader, who is outward looking and employs a proselytizing ideology. The main problem, as Weber first pointed out in terms of charismatic authority, is the ritualization of leadership and the decline in belief leading to self-interest rather than community interest, which proves inimical to the latter.

2. *Reconciliation systems* are not necessarily democratic, although they are representative. Examples include democratic countries, as we know them, as well as "single-party" states such as Senegal, and possibly socialist countries such as Yugoslavia. Consummatory values exist, but they are relegated to the private sphere, and are believed to be inherent in the individual. Public behavior is seen in terms of instrumental ends.[15]

3. *Bureaucratic systems* tend to result from a change from one of the other systems. For example, the military sub-type of the bureaucratic system would be of a "Kemalist" or possibly "Nasserist" type, in which the main problem would be the accessibility of the elite. Here the danger of institutional formalism would arise in the fashion described by Crozier. The advantage of this type of system is that it sustains specialized instruments of political control in order to maintain integration. Examples include Egypt, Argentina, and post-Nkrumah Ghana. Sub-types other than the military form are also common.[16]

4. *Theocratic systems* were seen classically in feudalism, when, by virtue of the local pattern of government based on proprietary and manorial rights and local and reciprocal allegiances, they were held together through lines of unstable kinship. The entire feudal system was infused with devotional extremism and a religious ideology. The problem with this type of system was that its stability depended heavily on ideological or religious unity, and this dependence contradicted the realities of local power, with consequent conflicts ensuing over the proper roles of church and state. There have been more stable theocracies, however, such as small New England religious communities.[17]

We should point out that these types of political systems are not real or concrete in the sense of membership group; instead, they must be seen as analytical models and applied as ideal types (although they are not ideal types in the Weberian sense). More important, each system tends to give priority access to different kinds of claims to representation. Mobilization systems, although they may be populist in character as suggested earlier, tend to favor functional claims to representation. However, such functional claims may not be restricted to purely development

[15]The problem is that the instrumental ends are in danger of becoming completely separated from consummatory ends, so that the latter are randomized. The resulting conflicts strain the legal framework or mechanism of bargaining by affecting the sanctity of their rules. A high degree of self-restraint in behavior is required. The emphasis on instrumental ends tends to wear this away, and a loss of generalized meaning ensues.

[16]One we have called the "neo-mercantilist" sub-type, with civilian bureaucratic control; and the other, which (like Afghanistan, Thailand, or Morocco) employs monarchical leadership and components of a military, party, or army bureaucracy for political rule, we call a modernizing autocracy.

[17]To reject the publicly defined consummatory norms would normally mean expulsion from the community, or constitute grounds for terminating any meaningful participation. Control in the system is in the hands of those claiming a special quality of religious or devotional inspiration.

functions, but may also include catering to party organization. Bureaucratic systems will tend to favor claims to representation based on interest and will regulate these according to recognized and institutionalized standards. Theocratic systems (and here we have in mind only historical cases, not contemporary ones) tended to favor popular claims to representation in the context of a widespread religious reform or messianic movement, yet allowed scope for interest claims by means of which the more instrumental qualities of social life were realized. In reconciliation systems all three claims to representation—popular, interest, and functional—tend to compete with industrial sub-types, with considerable conflict between the first and third. We can diagram these propositions as follows:

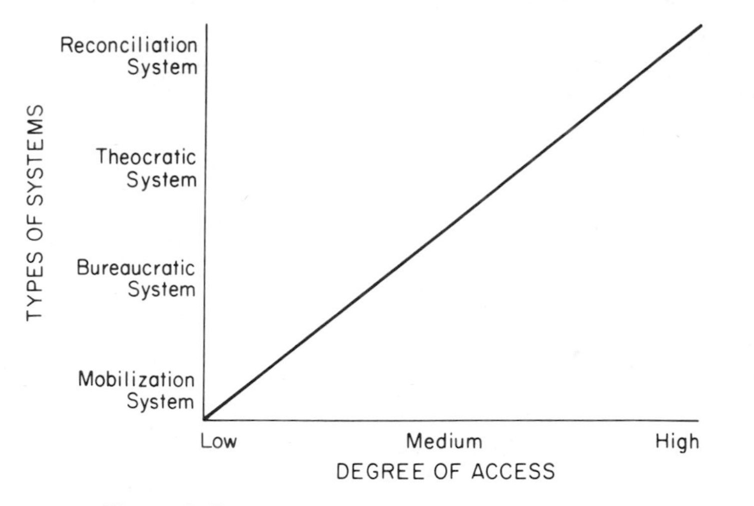

Figure 4. *Representational Access by System-Type.*[18]

1. Mobilization systems respond to pluralism and "embourgeoisement" by restructuring society along political lines in which popular representation becomes a symbolic gesture of unity; interest group representation is made public, and functional representation is bureaucratized.
2. Reconciliation systems respond to pluralism and "embourgeoisement" by oligarchical manipulations, corruption, and the use of economic advantage to restrict popular representation, and to expand interest group representation with functional representation subordinate to interest group representation.

[18]It must be pointed out that the variable of access and type of claim is not merely a function of the type of political system which prevails, but also of the degree of development. Hence early stage reconcilation systems may show some popular representation; however representation tends to be limited to "citizens" who represent only a small part of a total population, excluding slaves and other categories of "non-citizens" from participation, as in the Greek city-states.

3. Theocratic systems respond to pluralism and "embourgeoisement" by allowing popular representation, interest representation, and functional representation to occur as long as none threatens the sanctity of the religious values, thus ensuring a good fit between consummatory religious values and popular belief.

4. Bureaucratic systems respond to pluralism and "embourgeoisement" by manipulating interest group representation and functional representation and restricting popular representation.

To translate these propositions into more operational terms would require ranking the type of claim and the degree of significance within that claim of various concrete groupings in the system. Hence we could rank representative groupings from the various sectors of the stratification system in terms of their significant access on the basis of right, on the basis of function, and on the basis of interest. A number of interesting hypotheses would emerge almost immediately. For example, in the case of Argentina it is possible to show over time how various groups, such as landowners or trade unionists, shifted from popular representational significance to interest representational significance as the system of government changed from one type to another, when the bureaucratic government of Perón changed, to eventually become a reconciliation system under Frondizi. Hence differential access on the basis of claims, although it may occur for a variety of reasons, needs to be seen in the context of changing patterns of stratification on the one hand and alternative model types of government on the other. As we already suggested, both "systems" are linked by representation.

The result is a sequence of differentiation reflecting the proliferation of need and the instrumentalization of ends embodied in the development process as it moves from a state of traditionalism to industrialism. Each stage of the process presents a problem for each type of government, namely its response, by virtue of its own "systems-properties," to the problem of managing and controlling pluralism and "embourgeoisement." To summarize the discussion so far, the variables can be arrayed in diagrammatic form (Figure 5).

THE FUNCTIONS OF ELITE REPRESENTATION AND THE GENERAL MODEL

So far, we have concentrated on the evolving relationships between changes in stratification resulting from development and government according to system-type. These have been linked by representational access on the basis of access claims. The precise nature of these claims and the rights and properties they imply form an important part of the normative dimension of politics. Moreover, they define what kind of information

Stage of Development	Stratification Relationships	NON-DEMOCRATIC POLITICAL SYSTEMS TYPES: Theocratic	Bureaucratic	Mobilization	Reconciliation
Industrial	Class B Functional status Residual class A	–	Representational claims (popular, interest, and functional)		
Modern	Class A Class B Residual caste	"	"	"	"
Traditional	Caste (ethnic)	"	"	"	"

Figure 5. *The Developmental Typology as a General Model and Representational Claims.*

government should have at its disposal by recognizing the legitimacy of the claims implied. Much political struggle has been precisely over the degree of access each type of representation can be allowed in a political system.

However, we have said nothing about the various types of participation in decision-making by virtue of these claims. To do so we need to turn to the analysis of elites and the competition between them. Elites, as used here, constitute a set of variables intervening between society and government which have significant sub-system properties of their own. By representational elites we mean those with special access to power and prestige by virtue of the wider grouping they represent in society or the functional significance of the roles they perform for some object of government.[19]

We can now turn to the functions themselves and define them as follows:

[19]By organizational elites we refer concretely to a wide variety of roles, including administrators, chiefs, army officers, civil servants, priests, businessmen, etc., behind which stand particular organizational groupings, administrative bodies, clans or castes, armies, bureaucracies, churches, and industrial enterprises. How elite functions are distributed is not only the key to non-democratic representation, but it is in conflicts over which groups shall monopolize these functions that the case of non-democratic policies can be isolated. In bureaucratic systems (with government the independent variable) priority is given to functional elites relating to discipline and administration, i.e., armies and civil servants. In mobilization systems (where government is the independent variable) popular representation cannot only be expected to be restricted within a single-party framework (in which party serves to distribute the elite functions and allocate access at the request of government), but it is also non-functional. In theocratic systems (where society is the independent variable) popular representation needs to be managed by religiously organized functional elites, who thereby restrict government policy and shape it. In reconciliation systems, the manipulation of popular, interest, and functional elites is a basis of political bargaining and negotiation.

1. *Central control*: the ordered maintenance of discipline in a political system on a day-to-day basis.

2. *Goal specification*: the identification and priority ranking of policies; hence, a sharing in policy formulation on the basis of a longer term.

3. *Institutional coherence*: the continuous review, reformulation, and adaptation of the fit between boundaries of sub-systems, including the regulation of overlapping jurisdictions, and including as well, ideological adjustment.

With such a formulation it is possible to determine in each case whether the concrete organizational elites are specialized vis-à-vis these functions or whether they are engaged in a constant conflict to extend their degree of access.[20]

By combining these categories with those already employed we obtain the following diagram:

Figure 6. *The General Structural Model and Representational Functions.**

TYPES OF POLITICAL SYSTEMS AND FUNCTIONS OF ELITE

Stage of Development	Types of Stratification and "Embourgeoisement"	Theocratic System			Reconciliation System			Bureaucratic System			Mobilization System		
		Central control	Goal specification	Institutional coherence	Central control	Goal specification	Institutional coherence	Central control	Goal specification	Institutional coherence	Central control	Goal specification	Institutional coherence
Industrial	Class B Functional status Residual class A												
Modern	Class A Class B Residual caste												
Traditional	Caste (ethnic)												

*N.B. Shaded boxes refer to illustrative cases discussed later.

[20]In the first instance, the claim to legitimate access is likely to be on the basis of functional expertise. In the latter instance, functional expertise and representation by virtue of public participation are likely to be employed.

Just as it was possible to operationalize the access claim of various groups in terms of their claim to representation, so it is possible to evaluate the significance of an elite in terms of its degree of access in decision-making by functional significance. Particular elites, such as landowners, members of government, civil servants, businessmen and merchants, trade union officials, and the like, can be seen in the context of their access to decision-making by means of their ability to perform functions of central control, goal specification, and institutional coherence. For example, it is quite possible for businessmen in the United States, with claims to access based on interests, to take part in goal specification and institutional coherence to a very high degree. However, their degree of access will be limited by competing claims based on popular and functional claims from other elite representatives of the system. Since the United States is a democratic sub-type of a reconciliation system, the general pattern of competition is built into the political system and is quite acceptable. In a quite different situation, as in a mobilization system such as Guinea's, the claim to representation from the same group (whether public or private) would be far less acceptable; even if the claim were acceptable, the group's share in functional access to decision-making would still remain less.

Assuming we could find numerical values for these rankings, what would we be able to factor as significant but derived theories from the data? One answer is that we should be able to account for many specific structural relationships within society and between society and government. Moreover, since ours is a predominantly structural model, we should be able to determine the major sources and gains and losses of information in a system. This is of far-reaching theoretical significance, because the general efficiency of a type of political system can be related to various levels of development. If the theory is correct, we should be able to make some predictions about the capacity of different political systems to handle integrative and developmental tasks at different stages of development—a useful object in its own right, which also sets the stage for further studies concentrating on behavior within the structural context.

We can now review the dimensions of this model:

1. The traditional-industrializing continuum is a statement of the growth in complexity of social need leading to demands.

2. The differentiation in stratification indicates the group basis of competitive claims to access—popular, interest, and functional—which arise from social need.

3. The degree of hierarchy in a system indicates the differential pattern of access which government will allow in terms of the functions of the elite.

4. The degree to which ends are consummatory and non-empir-

ical, or instrumental and empirical, will determine the quality of political response.[21]

We can now restate the central propositon as follows: *The greater the degree of hierarchy, the narrower the participation in central control, goal specification, and institutional coherence.* To which, we can add one further point: *the lower the supply of information available to government.* In other words, we use the functions of the organizational elite to indicate the amount of information available in the system which the government is able to obtain. This leads to another proposition: *Where the amount of information available to government is small, coercion will be applied in order to maintain the balance between government and society. Coercion is a substitute for uncertainty.*[22]

Coercion, which we define as the application of violence or the threat of violence by the state, in turn causes a loss of information. It does so by using the organizational elites as a coordinating and punitive arm of government. Hence the following proposition: The more advanced the system in developmental terms and the greater the degree of hierarchy, the more the organizational elites will be used to *control* the sectors of society. The greater the degree of development and the smaller the degree of hierarchy, the more the organizational elites will be used to *coordinate* the sectors of society. The first set of conditions implies coercion through the elites. The second implies a sharing in power through the application of information.

Our main points should now be clear. When representation is viewed as the link between social need and government decision-making it defines the relationship of public need to access in government. The pattern of representation will vary with the system-type, both in terms of participation and function.[23]

In mobilization systems, where government is the independent variable and society the dependent variable, representation is therefore a control device "representing" government to society through the organizational elites. The result is minimum information and maximum coercion. In a reconciliation system, where society is the independent variable and gov-

[21]These four propositions suggest a relationship in which empirical patterns emerge from the analysis of real or concrete units through developmental-time and between systems-types. It is thus possible to use them for heuristic comparative purposes.

[22]On the variables of coercion and information, see the discussion in *The Politics of Modernization*, p. 40.

[23]It would be possible to devise a scale of participation and a scale of functional access in each general type of political system at each stage of development (including the variable access between those who claim technical knowledge, i.e., technocrats, and those who claim information about public needs). We can ask how effective is the role of the expert in monopolizing the functions of the elite, and how competitive with popular representation.

ernment dependent, the organizational elites share in power, provide information to government, and help coordinate society through participation in decision-making. Information is at a maximum, coercion at a minimum. In both cases the intervening variable is representation. Thus, by determining how well social need combines with political effectiveness, it is the most sensitive general indicator of structural balance in a system.

THE REPRESENTATIONAL MODEL

We have attempted a development approach using stratification to indicate the formation of group needs and interests by means of which representative elites can be identified in a general model and organized separately in a representational model. We have seen that such needs produce three types of representation: popular, interest, and functional. Access has been defined in terms of legitimate claims (popular, functional, and interest) operating within each governmental type: mobilization, reconciliation, theocratic, and bureaucratic. The role function of the representative elites varies in each. These functions are central control, goal specification, and institutional coherence. Since we have treated representation as an intervening variable, the three types of representation and the three functions will result in very different consequences and purposes of representation in each political system as well as in each stage of development. Operationalizing representation in these terms thus emphasizes its multiple purposes, its many different aspects, rather than the habitual although often implicit assumption that a particular combination of representational forms or functions leads to a particular political type or pattern of balance.

My emphasis has been entirely the other way around, primarily in order to enable us to develop a true theory of representation. To do so we should be able first to correlate certain types of representation with certain functions; second, to universalize the correlations; and third, to find a generalized explanation of why the correlations appear. It would then be possible to make representation the independent variable, with political system and developmental stage as intervening or dependent. Hence, my object in these notes, though this is perhaps only the first step, has been to specify the conditions under which a theory of representation is possible, namely, to establish the matrix for empirical correlations. The matrix is:

At the present stage, however, we can see only the variable consequences of each box in Figure 6, rather than correlations or syndromes.

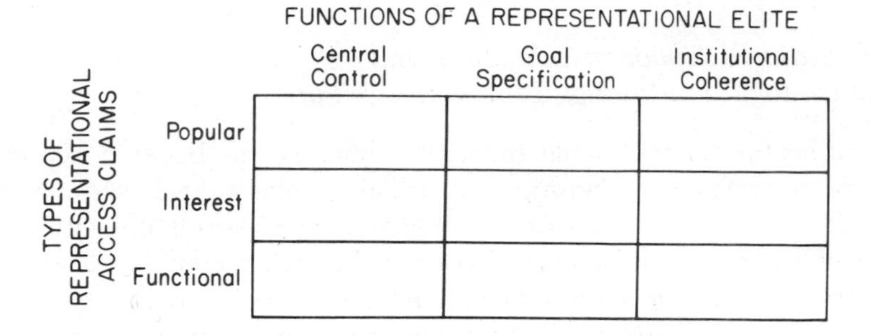

Figure 7. *A Matrix for a Theory of Representation.*

These remain entirely problematical. Still, the possibilities are interesting; and we can speculate, as I will now attempt to do, about which relationships are significant. I realize that proper speculation would require much more systematic work. The applications which follow are merely "trial runs" on a purely descriptive and impressionistic basis for illustrative purposes.

A PRELIMINARY APPLICATION OF THE TWO MODELS

Applying so many variables presents severe problems of language. Not only is it difficult to handle the simultaneous relationships involved without distortions imposed by our ordinary notions of sequences, but also, in this case, we are dealing with two "sets." In one the development process is the independent variable, the functions of the elite and government are intervening variables, and "political balance" or the stable relations between rulers and ruled is the dependent variable. Here we want to know how, in the absence of freely representative relationships in a political system, governments manage the growing complexity of need and provide suitable satisfactions to the members of a society. In the second "set" government is the independent variable, the functions of the representative elite are intervening, and the development process is the dependent variable. In the first "set" we find concrete systems which fall predominantly in the pattern of theocratic and reconciliation systems. In the second are those systems which fall mainly in the pattern of bureaucratic and mobilization systems.

Using these differences as our guide, we can now discuss the dimensions of the model employed in terms of its implications for non-democratic representation as well as for different stages of development. We will not discuss all the possible types but will use several for illustrative purposes.

A Traditional Theocratic System and Change to a Traditional Bureaucratic Type

Stratification in traditional theocratic systems was based on caste relations determined by kinship, i.e., tribal ethnicity. Such systems tend to link kinship with ancestors, in which case ancestral obligation is a form of shared central control between the living and the dead. Conflicts between ethnic groups define the central political problem; elites emerge from kin groups. Institutional coherence derives from priests and others, such as elders, who ensure the propriety of religious beliefs. Representation thus combines lineage and kin or clan leaders with ancestors in the form of kin "interest" and client "function." Government is not separate or distinct from the kinship elites, but rather, the central figure. Indeed, priest, king, and lineage merge. The combination results in the performance of the central control function by government.

What ensures the balance of the system is stability in the stratification sphere and the harmonization of social relations with sustained belief in imminent practices by a kinship elite with popular links through clans or other familial units. There is minimum emphasis on functional representation. Popular forms of pluralism are managed on the basis of reciprocal kinship or ethnic relationships. This arrangement is accepted as a divine expression. The problem of control is, therefore, to sustain the relationship between consummatory and instrumental values. Kinship representation combined with priestly authority is the general method employed.

We have chosen as an illustration the case of the Arab caliphate, because it was in our terms "traditional" in its developmental stage, i.e., organized on caste-ethnic lines (Semitic tribes) which originated in a theocracy (founded by the Prophet), and transformed itself first into an expansionist mobilization system (the Arab conquest) and then into a bureaucratic system (the Arab Empire). Our primary purpose is to use the typology first in a dramatic, historical way to illustrate some of the categories suggested above.

The Arab caliphate was organized for war in order to spread the faith. Its first phase was purely religious. After the death of Mohammed a military organization developed, which represented hierarchical authority but with instrumental values subordinate to religious values. This combination has frequently been a compelling force in history. Ibn Khaldun notes that "religious propaganda gives a dynasty at its beginning another power in addition to that of the group feeling it possessed as the result of the number of its [supporters]."[24] (The quotation notes the temporary qual-

[24]See Ibn Khaldun, *The Muqaddimah*, trans. Franz Rosenthal (New York: Pantheon Books, Inc., 1958), I, p. 320.

ity of this form of religious power.) Bernard Lewis, commenting on the caliphate after the death of the Prophet, suggests that those who elected Khalifa (the deputy of the Prophet) "can have had no idea of the later functions and development of the office. At the time they made no attempt to delimit his duties or powers. The sole condition of his appointment was the maintenance intact of the heritage of the Prophet."[25] So established, the Arabs, organized along military lines, began the twin tasks of conversion and conquest.[26] If the early caliphate was hierarchical in its system of authority, its very imperial successes meant that military commanders and governors could exercise increasing antonomy and control. The principal of election to the caliphate by powerful governors was followed. In theory at any rate, the Muslim community as such was represented.

The forms of representation during the early expansion period of the Arab empire were extremely limited. Important family dynasties exercised influence in court. Administrators, tax collectors, and other officials associated with the organization of public lands and rents occupied central decision-making positions. The key to representation was military, administrative, or familial power, with each serving as a claim to wealth. In Mecca a wealthy class of patricians dominated the elections to the caliphate. Their representation, based on political skill supported by great wealth, quickly turned them into an oligarchy, which in turn, led to a decline in religious commitment. Subsequently, conflicts arose between civil administrators and the oligarchy. Competition for support from non-Arab converts to Islam, who were anxious to obtain advantages as well as the financial success of the empire, caused the priority to shift away from consummatory towards instrumental values. "The assumptions of this system were the identity of Arab and Muslim and the maintenance of the religious prestige by which the Caliph exercised his authority. Its breakdown became inevitable when these assumptions ceased to be valid."[27] The result was a growth in oligarchical corruption and nepotism, which eventually led to civil war.

"The administration of the Empire was decentralized and in disorder and the resurgence of nomad anarchism and indiscipline, no longer restrained by a religious or moral tie, led to general instability and lack of unity. The theocratic bond which had held together the early caliphate had been irrevocably destroyed by the murder of 'Uthman, the civil war that followed it, and the removal of the capital from Medina. The oligarchy in Mecca was defeated and discredited. Mu'awiya's problem was to find a new basis for the cohesion of the Empire. His answer was

[25]See Bernard Lewis, *The Arabs in History* (New York: Harper and Row, Publishers, Inc., 1960), p. 51.
[26]*Ibid*, p. 52.
[27]*Ibid*, p. 59.

to start the transformation from the theoretical Islamic theocracy to an Arab secular state, based on the dominant Arab caste."[28]

What were the dominant groupings to be represented? They were first organized around war and administration by means of appointed chiefs who came to have territorial jurisdictions. Their importance to the caliphate was so critical that they formed a "court" in which intrigue was a key characteristic, particularly against the Mecca castes. Functional "representation" based on administration was thus arrayed against group "representation" based upon caste. The former prevailed, resulting in the secular, bureaucratic Arab state.

Our case emphasizes forces that tend to limit the effectiveness of a mobilization system and lead to its demise. Success is likely to produce limited accountability but many claimants to power. In a mobilization system, representation as such barely exists and is more likely to result in intrigue than in responsible actions. There is virtually no representation because the leader personifies the total community, and any publicly defined pattern of accountability is seen by him as a division in that community. Harmony and devotion, not division and conflict, are the aims of such a system. When the consummatory values associated with such devotion begin to decline, then de facto representation leads to civil war between rival chieftains and the rise of a bureaucratic system.

A Traditional Reconciliation System and its Consequences

Traditional reconciliation systems are organized in stratification terms around kinship. Kin groupings clustered into caste-like relationships are entered by marriage, adoption, or co-optation. Coalitions of caste relationships hover somewhere between caste and Class *A* and are characteristic of historic European reconciliation systems about which we have some knowledge, such as Athens, the Roman Republic, or the Florentine city-state. In each of these cases and within the general category of caste-type relationships, there was to be found a dynastic pattern of stratification. However, such general characteristics hold for more than antique European prototypes and would even include those age-grade segmentary systems in Africa in which entry is on the basis of generation. Central control in such reconciliation systems is normally through a king in a council dominated by senior castes, coalitions of castes, or age-grades. These last may vary in type from dynastic familial organizations to other groups which maintain stewardship over land and possess other property rights not easily attainable by the ordinary public. Goal specification consists primarily of special protection for the various major

[28]*Ibid*, p. 64.

economic and ethnic groupings. Institutional coherence rests with the consultative and conciliar procedures worked out, including courts and councils, magistrates and priests, and shared participation of overlapping caste-like groupings in the reconciliation of conflicting interests. The traditional reconciliation system thus emphasizes representation on the basis of familial seniority. For a more complete illustration we will analyze the case of the Roman Republic.

The Arab case demonstrates how systems change from theocracy to mobilization to bureaucratic representation. Another case of a traditional system is better known because it is closer historically to the European experience, namely, the traditional reconciliation system of the Roman republic, particularly at the time of the attempted reforms of the Gracchi. Government of the republic had been primarily aristocratic, with the burgesses dominated by the old senatorial families. During the expansionist phase of the Roman empire this type of government worked reasonably well. But, at the height of Rome's glory, as Mommsen suggests: "The government of the aristocracy was in full train to destroy its own work. Not that the sons and grandsons of the vanquished at Cannae and of the victors at Zama had so utterly degenerated from their fathers and grandfathers; the difference was not so much in the men who now sat in the senate, as in the times. Where a limited number of old families of established wealth and hereditary political importance conducts the government it will display in seasons of danger an incomparable tenacity of purpose and power of heroic self-sacrifice, just as in season of tranquility it will be short-sighted, selfish, and negligent—the germs of both results are essentially involved in its hereditary and collegiate character."[29]

The Roman case would indicate a shift from claims to popular representation on the basis of a narrowly limited definition of citizenship to rural interest representation on the basis of clanship estates. Struggles over access to decision-making resulted in a corresponding decline in institutional coherence (and in the formation of a religious vacuum which prepared the ground for the successful entry of Christianity at a later stage), struggles over central control and goal specification between various clans, and in the development of different classes.

Attempts to prevent the senate aristocrats from plundering the system and to make them recognize the needs of the public gave rise to conflict between "optimates," who wished the rule of the best, and "populares," who favored the will of the community. The result was conflict over and struggles between rival "classes" as well as between "estates." Attempts to create major reforms, first by Tiberius and subsequently by Gaius Gracchus, ended in their deaths.

[29]See Theodore Mommsen, *The History of Rome* (New York: The Free Press, n.d.), III, p. 297–98.

The Roman example is interesting because it demonstrates the difficulties as well as the typical problems of reconciliation systems which are not democratic, i.e., which exclude part of the community, from effective representation. The Roman system excluded slaves, foreign burgesses, and in effect, the urban poor, yet, nevertheless considered them part of the society. The civic community was thus only a part of the whole. Magistrates, for example, were chosen from a relatively small number of families. Nevertheless, the citizens could record a vote on important issues, and politicians, in order to be elected, needed to have a faction behind them. The basis of faction was in the *gens*, the family. Hence, family connection and political marriage were extremely important.

Personal obligation and the resulting patron-client stratification system were also important. Faction, intrigue, and personal connection are all characteristics of representation in reconciliation systems which provide for accountability through conciliar bodies which represent the "weightier part" of the community but not necessarily the most functionally significant part. What H. H. Soullard suggests for Rome is certainly true of reconciliation systems more generally: "It is this far-reaching nexus of personal and family relationships and obligations that underlies the basis of Roman public life, a fact which the nobles themselves may have sought to obscure. Its form naturally will have varied at different periods of Rome's history. Thus in the early days the tie of the clan was probably the predominant factor; families would group themselves around such leading patrician clans as the Fabii, Aemilii, and Claudii."[30]

The Roman case merely illustrates in a historically familiar context a general phenomenon found in many modernizing societies today. If we take the same characteristic case, the separation of society from the effective civic community, and place it in the context of modernizing nations—whether old ones, as in Latin America, or new ones, as in Africa—we see many of the same problems arising again. In the Latin American case the result has been the growth of Class *A* conflict and Class *B* coalitions, thereby providing various oligarchies with manipulative control over representative organs. Representation has been on the basis of family. Although such representation was originally based primarily on rural landowning wealth, it has expanded laterally in the form of controlling dynastic commercial and industrial oligarchies. Hence, there has been over-representation of the "weightier part," and the patron-client relationship has extended into every aspect of political life. It is precisely to alter this type of situation that many of the modern "democrats" in Latin America, such as Frei in Chile, have attempted to create a theocratic modernizing society by means of land reform and more effective representation.

[30]See H. H. Soullard, *Roman Politics 220–150 B.C.* (Oxford: The Clarendon Press, 1951), p. 3.

The Modernizing Reconciliation System

Modernizing reconciliation systems are likely to be extremely unstable in the primary stages of modernization because of the survival of many traditional practices. Overlapping caste, Class *A* and Class *B* relationships provide the basis of competing coalitions. Here interest representation predominates; central control is weak and bureaucratic; goal specification of the developmental variety is manipulated by politicians with only marginal participation by technocrats; and institutional coherence is based on corruption, mobility, and pay-off. If there is popular representation, it militates against developmental planning. Uneven access to power accentuates inequality and social discrimination. Many Latin American countries fall into this category.

In later stages of modernization, with the growth of class of the *B* type and its intermediary status clusters between Class *A* structures, central control tends to become more organized around a bureaucracy. Goal specification is shared by competing class and status groupings, while institutional coherence is sustained through multiple and overlapping institutional groupings. This pattern is likely to lead to organized plunder, with repeated interventions by the military. The combination of political and economic stagnation, popular representation in voting, and functional representation through the bureaucracy, army, and developmental agencies creates conflict between popular and functional principles of representation.

As we have suggested, reconciliation systems are not necessarily democratic in the western sense of the term. Caste, Class *A*, and Class *B* relationships are linked to familial and personal ties. Such overlapping role sets combine within a single community elements of caste opportunism and class conflicts (as in campasino movements), so that the development of multi-bonded class and status relationships uses the structure of representative government as an umbrella to protect its interests from demands produced by caste and Class *A* types of conflict. Moreover, when such conflict gets out of hand; the Class *B* elites, faced with a management problem, tend to favor military intervention leading to a new constitutional framework.[31] Such efforts attempt to link by political means the structure of social relationships and roles established in each sector of the stratification system with government on the basis of interest representation. A new round of corruption occurs, as well as a new tendency to plunder the system in the absence of more positive representational

[31]See the interesting theory of military intervention advanced by José Nun in "Amèrica Latina: La crisis hegemonica y el golpe militar," *Desarrollo Económico*, VI (July-December 1966), 22–23.

links and associations. The crisis in central control soon repeats itself; hence, the predicament. Sharing power through popular representation by means of the proliferation of voluntary associations, committees, and local governments, and by means of general participation in assemblies and councils throughout the structure of pyramidal authority only intensifies the conflict between popular and interest claims to representation; but in the exercise of their functions the elites emphasize distribution rather than development. This exaggerates a "plunder" psychology with few possibilities for managed and enforced savings in the community. Representational access in terms of any organized interest—whether based on class or function—becomes dominant at the expense of the others.

The problems of the non-democratic reconciliation system are thus accountability without constraint and political participation for short-term gains. The result is likely to be political and social stalemate, punctuated by periods of conflict.

An Industrializing Reconciliation System

The third type of reconciliation system—a type which occurs in industrialized countries—represents the most acute stage of the "crisis of meaning" inherent in the model itself. In this type of reconciliation system class conflicts have given way to status coalitions, each supporting popular and interest representation in competition with functional representation. Central control has become a function of conflict between bureaucrats, technocrats, and politicians. Goal specification is a tug-of-war between interest and functional representation. Institutional coherence is based upon popular representation. Here lie many of the familiar problems confronting pseudo-democratic societies, such as the inadequacy of representative mechanisms and restricted access.

Yugoslavia and Poland might serve as examples of industrialized reconciliation systems, and even the U.S.S.R. is moving in that direction. A few Latin American countries, such as Brazil and Argentina, might also fall into this category despite their military regimes, except for the fact that they are not yet sufficiently industrialized. Representation in an industrial society is much the same as in the modernizing society, except that in the former case either a party, a bureaucracy, or a military group is responsible both for central control and goal specification, while institutional coherence is left to whatever class and associational groupings are found available, perhaps those surviving from the previous system. In other words, non-democratic reconciliation systems in industrial societies tend to be "tolerant" of the social system and to allow institutional coherence to be handled locally by the community itself, while functional access is increasingly prominent.

Modernizing Mobilization Systems

Characteristic cases of modernizing mobilization systems would include Guinea, Ghana, and Mali immediately after their independence. The stratification relations of such systems are of both the caste and the Class *A* types. In other words, we find a typical traditional caste/colonial or expatriate caste stratification system alongside a "middle class" conscious of its position and performing modern tasks.[32] A mobilization system tries to eliminate the colonial caste root and branch and to integrate class and remaining traditional caste relations around new political clusters—a political "class" of the *A* type which embodies the community, such as the P.D.G., the Union Soudannaise, or the C.P.P.—while manipulating populism as a substitute for popular representation.

Party organization creates representative clusters and attempts to define participation in functional terms: the socialization function (youth movements); the production function (trade unions and corporations); the rural innovation function (cooperatives and farmers associations); and the ideological function (ideological institutes). Interest representation is likely to be suspect and regarded as "neo-colonialist" or imperialist. Attempts to alter caste relationships are made by changing the principles of representation and by modifying sources of mobility—both politically, through a "single party," and by bureaucratic co-optation. Central control is likely to be in the hands of a party-government coalition in which the key posts in each are occupied by the same individuals. Goal specification is expressed in terms of planning based on a combination of ideological and technical goals in which technocrats, engineers, economists, statisticians, and the like play a large part, normally in some conflict with political leaders. Institutional coherence is based on increasing bureaucratization, again with a high ideological component. Two characteristic principle conflicts exist between government-sponsored elites and the remnants of traditional elites, and between ideological specialists in the party and civil servants and technocrats. Here we find representation on the basis of function ideologically linked with relevant groupings in the society. Counter-elites are excluded, but even these may not necessarily be restricted in terms of social mobility within the system.

The principal differences between the traditional and modern forms of mobilization systems are, first, that populism is used to support func-

[32]In this usage I would reject the notion advanced by those who claimed that there was no "class" in Africa. Vertical caste (European/African) was followed by Class A/caste (African elites versus tribal groups) and Class A/Class A relationships relatively quickly.

tional representation in the modern forms, and second, that populism requires a consultative base, while functional representation requires a special access to functional elites. Populist and functional elites contend with each other for power. Popular representation is limited to being of the testimonial variety of populism. Access to central control and goal specification is restricted to those concerned with development or maintenance of support. The institutional coherence function is restricted to programmatic ideology, with organizations modified according to the degree to which they fit the ideological pattern.[33]

In general, we can say that even where there is a minimum of popular representation, growing competition between populist and functional elites for access to central control and goal specifications produces considerable accountability. Even the functional elites seek to expand their competitive access by broadening their recruitment base in society. The tendency is to move downward through the restratification of the public into corporate functional groupings relevant to development and systems-maintenance. Not class, but *corporate* grouping is characteristic; hence, a kind of "corporate representation" in primary stage modernizing mobilization systems is seen as the means of reconciling populism with functional expertise.

The solution just mentioned is rarely achieved, however, because of the appearance of the "embourgeoisement" phenomenon, which breaks up the stratification along corporate-functional lines. Moreover, even caste elements prove difficult to eradicate, not to speak of Class *A* type groupings. The middle class of the *B* type, growing as modernization proceeds, makes demands based on wider needs. Thus, central control needs to be even more tightly organized in a military or para-military type of formation. The result is government versus the elites. Goal specification then relies more heavily on systems-maintenance than on development. Institutional coherence tends to be a combination of ideological orthodoxy and coercion. Government-monopolized central control is allocated on an appointive basis to administrators.

Goal specification is toward a future objective. An elite of ideological specialists is required both to create such goals and to insure their status as consummatory values. Institutional coherence is handled by administrative magistrates or tribunals dedicated to the preservation of ideological uniformity. The functions of an elite are joined within a narrow circle, closely associated with government and hostile to other groupings, particularly other caste groupings in the system. When there is weakness or failure in the performance of any of the elite functions, government is likely to apply coercion. Hence, "embourgeoisement" creates the

[33]See Aristide R. Zolberg, *Creating Political Order* (Chicago: Rand McNally & Co., 1966), pp. 93–125.

conditions for mobilization and also prevents the mobilization system from working.[34] Under such paradoxical conditions, popular representation in the form of a party elite would collide with the governmental functionaries or technocrats over an increasingly restricted access to elite functions.

The Industrializing Mobilization Systems

During industrialization, the problem of the decline of consummatory values in combination with the primacy of instrumental values tends to fit directly with a structural pattern of differentiation, in which class conflict gives way to multi-bonded class with coalitions and groups forming on the basis of functional significance. Party leaders and technocratic elite are likely to compete for central control, as in the case of the modernizing mobilization system; however, party leaders and bureaucrats are likely to handle goal specification by means of consultative instruments, while institutional coherence is similarly dealt with by party leaders and plant managers. The industrial system injects new and mutually opposing elements into the picture: On one hand, there is the need for decentralization of command units (as the complexity of the system grows), and on the other, there is increasing bureaucratization occasioned by the effort to retain command over a decentralized decision system. Representation is thus likely to be functional on the basis of the productive system and consultative on the basis of the hierarchy. We can call the resulting sub-type *consultative* (as distinct from popular) representation, as exemplified in China by the direct contact between cadres and the masses.[35] But even in China, the emerging stratification pattern creates an interesting problem, namely, the "embourgeoisement" phenomenon, which breaks up society into competitive status groupings, making it difficult to treat the population in terms of any given class or corporate interest, but rather as representative of elaborately distributed needs.

Breaking up the class pattern into multi-bonded class emphasizes competitive claims to popular representation under the guise of consumer interests. If a few technocratic elites, crucial to the developmental process, gain supremacy over the party elite, central control would be shared by administrators, civil servants, and managers. Goal specification would be decentralized with a corresponding depoliticization of many aspects of social life. Institutional coherence would be provided by the shared and overlapping organizational pluralism associated not only with production and distribution, but also with local government. At this point consult-

[34] *Ibid*, p. 127.

[35] See James K. Townsend, *Political Participation in Communist China* (Berkeley: The University of California Press, 1967), *passim*.

ative representation may be transformed into popular representation. If this should occur, then the political system could become democratic.

The industrializing mobilization system is of great importance because it seems to produce a contradiction between political and economic needs. In highly industrialized societies the multi-bonded pattern of class spreads throughout the system. It becomes virtually meaningless to speak of classes in the Marxist or Weberian sense.[36] The new types of status groupings, each with special claims to representation and power, are competitive in terms of the function of the elite and their type of claim to representation. Most important is the role of the new technocrats, whose functional value is based upon knowledge or innovation. They are opposed by the bureaucrats, whose claim is based upon continuity and efficiency, and by the politicians, whose claim is based on instrumental or consummatory values of a populist variety. The conflict arises because of the role of information. The modernizing society has a model to follow and a goal, industrialization. It can afford to be imitative. The principal difference between modernization and industrialization is that the latter creates a revolution in innovation and technique. In industrial systems it is necessary to reconcile representation of interests and function with new knowledge (innovation). Each of these types of representation involves a form of information which government requires during industrialization. Hence the effect of high industrialization is to diversify need as a basis of information, setting up the following causal chain: *The need for information results in more diverse representation on the basis of complex interests. This emphasizes instrumental values. As consummatory values decline and the need for information grows, the mobilizing industrial system will move toward a reconciliation system.*

SOME TENTATIVE GENERALIZATIONS

By putting so much emphasis on development, we have related system-type to representation in terms of changing needs and information. Our formulation does not deal with democratic systems, but could include them. In modern pre-democratic developing societies, and some industrial ones as well, democracy is a goal based on developmental priorities rather than an independent normative aim, based on a prior, if implicit, agreement on popular representation. The maintenance of representative government in democracies over time is partly a function of an ability to convert potential conflicts over values into conflicts over interests, *without, nevertheless, allowing interest representation to become domi-*

[36]The concept of false consciousness seems merely a presumptuous convenience, adopted by messianic intellectuals as a warrant of superiority in a world which otherwise largely ignores them.

nant. This implies an effective blend of consummatory and instrumental values and high accountability on the basis of popular representation, both of which imply agreement over the balance of representational claims with regulated competition of functional access by elites. Such a system is subtle, complex, and delicate.

In a mobilization system on the other hand, consummatory values clearly dominate. There are few overt challenges to hierarchical authority and there is minimal popular representation. Indeed, pluralism is the enemy. The corporate community is, at least formally, highly unified, and dissidents are silent. However, over time there is a tendency toward functional representation. During the early stages of development, particularly in pre-modern systems, these functional representatives include military and administrative figures in bureaucratic roles.[37] In mobilization systems at the highest stage of development, industrialization, these roles tend to become more specialized around those most germane to generating information and technique, and the clusters of functional roles facilitate central control and goal specification.

We conclude with the following propositions:

1. Both mobilization and bureaucratic polities are limited accountability systems, with government the independent variable and society dependent. Emphasis in the former is on functional representation. In the latter, functional representation is mixed with various forms of patron-client interest relationships.

2. Both reconciliation and theocratic polities are high accountability systems in which society is the independent variable and government dependent. Emphasis in the former is on a mixture of interest, functional, and popular representation; emphasis in the latter is on popular and interest representation personified in a religious/ethical authority.

Although representation is treated here as an intervening variable, it does have several generalized sub-system characteristics. First, information is created through the functions of the elites. The greater the access to central control, goal specification, and institutional coherence by the elites, the more broadly is power distributed, the more likely are the elites to engage in competition to represent diverse groups, and the greater is the degree of information available to decision-making. When the system begins as a mobilization system, the competition among elites constitutes a disciplinary problem for government; elite functions are reduced and information is lost. The proposition which emerges then is as follows: *When a society of the mobilization type is at the stage of late*

[37]It is important to stress that quite often the role is created by the individual, i.e., a trusted lieutenant is made an administrator. If he, as occupant, can be replaced, but the role is retained, then role institutionalization has occurred; and it is possible to consider the role independently of the occupant.

modernization or industrialization on the development continuum, it develops a multi-bonded/status social system. The competition for access by elites leads to decentralization of power but to no change in the principle of hierarchy, thus posing an authority problem for government likely to lead to coercion on the one hand and intrigue on the other. Intrigue will be the main activity of the elites competing for access to central control, goal specification, and institutional coherence. In the absence of good information, government will apply coercion.

In reconciliation systems, such competition between elites is likely to lead toward a greater degree of elite participation by wider sectors of the public, with two main tendencies emerging: representation on the basis of multi-bonded class, or *popular* representation; and representation on the basis of modern status, or *functional* representation. Competition between elites consists of conflicts over the role of experts (civil servants and technocrats) versus politicians (elected representatives). Such competition profoundly affects the effectiveness of participation by the public. Under conditions of high industrialization, a sense of powerlessness can lead to public feelings of alienation as well as to a decline in the over-arching shared consummatory values of the systems; in this case the conversion of issues of values into conflicts of interest produces an excessive fractionalization of power which renders effective decision-making impossible. Under the circumstances, freely available information becomes unusable. The proposition which thus emerges is that *in reconciliation systems, if the competition between elites for access to elite functions and the differing claims to representation produce an excessive fractionalization of power resulting in the privatization of wants and randomization of ends, then the rules of the system themselves become vulnerable. Such systems produce increasing amounts of information and little coercion, but the communications net is so overloaded, and the claims to participate in central control, goal specification, and institutional coherence so competitive that the systems tend to be ineffective.*

The conclusion to these notes is really to state a problem, namely, that the long-term process of industrialization polarizes social structure into groups that are counterposed against each other in a competition for representation that is imposed by the need for information. Although I believe that these conditions produce a long-run tendency toward a reconciliation system, the likely possibility is a "dialectic" between a modern form of the corporate state, with a high emphasis on functional representation, and a democratic state, with a high emphasis on popular and interest representation.

In sum, we have attempted to identify the types of representation which are functionally distributed to particular elites under conditions of variable access and growing need.

Political Systems and Developmental Change

INTRODUCTION

This essay is one of several I have been working on recently which deal with modernization as a form of social change and particularly with how the modernization process is affected by different types of political systems. The papers share two general objectives, namely, clarification of a theoretical dimension relating to the study of modernization itself (clarifying the general models suggested in *The Politics of Modernization*[1]), and preparation of the ground for a broadly comparative empirical study of seven societies at different levels of development.

Here we are primarily concerned with the following question: which type of political system is most appropriate for each level of development? The short answer is that the modernization process creates such problems of coordination and control that "democratic" political systems, in the usual sense of that term, are not very relevant. Moreover, their relevance appears to decrease as a society moves closer to the transition to industrialization. On the other hand, in contrast to modernizing societies, highly industrialized societies, by virtue of the need for multiple sources of information, have a "systems-tendency" toward some form of "democracy." The key to this formulation suggests a proposition as yet

This paper was prepared for presentation at a seminar on the Methodology of Comparative Research at the University of Minnesota and will be published with other papers of the seminar in a volume on the methodology of comparative research.

[1]See David E. Apter, *The Politics of Modernization* (Chicago: The University of Chicago Press, 1965).

unconfirmed, namely, that there is an inverse relationship between coercion and information.

The present formulation, which originated in my book on modernization, advances a theory which identifies expanding choice as the central consequence of modernization and suggests certain political types appropriate for the management of choice at different stages of political development. Development is seen as a continuous process of differentiation and increasing complexity, somewhat along lines recently suggested by Marsh, with stratification serving as its social measure by defining the group basis of political action.[2] In turn, political action, manifested by political parties and other concrete groupings, is seen as the link between society and government, through which the latter responds in terms of coercion and information. The relationship between coercion and information is considered crucial for determining how political systems change.

The original models employed a combination of concrete and analytical units, which seemed useful in carrying the analysis forward but proved less than satisfactory from a purely theoretical point of view.[3] A first essay dealt with the normative, structural, and behavioral aspects of choice in relation to politics.[4] A second focused on the relationship between government and society, concentrating on representation based on a type of legitimate claim and elite access (rather than concrete groupings, such as party, bureaucracy, or interest groups per se—although each of these, and others, could be fitted easily into the model of representation employed). This treatment specified the source of information in the relationship between representative elites and government as well as the means for applying coercion. In this essay, the characteristics of information and coercion will be discussed more fully in relation to political types, although at the present stage, the presumed relationship between them remains speculative, extremely hypothetical, and necessarily very tentative.[5]

Perhaps some attempt to justify these efforts will help to clarify our purposes. The comparative analysis of political systems is particularly difficult from two points of view. First, when dealing with the complex processes of development and modernization, virtually all aspects of social life come to have potential political significance, whether they be recognizable political actions and familiar methods or unfamiliar and

[2]Robert M. Marsh, *Comparative Sociology* (New York: Harcourt, Brace, and World, Inc., 1967), pp. 33–37 and 155–86.

[3]In collaboration with several colleagues from the Politics of Modernization Project at Berkeley and in the practical context of comparing four West African and three Latin American cases, I have attempted to clarify the conceptual bases originally employed.

[4]David E. Apter, "A Paradigm for Political Analysis." [Printed in this volume.]

[5]David E. Apter, "Notes on a Theory of Non-democratic Representation," *Nomos* X (New York: Atherton Press, 1968). [Reprinted in this volume.]

remote ones. In each system undergoing modernization imbalances occur between norms, structures, and behavior, which we can describe as a lack of "fit." To analyze this lack of fit is a difficult but important task of comparative analysis.[6] It is also difficult to find the appropriate intermediate conceptual level necessary if we wish to make comparisons of modernization by the use of political studies which serve diachronically (through time) and synchronically (between systems). Moreover, such intermediate conceptualization needs to be capable of operationalization.[7]

Our efforts have included field work leading to explicit comparisons between different types of systems at various stages of development (synchronic), and to studies of systems with different, but culturally significant historical experiences (diachronic), e.g., Spanish, French, and English colonialism. Our research is still in a preliminary stage, and this manner of working back and forth between concrete research and conceptual reformulation has its problems. For one thing, it is certainly very slow. For another, many of the attempts at conceptualization prove too cumbersome or useless for research purposes. Nevertheless, despite the episodic character of events and the research "rush" which results when the fashion in governmental style shifts (such as a concern with "single-party systems" or "the military in politics"), our attempts seem to be worth the trouble. The speed of events is such that it is important to find that level of analysis which improves our level of analytical understanding by means of the comparison of many systems, even when we are not at the level of events themselves, and there is some cost in empirical efficiency. What "events" have clearly shown, however, is that the political aspects of development are far more complex than they appeared to observers a decade or so ago. It seemed at that time that the description of developing areas would project in bold outlines the key variables of which all politics is composed, bringing us back to "fundamentals" in a fresh way, unencumbered by the orthodoxies with which we had become accustomed to study American or European governments. Now even the new "fundamentals" are lost in the bewildering array of political problems which succeed one another in Latin America, Asia, and Africa.

Consider the thinking a decade or so ago. Then it was the fashion to regard "decolonization" as a process by means of which colonial authori-

[6]We need theoretical categories which, while less general than those offered by Marx, Durkheim, Weber, or Parsons, are more analytically refined than those employed by Russet *et al.* who use primarily available indicator data.

[7]Several efforts have been made, both in the Politics of Modernization Project and elsewhere, to test the logical coherence of the general models employed. In particular, Mr. Mario Barrera has attempted to incorporate the variables using a wide sample of countries and computer techniques, while Professor Donald W. Katzner of the Department of Economics, University of Pennsylvania, has made a logical test of a somewhat simplified version of the earlier models (see his "Political Structure and System and the Notion of Logical Completeness" [unpublished manuscript]).

ties could devolve power to nationalist groupings until the goal of popular government would be achieved. This approach, more common in Europe than the United States, sounds almost as quaint today as do the theories of nationalism which were the preferred explanatory devices of American scholars. In the contemporary perspective, nationalism or socialism or even development itself represent "fading" strategic variables, because individually neither has explanatory power. We still lag behind conceptually, and this is particularly the case in structural analysis; the methodological promise of a few years ago has not sufficiently materialized. We are still caught by surprise by the rise and fall of governments, the failure of policies, not to speak of the effect on developing societies of those drastic alterations occurring within highly industrialized societies, the consequences of which are to create modernization itself.

Obviously, present efforts at reformulation will fare little better than their predecessors unless we first establish some criteria to be met. The criteria suggested are as follows: first, we want to create a "systemic" theory which shows a "circular" flow of "causes and consequences." Such a chain of linked variables themselves need to be analytical, while the units which are under study remain concrete. Second, the analytical variables should be operational, in the sense that they can be quantified. Several strategies for quantification are possible, but the simplest is to rank the concrete units on a simple scale to see their relative weights vis-à-vis the analytical variables. Third, the combination of theory applied quantitatively to concrete units should produce factored clusters of variables which correspond empirically as well as in terms of the theory, i.e., it should be possible to obtain syndromes which can be inferred logically from the models for which empirical validation occurs. This remains our goal.

Before going on to a consideration of the problem of development and the types of political system optimally suited to a particular level, it might be useful to summarize the general model with which we are presently working. As matters stand now, we intend to use the structural models employed here for the analysis of differentiation and complexity due to modernization. Concrete groupings are seen according to stratification; e.g., caste and ethnic strata; class based on occupation and solidaristic consciousness (another form of class based on multi-bonded factors, such as residence, income, occupation, and education); and functional status. Elites representing these groups by their degree and type of access to government provide the major source of information inputs and, as well, serve as coercive outputs. Different political systems have governments which handle such information differently. Cases under study include Senegal, Mali, Ghana, and Nigeria (early stage modernization), and Peru, Chile, and Argentina (late stage modernization).

Each concrete group; e.g., landowners and peasants, army and bureaucracy, trade unions and intellectuals, will be ranked in terms of its predominant type of claim to participation in politics as well as the claim to access made by leaders on its behalf. Claims to participation are seen as popular, functional, or interest. Types of elite access to government decision-making are defined in functional terms as follows: goal specification, central control, and institutional coherence. The combination of empirical rankings can then be correlated with the type of system which prevails—mobilization, theocratic, reconciliation, or bureaucratic—in order to evaluate the types of information emerging at the governmental level and the degree of coercion applied. Part of the model is being tested on computers with coercion ranked on a multi-factored scale.

Of course, despite the bewildering array of theories about development and, in particular, "political dcvclopmcnt," thcrc is no general agreement with regard to terms and categories or especially strategic problems. A concern for political "stability" as a problem focus is common, but many difficulties arise here. For one thing, indicators of instability (coups, armed revolts, secessionist movements, etc.) are very rough and lead an observer to emphasize more "epiphenomenal" variables. Often, too, analysis is based on the simplistic assumption that stability is "better" than instability; that it is possibly the "silent" prerequisite of economic growth.

Whatever the merits of these indicators, however, I would like to take a somewhat more complex position, if only because the causes of political development cannot be confined to or located in a single variable. Moreover, while political stability may be quite a good indicator and a desirable condition for certain purposes relating to development, it may also be undesirable for others and give misleading impressions (i.e., that societies with unstable governments are ruled badly). Our position is that during the modernization phase of the development process, a government's ability to affect development itself generally reaches an effective ceiling quite quickly. When this ceiling is reached, the system of government, as distinct from its occupants, will need to change. This approach follows from our original assumption that the political difficulties confronting government increase as modernization proceeds. To put it another way, a management problem is produced by modernization which causes the political system to reach its ceiling rapidly. Then, once the ceiling has been reached, pressure will build up for the system to change.[8]

[8]Indeed, if at early stages of the development process it is possible to "manage" through some kind of bureaucratic political system—whether an army, a single party, or a civil service—at later stages of development, as a country moves toward major industrialization, political systems are likely to succeed one another more and more rapidly unless a powerful and highly centralized type of political system is established to control the process. Only after the shift to industrialization does such a highly centralized type of political system rapidly outlive its usefulness.

THE CONCEPT OF DEVELOPMENT

Before elaborating the model, some of the concepts used here should be clarified. "Development" is a generic term at the most general level of analysis, including various types of "growth": economic (as in the increase in "roundabout" production); "differentiation" (which results from necessary specialization of function); and increasingly complex patterns of social integration (as in the formation of solidaristic groups). In this context, development has various indicators: such as, increased per capita income or GNP numbers of civil servants; and the proliferation of specialized instrumental roles (financial, technocratic, etc.).[9]

"Industrialization," as used here, refers to a specialized process in which the expansion of productive enterprise is the integrating factor in social life, creating both a demand for skills and education as well as providing the central allocative and distributive mechanisms. Industrialization thus defines utility. It produces certain structural and organizational uniformities. These structural similarities render obsolete certain once powerful distinctions, such as those between capitalism and socialism or between private and public ownership—particularly as organizational types. And while these distinctions are becoming less and less significant, problems of bureaucratic decision-making, optimum organizational size, and efficient utilization of resources are common concerns of growing importance in all industrial systems. More significantly, perhaps, the United States is entering into a period of what might be called a "post-industrial" stage, in which the distinguishing feature is the generation and utilization of new information at an increasingly high rate. Several other industrial societies will soon find themselves in the same situation.[10]

"Modernization," the process with which we are particularly concerned, is a special case of development defined by industrialization, but more general than the latter phenomenon. Here modernization is used primarily with regard to the spread and use of industrial-type roles in nonindustrial settings. We can diagram the characteristics of modernization as follows:

[9]As a concept, it originated in the sociological literature of the late nineteenth century concerned with the growing differences between agricultural and industrial societies. The work of Durkheim is the simplest and clearest of these formulations, while Weber's is the most complex and interesting. Toennies's, although commonly used, is the most superficial. From these and other sociological thinkers (Sombart for example) modern structural analysis arose, of which Parsons's is the most recent example.

[10]The post-industrial stage imposes very special problems, including the "meritocracy" problem posed by Michael Young in which talent, ability, and informational creativity form the new basis for ordering society. Accordingly, a functional elite is produced, while, on the other hand, society casts out "superfluous men." See Harold L. Wilensky, *Organizational Intelligence* (New York: Basic Books, Inc., Publishers, 1967), *passim.*

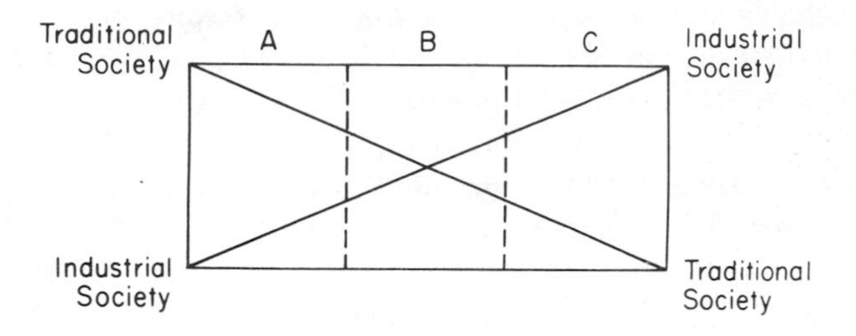

Figure 1. *Stages of Development.*

We can see that the relationship between traditional society and modern society is such that the latter emerges at the "expense" of the former. However, it makes no sense to follow the same procedure in regard to the relationship between modern and industrial society. In other words, it cannot be said that as industrial society emerges modern society disappears. Quite the contrary: they merge and become the same. Hence the relationship between development, modernization, and industrialization is a logical progression resulting in the decline of traditionalism, with modernization a consequence of industrialization.

This formulation has a number of advantages. For one thing, it can be operationalized. It is possible to examine the empirical spread and functional consequences of modern roles in traditional systems. Also it is possible to describe the general process as genetic and in terms of stages. If we consider Stage *A* early modernization, Stage *B* midpoint modernization, and Stage *C* the transition to industrialization; concretely, most African nations would fall in Stage *A*, most Latin American nations in Stage *B*, with a few—Brazil and Argentina—in Stage *C*.

In this context, development also implies change from traditional society, the base-point, to industrial society, the goal. However, this is a bit misleading; for, although we may think of development analytically as a shift from a traditional to an industrial society, the process of modernization works the other way around, i.e., from industrial to traditional. Modernization, thus defined, represents the spread of roles originating in societies with an industrial infrastructure, serving functional purposes in the industrial process, to systems lacking an industrial infrastructure. This is why we spoke earlier of a lack of "fit" in the system as well as a political management problem which intensifies with the proliferation of such roles in the absence (or very limited partial development) of industrialization.[11]

[11]I prefer the present formulation to the technological notion of modernization used by Levy and others, although I would be more inclined to accept the latter as appropriate to a definition of industrialization. See Marion J. Levy, Jr., *Modernization and the Structure of Societies* (Princeton: Princeton University Press, 1966), pp. 9–15.

To reformulate our primary assumption: As a society experiences modernization, conflict produced in the absence of an industrial infrastructure requires government to organize and integrate the various sectors of the community. Hence the following proposition: the closer a modernizing country comes to the stage of industrialization, the greater the political problem of controlling and integrating the process. If this assumption is correct, the transition to industrialization requires an exceptionally well organized political system able to maintain a high degree of control. It is because the problem is so complex that I suggest that high control systems are necessary to make the transition to industrialization. However, after that phase of development has been completed, because the special emphasis of industrialized societies is on the generation, dissemination, and application of new knowledge at an ever increasing rate, the need in post-industrial societies is for greater decentralization of high control systems. If the industrial infrastructure can also carry with it certain organizing properties which reduce the need for direct government control, a non-coercive, high information situation will result, with government playing a mediating and coordinating role.

The central significance of the total development process is in its capacity to widen human choice and alternatives. This represents simultaneously a normative problem (how can choice "best" be widened?), a structural problem (how can the system of roles be held together under various conditions of choice?), and a behavioral problem (what constitutes the permissible levels of action as seen from the point of view of members of the system?). At its widest extent, when development is linked with choice as the "venue" for contemporary political analysis combining normative, structural, and behavioral elements, it is possible once again to talk about "fundamentals," and thus to fulfill the first step in the criteria for reformulation suggested above. Using the three main dimensions of the choice problem as our focus, we can suggest the following propositions: (1) As societies modernize, the normative integration of the previous system begins to weaken, thereby widening the area of public meaning and reducing the area of prescriptive values. (2) From a structural standpoint, modernization creates more complex systems of roles which need to be managed. (3) From a behavioral point of view, there is more ambition and less predictability in social action, producing greater uncertainty among individuals both about themselves and about the anticipated responses of others.

Modernization then is a direct cause of the lack of "fit" between normative, structural, and behavioral aspects of choice. It is the critical problem with which a government needs to deal. A solution requires political expertise under conditions of weak legitimacy and a low ceiling on political options.

POLITICAL SYSTEMS-TYPES

Development and choice are the parameters within which a political system must operate. Development has been divided into three stages: traditional, modern, and industrial; choice has been discussed in three dimensions: normative, structural, and behavioral. However, just as the process of modernization proceeds from industrial to nonindustrial systems, so the complexity of choice increases in the same manner, with rapid proliferation of contradictory norms, alternative role systems, and uncertain behavior. The political response to this situation is to control the normative and structural aspects of choice—on the assumption that this in turn will control behavior. As used here, a political system is a structural response to a behavioral problem of uncertainty resulting from randomness in public action. Such a response can be seen as a political type combining normative and structural variables.

Hence, the political system (which I define concretely as a relationship between society and government) responds to pressures of modernization, which, as reflected in the emergence of class and status conflicts, not only represent claims to redress and power, but claims to key conflicts of values and interest as well. Such claims, whether based on values reflecting proprieties of rank in the society or on interest in whose views should prevail and what groups should enjoy special advantages, may give rise to powerful ideologies, which political leaders wish to endow with much wider moral claims than ordinary proprieties. In conflict, these ideologies define the phenomenon commonly referred to as "legitimacy," which together with its values forms one basis of our structural model of government. If these moral issues should reach such proportions that they define a new basis of legitimacy, we can say they embody nonempirical ends in which a high component of symbolic meaning is associated even with ordinary acts. We call such normative ends in application with empirical means consummatory values. They are commonly expressed in ideologies and represent a moral synthesis directly opposed to an appositive or antithetical moral synthesis.

The alternative situation is where ends and means are empirical. Ordinary demands, which are generated through the system during modernization, normally arise through the competition of groups, such as those based on interest, function, and the like. These are found in both the traditional and more modern sectors of the society. When competition of interest results in the identification and articulation of empirical means germane to empirical ends, what we can call a condition of instrumental values emerges. Most ordinary demands are of this nature. If consummatory values embody normative conflict, instrumental values embody interest conflict. Combinations of these are possible, as when ordinary issues are seen in a wider ideology with a hortatory or utopian objective enabling the ideological expression of a synthesis of consummatory and instrumental values: for example, the Catholicism of medieval Europe, Protestantism during the late Reformation and the industrialization of the West, Japanese nationalism with its high component of political religion, or communism with its elevation of the community to a sacred value. Such powerful syntheses are the moral punctuation marks of political life. They define the issues for all societies—whether they are accepted or rejected by individual governments—and have a great impact on structural and behavioral aspects of choice.

Two other variables of equal importance need to be identified. These are structural categories, which we call hierarchical and pyramidal authority. Here we refer to the degree to which a government is accountable to the public. If accountability is very low, we call this a condition of hierarchical authority. If it is high, we call the resulting authority structure pyramidal. Hierarchical authority is that authority analogous to a command system. Pyramidal systems have semiautonomous decision-making powers, as for example, the several states of a federal system.

Putting these categories together gives us the following types of political systems:

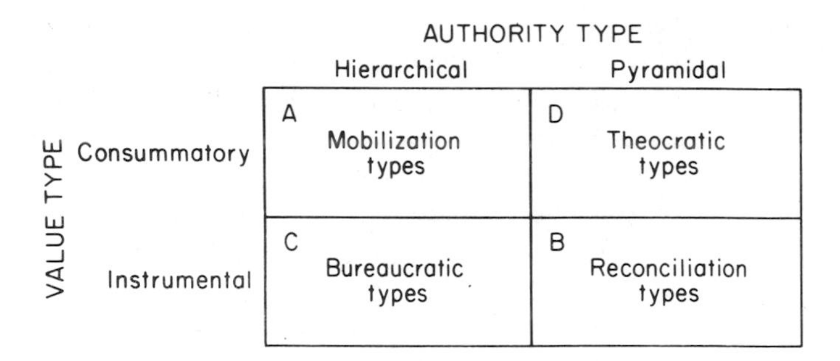

Figure 2. Political Systems-Types.

As modernization proceeds, the complexity of the process creates a need for more and more hierarchical authority to control it. As I have suggested, this is partly due to the inequalities in a system (reflected in class and status solidarities and conflicts) which generate political grievances and can be exploited by political entrepreneurs, as well as to heightened political competition, which creates estrangements preparing the ground for carriers of political consummatory values of either the "left" (as in Cuba) or the "right" (as was the case in Peron's Argentina). One characteristic response to the problem of modernization is seen when a government which is hierarchical in its authority and consummatory in its values comes to power and creates a powerful synthesis of consummatory meanings in instrumental acts. Such a government we call a mobilization system (Type *A* in the above diagram). Mobilization systems have a limited but important, role reaching optimum effectiveness in the transition from high modernization to early industrialization (as was the case in Russia in 1917 and is today in China). However, they have very limited utility for transforming traditional to early stage modernizing societies (as is shown in the cases of Ghana, Guinea, and Mali) and reach their ceilings very quickly. Such systems try to create a new synthesis between normative, structural, and behavioral dimensions by limiting choice and the criteria for choice to "normally valid" goals.

An alternative model, the reconciliation system (Type *B* in the above diagram), in which pyramidal authority and instrumental values prevail, is common during periods of modernization, particularly in Latin America. It has produced certain endemic problems, however. By permitting prevailing differences in the community to sustain themselves through the competitive conflict of interest groups, pyramidal authority results in an allocation of rewards in the system according to the strength and persistence of organized sectors of the society. In addition, when there is a high degree of instrumentalism, a situation which may be described as a "gambler's choice" prevails; the result is great inequality and very little commitment to the system as a whole. At best, the government's role is restricted to mediating between competing power blocs; if it is sufficiently restricted in what it can do by high degrees of accountability, the result is stagnation.

Reconciliation systems can work well only when one of two conditions is present: (1) when the system "descended" from a previous level incorporating highly consummatory values which had defined a "New Jerusalem" in ethical terms (as was the case in the New England communities of the United States, which had institutionalized the values of corporate responsibility so effectively that they spread throughout the system to act as silent monitors on instrumental behavior); or (2) when the system shows an exceptionally high rate of growth and a correspondingly high "payoff" (as is the case in Venezuela). Without one of these two conditions, the reconciliation system is likely to result in the rise of such inequality and concomitant corruption in government that it produces little commitment to the society on the part of its members or its government. In this case, the relationships between norms, structures, and behavior are a result of a kind of political *laissez-faire*.

On the other hand, as industrialization proceeds those aspects of a reconciliation system are produced in which the relevant conditions of success just described are likely to be present, especially if a "New

Jerusalem" was created by a previous mobilization system. If, in addition, industrialization has produced the promise of a high rate of payoff, the result may be a well-functioning reconciliation system which, although it may or may not be "democratic" in the sense of representative government, would nevertheless be characterized by the accountability of its government and the increasing primacy of its instrumental values. Thus, movement between *A* and *B* situations in the model is possible as a society goes from early stage industrialization to "mature" industrialization. More important perhaps, because they are more characteristic during modernization, are two other movements: namely movement from *A* to *B* to *C* and from *B* to *D*. The first two shifts, from mobilization type and reconciliation type to bureaucratic type, recently occurred in Ghana and Nigeria. The second, from reconciliation type to theocratic type, is being attempted today in Chile. However, the long-term prospect in modernizing countries is a movement back and forth between bureaucratic and reconciliation types. Latin American countries have experienced this. Oligarchical reconciliation systems reach a certain stalemate, and a caudillo or military leader or other personalized figure takes over. He is overthrown and "democracy" is restored. The same situation is now coming to prevail in Africa in the form of military regimes.

The mobilization and reconciliation systems share one characteristic in common: they articulate a process which is the key to their functioning, namely, the organization and direction of the entire system toward given goals in the first instance and the mediation and reconciliation of interests in the second. They have a certain political coherence.

The theocratic and bureaucratic types are "states of affairs" systems. They lack a political blueprint, but represent a more immediate and direct balance of forces. The theocratic system is based on a high behavioral commitment to consummatory values; its structural form is whatever sustains that commitment. The bureaucratic system is based on a powerful and effective organizational mechanism, e.g., army, bureaucracy, party, etc. In this case, consummatory values are largely irrelevant, and, while behavior is controlled, all values are "instrumentalized" to serve organizational or structural needs. If the belief system of the one or the organizational sub-system of the other is threatened, the system will change.

Thus, with the four types of political systems, we can speak of two "process" types, two "states of affairs" types and four criteria of maintenance. These criteria of maintenance are important because they can serve as a means to identify when a system-change takes place. Let us take two possibilities: If in a mobilization system the mobilization process falters and the system comes to depend on an organizational sub-system as the critical organizational mechanism and the pattern of consummatory values begins to decline in favor of instrumental values, then the system has shifted to a bureaucratic type. If in a reconciliation system mediation between various groupings terminates and a mobilizational process takes over with a particular sub-system assuming control over all the others in the presence of consummatory values, then the reconciliation system will have changed to a mobilization system.

To summarize the discussion so far, we have suggested that the modernization stage of the development process creates a widening of choice which creates severe management problems in normative, structural, and behavioral terms. A political response is to combine normative and structural controls in political systems, each of which restricts behavior in some particular manner. Each political system reaches a "ceiling" in which the resources of development at its disposal are no longer capable of being redeployed.[12] The ceiling affects the process or state of affairs on which the system is functionally based, and a change from one type of political system to another becomes more likely. We can now turn to the political system itself in order to see how this situation occurs.

From the foregoing analysis it should be clear that there is no single "best" political system for a particular stage of development. Rather, what seems "optimum" is the system which has not yet reached its effective "ceiling." Moreover, we can tentatively suggest that different types of systems will vary in their ability to prevent that ceiling from being imposed on them too rapidly. This in turn suggests that there are possible optimum types for each stage of development. Mobilization systems are "optimal" for late stage modernizing societies in transition to industrialization. Bureaucratic systems are optimal for midpoint or intermediate modernization. Both mobilization systems and reconciliation systems are useful at the primary stages of modernization insofar as they create a framework for society, however, the transition from traditionalism to early stage modernization produces extreme difficulties for both. Theocratic systems are not likely to be useful at any of the stages of modernization or industrialization, but the category has relevance historically, as well as in certain traditional cases.

[12]By a ceiling, I mean the limits imposed by the political system-type on the deployment of natural and human resources for developmental purposes. To take an extreme example, if we compare India with China, both high population-increase countries, in terms of per capita income rises during the 1950's, we can see that Chinese per capita income between 1950 and 1958 grew at an annual rate of 11.5 percent, while Indian per capita income growth during the same period was about 1.5 percent. While the differences are obviously not entirely due to the fact that the former represents a mobilization system-type and the latter a reconciliation system-type, the political system "ceiling" for each is a critical factor. See the discussion by S. K. Nath, "Indian Economic Development," *Planning and Growth in Rich and Poor Countries*, eds., W. Birmingham and A. G. Ford (London: George Allen and Unwin, 1966), pp. 144–45.

It is now necessary to specify more clearly what we mean by "optimal" system. By optimal system I do not refer to the most democratic or most libertarian. My personal view is that democratic and libertarian systems work "best" in industrialized societies where the need to create and apply new information is critical. But modernizing societies can be more emulative, in the sense that they can observe industrial systems and utilize some of the information which they produce. The peculiar difficulty of modernizing societies is, however, that the more they modernize, the more roles are drawn from an industrial context, and the greater becomes the complexity of the system, the organizing functional principles of industrial society are still lacking. Hence the goal of modernizing societies, i.e., industrialization, is a simple one, but the political problem, managing the complexity of roles, becomes greater the closer a country moves toward the goal. The "best" system, then, is that which handles this management problem most effectively, allowing modernization to proceed in a relatively efficient manner.

I have suggested that a mobilization system shows relatively low accountability, the principle which defines the basis of the hierarchical organization of government. Conversely, reconciliation systems show relatively low hierarchy, or high accountability, with accountability taking a concrete form vis-à-vis political parties, the military, civil servants, business enterprises, trade unions, international technical bodies, overseas missions, etc. However, as modernization increases, the problems of coordination and control grow greater for both types of systems as described above.[13]

Having described the political systems-types and the characteristics of systems-change, we can now restate some of these concerns in terms of several functional categories, relating these to the analysis of information as an input and coercion as an output of government. In the following discussion, it should be possible to see the relationship between the formulation of the general model (in terms of mobilization and reconciliation types) and the responses of each system to the pressures of modernization.

UNCERTAINTY, INFORMATION, AND COERCION

We begin with a basic problem of systems-change: When does a government reach its "ceiling" beyond which it cannot make major structural changes vis-à-vis human and natural resources? To answer this question, we will examine the matter of systems-change in the context of several

[13]In addition, we need to add a more interesting possibility, namely, that each type is increasingly vulnerable to the other and acts as a potential "withinput" for the other.

definitions and relationships. Although the analytical units are the political systems-types suggested, the concrete units are government and society.

In mobilization and bureaucratic systems, government is the independent variable with society dependent. In theocratic and reconciliation systems, society is the independent variable and government dependent. The link between government and society is what we call representation. Representation can be popular, interest, or functional, with different emphases prevailing in different systems-types; for example, mobilization systems emphasize functional representation, while reconciliation systems emphasize all three forms. However, every society shows some mixture of the three. Representation is carried out by representative elites who exercise three major functions: central control, goal specification, and institutional coherence. Central control refers to access to decision-making on a day to day basis; goal specification refers to access to planning and the establishment of political objectives; institutional coherence refers to mediation between organizational jurisdictions and ideological positions. These functions are the result of elite roles which respond concretely to problems arising in the stratification sphere and convert them into a series of inputs. This is why we say that representational elites have linkage roles between society and government. Nor are these elites merely passive transmitters of information. They may serve as "triggers" for government action, affecting values which have a wide moral significance (consummatory) as well as those with developmental significance (instrumental).

Several assumptions can now be specified: the greater the amount of participation by elites in government, the greater the degree of information available to government. The idea here is that elites "create" information by participation. In this context, "information" means that knowledge which reduces uncertainty, and "uncertainty" is the ability to predict a reasoned sequence of events. Given the foregoing analysis, we can recapitulate the problem as follows: (1) The greater the degree of modernization, the wider the range of choice. (2) The wider the range of choice in a system, the greater the degree of normative, structural, and behavioral imbalance. (3) The greater the normative, structural, and behavioral imbalance, the greater the degree of uncertainty. (4) It is to uncertainty that the various political systems-types respond.

The relationship between type of representation and access to government differs depending upon whether government is the independent or the dependent variable. In a mobilization system there is minimum representation by type and minimum access. In a reconciliation system there is maximum representation by type and maximum access. The combination of access and representation is an index of participation.

We can summarize the analysis so far in the following diagram:

Figure 3. *The General Model of Political Development.**

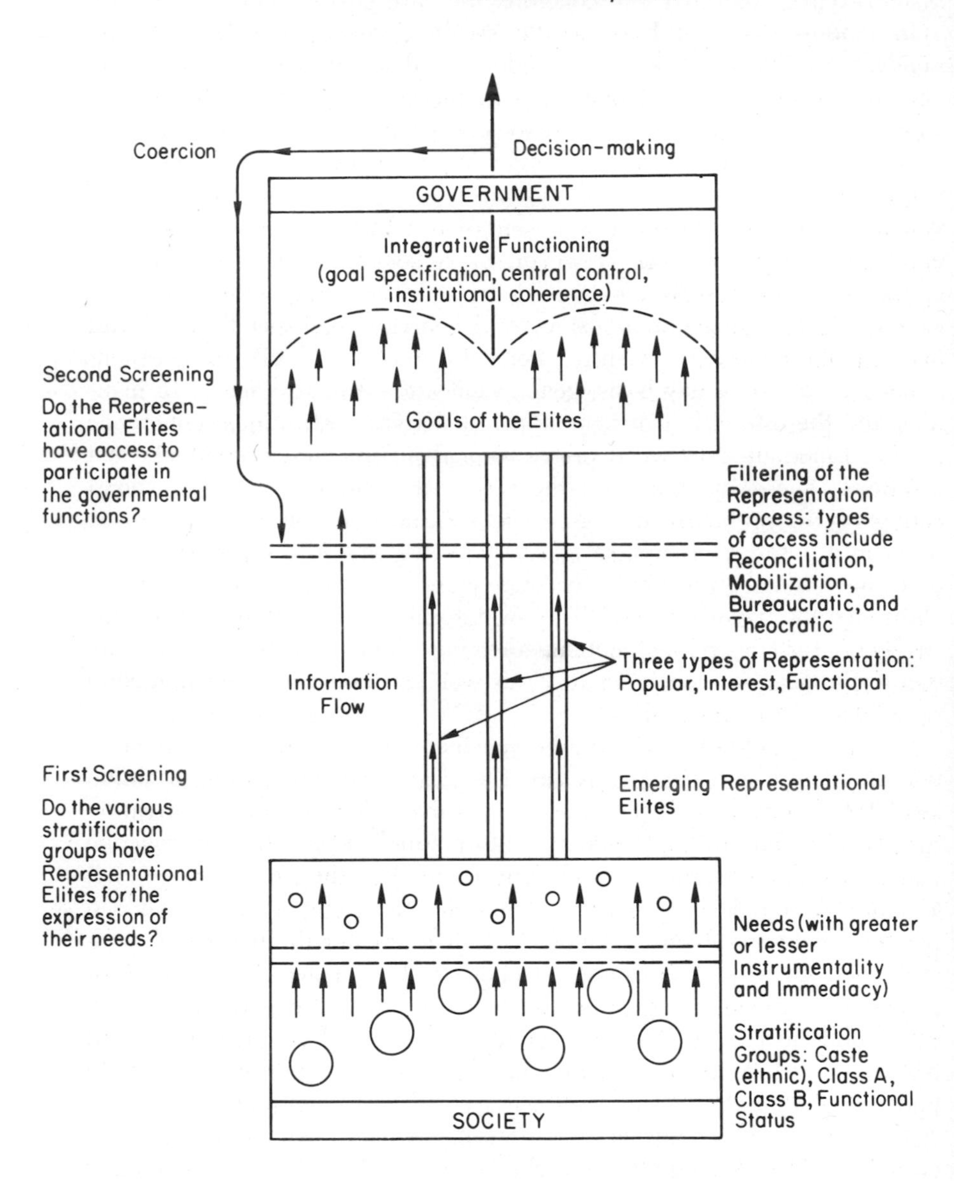

*I am indebted to Professor Tarcuato DiTella for the organization of this diagram.

To carry the analysis a step further, let us see how each of the two systems, *A* and *B*, mobilization system and reconciliation system, handle these problems. Let us assume that both types of system seek to maximize the information at their disposal and to increase the efficiency of their decision-making. At any point in time the total amount of information available in a system is the product of consummatory values (normative preferences), instrumental values (interests), and technical knowledge. Moreover, modernization increases the total amount of information available in both the instrumental and technical spheres. Hence, the following propositions: (1) The lower the degree of hierarchy, the more difficult it is for the government to act on information—unless there is a high degree of consensus from accountability units. (2) The higher the degree of hierarchy, the easier it is for government to act upon the information at its disposal. (3) In order to ensure freedom of action, hierarchical governments tend to maximize technical information and to employ coercion to control consummatory and instrumental values.

In other words, both systems attempt to increase their decision-making effectiveness through the application of coercion. In the case of the mobilization system, such coercion tends to be in the form of direct government control, and it is applied in terms of the information already available. The system is coercive, particularly in the sphere of consummatory values. Normatively, it restricts political values to a highly symbolic set of consummatory "templates" creating a special language or code. A high degree of symbolic coercion is prepared for violators of this code. They may be "cast out" of the community or put to death for violations of symbol. Political "witches" are publicly burned, especially those representing counter-legitimacy consummatory values. Instrumental values, more easily contained by police controls or a political party (the so-called single-party system being one device employed), tend to be concentrated in two forms of interest, economic and political, but these interests stand for the community as a whole, rather than for particular sub-groups.

In reconciliation systems political leaders also desire to use centralized coercion. However, the key characteristic of pyramidal authority is limited power, and a corresponding limitation on coercion is imposed by the diversity and strength of accountability groups. Nevertheless, the tendency to coercion exists for many reasons. In the absence of coercion, there is likely to be considerable private corruption. Dislike of the government as well as other forms of resentment are common. Many interests compete, but this competition may weaken rather than strengthen the system as the danger of converting interest conflict into value conflict arises and prepares the ground for either a mobilization system or some other alternative, including take-over by groups with a high coercive potential and instrumental values best represented in the military. Cases in point have been Burma, Pakistan, the Sudan, and most recently Nigeria.

In each case—mobilization or reconciliation system—the key to system-change is a functional change in the political system itself.

In *The Politics of Modernization* I put forward the proposition that there exists an inverse relationship between political coercion and information. Increasing coercion will result in losses in information. Such losses are not necessarily direct and immediate; nor are they all of the same type. Losses in information from increased coercion are likely to be highest in the sphere of counter-legitimacy consummatory values and lowest in the area of technical information resulting from industrialization itself. However, instrumental conflict is likely to be disguised and increasingly converted from interest conflict to value conflict. In other words, a two-step process takes place, including the loss of information about counter values and the increasing political significance of what would otherwise remain in the category of interest claims. This is the particular problem of the mobilization system.

The problem is the reverse in the reconciliation system. Thus, information about instrumental conflict is likely to be very high—so high, indeed, that it cannot be screened and evaluated. In addition, the content of the information is likely to be so confusing that a government is at a loss about how best to act upon it. With its sphere of action limited by diverse accountability groups, government is likely to find compromise necessary—itself a cause for that stagnation. This situation creates groups in favor of populist consummatory values which repudiate government or act as a regenerative movement against the government. If coercion can be applied against representatives of this moral force, it only reinforces their claims and gives them wider legitimacy. We can diagram these tendencies as follows:

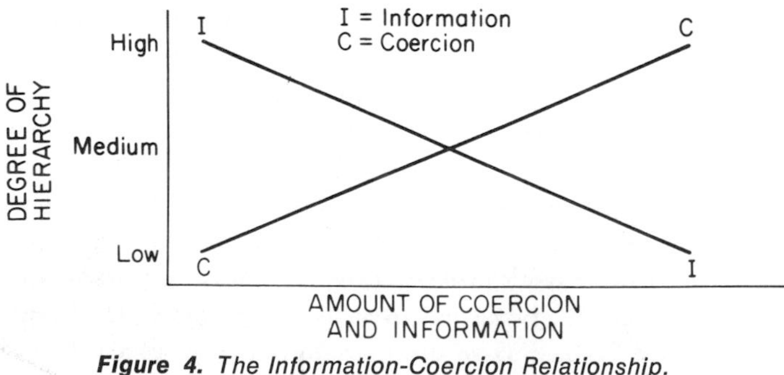

Figure 4. *The Information-Coercion Relationship.*

Now, we can restate these assumptions in several hypothetical propositions: (1) All governments engaging in modernization show a tendency to increase coercion to maximize the efficiency of decision-making. (2)

The point at which this tendency terminates is where coercion causes such losses in information that effective decision-making is reduced. (3) Changes in the relationship between coercion and information produce changes in the type of government involved, not only in terms of mobilization and reconciliation systems, but also into two intermediate types involving hierarchical authority and instrumental values or pyramidal authority and consummatory values (the latter change occurring much less frequently than the former).

We can diagram these points as follows:

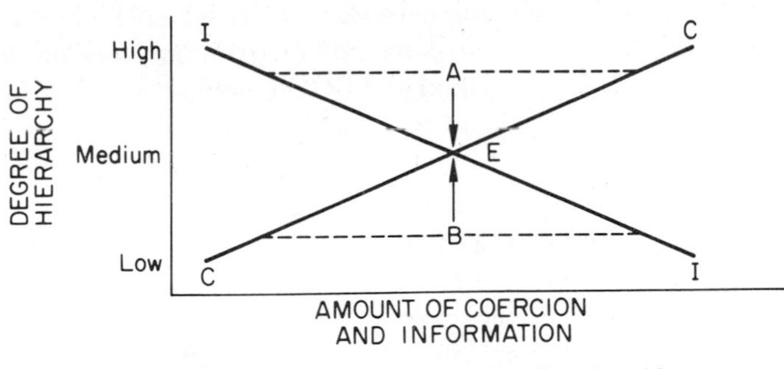

***Figure* 5.** *The Information-Coercion Relationship.*

The tendency $A \longrightarrow E$ illustrates the need for greater information on the part of a mobilization system, while the tendency $B \longrightarrow E$ indicates the need for greater coercion on the part of the reconciliation system.

Quite aside from their theoretical interest, there are several reasons why these tendencies are significant. As a practical point, particularly for countries in the early stages of modernization, erstwhile mobilization systems such as Ghana, Guinea, or Mali, which showed a high degree of hierarchy through the mechanism of the single-party state as a vanguard instrument, did not apply much coercion in the first stage of their regimes. Moreover, having replaced colonially sponsored reconciliation systems (at least in the last stage of colonialism), they were exceptionally high information systems. However, as the pressure to pursue rapid modernization created problems of organization and discipline, the coercion outputs rapidly increased and the process of declining information manifested itself in several ways. In the Ghanaian case the conversion from *A* to *C*, as in Figure 2 above, occurred through a military coup d'état, while in Mali and Guinea it resulted in bureaucratic formalism and the drying up of sources of activity and enthusiasm.

In the case of a reconciliation system, the problem is too much information. The failure of the federal government of Nigeria to act on information received was a result of the excessive degree of regional and local accountability, which made necessary action impossible. The recent military take-over has resulted in the formation of a more hierarchical system with corresponding increases in coercion. Information previously available through the reconciliation system is still available for the new regimes, while the newly present coercive opportunities have been manifested in domestic military action against the Eastern Region (Biafra).

I cite these cases because their theoretical formulations were well worked out before the actual changes in government occurred in both Nigeria and Ghana, and because they are perfectly explicable by the model. Both new regimes have medium hierarchy, medium coercion, and conform to the type I have called bureaucratic, which includes as subtypes military oligarchies as well as neo-mercantilist and modernizing autocracies. These can be described as ABCD below:

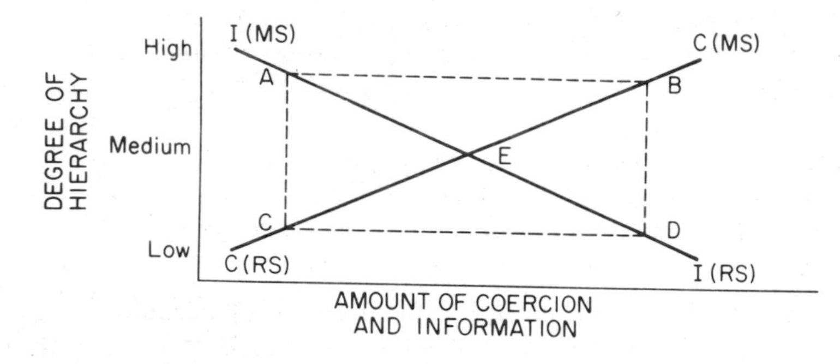

***Figure 6.** The Information-Coercion Relationship.*

The reasoning underlying both the concrete cases and the theory can be described in a number of propositions emerging from this formulation: (1) Increasing the degree of hierarchy narrows the circle of decision-makers and enlarges the excluded range of representational elites. (2) The greater the degree of hierarchy, the more concentrated the power of the decision-maker. (3) To maintain this power, decision-makers may employ coercion or payoff. (4) To the degree to which potential representational elites are eliminated, competition for power between remaining decision-makers becomes greater, as does the need for manipulative skills on the part of the central leadership. (5) The greater the loss of representational elites, and the greater the competition between remaining decision-makers becomes greater, as does the need for manipulative The greater the loss of information, the greater the need for a regulative coercive force, such as an army or police unit. (7) The greater the reliance on coercion, the more significant the role of the army and police, and the greater the need to control them.

To summarize:

1. Increasing hierarchy—lower accountability
2. Lower accountability—greater coercion
3. Greater coercion—lower information
4. Lower information—greater coercion
5. Greater coercion—increasing hierarchy[14]

CONCLUSION

We conclude by restating the general hypothesis: As modernization grows in a system, the greater the complexity of differentiation in stratification-group competition, the more quickly a political system-type will reach its "ceiling" of effective response, and the greater will be the need for coercion. Thus, in early and middle stage modernization, we can expect a succession of political system-types, with the bureaucratic type providing the greatest degree of stability. If the goal of industrialization is central and overriding, during late modernization a mobilization system will emerge to "take" the society over the "hump" from late modernization into early industrialization. At this point, the need for information will grow and coercion will become increasingly dysfunctional to the system.

To recapitulate briefly, our task is to evaluate the political consequences of the differentiation of social structure from traditional to industrial stages according to stratification with caste (and ethnic), class based on occupational criteria and consciousness, class based on multi-bonded factors, and finally, functional status groupings forming the basis of social life. These patterns of differentiation represent the empirical dimension of differentiation of choice, to be located and identified in particular group-related action in categories, such as, landowners and peasants, army and bureaucracy, trade unions and intellectuals, etc. Each one of these groups can be ranked in terms of its predominant type of claim to participation—popular, functional or interest, as well as in terms of its degree of access to decision-making by means of goal specification, central control, and institutional coherence. The combination of empirical rankings can then be correlated with types of political systems to evaluate what types of information emerge in relation to the degree of coercion applied. The general hypothesis is that if the level of differentiation reflecting changes in stratification increases, the political result will be more and more fragmentary changes in the political system-

[14]The situation would be different for highly industrialized societies, where, I would argue, the greater the degree of industrialization, the greater the need for information; hence, the long-term tendency is toward the reconciliation system.

type until late modernization, when a mobilization system will emerge with the capacity to "take" the society from late modernization into early industrialization.

A Paradigm for Political Analysis

THE NEED FOR A PARADIGM

General theories of relevance to political scientists seem, for the most part, to have been produced in other disciplines, particularly economics, anthropology, and sociology. The field of politics has not always been so derivative in character. When politics was a specialized subject matter it belonged to a tradition, now considered gratuitous, which held that civic virtue was a goal for all, and the mechanisms with which to produce it were the means to that goal. The study of the first was political philosophy, and the study of the second political science. The field of politics combined both, with particular syntheses representing theories. When agreement broke down over what constituted civic virtue, then the appropriateness of the mechanisms became more doubtful. The field now lacks unity, and there is little likelihood that it will be restored on its old terms.

Nor does it help much to "import" ideas from other disciplines. These only complicate matters, especially when "civic virtue" has become a good deal more elusive than we had supposed, and many of the mechanisms have lost their habitual connotations. If we use new methods in an old context, empirical precision may be increased, but so will our theoretical errors. To insert improved methods and borrowed theories into the antique body of the field of politics is one of the more embarrassing forms of violation. Our present circumstances justify attempts at general theory in politics, even though in other disciplines this is now becoming obsolete.

Sociology and anthropology, for example, are giving up the large architectonic theories which for a time gave them an intellectual unity. Indeed, Parsons, no less than Marx, has become obsolete. But general theory is a matter of first principles rather than last ones, to be undertaken only when it is necessary to go from the new to the old, an infinitely more frightening procedure than going from the old to the new.

The field of politics is undergoing a bewildering and strenuous theory building. It is a phase, but a necessary one, tempered also by the criterion of operationalism in that there is widespread recognition of the need to link systemic with operational variables. The mixture of the systemic and the operational is often called "political sociology," because its problems are drawn from the classic concerns of politics, its theories from sociology, and its methods from empirical studies and fieldwork. Such a mixture has consequences for both disciplines.

The original interest in political sociology was the work of the historical sociologists. They were the first to recognize that the relationship between society and government was more complex than most political scientists allowed. More important, their sociological interest derived from a political one. This was particularly the case with those concerned with society as such, rather than with some of its specialized aspects in the field of education, demography, criminology, or social welfare. Indeed, these fields are splitting off from the mainstream of research at the "societal" level to become either more applied, as in the case of social welfare, or more theoretical, as in the case of demography. A similar procedure is at work in political science. Public administration is the equivalent for "social welfare." Other "fields" in the discipline overlap extensively (comparative politics and international relations for example). More and more what remains are schools in research theories, with interesting bodies of descriptive materials as divisions. These reach out across both disciplines and share the same rules, tendencies, and training requirements. They only differ on the old issue of political philosophy. In political science the civic virtue focus becomes a battleground. The political philosophers want to hold it aloof or make it into a single universal field; the rest recognize that without integrating it there is no way to establish a unity of discourse in the study of politics.

The relationship between politics and sociology is particularly close on a theoretical level when we come to the study of development and modernization. So many of the problems of political relevance today were first examined by historical sociologists in the latter part of the nineteenth century that we share a common point of departure. Our question is how we can translate into contemporary research terms our knowledge of the discontinuities which arise at the levels of norms, structures, and behavior during major cultural transition. More particularly, from a political science point of view, we must find out how to translate into components of authority, or categories dealing with power, the consequences or breakdowns in the congruence of fit between all three brought about by the impact of industrialization, modernization, urbanization, and mass participation.

The political emphasis is thus a matter of degree rather than kind, and the overlap with sociology is very great. If we recognize this at the theoretical level we can avoid the danger of borrowing concepts from sociology to be employed in a conventional political science approach. Such borrowing does violence to both disciplines and, what is more, the borrowed concepts are often applied in a faulty manner. (Nowhere is this more manifest than in the now commonplace application of "systems" of "functions" or "structures" to political problems). Another concern, if we use a more conventional political science, is the expropriation and use of empirical data from other disciplines. Since we lack good criteria for selection and employment of such data, we merely expand our descriptive coverage in a hit or miss manner and, as well, overburden our conventional categories.

Of course, the need to borrow theories arises for very good reasons. In studying modernizing societies, for example, the role of kinship will suddenly pose political problems which do not fit easily into our conventional categories. The natural tendency is to see how anthropologists have dealt with the subject. On closer inspection, the matter turns out to be complex, mainly because of a tortured language of classification. A few might have the patience to trace the concepts back to the structural theories on which the categories are based, carefully working their way through the theories of Malinowski or Radcliffe-Brown, only to find (at the moment of triumph) that anthropology has gone well beyond the models which were employed.[1]

Similar problems arise with sociology. Indeed, there, if anything, the situation is worse. Although structural theories in sociology have proved a rich source of hypotheses, helping political scientists to relate social structure to government, they tend to draw attention to problems at an excessively generalized level. Concepts, such as Durkheim's notion of differentiation, complexity, and the emphasis on the strains placed on solidarity—all of which have been important in focusing the political interests of political scientists—are now rather dubious. What does solidarity really mean? Is it any better than that other appealing but overworked concept "alienation"? Even Weber, the source of many political ideas about urbanization, religion, bureaucracy, and entrepreneurship, who has probably served as the most important original source of ideas

[1]See A. R. Radcliffe-Brown, *A Natural Science of Society* (Glencoe, Ill.: The Free Press, 1948) and *Structure and Function of Primitive Society* (Glencoe, Ill.: The Free Press, 1952).

for contemporary political studies of modernization, is becoming the subject of increasingly hostile scrutiny.

The predicament of the political scientist using a conventional set of categories is thus exacerbated as much by crises within theory as by the difficulties he confronts in selecting between theories. It is not surprising that many political scientists view the spectacle with extreme sourness, as they cling to well-used categories, if only to prevent the confusion which grows as the discipline develops. What they fail to see is that their cure for the difficulty is in large measure its cause. Pointing this out does not help very much, however, because we cannot supplant an old tradition by a new one if the latter is not simpler, clearer, and includes the old within the new.

What is more, political science has a tradition, developed in the West, of preoccupation with specialized instruments of government. This preoccupation accounts for the importance attached by political scientists to the study of the ancient constitutions of Greece and Rome, and, to a lesser extent, of medieval and conciliar theories of the corporation and representation. Studies that were undertaken were by and large designed to show how present-day institutions of government evolved from a lower to a higher stage, and from less perfect to more perfect systems of government. These historical and evolutionary assumptions embodied the notion of progress, which, when attached to specific mechanisms of government, such as parliaments and committees, methods of voting and representation, bureaucratic organization and administration, and the courts and judicial review, was considered to have universal significance. Moreover, during this period, when political science stood in direct relation to law and economics, each field had the virtue of clarity. Not only were all three disciplines considerable, precise, and clear, but, as well, the field of political science derived its concepts from the other two and had a clear perspective on power and its distribution. An implicit but widespread view of politics assumed that power was generated and distributed by means of economic activities. The central problem was its containment by regulative procedures, particularly those produced by representatives and constitutional bodies. The civic concern was freedom with responsibility. A central characteristic of this implicit view was how these various dimensions could realize their substance in law.

Today our emphasis is different. Such views were ethnocentric, based on inadequate knowledge of the ways of social custom and behavior. The old boundaries were found in law. Our notions of progress, although they remain, are more cautious; our view of the political universe is more problematic. And therein lies our paradox—disappointed in our conventional categories, we are also suspicious of the conceptual formulae which have been imposed upon us, whether from outside by other disciplines or by fellow political scientists concerned with formulating new categories for analysis.

If we have lost the sharpness of a legal approach and the simplicity of an economic analysis of power, we have gained a widened theoretical scope and more enlarged theoretical sophistication. We are moving away from simplistic notions, such as the notion of time as sequence, toward more abstract analytical models such as those which would treat time as a variable without necessarily involving sequence.

These changes in emphasis are no cause for complaint. They only highlight the plight of the political scientist today. His concrete concerns can now include virtually all the potential problems of society and its component parts. His theoretical interests must encompass at least a sufficient understanding of the other social science disciplines, so that he can appropriate their findings and use them in his work. He must be proficient in modern methods of field work and data gathering as well as in forming analytical models appropriate to the complexities he encounters. Because of this, one priority emerges as central for the next few years: For the time being, our analytical needs must take precedence over the more narrow technical questions. If we simply expand our technique with our present descriptive categories, we will hardly move the intellectual boundaries of the discipline at all.

However, when we leave aside the conventional in order to adopt the new and untried, we cannot cope with the data produced in enormous quantity by various research disciplines and subjects since the war. Once exotic areas and languages are now being explored in depth. The periphery and the center, the metropole and the field, divisions which in the past helped to divide our studies so that educational priorities could be established, have also become confused. If we add to this the revolution in quantitative research technique, it is easy to see why we must cling to our categories, descriptive or not, conventional though they might be. Without them we are lost—both in regard to our present research and to the utilization of our knowledge to date. Recognition of this predicament does not help much. The danger is that in trying to clarify we simply compound the problem.

Moreover, broadening our geographical or regional knowledge has not only piled on descriptive data, it has also shown the range of problems for study to be infinite. If we have no "discipline" beyond the conventional, and the conventional is inadequate, then we are likely to be overwhelmed, inundated by what there is to be known. The purpose of a discipline is precisely to delimit some range of experience and make it finite, and susceptible to analysis. This is why we need to return to general political theory and first principles. We face the threat of the disintegration of the field—both empirically, since we need to know everything and everything is "relevant," and analytically, since conventional categories do not produce useful results.

Curriculum changes have not solved the problem. Courses proliferate, overlap, and duplicate, not only within political science but, more descriptively, in "outside" or cognate fields, which specialize in modernization, development, de-colonization, industrialization, ideology, and political movement. Problem emphases vie with area approaches in Africa, Latin America, Asia, and the Middle East. It is no wonder that we do not treat America and Europe as "areas"—they represent the bases for our analytical emphasis; they remain our "yardsticks." If we treated the United States or Europe on a par with other cultural or geographical regions (where our conventional categories apply), our conceptual system would vanish. Yet, sentiment apart, from the standpoint of research emphasis they are no different than our so-called "areas." Before "putting them in their place" a rethinking of our basic categories and formation of new intellectual paradigms is necessary. This is precisely what Almond, Pye, Coleman, Verba, Binder, Riggs, and others have been trying to do. Today we know that it is not sufficient merely to add new substantive areas or geographical regions to our curricula, nor is some smattering of ignorance in anthropology, sociology, or economics enough. (Indeed, one of the great fallacies of political studies is to think that an "interdisciplinary" focus would help. It only confuses the problem further and leads to muddy thinking.)

To make more explicit the types of analysis to be found in contemporary society and to indicate some possible strategies which political scientists can use, we must take a step back from the immediate and bewildering array of theories in the various disciplines in order to ask ourselves something about more general analytical modes common to all disciplines, just as in field research we look for patterns behind the bewildering array of behaviors and customs in the real world. In other words, we must treat the proliferation of theoretical approaches as items of experience to see what patterns they form. Hence I intend to try my hand at a preliminary clarification. Although I am concerned with finding more meaningful modes of thought in the social sciences, I write from the standpoint of political science. As I see it, the task requires first, an attempt to define some of the main dimensions of work with which we all deal, e.g., to put analytical boundaries around them.

AUTHORITY AS A SYSTEM

Contemporary political studies show two central but divergent tendencies: The first, which originates in the tradition of normative political theory, is the consideration of society (and more particularly the state) as a moral phenomenon. According to this view, authority is determined by reference to abstract moral principles, whether embodied in religious prescriptions, political ideologies, or other prescriptive statements regarding relationships between men. The second treats politics from the standpoint of power. Here the principal problem is finding the best method for balancing individual wants in a manner capable of sustaining political order. Emphasis is on the governing of means, rather than on abstract morality. Authority is derived from sources such as the power of numbers, access to resources, and political skill, and is regulated by a mechanism which is often elevated to the level of abstract principle, such as majority rule.

These two alternative positions have served us from the beginning of political philosophy. Their divergence can operate as a matter of emphasis, as, for example, between Plato and Aristotle, or as a matter of deep-rooted principle, as between ultilitarians and neo-Hegelians in the nineteenth century or political monists and liberal pluralists today. Many doctrinal efforts have been made to merge or blend these two approaches (as in modern social democratic movements), just as there have been efforts to sharpen the distinctions between them (as in Leninism and the attempt to strip liberal democratic features from the Communist movement), but in practice the former is difficult to achieve, while the latter is exceedingly puristic and totalitarian. The practical difficulties of both approaches have been most recently observed in new nations, where inadequate liberal constitutions (on the basis of which, in many cases, new governments won autonomy from metropolitan powers) have been swept away shortly after independence. On the other hand, most of the attempts at more monolithic political systems have also broken down. If we look for a moment at the way the emphasis shifts toward or away from nationalism or socialism, we begin to understand how people can alternate so frequently between one approach or another in a practical setting. And of course, fashions in political attitudes change among political theorists too. When the political analyst opts for one or another orientation, he revises his models of the polity.

Today's preoccupations focus on new and better combinations of the political tendencies described, and the array of such formulations has never been more numerous or complex. Consider modern group theories, for example. Proponents of this orientation view politics in terms of a competition between groups and individuals, which generates both power and the conditions necessary for its control. Methods of analysis appropriate to such study are increasingly statistical and quantitative. Modern anti-pluralists find this approach and its methods repugnant. They are anxious to define a basic pattern of reform or revolution which will provide a permanent solution, and they regard group approaches to political life as not only amoral in reference, but immoral in consequence. As the necessary prerequisite to freedom, they turn toward a higher moral basis for authority. Their methods are less empirical and more logico-dialectical. An enormous philosophical as well as technical literature testifies to the vitality of both approaches, and the battles between orientations will most certainly continue.

If this viewpoint is correct, it seems possible to suggest that what represents competitive norms for protagonists in politics results in different dimensions of authority, or, to put the matter another way, the two views presented represent alternative normative boundaries for the establishment of authority. The difference between them allows us to establish a continuum at the normative level against which authority in real systems can be compared. We can therefore treat the two basic normative orientations not as concrete, but as analytical polarities, since concrete systems show some empirical mixture of both. Determining characteristics of that mixture for any concrete political system represents a strategic problem for analysis, just as the study of values represents an important aspect of the study of culture undertaken by anthropologists.

However, the problem of determining strategic approaches to the boundaries of authority is not exhausted. A second set of boundary alternatives in political studies has characteristically been derived from accountability, or how power, no matter how derived, is distributed. *Accountability* then is a structural dimension in politics which has formed a basis for most of the typological models employed by political theorists. To go one step further, we can say that structural analysis in politics has dealt with descriptive statements of accountability, while accountability is itself a function of representation. The "systemic" character of political analysis has thus come to depend upon descriptive propositions about mechanisms of participation and representation, particularly devices such as electoral procedures, methods of voting, party organization, the franchise, and the like.

The normative-analytical and the structural-descriptive approaches have been related by concepts such as responsibility, political conscience, and citizenship. Thus, in the case of "citizenship," for example, authority derives from the participation of citizens in the polity. High accountability by government generates citizen support, which creates powers to be employed in their own interests. Those interests have a normative side in the liberal formula and define the ends of the polity itself. I cite the liberal formula, because it has the great virtue of simplicity, but even this view allows complexities to emerge, such as "populist" and "elitist" theories. Whatever the approach, however, what emerges, with the emphasis on obligation, responsibility, and citizenship, is in reality not a true analytical link between the normative and structural dimensions of authority, but something else, a third dimension of politics, namely, behavior. If this is correct, then the basic paradigm we have been following in political analysis is not so much wrong as incomplete. The purpose of this paper then is to complete the paradigm.

Interest in behavior is, of course, not new in political studies. In the past it has been identified with certain simplistic assumptions regarding man's nature. According to Rousseauean and Lockean views, man possessed natural tendencies to goodness—provided the appropriate normative (religious) and structural (economic) environment was there—while to others, man possessed a hostile and competitive nature, to be regulated by moral imperatives or norms, or rationality, or structures of control through which the same behavioral principle suitably mutated could serve to check man's moral appetite. Today we have a more elaborate concept of man in society, we speak of socialization, motivation, the effect of the internalization of norms, and commitment and responsibility. Interest in behavioral dimension has led to its occasional use as an independent variable, with norms and structure implicit and dependent or derivative. (For the most part, however, political scientists hold norms and structures independent in determining man's social nature.)

No matter how one feels about the status of the behavioral variable, however, the dimensions just indicated can be made to form a paradigm for contemporary political analysis. In political theory this paradigm has remained implicit, but I think it is possible to clarify it by identifying authority as falling within normative, structural, and behavioral boundaries. These boundaries can be "rotated" quite arbitrarily; which of the variables shall be held independent or dependent is a matter of procedure, and while the paradigm should apply to all authority systems it is particularly interesting to employ it in the context of new nations, where the behavioral and structural boundaries of authority do not fit together very well. It is the problem of fit, in particular, which has by no means been sufficiently elaborated. Structurally, if a new nation employs the liberal formula with high accountability, a system of stalemate may result. If, on the other hand, it reduces accountability, it runs into the danger which accompanies the arbitrary and capricious use of power. Normatively, higher emphasis on social discipline could produce moral authority, but if this fails to result, abuses are likely to follow. Meanwhile, behavior tends to be ambiguous and diffuse. There is a lack of effective socialization in relation to norms, since no normative authority is likely to prevail. At the level of structure, with the liberal formula, competition leads to corruption—alternative behavior becomes devious and disguised.

Discussing this paradigm in the context of new nations immediately sets up certain "systemic-paradoxes" which are focal points for analysis. We shall define authority itself as a system containing *choice*. The various components of authority establish the conditions of choice—choice in terms of whole systems or polities, or choice for individuals within those systems and the relations between both. For us, the problem of the regulation of choice is thus the object of authority and constitutes "the political problem." If we use the context of new nations for such study it is because such a context is useful for putting into bold relief problems of unusual significance, namely, the degree of coherence or fit between each of the components and the consequences for political life. However, new nations, while they may illustrate these matters in a contemporaneous setting, are in this respect no different from all others, except for the fact that in some of the problems attending authority and its establishment they are subject to more sharply distinguishable cleavages. Another advantage of studying them is that they are susceptible to contemporary, rather than historical, research.

The problem of authority and choice determines the dimensions of the paradigm. Empirical applications in my own work are based on an interest in development, and, more specifically, modernization. Modernization in my view is a particularly instructive setting for choice and authority, because it establishes the larger setting within which choice is possible, while authority systems operate in such a manner that they affect its pace and direction. Development, modernization, and industrialization are defined as parts of the same phenomenon, with modernization a consequence of industrialization, and development the descriptive process of both.[2] Viewed from this standpoint, the process of development is, from a diachronic point of view, linear, i.e., progressing from traditional to modern, from agricultural to industrial. Political development and changes in system types are nonlinear, however. We treat modernization synchronically or comparatively, as it is measurable in terms of the spread of industrial roles in traditional societies. These two main emphases, the dimensions of choice and the polity in the setting of modernization, establish a linear-nonlinear set of relationships and form the basis of the empirical work in many contemporary studies of modernization. Much effort has been devoted to determining the empirical variables involved in both sets. Moreover, there is an increasing effort to establish systemic relationships for each separately and then to combine systems in new analytical models drawing on theories useful for each set. There are, of course, many difficult problems which arise when such ambitious efforts are undertaken. Some of these center around the particular models themselves: their suitability, whether they conceal

[2]Development thus refers to differentiation and complexity, modernization to the establishment of rules relevant to industrial societies in hitherto non-industrial settings, and industrialization to the creation and integration of roles organized around manufacturing.

practical prejudices or disguise political preferences by elevating them to the level of theoretical statements. In addition, we should emphasize again that although modernization represents a linear continuum (and the concept of development is itself a recognition of change in a particular direction), alterations between political systems do not follow some linear pattern. They represent alternatives within the linear pattern itself. The reason for this formulation is that it raises the question of "fit" between the components of choice and authority—normative, structural, and behavioral—and of their relationships to various stages of development. This allows us to state an overall long-term objective to these studies: We wish to establish criteria for determining optimal modes of authority for different developmental stages and purposes in order to arrive at some solutions.

THE DIMENSIONS OF CHOICE

I would like to consider the unity of the social sciences in relation to a concern with choice. This includes the analysis of types of choices, conditions, means, ends, and options. A theory of choice would include at least three main dimensions, each subject to theoretical development: a *normative* dimension, involving ethical and proprietary conceptions which organize thought and action to give it meaning; a *structural* dimension, creating conditions in which alternatives are possible; and a *behavioral* dimension, representing the options in life actually identified and selected. Each dimension can be handled in many different ways. In political studies, two common approaches are historical, involving sequence as cause and relating appropriate subject matter, as it were, diachronically, and comparative, showing different settings of choice and indicating choice relationships synchronically. Using these categories to evaluate the work of the field, we could say that in political studies normative analysis seen in diachronic terms has been highly developed with (as we have already suggested) universalized ethical manifestations expressed in legal terms. Comparative or synchronic normative concerns have been dealt with more in economic terms. However, as the subject matter has grown more complex, emphasis has shifted to other possible dimensions.

Indeed, if we use a five point rating scale to evaluate analytical tendencies in political science, as in Figure 1, the historical-normative combination receives great emphasis. Also the history of ideas (or what passes for it) becomes an evolutionary political theory. The historical-structural dimension is only slightly less developed. It came into fashion in the nineteenth century as a utilitarian interest in reforms of systems

TYPE OF ANALYSIS	DIMENSION OF ANALYSIS: Normative	Structural	Behavioral
Historical (Diachronic)	5	4	0
Comparative (Synchronic)	1	3	1

Figure 1. *Main Lines of Political Study.*

of representation, bureaucracy, political parties, and the like. It too was expressed in historical-evolutionary terms, e.g., beginning with the Greek city-states and progressing through the organization of feudalism, the "medieval synthesis," the "rise" of the nation-state, and so on. (Our course titles and sub-field specializations still reflect these two emphases, since the discipline was founded around them.) Indeed, the traditional form of political science rests upon the implicit implication that the historical-normative (universalization of ethical principles) in combination with the historical-structural (the universalization of principle political types), when brought into the proper legal framework (constitutionalism) and translated into a useful set of controls over economic power (checks and balances), will: (1) show the superiority of democracy as a political form, and (2) treat the historical-normative and historical-structural as a set of independent variables. Hence the traditional paradigm of political science stacked the cards in our favor. The good and ethically sound principle in combination with the structurally superior political system is equal to democracy. To universalize this experience becomes a practical problem of policy, including both internal reform and international relations. But what happens when the sequence does not work, and behavior does not conform? We do not question the paradigm, but rather define the situation as deviant.[3] If studies of behavior show that presupposed normative and structural conditions cannot be met or are inadequate, then the historical tradition of political science has little to offer us.

In the comparative-normative area, political science has done very little until recently to examine new moral-ethical planes and sets of ideas. The most important normative ideas have come from the study of ideologies of new nations and socialist societies. There has been greater

[3]If studies of behavior show that presupposed normative and structural conditions cannot be met or are inadequate, then the historical tradition of political science has little to offer us. The historical-behavioral field has included, in the past, mainly biography.

progress in the comparative-structural combination. This field has developed well beyond the study of western institutions (and some totalitarian ones) to the examination of polities in all parts of the world. Here we have seen the emergence of a non-typological interest, the first step in the deviation of analytical paradigms. True, the typologies are still mainly descriptive; new developments have had the advantage of keeping them close to data. The development of new and more analytical comparative-structural models is the next step. Work on the comparative-behavioral side is just beginning. We are only now becoming concerned with the new problems associated with development in this area. However, in the next few years the comparative structural-behavioral combinations will attract the most creative attention.

So far, it has been suggested that the common core of all social science theory can be seen as a problem of choice. We have described choice as a series of changing alternatives. To review briefly, each succeeding situation is contingent upon preceding choices. Disciplines, as we know them, simply segregate pieces of the problem. For example, economists segregate the choice problem in terms of the allocation of scarce goods and services. Anthropologists deal with the cultural aspects of choice. Sociologists confront societal elements. Political scientists, concerning themselves with choice in terms of power and responsibility, rulers and ruled, need somehow to incorporate all the other aspects as well. This is the analytical difficulty of a discipline which also includes the containment of choice as its special subject matter. Political science will not become more useful than it has been hitherto by simply adding some relevant theories from related disciplines. We need to establish new boundaries for it around authority and to treat choice as a problem of authority in its *normative*, or moral dimension (embodying both its wider objects and obligations), its structural dimension (involving the patterns of social relationship and organization which, analytically defined, contain social life), and its *behavioral* dimension (including the selection between alternatives presented by the other two). Theories relevant for each dimension can be selected as they illuminate problems of authority. Hence the normative and structural dimensions may be seen as defining *what* choices are possible, the behavioral dimension as referring to *which* choices are made. A focus on choice draws attention not to disciplinary priorities but, rather, to possible and alternative modes of conceptualization and theory construction.

I stress too the arbitrary quality of the enterprise. An observer can hold norms as the independent variable, using structure as the intervening variable with behavior dependent. Each of the resultant six alternative sets of relationships represents a main theoretical possibility. For example, if norms are the independent variable with structure intervening and behavior dependent, then we would anticipate analysis on the basis of the independent role of ideas in action, linked to action by structures, such as stratification, organization, and so forth. If an approach deals with structure as independent with norms intervening and behavior dependent, then organization of authority or bureaucracy or the working class, for that matter, may be seen as imposing its normative imprint in such a manner as to effect behavior (as in Marxist or neo-Marxist approaches). If behavior is the independent variable with normative variables intervening and structure independent, then we would expect to find theories involving belief or attitude formation effecting the internalization of norms leading to changes in structure. Whatever the particular set selected as a mode of analysis, however, it seems to me that because they define the character of the theory to be employed, basic decisions about the variable to hold independent represent the first step toward clarification of the field.

In addition to conceptualizing the problem of choice, with all the intellectual unity that I believe this implies for political science, there are also practical research aspects to the present formulation. These include the selection and identification of concrete units and sub-units for examination, i.e., the empirical variables, how they cluster, and how these can be made to serve as validating tests for more generally defined hypotheses. For example, in the context of modernization, normative, structural, and behavioral hypotheses can be applied through the empirical observation of social units which are concrete in the sense that they are membership units, such as trade unions, churches, clubs, kinship systems, class systems—the list is virtually inexhaustible. In developmental terms the present formulation becomes the means of dealing comparatively with stages of development, with the movement from primitive systems of choice under traditionalistic structural and normative conditions, to wider choice systems resulting from modernization. We can compare large-scale systems with small ones, use gross aggregate statistics (population, size, densities, productivity), and organize the apparently bewildering array of information in an orderly, and comparative manner.

THE PARADIGM

Having sketched out a point of view and a review of some of the conceptual problems of contemporary political analysis, I would like to put these in a more systematic context. We have suggested three dimensions of choice: normative, structural, and behavioral. Each dimension imposes certain methodological obligations, a *method of generalizaton* and a *method of observation*. The latter is essentially a statement of the type of observation toward which each theoretical dimension is predisposed. The former involves a description of the likely process whereby generalization from that which is observed to that which is inferred takes place.

Let us begin with the case of normative theory, which is concerned with the question of predominant values in a system. These predominant values represent a definition of meaning for the system, and may take the form of ideologies, religious beliefs, or more generalized moral preferences.[4] Many anthropologists and sociologists in trying to organize and delimit such values to a core or central group have found them elusive, incoherent and ambiguous. Clarification has involved linguistic analysis as a technique as well as other devices for measuring the significance of values in action. The problem is that the discussion of norms and the identification of central values tends to be confused with the procedures and techniques used for identifying them, a problem preceding the structural one of determining the effectiveness of these norms in social structures or behavior. From the present standpoint, however, we can say that the method of observation of norms begins with the observer's definition and articulation of his own values in a context of personal moral predicaments. This method of observation has been called "participant observation." Hence we say that the meaning of values can never be identified without the prior identification of the values by means of their significance to the observer. This process of participant observation, by identifying the values of the observer in a concrete situation, articulates a counter set of competitive normative alternatives: Every value allows the identification of an opposite value. This implies that normative meaning is based on matched antinomies, the useable components of which provide multiple opportunities for behavior. Identifying these antinomies implies a method of generalization which is essentially dialectical. Through the exploration of sets of antinomies it becomes possible to discern operative norms, normative dilemmas, and clusters of values in concrete systems. Thus normative theory depends on participation as a method generalized, dialectically respective of the techniques employed.

Structural theory depends upon the organization of role paradigms in concrete systems. Its object is to define the consequences of different types of role sets for the unit of which they are a part. This requires the description of patterns of social relationships according to principles such as kinship, stratification, and organization. Such role sets, as we pointed out earlier, make sense only when seen phenomenologically. This phenomenological bias implies a quite different concept of the observer than was the case with normative theory—namely, an "external"

[4]These represent an identifiable source of relevant meanings in the sense that we are using this term. See Clifford Geertz, "Ideology as a Cultural System," *Ideology and Discontent*, ed. David E. Apter (New York: The Free Press, 1964).

observer capable of perceiving the relationship of wholes. The method of observation begins with the external observer. Meanings attached to relationships so identified are essentially functional. The method of generalization then depends on taking whole units and asking what consequences for the system their various components or sub-systems demonstrate. When the observer identifies a set of functional and structural "essentials," the particular form of functional analysis is known as requisite analysis. Hence structural theory depends upon principles derived from functional relationships transformed into deductive generalizations or propositions.

Behavioral theory is concerned with motivation and perception, learning and adaptation. It does not, of course, apply exclusively to individuals as actors, but refers also to groups. Just as individuals have memories for the storage and organization of information leading to an understanding of which choices to make, so groups may have official "memories." The method of observation is essentially experimental. Such experiments may include small groups or individuals, and the techniques of experimentation may become highly mathematical and technical. The method of generalization tends to be inductive and based on replication, where functional analysis emphasizes deduction and logical consistency.

In sum, each major component of the theory of choice involves a compatible method of generalization and a component method of observation. Much confusion in contemporary analysis results from the fact that methods of observation or generalization appropriate to one type of theory are used in another. Obviously there is no one particular approach suitable to one particular theory. These categories are designed as general guidelines in Figure 2 on the following page.

We can now turn to each of these categorical sequences and discuss them in greater detail. The first sequence, *A*1, *A*2, *A*3, begins with the observer as intellectual and actor. Here experience of the world is derived from a problem beginning with the observer himself. To the extent that an intellectual is at the center of his relevant moral universe, he can use personal commitment, moral pain, puzzle, and predicament to sensitize his relationships with others in the wider community in the context of the problem of meaning. Without this point of departure, the normative dimension of political analysis remains alien or normally parched.

The problem is to universalize this method of experience, essentially a "sociology of knowledge" problem. As I indicated earlier, I call the generalization process dialectical, because it means the identification of valued commitments in terms of their opposite alternatives leading to the formation of some symposium of values or complex of beliefs which may be regarded as general "orientations" toward norms defining proprieties and proper forms of conduct in specific situations of action, such

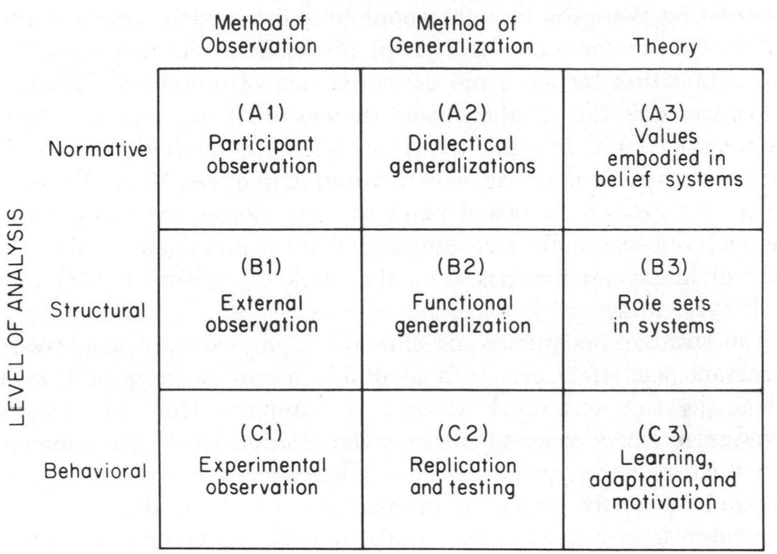

Figure 2. Dimensions of Choice.

as universalism, rationality, and pertinence. These values may be more specifically embodied in an ideological point of view or more diffused in a less identifiable form, but they and their alternatives need to be translated into "dominant" and "recessive" normative syndromes while avoiding idosyncratic conclusions, to create a totalistic normative view encompassing diverse value sets which are the properties of the system and do not inhere in the observer's selective perception. Mannheim puts the situation and predicament very well.

> To draw a simple illustration from everyday experience of the striving towards a total view, we may take the case of an individual in a given position of life who occupies himself with the concrete individual problems that he faces and then suddenly awakes to discover the fundamental conditions which determine his social and intellectual existence. In such a case, a person who continually and exclusively occupies himself with his daily tasks would not take a questioning attitude towards himself and his position; and yet such a person would, despite his self-assurance, be enslaved by a particularistic and partial point of view until he reached the crisis which brought disillusionment. Not until the moment, when he for the first time conceived of himself as being a part of a larger concrete situation, would the impulse awake in him to see his own activities in the context of the whole.[5]

[5]See Karl Mannheim, *Ideology and Utopia* (New York: Harcourt, Brace, and Co., 1946), p. 95.

Mannheim's point is close to the mark. It is the moral predicament, imposed by the crisis brought about by participation, which is the "situational" basis for social analysis of norms. It is the necessary, but not sufficient, cause for adequate generalization of normative theory.

We can now turn to the second dimension of analysis, the structural. By relating norms to structure via a functional method we can observe modes of expression, ideas, in structured action, i.e., roles. To put it another way, from a structural point of view, norms are cultural items to be observed externally and generalized by a functional method. In the field of linguistics this has been the work of anthropological theorists, such as Levi-Strauss.[6]

The structural sequence, *B*1, *B*2, *B*3, is, as we have suggested, phenomenological. It incorporates identified norms as parts of role sets of which the units examined are parts of sub-parts. Here we observe patterns of action in order to perceive the relationship to the concrete unit of which the actors are a part. Such behavior is never random, but organized in relatively prescribed patterns. Some of these patterns are cliental relationships of various kinds: doctor-patient, civil servant-citizen, lawyer-client, teacher-student, master-slave. Others are organizationally determined (employer-employee), ethnically determined (Negro-Caucasian), religiously determined (Christian-Jew). They occur concretely in trade unions; religious bodies, such as churches; military bodies, such as police forces; in armies, and so forth. Whatever the origin of a role, each individual plays several, more or less simultaneously, and moves in a partially prestructured set of ways. Departure from these ways or excessive deviance induces social controls.[7]

Functional generalization (*B*2) centers around the organization of analytically defined boundary exchanges which identify how role sets handle diverse functions. These lead to generalizations about structural tendencies: about the identification of characteristic entrepreneurial phases during different stages of industrial differentiation; about the growth of functional specificity and universalism as a consequence of modernization; about the conditional relationships of religious modes of orientation with adaptability in social institutions. The first is dealt with in Smelser's *Social Change in the Industrial Revolution*; the second is a concern in Marion Levy, Jr.'s., *Modernization and the Structure of So-*

[6]See particularly, Claude Levi-Strauss, "The Structural Study of Myth," *Journal of American Folklore*, LXVIII (1955). See also Edward Sapir, *Culture, Language, and Personality*, ed. David Mandelbaum (Berkeley: University of California Press, 1956).

[7]For the analysis of social roles, see Florian Znaniecki, *Social Relations and Social Roles* (San Francisco: Chandler Publishing Co., 1965); S. F. Nadel, *The Theory of Social Structure* (Glencoe, Ill.: The Free Press, 1957); Michael Banton, *Roles, An Introduction to the Study of Social Relations* (London: Tavistock Publications, 1965); and Talcott Parsons, *The Social System* (Glencoe, Ill.: The Free Press, 1951).

cieties; the third is discussed in Robert Bellah's *Tokugawa Religion.* Each of these books uses a functional method leading to a structural generalization. Each takes a concrete unit as a point of analysis.[8]

Structural theories have by and large applied functional methods to macro units in order to make generalizations about their properties. Such generalization depends heavily on logical consistency and deductive propositions. Important structural theories use a notion of unit variation and boundary change resultant from disequilibrating relations between norms and role sets. Integration is thus seen as a central and highly generalized "system-problem," the components of which can be found in conflict between roles, role sets, and role prescriptions.

The link between the normative and the structural dimensions is an obvious one; in the past the combination has been referred to by the term "institutional" analysis. The term is a bit misleading, since it recalls a particular period of political studies when institutional analysis was centered about western democratic beliefs, and the relationship of these to constitutional government widened to include matters of culture and religion. Studies in institutional analysis ranged from literary exercises to the most directly political. The contemporary structural emphasis could be called "neo-institutionalist"; its theories combine elements of both the structural and the normative in more directly deductive-empirical synthesis.[9] In the relationship between normative and structural theory, identification of the former leads to its employment in the latter. It is this combination which I have called neo-institutionalist, a combination of Set *A* and Set *B* in which the two set the limiting conditions within which choice takes place. The question of which choice actors opt for is another matter.

We can now turn to some elements of the behavioral dimension of choice, *C*1, *C*2, *C*3. The behavioral problem begins with the need to establish a scientifically "clean" situation, by means of which experimentation is possible and controls are readily available. This is difficult to achieve with human beings, whose complexity prevents most experimental observation which would be of direct use in political studies. Hence behavioralists have had to devise elaborate strategies for the identification of dependent variables, in order to observe learning patterns and motivation analogies between human and animal behavior, as

[8]See Neil Smelser, *Social Change in the Industrial Revolution* (Chicago: University of Chicago Press, 1959); Marion J. Levy, Jr., *Modernization and the Structure of Societies* (Princeton: Princeton University Press, 1966); and Robert N. Bellah, *Tokugawa Religion. The Values of Pre-Industrial Japan* (Glencoe, Ill.: The Free Press, 1957).

[9]I do not mean to imply that the earlier form of institutionalist analysis is displaced. The bulk of the work in comparative politics, for example, remains in this tradition. There are some delightful recent literary examples, such as Raymond Williams, *Culture and Society, 1780–1950* (London: Chatto and Windus, 1960).

in animal psychology, as well as more social, but controlled, situational experiments, as in schools. Analysis of small groups, especially observation of their internal capacities for adaptation, has been central. Much experimental work has centered around the derivation of various learning-drive reduction or stimulus-response situations to evaluate duration, intensity, and adaptive consequences or avoidance patterns. Once identified, the task is to replicate the results, partly by mathematical means of translation into further experimental situations. Hull is perhaps the most rigorous exponent of this "experimentalist" behaviorism position. His attempt to identify "molar" (non-physiological) or intermediate mechanisms in a system of linked corollaries helped to create modern behavioral theory.[10] Another key figure in this field was Edward Tolman. Both of these men postulated the kind of "behaviorist" or molar theory which identified a level of analysis which made it possible to go from behavioral experiment to behavioral theory without reducing the latter to physiological causes.

In a general sense, the "behavioral" theories of Hull and Tolman have been adapted for the analysis of political attitudes, such as in the study of psychological readiness for ideological preferences, and increasingly in the analysis of normative variables in terms of conditions and propensities of actors to shift from one pattern of norms to another. For a political scientist, the relationship between socialization processes and the persistence or duration of institutionalized preference is of major interest in any situation where political change is dependent on an altered motivation of members of the system. Many of the superficially outlandish acts of governments, such as building showpiece projects and organizing youth movements which chant absurd slogans in unison and march *en masse* in lock-step, are partly understandable as methods dictators may employ to change already socialized individuals, i.e., to manipulate or alter previously institutionalized values. (This should remind us of the relationship between normative and behavioral analysis. The norms which govern behavior are translatable into ways people sustain norms as well as into ways people alter them.)

In my view, as already suggested, the relationship between structural analysis and behavioral analysis (rather than the normative-behavioral) will be the most useful focus in coming years. (It is also the direction in which I choose to work.) However, before going on to discuss this point of view, I would like to review some of the methodological implications raised in the discussion so far.

We have suggested that at each of the main theoretical levels of analysis there is a particular problem. For the normative level it is how to

[10]See the discussion in Ernest Hilgard, *Theories of Learning* (New York: Appleton-Century-Crofts, 1950), p. 184.

move from the subjective mode of the participant observer to the objective generalization about norms, their spread, and significance. In a real sense this is the classical task of political theory: to pose questions about the good state, the ideal society, the purpose of political life.

Structural analysis confronts the problem of generalizing "wholes" from static equilibrium assumptions (particularly important in the requisite form of structural analysis) and moving from generalization to the identification of dynamic variables. It is necessary to move from a "grid" or conceptual scheme, which represents not a set of variables but rather a net to "catch" them in, to the selection of variables in process terms. This is what Durkheim did with respect to differentiation and complexity, what Weber did with the analysis of bureaucracy, and, for that matter, what Marx did in the analysis of class and capitalism. Problems arise in structural analysis if process variables so identified are mistaken for an evolutionary ontology. If the structuralists have been attacked for excessive reliance on static (and therefore, normatively speaking, conservative) biases in their work, it is also true that when they talk about process or dynamic variables, they have also reified the development of evolutionary approaches for analysis as inherent in the subject.[11]

Finally, in the behavioral field the problem is to move from the precise conditions of the laboratory to a valid generalization about behavior in various structural and normative settings. Perhaps the most pressing problem here has been to link behavior found to be predictable in small group settings to larger settings which drastically vary the structural parameters. (Group dynamics or organizational behavior theories have thus been applied to "international systems" in stimulation strategies with mixed success.)

THE NORMATIVE-STRUCTURAL COMBINATION

Particular combinations of theories and approaches are of special relevance at different stages of understanding. For example, it is very difficult to engage in highly experimental behavioral research under conditions in which the normative or structural variables are largely unknown. Moreover, where basic knowledge of the situation is lacking, i.e., while a research area remains exotic, many problems arise from false appearances and misleading evidence. The combination of normative and structural analysis is a most useful strategy for gathering data at this preliminary stage of knowledge. The first object then is to lay out

[11]While it seems to me appropriate to treat a dynamic problem focus, such as political stability *vis-à-vis* modernization, one must be sure to refer to evolution as a dependent variable. If it becomes an independent variable in the sense of a new social-Darwinism, then analysis is on extremely shaky ground.

the properties of systems, both in terms of their subjective meanings and their objective relations, norms, and structures.

At the normative level we have the problem of discovering what constitutes the meanings by which men live as well as the dominant norms from which authority is derived. The observer seeks such information through participation. He learns the languages, myths, and metaphors by which men organize their explanations. Indeed, normative theory, in this sense, results in that participation in metaphor which allows the observer to identify analogies and to establish through them a set of value antinomies which forms his hypotheses about values. If he learns the meanings of certain holy phrases, ideologies, political festivities, and the like, he can also identify the alternatives against which these are posed. Hence the language of norms is the language of contradiction. Participation is necessary in order to establish the conditions under which contradictions are resolved in a dominant set of authoritative normative beliefs—both in terms of their content and qualities. The contents are often composed of specific ideologies, the qualities mainly involve the types of ends or objects which they embody and the means by which meaning is in this wider sense defined for the members of the system under analysis.

At the structural level, we do not follow this dialectical pattern. Here we use generalized functional categories to classify and factor activities which seem to follow patterns laid down by roles organized in institutions. Each institution embodies mutual expectations with defined limits of deviance. With respect to the specific problem of modernization, it becomes possible to identify those institutions most directly derived from industrial systems and to ask how far they depart from their origins in a new setting (i.e., what functions they perform which are similar as well as those which are not), just as it is also possible to ask what functions are then performed by non-modern institutions. Thus we are led from what we know to what we do not know, for example: How do political parties in Africa differ in their functional consequences from those of England or France? Similar questions arise in the case of the bureaucracy, and the like.

In political terms we define structural problems of choice around certain types of political system. The way in which these political systems operate is translatable into a set of predictions. The roles which function within the political systems become the units for functional observation. A major problem of functional analysis is how the political roles mesh with the larger social system. The notion of authority serves as the limiting factor, in which the concept of choice and two of its dimensions are articulated in the context of the relationship between society and government, the key concrete units of the political system. The boundaries of this relationship are ultimately dictated by the degree of modernization in the system. The variables, determined by a dialectical examination of values and a structural study of group relationships in government and society, are linked in terms of institutions, such as, education, ideology, religion, and organization. The primary emphasis is on solidarity or authority.

With a developmental focus there are, of course, dangers in this approach. It is all too easy to assume that because modernization spreads, its consequences are always the same in institutional terms (the familiar problem of ethnocentrism), or, more surprisingly, in functional terms, as Levy would have it.[12] In our terms, however, the normative and structural dimensions may vary in context and meaning, despite the same degree of modernization in several systems. The result would be differences in political systems. And in the present formulation, the boundaries of behavior are dictated to the degree that the political system is determined by a normative or structural dimension. Hence the analytical combination of normative and structural theory implies a restricted theory of choice—the political—and a means of determining behavior by political analysis. We can call this combination neo-institutionalist analysis.

THE BEHAVIORAL DIMENSION

As the normative-structural combination—or neo-institutionalist approach results from theories which arise through the integration of normative and structural theory, a similar link relates structural and behavioral theory. This connecting link is *role*, just as in the normative-structural combination it was *institution*. Role has its structural side, insofar as it consists of generalized functional positions in a social system with institutionalized characteristics and proprieties. Motivations to perform roles—not to speak of social learning itself, which takes place within roles—represent some of our main concerns here. Structural theories which deal with roles seek to explain their properties as sets, as does the work of Znaniecki, Parsons, Nadel, and Banton. Role integration, compatability, coherence, deviation, and the like represent a structural emphasis to which I refer.[13]

However, the more behavioral side of role analysis tends to emphasize role performance and, most particularly, the discrepancies between ideal and actual patterns of behavior. There is, as well, the question of role creation: How do different functional sets arise, and how are they affected by individual leadership? Here a complex literature includes the "inter-

[12]See Marion J. Levy, Jr., *Modernization and the Structure of Societies* (Princeton: Princeton University Press, 1966) *passim*. See also C. S. Whitaker, Jr., "A Dysrhythmic Process of Political Change," *World Politics*, XIX, No. 2 (January 1967).

[13]See Znaniecki, *op. cit.*; Parsons, *op. cit.* Nadel, *op. cit.* and Banton, *op. cit.*

personal relations" tradition in psychiatry and the research centered around therapy (as with Harry Stack Sullivan, Karen Horney, and others) and, more particularly, the analysis of role relation to personality. Here the works of Lewin, Newcomb, Merton, and Erikson are particularly relevant, insofar as personality variables determine choice in the sense we are using that term.[14]

The attempts to associate the behavioral dimension with the normative and structural dimensions has involved very different kinds of methodological considerations in each case. The normative-behavioral dimension involves theories of self-identification and meaning in terms of the learning and socialization phases of the individual, including the study of symbol formation. By and large, however, it has been based on therapy, rather than experiment, with functional methods of generalization and a participant observational role, as when the psychiatrist interacts with his patient after having been analyzed himself so that he can generalize his own participation. Work here in political studies has been suggestive, but not very satisfying. An attempt to give more precision usually involves the employment of useful techniques, such as content analysis, but many problems remain. Works, such as Erikson's *Young Man Luther* and Nathan Leites' *Ritual of Liquidation*, are cases in point. The founder of this normative-behavioral combination was, perhaps, Harold Lasswell.[15] Recent studies include work on political socialization and the study of attitude formation.[16]

THE STRUCTURAL-BEHAVIORAL COMBINATION

So far, we have moved along the following lines in our general diagram (Fig. 2). We have suggested that the set including *A*3, *B*3, and *C*3, constitutes a basis for a total theory of choice. Each of these dimensions, however, is separate, embodying general theories of its own. In addition, we have been concerned with sets 1 and 2, i.e., observational and methodological propensities. We have associated these with a particular category of theory.

[14]See Erik H. Erikson, *Childhood and Society* (New York: W. W. Norton & Company, Inc., 1950); Theodore M. Newcomb, *Social Psychology* (New York: The Dryden Press, 1950); Kurt Lewin, *Field Theory in Social Science* (New York: Harper and Row, Publishers, 1951); and, perhaps most basic of all, George H. Mead, *Mind, Self, and Society* (Chicago: University of Chicago Press, 1934). See also Meyer Fortes, *Oedipus and Job* (New York: Cambridge University Press, 1959).

[15]See Lasswell's "Psychopathology and Politics," in *The Political Writings of Harold D. Lasswell* (New York: The Free Press, 1951); Leites and Bernaut, *The Ritual of Liquidation* (New York: The Free Press, 1954); and Erik H. Erikson, *Young Man Luther* (New York: W. W. Norton & Company, Inc., 1958).

[16]See, for example, Herbert Hyman, *Political Socialization* (New York: The Free Press, 1959).

Moreover, it is also possible to move along the diagram in other ways. For example, it is possible to begin at point *A*1 (participant observation), move to *B*2 (functional generalization), and on to *C*3, in order to derive theories about learning, adaptation, and motivation. Many theories of social philosophers today follow this line, such as George Herbert Mead, and possibly Levi-Strauss, although the latter is also concerned with the *A*1, *A*2, *A*3 sequence. Classical Marxism, as distinct from the more psychoanalytical and contemporary forms of neo-Marxism, would follow the pattern of *B*1 (external observation), *A*2, as a method of generalization, and *B*3, particularly in the analysis of class and class conflict. When confronted with the problem of explaining why revolutionary behavior would ensue without being derived from his own ideological prognostication (a position which he explicitly rejected), the behavioral problem involving the separation of true from false consciousness and the identification of genuine class interest, Marx had a behavioral theory which followed along the *A*1, *B*2, *C*3 pattern—namely, participation in the material mode of existence which generalized man's condition into a shared sense of solidarity, developing a revolutionary motivation which allowed groups of individuals to make choices not hitherto perceived possible in a system, leading to the transformation of that system into another structural type (capitalism into socialism). Development of the line *C*1, *B*2, *A*3 is just beginning to be promising, and has been largely concerned in political science with the analysis of political socialization. The works of Easton, Hess, Verba, and Hyman are particularly significant here. Moreover, contemporary studies of organizational behavior following the line of *B*1, *B*2, and *C*3 are becoming common. This is a major focus in several recent studies in this field.[17]

Each of these sets represents methodological and theoretical options. The options selected would depend in part upon which combination of choice variables is held independent or dependent. For example, it is possible to consider (as the "institutionalist school" of comparative politics originally did) the normative factor as the independent variable with structure as intervening and behavior as dependent. One looks at the moral basis of the community for a definition of purpose and examines structural variables to see how they transmit these norms into a set of organized structural constraints so that a prediction about behavior is possible. In politics this was the particular significance of those able constitutionalists who related normative analysis to philosophical conceptions of the good à la J. S. Mill or T. H. Green. Political theorists of the institutionalist school, like Friedrich, Finer, and Laski, could translate these prescriptions into an organizational formula relating to such struc-

[17]See James G. March, ed., *Handbook of Organizations* (Chicago: Rand McNally & Co., 1965).

tural variables as judicial propriety, parliamentary checks on executive authority, methods of electoral representation, and the like. These were functionally defined in terms of the maintenance of a particular structural type, such as democracy. If the proper normative and structural fit was achieved, then the appropriate behavior could be expected to follow.[18]

This paradigm is by no means obsolete. What has changed in normative and structural theories today (the neo-institutionalist as compared to the institutionalist approach) is the emphasis on general theory and the recognition of the need to become more analytical in order to cover many types of cases. In addition, our functional methods and observational techniques are developing rapidly to the point where structural-behavior combinations are now possible. This transition is best exemplified in the work of Gabriel Almond (and his associates in the Social Science Research Council Sub-Committee on Comparative Politics), as well as in the work of a number of other scholars working independently: Harry Eckstein, Samuel Huntington, Dankwart Rustow, Reinhard Bendix, and Amatai Etzioni. The series edited collaboratively by Almond and Coleman, Joseph LaPalombara, Leonard Binder, and Myron Weiner is in a very loose way organized around the functional categories explicated by Almond in *The Politics of the Developing Areas.*[19] Perhaps the most important single work in this field is Lipset's *Political Man,* which has had extremely important methodological as well as theoretical consequences.[20] All these share in common an explicit concern with behavior as the dependent variable with structural theories independent.

The burden of explanation of structural situations also rests with an analysis of the behavioral syndromes on which structures depend. Studies of authoritarianism and civic attitude, as well as comparative studies based on these, allow the use of the behavioral factor as the independent variable. Here the study made by Almond and Verba in five different political cultures is extremely important. In that work behavior is the independent variable, norms are the intervening variables, and structure is the dependent variable.[21] Much of the important work in the struc-

[18]Perhaps the best work here was done by Sir Ernest Barker and Carl Friedrich.

[19]See Gabriel A. Almond and James S. Coleman, *The Politics of the Developing Areas* (Princeton: Princeton University Press, 1960).

[20]See S. M. Lipset, *Political Man: The Social Bases of Politics* (Garden City: Doubleday & Company, 1960).

[21]See Gabriel A. Almond and Sidney Verba, *The Civic Culture: Political Attitudes and Democracy in Five Nations* (Princeton: Princeton University Press, 1963). This work can be critcized for the linkages made between the independent variables and dependent variables in terms of a rather ethnocentric set of intervening variables. It is also possible to criticize the methodological assumptions (replicability) of its more experimentally grounded propositions, but I am not concerned with evaluating this work now. Rather, *The Civic Culture* fits the scheme used here as an illustration of a central political study combining structural and behavioral variables in its general strategy of development of dependent and independent variables and the relationship between observation, generalization, and formal theory.

tural-behavioral area involves a behavioral theory mixed with functional methods of generalization (so that analogy replaces replication on the behavioral side). This would be true of David O. McClelland's *The Achieving Society*, in which an experimentally observed personality variable is generalized in functional terms in the context of innovation, with cases treated historically as well as cross-culturally.[22] More directly, in the area of political studies, the examination of both structural and motivational aspects of roles has been a central concern in Lucian Pye's work, particularly *Politics, Personality, and Nation Building*, and, as well, in Daniel Lerner's *The Passing of Traditional Society*.[23] In the latter, the application of survey techniques to behavioral questions widens the scope of the method of generalization appropriate to behavioral studies.

Clearly, at the level of structural-behavioral analysis, the possibilities of combined strategies for observation and generalization have hardly been adequately explored. Experiments being pursued in mathematical analysis may enlarge the possibilities of replication as a method of generalization by means of quantitative logical systems, which would provide a closer integration between functional method and replication itself. Here an entirely new set of research obligations becomes pressing. Indeed, for further development the structural-behavioral combination needs perhaps not so much new theory (because there is already considerable richness in that area), but rather good methods of generalization which can be integrated to fit present theoretical requirements. The work of the more mathematical sociologists is promising here.

CONCLUSION

Political science as a discipline lost both its innocence and its purity when its original boundaries, law and economics, disappeared. However, to replace boundaries is not an easy matter—we cannot look to another set of disciplines to do the job. Rather, we need to be aware that a political focus draws on a normative point of departure aimed at articulating properties of a good society. Beyond that, theories may be derived from any discipline. Indeed, highly generalized theories should be viewed less in terms of their subject emphasis than in terms of the relationship between types of independent and dependent variables, which are united by a central concern with choice.

The attempt to articulate theory in terms of choice has also involved a concern with the methods of observation and generalization implied

[22]See David C. McClelland, *The Achieving Society* (Princeton: D. Van Nostrand Company, Inc., 1961).

[23]See Lucian W. Pye, *Politics, Personality, and Nation Building: Burma's Search for Identity* (New Haven: Yale University Press, 1962); and Daniel Lerner, *The Passing of Traditional Society* (Glencoe, Ill.: The Free Press, 1958).

by each level, normative, structural, and behavioral. Affinities at each level, involving philosophical and technical problems, have been suggested; a self-conscious concern with such problems is central to our understanding of the relationship between theory and research. In addition, I have suggested two main guides for the future. I mean that on the theoretical level promising combinations include (1) neo-institutionalist analysis, and (2) structural-behavioral analysis. These involve more complex integration of methods of observation and methods of generalization. It has seemed to me essential, however, to separate all these ingredients arbitrarily in order to make new combinations explicit and clear. In terms of our diagram, Figure 3, these two tendencies embody the following combination of analytical sets for political analysis.

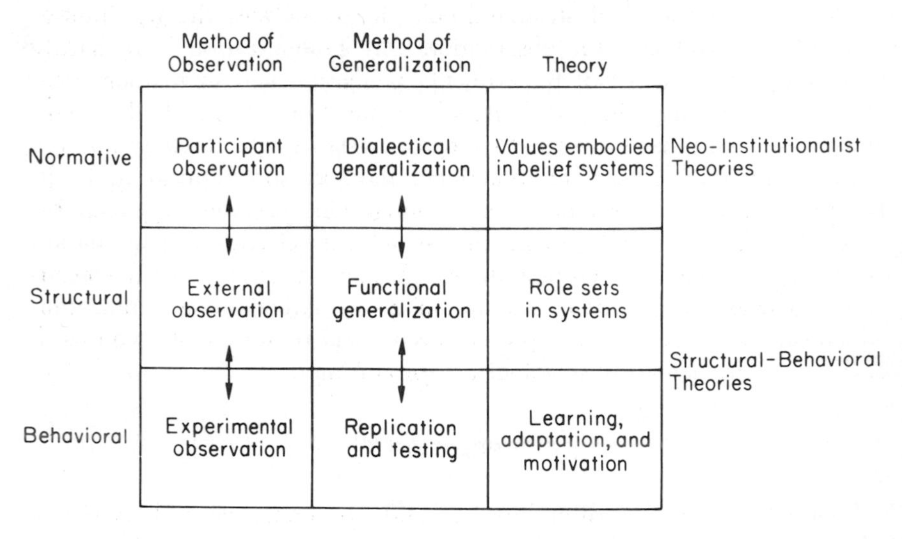

Figure 3. *Some Contemporary Emphases.*

A double standpoint of observation for both neo-instiutionalist analysis and structural-behavioral analysis is needed, as well as a combined method using a dialectical-functional system for generalization for neo-institutional theory and a functional-replication method for structural-behavioral theory. Certainly the limits of requisite analysis using macro-survival models are too easily exhausted without establishing good empirical standards of verification. Only replication and prediction can do that.[24]

What implications can be derived from the present discussion? First of all, it seems clear to me that without a conceptual map of these main problems and approaches in the field it is impossible to teach students

[24]See Etzioni's comments in *A Comparative Analysis of Complex Organizations* (New York: The Free Press, 1961), pp. 58–59.

at a professional level what constitutes the meaningful scientific landmarks in their disciplines. As the old disciplinary boundaries fail, proliferation of relevant theories and subject matters creates, not intellectual excitement, but desperation and frustration. The analytical confusion is immense. I have suggested that it is necessary to identify some of the universal problems at each level of analysis in the observational and methodological dimensions, because at present students are asked to opt for different alternatives without knowing what their options are. It is one thing to discover the problem of the participant-observer, as Mannheim does; it is quite another to recognize that this position is alternative to others, each of which has a predictable methodological consequence. Perhaps I am claiming too much for this paradigm—I would be the first to admit this. But such a scheme is necessary, not only as a guide to the bedeviled student, but also as a basis for reorienting graduate curricula away from the overworked "job" market categories toward a more analytically and methodologically coherent pattern.

Many problems remain regarding our movement from the manipulation of concepts in terms of analytical systems to the concrete units of our analysis. The paradigm suggests methods to perceive and identify analytical structures, how to manipulate them for theoretical purposes, and how to "plough" theories back again into concrete structures as a kind of productive intellectual investment. All these matters will remain a permanent source of difficulty, and in none of our three dimensions—normative, structural, or behavioral—is there agreement about their resolution. At the structural level, my own solution is to accept a generally phenomenological mode of perception, a notion of analytical structures as the basis of theory construction, and the selection of indicator variables from concrete systems to illustrate the properties of the analytical ones in order that eventually we will conceive of real or concrete units in a different way. The research analogy implicit in structural analysis is perhaps closer to pure mathematics than anything else. It is the logic of sets. The structural sets one uses stand somewhere between purely logical set of symbols and a defined notion of real things and events.

The approach suggested here is as follows: (1) Take the concrete unit of the most general type-case as a point of departure for analysis, selecting it according to its appropriateness and significance for the problem under analysis. (2) Before locating additional sub-systems, examine units and sub-units functionally in order to determine their characteristics, as they are useful in holding together or sustaining the concrete system itself. (3) Regroup these analytical functions into a series of analytical structures which form models as sets. (4) The resulting models are static. To discover their dynamic properties requires a process variable. (5) Defining the models in terms of their process variables is a way of saying that we discover what synchronic or diachronic relationships they produce. (6) These define generalized tendencies to be tested against changes in the concrete units with which the analysis began.